Finding God's Will

In The

Redeemed View Of Life

Toward A Reformed
Definition of Grace

T.L. Parker

Parker, Timothy L., 1953-

Foreword

Within the Christian life, many trivial and troubling issues arise that challenge our beliefs, teaching and understanding of theology. The trifling things we encounter only trifle us as we lose sight of the intended perspective of God's theology. The proper intent of the Christian life is to make much of God by bringing Him glory in all that we think and do through our lives in the world in which we live.

In his book, Tim provides the reader with a way to consistently view the world and life as God would have you to do, all the while providing practical analogies to prove the points he develops within its pages. Tim addresses many areas of theology in order to show a good foundational view of the Christian life. Addressing the necessity of Scripture and its clarity is one way the author shows the reader the critical importance of understanding a Holy God. Scripture is the only place to start! With a good understanding of God in the Scriptures, Tim develops his plea to his reader to have a proper life-view through the Scripture you read and claim to love.

The urgency of this book in today's world is evident. With many religious options that allow you to choose the most comfortable philosophy for your life, a true reading and understanding of Scripture is vital for our current and future generations. Without it, many more heresies will arise and many more people will live by a false gospel.

As Tim divulges lots of information regarding a theological worldview within these pages, this book should be read slowly in order to properly digest its content. If read according to the author's intent a clear, reformed and adequate view of God and His Holy Word is ever present. My prayer for each person that reads this book is that you will be blessed by the scripturally supported, prayer-bathed and heartfelt call to holiness by the author, and most certainly by God Almighty.

Shawn Golden
Pastor, Campbellsburg Baptist Church, Campbellsburg, KY

Dedications

This book is dedicated to three living pastors who spurred me on in the faith and gave ministry opportunity and spiritual vision. I honor a fourth pastor to celebrate his memory and legacy he built.

First, Al Titus asked me to teach my Grace Series in his flock where God fanned my pastoral-ministry flames. Al modeled an eclectic ministry that embraces truth no matter from what doctrinal camp it comes. In this Grace Series teaching I met my wife Elizabeth.

Second, Mickey Nardin invited me to join him in ministry. He mentored, pushed me and provoked regeneration/salvation/gospel questions contained in this book. I thank God for his ongoing effort to help pastor-less flocks and mentor saints in the faith.

Third, Michael Shea invited me to join him in ministering to his flock. He embraced my questing mind and pushed me to inquire into the pastoral job I currently enjoy. Thanks Michael.

Fourth, David Mercer showed a love for Christ-reflection like few men I've known. God called him home to glory on December 9, 2012 doing missions work in Nicaragua. He was passioned for lost souls – his passion inspired me. One favorite saying was: "Love God, Love People, Prove it!" Thank you Dave!

I want to honor the two people who laid the most significant foundations in my life – my parents, William and Frances Parker. My questing mind always yearned for answers – it still does! As a very young boy, I remember asking some deep questions. I spent much time discussing the faith and talking theology – mostly with my mother over the years. Her humble prayerful living still burns in and inspires my soul. She went to be with our heavenly Father on Father's Day, June 17, 2001 and I look forward to seeing her again. My father is one of the finest Christian men I've known. Through differences, I've greatly respected my father as he lived gracefully and boldly before the world – to shamelessly share the Gospel of His Savior. As a school teacher, I remember the Bible Clubs he mentored. In his Assisted Living facility, in his dilapidated 85 year-old-tent, he still shares his faith to any who have a functional ear. I thank God often for my parents' godly training, bravery and influence.

To all who taught me in the faith – even those who have gone before or those who may not have seen the outcome – thanks for your godly input. There are many names that I do not list but their memory spurs me on. I thank God for many who endure my peculiarities and still push me onward. May I do likewise to the glory of His Gospel of Mercy and Grace. To Him Alone is the praise!

Outside Acknowledgments

It has been a delight to become acquainted with Tim Parker. He has allowed life's experiences to propel him to find a deep relationship with God. He has a deep thirst for knowledge, but does not rest until it is understood in the context of daily life. It has been my privilege to offer some guidance in the publication of this work. I believe you will find it stimulating. It is not just another treatise on knowing God but is this author's finding in his personal quest the proactive truths of the Almighty!
-    Dr. Bob Bedford

Much is written about Christianity but few endeavor to illuminate the foundation of our beliefs further than a predictable regurgitation of accepted dogma. In *Finding God's Will in the Redeemed View of Life: Toward a Reformed Definition of Grace,* Tim Parker provokes the reader to enlighten their perception of Grace, Regeneration, Sanctification and God's will for His people through a step by step walk through Scripture. At the beginning of this work, we talked about how professed believers neglect or dismiss the value of good doctrine but we cannot get around study and embracing right doctrine if we are to live in a God-pleasing way. Are you reluctant to study theology? Open your heart, mind and will to the greatest necessary endeavor of your life. More than you know, The Redeemed View of Life is your lifeblood and can lead you to the throne room of Heaven itself.
-    Pastor Arnie Koontz

When I first heard Tim speak at Smiths Creek Bible Church in 2011, I was struck by his passion for Christ's message. He spoke sincerely and right from the heart. His book, *Finding God's Will in The Redeemed View of Life: Toward a Reformed Definition of Grace* shows his sincerity and passion for what he believes the Bible teaches for Christ-reflectors. This book took me to Biblical issues that I didn't even know existed. The writing made me think, and think *deeply.* As a fairly new studier of the Bible, the issues taken on by this book are some of the most important ones I have ever read about. My Christian lifeview has changed – for the better. Thanks Pastor Tim for helping me on my spiritual journey.
-    Darci Danhausen

It's the glory of God to conceal a matter and the glory of kings to seek out a matter. Tim spent much of his life studying the Word of God to seek out depth of its wonderful riches in Christ. At times, I've been amazed at the insight Tim receives on a spiritual matter. He has experience in many areas of life and is capable of identifying with many whom he comes in contact. While the import of this book is truly God-revealing, it offers varied perspectives of society in which Tim has experience. I recommend this book to your reading and pray God will bless you as a result. I've known Tim all his life since we are first cousins. He always shows a passionate love for God and is a devoted disciple of Jesus Christ. I know him as a true man of God who has received the comfort of the Comforter – may it bring comfort to you too.

- Bruce Kaufmann, B.A., M.B.A., J.D.

While each chapter within these pages could be books in themselves – and maybe should be – Tim provides an extensive overview of each topic. I delved into these topics through the years of my own spiritual journey as I sought to understand. The subjects are all too familiar to me; you see, I well remember discussing and debating these topics with this author – my brother – through the years.

Writing about God and the study of Him and His Word as Tim does may not be the most readily received view in today's hyper-critical and politically correct world yet these topics are extremely important for any student of Scripture or individual who truly seeks to understand truth.

Understanding the framework of God, His Word, Will and Ways provides us with a depth that is sadly missing today. While many religious skeptics, ultra extremists and the like exist today, few see the topics covered as they need to be seen. Fewer still study these vital topics from a redeemed perspective.

It's critical for us to believe the authenticity of God's Word, Will and Ways – and see life from God's vantage point. Without this, many lives will be lost – bankrupt of these vital truths. The only way to understand these subjects is through prayer, reading and study – all of which take time and effort. I urge you to listen to Tim's words and heart to allow God to speak to you in your journey of faith.

- Bill Parker

I've had the benefit of knowing Tim Parker for many years now. Over lunch or coffee, we've had many conversations. I've seen time and again that once we move past common questions about family, work and weather the conversation will inevitably be launched into grace. This is because grace is the passion of his heart as it connects the fabric of Scripture. Tim has written a book to show just that!

Grace is a topic Tim has wrestled deeply with for the last 20 years, not because it's a matter of personal interest alone but because it's of interest to the well-being of the church and her mission that Christ has given. Tim writes about these matters, not from a mind trying to play intellectual chess – easily moving around concepts, definitions and logical arguments trying to advance one school of thought over another – No! Tim works through many detailed and fine arguments in a desire to uncover and display the gospel in its fullest expression through the two sides of the Cross in mercy and grace.

Because of his passion, Tim covers the themes of grace with detail and precision while seeking to make it accessible to the general reader who is willing to think a little harder. The reader may not agree with every point but, after reading his points, will be gripped with the conclusion that grace is such a magnificent reality that it will be rightly put on display "in the coming ages" (Ephesians 2:7). I am encouraged that Tim brings this topic into fresh and relevant perspective in our day. May God use this to further your life that is lived by and in His grace.

- Pastor Anthony Ferriell

One of the blessings of being a teacher of adult learners is that every once-in-a-while a student will contact me about something significant in his or her life. Almost always, it's good news and it usually involves a professional milestone in their life. This was the case a few months ago when I heard Tim Parker was completing a book.

Of course, I was not the least bit surprised that Tim was now an author. As his writing instructor at Spring Arbor University I had the joy of teaching "Critical Analysis and Research Writing." To my delight, Tim took to the coursework as a natural with the kind of respect for words and the constructing of sentences that would make any writing instructor proud. It was evident that Tim would build on the Christian education he received at Spring Arbor to direct him toward greater work in serving the Lord. The book in your hands is the result of this wonderful convergence.

With opportunity to assist in some editing chores, I say quite candidly this book is a great representation of Tim – the man of God, and Tim – the eloquent writer who strives to get better at the craft. If there is one quality I point out in this book it's that Tim is totally transparent. He speaks from the heart and soul, pressing intentionally forward with an agenda to build strong, capable leaders for the Lord's work. Every bit of instruction that he offers is supported by sound experiential and scholarly information.

The reader is set to undertake a journey – one to create important learning experiences that can be built upon for years to come. My prayer is that every consumer will approach the reading experience prayerfully. Doing so will ensure that the many rich nuggets of information and revelation will be fully realized – and ultimately internalized. Tim planted and watered, and God will give the increase.

- Professor Robert McTyre, Sr. - Director of Writing, Spring Arbor University; School of Graduate and Professional Studies

My Acknowledgements

Saints allow me to teach this material after fleshing out its principles and I enjoy every opportunity. God often pushes me to "Say it again differently" but I need sounding boards. I am often too blunt and dogmatic and need others to smooth out rough edges. At times my mind gets trapped by my pea-brain-approach; therefore I greatly appreciate those who helped make this an acceptable reality.

Arnie Koontz encouraged me to publish a book long before it happened and offered great insight. Bruce Kaufmann encouraged me to join him in a doctoral course; this book is part of our requirement. My professor, Bob Bedford pushed spiritual buttons. My brother Bill offered tremendous help by listening and questioning over the years. Shawn Golden committed a Christmas holiday to read the manuscript and give input. John Hafner endured rough drafts to give invaluable advice. Dave Mercer gave valuable feedback; God called him home 'early' and cut short our graceful conversations. Darci Danhausen provided helpful questions and feedback. Steve Webb offered his younger perspective. My sister Marcia Adams offered perpetual encouragement. My writing professor, Robert McTyre did final editing. Pastors Jason Pittman and Keith Miller read early manuscripts to offer insight and encouragement. Shawn Wilhite from Southern Baptist Theological Seminary gave invaluable help with chapter structure and footnotes. Anthony Ferriell spent many hours discussing and provoking. Many nameless ones provoked – maybe negatively – but God used it for good. Kristopher and Kristina Stephens did my art work; their two daughters Crista and Cecilia are playing in the hay. Darin Magneson of Thorpe Printing did the cover graphics with Kristopher's art on the front cover. Ryan Vangel cleaned up two charts. Larry Van Beek offered feedback and Skype time. My sons, Tim, Todd and Brad encouraged my efforts by discussing different teachings. My 11-year old son Charlie performed tasks that electronically-illiterate dads need. My son Jeremiah installed graphics into the text and tweaked a couple charts.

I'm indebted to my wife, Elizabeth, who initially challenged me to get a degree; I keep working toward an ever-changing goal. Her motivation resulted in a pastorate and this book, though she did not choose either. I'm indebted to her for the resulting joy from her provocations even as we look toward how God will use us ahead.

Lastly I am eternally grateful to my God and Savior Jesus Christ who gave his grace in regeneration, sanctification, in preaching and writing this book. I trust this book glorifies His grace as much as I desire. May God use it to push us higher in our pursuit to Image Him. Your personal Christ-reflection might be a valuable indicator but I offer His grace back to Him for His praise. I could wish all this help means a product without holes or mistakes; in the end, all mistakes are mine. I trust you are challenged to comment or question.

Finding God's Will in The Redeemed View of Life: Toward a Reformed Definition of Grace

Table of Contents

Introduction to God's Will and Ways

A nine year old leaving his flag football game approached the busiest intersection he had to cross to return home. As the busiest, it was also dangerous. Soon great turmoil sprang up in front of me. Sirens wailed and a small crowd of people were buzzing about how a boy had been hit by a car. I heard "No one was dead" and as I worked through the leg-maze I saw the boy – still under the car – and thought "How sad!" He was about my size but I did not recognize him. I vividly saw the stark effects of a car wreck that could have been deadly. Only later I learned he was my good friend. I could not believe it; we planned to walk home together – it could have been me in *that* wreck too!

The reality of a car wreck offers a worthwhile starting analogy. My friend was in a body cast for 6 months and eventually healed. As humans, if we could, we would avoid car wrecks and death; however, we were all in a wreck and may be in another one as our mortal life ends. If we could avoid *that* car wreck, someone please tell us how!

The car wreck we endure is the tragedy of sin and death, and we look through a maze to see what happened. The great wreck at the end of mortal life is God's judgment. Some think that to avoid the tragedy of sin and death is the Great Remedy. It's a good one but the greatest remedy is to live in God's Righteousness that brings soul-joy *and* overcomes the final eternal wreck. David Wells says,

> This moral reality [judgment] is at the center of our universe and God's dealing with it. In the end, it is upon Christ's death and wrath that our hope rests, for he is the last line of resistance to the triumph of what is evil and fallen. It is because of his judgment, because of the day when he will put truth forever on the throne and evil forever on the scaffold, that hope can be sustained in the midst of a world in which there is not only much corruption but in which what is corrupt is so often rewarded and triumphant. God, who is at the moral center of the world and who sustains the moral order, is also the one who has provided in Christ the answer to the profound moral dilemma that his presence evokes.[1]

In our bobble-head culture where people profess to know what to do, yet lack the moral fortitude or character to pull it off, we are in a dilemma of our own making. It's sad when we cannot avoid or explain the car wrecks. Many profess belief in God but violate any Command without remorse or pricked conscience. For some, I might be the old dinosaur talking – not just in age but in gifting. With the gifting of a prophet, I point The Way to live the greatest remedy for our car wrecks.

Contrary to common thinking, man's attempts in and out of the church often miss God's Way. Confusion surrounds what salvation means, how it's gained or applied and effectively lived out. Some claim to know or possess salvation. Others are lost in a haze and won't come out favorably in the car wrecks. We will examine this broad haze, offer a redeemed definition of grace and present a working faith to discover right relationship with God through His applied means.

It's said, "Many roads lead up the mountain to find God and His Will" yet there's no higher pursuit than to experience salvation as God intended. The world offers well-intended but wrong mountain-paths that represent this confusion. Many live in self-actualization and autonomy, apart from God's Will, yet man-designed ways can't work God's Will. Only God's Work and Power for, in and through us can!

To approach a subject we do not know might seem intimidating but learning can be an epiphany. Something in our nature strives to be the best and most understand "If we're going to do something, it's worth doing right" even if we do not always succeed. Applying that learning to key ingredients can be revolutionary and redemptive.

The same goes for the Christian faith and lifeview.[2] If we miss an essential element in life, most want to know how to correct their oversight. My intent is to encourage us to **pursue God's best, seeing and practicing our faith through God's eyes** to obtain and live the Redeemed View of Life – a lifeview that practices life from Christ's Mind, Power, Faith and Sight – as God planned from the beginning.

If we miss an essential ingredient in baking a cake, our cake will not taste good or it will be a flop. We will likely kick ourselves for being forgetful – vowing to do better next time. To learn something that we overlook can be humbling. This book is not really about an edible cake but a spiritual cake related to salvation and becoming like Christ.

This book is about God's gospel and grace living strong in us. As God can make a divine reality in us, I refer to this divine reality as a cake to highlight regeneration. After regeneration, Christ-followers build His Plan into their whole being. Christ-imitation is the objective – only possible through organic new birth and ongoing grace.

Scripture encourages serious effort to find God's Will. In 2 Timothy 2:16 Paul said "Do your best to present yourself to God as one approved, a worker who has no need to be ashamed, **rightly handling the Word of Truth**." Once you know God as Father through the work of Christ, we can set our mind and lives to being what God desires.

Some think God instructs through osmosis. Give up on the idea as God does not teach in this manner. Computers and electronics provide advantages in our modern world but tools only facilitate progress. We must apply right attitudes, diligent work, serious study and a lifelong commitment to learn God's Will – the old fashioned way.

I know what it is to flounder in the faith as I once thought God would teach me by osmosis. God has a much better way than osmosis and I demonstrate a redeemed biblical way to find God's Will. This work can be viewed as a manual for the faith delivered once for all. As we systematically approach our Christian faith in a higher way, we will be eternally glad if we give great effort to experience His Will.

As God built sanctification into my life, I have a story to tell. I often dreamed of writing a book without a firm plan. I saw myself as a layperson called to unofficially pastor people in the faith. I studied theology for 30+ years but did not see myself as sufficient to write. I used to write for an audience of two – God and me; to make a book a reality seemed like a pipe dream. But this book tells how God produced Christ-reflection in me; may God illumine your mind and life too.

This book originally started as three papers, *God's Will,*[3] *The Redeemed View of Life*[4] and *The Two Sides of The Cross*[5] that I wrote to thank God for what He taught me. I heard it said of one seminary professor, "Listening to him is like trying to get a drink of water from a fire hydrant." As I laughed, I realized my writing and teaching can be similar – like eating bullets from a machine gun at times.

Every faith-journey is different but maturity in the Christian faith takes a similar path. God presents the "faith once delivered for all,"[6] "one faith"[7] and Faith Chapter[8] to demonstrate <u>continuity</u> of believing and following His Word. My story, encased in God's Cross-Story, can provoke, encourage and direct those who want to find and mature in the faith. For this reason I humbly offer my story to glorify His grace.

In reflection, learning is provoked. My life journey can help us know that learning God's Will is not a cakewalk but requires a cake. Learning to walk in Christ's Faith takes time and diligence. The Gospel's beauty is that God designs us to live with His power through Christ's Cross and – to know His Will, we must do His Will.

Plugging into R.C. Sproul's teaching and Ligonier Ministries[9] was huge for my spiritual development. Practical and theological foundations were laid in my life. Through *Renewing Your Mind*[10] radio programs, tapes, conferences, Ligonier Ministries' *TableTalk*[11] Devotional and recommended books, God taught me great things.

God took me through the School of Hard Knocks where I learned Paul's thorn-in-the-flesh message, "My Grace is Sufficient!"[12] Pursuing degree work encouraged many things. Becoming a pastor was huge. God continues to stretch theological insight in preaching Christ through grace and burdens me to incite Christ-reflection in my flock and those in my sphere of influence. God's provocation is ongoing as I gracefully learn to glorify Him.

It's not easy to ascertain how God wants us to study, think and live when competing and conflicting thoughts bombard our mind. As I wrote in 1995 for my audience of two, I wrote to what God taught me experientially and theologically through His Word. This book shares some of that journey. If we can see the forest rather than individual trees, we can see a laymen's systematic approach to God's Will.

Part 1 – Clearing the Land to Build a Redeemed Lifeview

We are designed to image God in Christ and see truth through His eyes but we often fail miserably. We struggle to see through various aspects of nominal Christianity that our flesh might embrace. Christianity is essentially about Life in the Spirit rather than life in the flesh as the world and Satan beckons to lead us *from* God's Will.

When we realize our lack, we turn to God for instruction and power to perform His Will through Scripture that gives a workable understanding of Law, Gospel and God's Will. As we sort through genres, periods, leaders, varied texts and apparently-different ways of salvation, we look through a fuzzy haze. **Chapter 1** explains this haze and offers help to see Scripture as one Redeemed Story.

Every person is commanded to seek God's Will and live mightily for Him; therefore we must seriously evaluate our approach to life. As God-in-the-flesh, Jesus was sent to <u>effect</u> salvation purchased on the Cross for those who believe Him and follow His gospel. I use <u>effect</u> rather than <u>affect</u> when referring to salvation because this is Scripture's emphasis. God can *effect* salvation; we can only *affect* salvation – but to reflect Jesus Christ, we must be hot after this pursuit.

Some live off their parents' or untested faith but each person needs vital personal faith. Until we experience transformation by being born from above[13] to reflect Christ's image, we do not know God's Will! God calls us to love Him with our heart, mind, body and strength. We are to be sold out to Him to diligently perform God's Will. **Chapters 2**

and 3 set the stage for right thinking and subsequent living, with Chapter 2 presenting a one-page synopsis (p.57) of Scripture's scope.

We can use worldview and lifeview as synonyms but my desire is to influence a _redeemed view of life_ or lifeview rather than a worldview per se. Worldviews are taught through broad presentations with higher-level worldly ingredients as their focus. My desire is to influence all-inclusive thinking parameters that frame our lives through redeemed living. With corrections in mind, this book can be viewed as a mini training Manual for Christian thinking and behavior.

It's amazing to look back over the years to see how God works in our lives even when we do not know it. We often _see_ after-the-fact as we evaluate God's moving. I was churched from birth and a student of the Word for many years yet if one thought they did not need correction and conversion, it was me! Seeing Scripture with God's eyes is the thrust of the Redeemed View of Life; it can challenge us all.

The common "Don't confuse me with the facts; I've already got my mind made up" attitude or position won't work. As God leads in sanctification, redeemed thought-patterns enable a Christ-reflecting lifeview where we see through God's eyes, if you will. **Chapter 4** presents _God's Thread of Continuity_, my basic foundation – with eyes.

Part 2 – Claiming a Literal and Objective Divine Foundation

God is One overarching Godhead who exists in three persons: God the Father, Son and Holy Spirit – what we call Trinity. All possess eternal life, are equal in purpose and concertedly _work_ redemption. The more we learn about God, His eternal plan of redemption comes into focus. God's Will, Ways and Word take up **Chapters 5, 6 and 7**.

God helps unpack His Word through His Story – redemption for His people in whom He applies the accomplished Atonement of Jesus Christ on the Cross. God challenges us 'Come see what I have done! See how I apply redemption to those who believe Me and do as I command!' As the Great Evangelist, God calls sinners to repentance, faith and conversion in the Redeemed View of Life.

God's Holiness, Character and Law go together in a neat package but are unpacked separately. In the church and world, these doctrines are greatly misunderstood but as God reveals Himself, we must seriously look in order to see Him as He is. God's Holiness and Character are presented in **Chapters 8 and 9.**

Part 3 – Clinging to a Redeemed GRACE-FULL Salvation

Part 3 speaks toward a Redeemed Grace-Full Salvation. If we are to overcome the scourge of nominal Christianity, we must understand and live Christ's Truth. First, I focus on a Redeemed New Covenant Cross-View because many doctrines are firmly planted here. Second, my soul's passion is Grace. Grace is a stand-alone doctrine without need of 'adjectival definition.' **We need a reformed definition in light of grace-confusion today**. A fresh look at Grace might provoke us to rethink practical and doctrinal foundations of salvation. Third, we need a grace-Full salvation – Full in the Cross and New Covenant truth. Fourth, I examine salvation from a Redeemed Grace-Full foundation. In the process, some might be driven to the reality of God's Salvation through His Grace.

Christ's disciples think of salvation in terms of Justification, adoption, Covenant, atonement, law, Holiness, Grace, sin, repentance, faith, conversion and belief. If however, we put the proverbial horse before the cart, confusion exists over how these terms and doctrines flow into God's salvation. I can't 'straighten out' anyone but as God stretched me in my journey, I answer difficult issues with redeemed answers. While others helped clear my haze, I offer what God taught through His Word. I trust my journey helps some find the reality of new life in Christ. With a backdrop of Redeemed Grace-Full Salvation, **we can overcome nominal Christianity** – especially inside.

The doctrine of grace was a huge theological stepping stone for me. The Spirit powerfully taught me a reformed definition of grace in what I call *The Two Sides of the Cross*.[14] **My understanding of grace is different,** not least because it's the greatest element God presents in Christ. It's crucial to realize this essential difference. I teach grace as Scripture's paramount doctrine of Holiness – in contrast to typical views. Hereafter I **bolden grace** and can use the adverb **redeemed** when I speak of **grace** to contrast common or 'faulty' views.

Six authors named John – what I call my six Johns – pushed my theology that budded into a passion for **grace**. *Living in the Power of Future Grace*[15] by John Piper was instrumental. The *Institutes of the Christian Religion*[16] by John Calvin was powerful. *A Treatise on the Law and Gospel*[17] by John Colquhoun was huge. *Principles of Conduct*[18] by John Murray was provocative. *Religious Affections*[19] by Jonathan Edwards humbled me greatly. *Primitive Theology*[20] by John H. Gerstner challenged theological paradigms. They all helped.

Unapologetically, my heart beats with **Grace as** I think **Grace** beats in God's heart too. I sometimes feel like a modern Jeremiah compelled by **Grace** to proclaim the message. Jeremiah 20:9 says, "If I say, 'I will not mention Him, or speak any more in His Name,' there is in my heart as it were a burning fire shut up in my bones, and **I am weary with holding it in, and I cannot**." I too must declare His **Grace**!

The vehicle God used to teach me **grace** was a neurological condition in my neck, probably from an undiagnosed broken neck. An emergency neck fusion, 5 years later in 1995, did wonders. God touched my soul significantly and, through this physical trial, I learned **grace** like Paul in 2 Corinthians 12. Understanding this reformed definition of **grace** continues to drive me and is contrasted against foundational mercy presented in **Chapter 10**. While I quote many men to support what I present on **Grace**, I don't parrot anyone but the Spirit as He speaks through Scripture and New Covenant **grace**ful reality.

The Holy Spirit rebirths those whom the Father draws to the Son's Atoning work. Once rebirthed, our heart, mind and life is opened to ongoing <u>sanctification</u> – <u>being conformed to His Likeness</u> – also called conversion. If God plugs the organic reality of regeneration into us, we are on the path to find His Will for and in us. The Three Step Process of 1) put off the old man, 2) transform your thinking and 3) put on the new man demonstrates how these doctrines flow together in the Redeemed View of Life. **Chapter 11** presents repentance, faith and conversion as this Three Step process – the jest of Christian faith.

As I ponder the Church's life-blood, the subjects of 1) **grace**, 2) salvation and 3) how people understand the mechanics and reality of salvation greatly concern me. I see *professed* believers struggle to know God and build their faith. I teach that God can build the salvation cake in us. **Chapter 12** speaks to the difference between believing a recipe versus having the reality of the recipe live in us.

God the <u>Father</u> sent Jesus Christ, His One and Only Unique <u>Son</u> to fulfill all prophecy for His Atoning Cross Work. The sending, life, death, Resurrection and Ascension of Jesus is the Bible's back-drop. The <u>Spirit</u> applies Christ's work, making formerly dead ones into born-from-above-ones – and God's Gospel seeks sons. Do not assume you are God's child; become an adopted son – the subject of **Chapter 13.**

The Spirit turned my lights on to His power for saints – God's empowerment – first in believers to be redeemed and then to be holy. This power does not come from the Law but through faith; however **this power of grace lives in the gold vein of God's Moral Law**. We can learn to embrace the Moral Law as God's Will in **Chapter 14.**

The applied reality of the Gospel is crucial to overcome our car wrecks. To find the Gospel fulfilled in us is one of life's greatest joys. The last chapter ties the book into a redeemed summary of the applied gospel of **grace**. **Chapter 15** presents this application and outgrowth as the culmination of Finding God's Will in a Redeemed lifeview.

FYI, I try to qualify topics through upper case versus lower case letters to distinguish between divine and human origins. For instance, Holy refers to God and His attributes whereas holy refers to the best humans can do with the empowerment of Divine Holiness. A huge difference exists between law and Law – we must learn this. I often highlight and underline when I read; I tend to write the same way. Rather than use break-out boxes, I tend to bolden key points.

An **Appendix** synopsis is 1) my life experiences are given for insight rather than a normative model; 2) John's presentation of Jesus as God; 3) Book suggestions; and 4) a Quickie Reference Guide.

I pray the following teachings cause us to see God, Christ and Scripture in a new way as **God commits Himself to those who believe and are converted**. Paul confirms this in Galatians 2:19-20:

> For through the law I died to the law, so that I might live to God. I have been crucified with Christ. It is no longer I who live, but Christ who lives in me. And the life I now live in the flesh, I live by faith in the Son of God, who loved me and gave Himself for me.

Jesus was God's final revelation and Scripture is God's final completed Word – although He still illumines and speaks. God wants us redeemed IN Christ – that's why it's His Gospel! Our faith needs stretched. Get rid of the "Don't confuse me with the facts; I've already got my mind made up" attitude. If you must, read one chapter at a time. I *try* not to speak above the average pew-sitter but when I do, **don't allow any teaching to discourage you**. Chew well before you swallow and pursue Truth like the Bereans because living His keys allows us to become healthy Christ reflectors of God's Will in **Grace**!

Since God <u>essentially</u> invests everything He is to gain salvation for those who believe, we can find the joy of living strong in the Power of Christ. Strange as this may sound, Jesus' dying words on the Cross, "It is Finished!" are the beginning and stamp of God's Will for salvation. Get started in redeeming your view of life. Look through the haze of history and corruption to see the Cross in its glory. Rather than a futile car-wreck-life, live a life that counts for eternity. **Through Christ we can experience God's empowerment to overcome life's car wrecks** – to find joy, rest and freedom for our eternal souls. We look at the trees to see the forest – to understand the trees as God desires.

---

1 David F. Wells, *Losing Our Virtue: Why the church must recover its moral vision* (Grand Rapids, MI.: Eerdmans Publishing, 1998) 36.

2 Teaching a godly *lifeview* is a major goal. I can't find a dictionary definition but will unpack its meaning throughout the book; be patient as this gets explained. I tie it directly to the Redeemed View of Life, God's Thread of Continuity and Grace.

3 *God's Will* is a paper where I attempted to answer the typical questions that pertain to ascertaining what God wants us to do in the decisions of life.

4 *The Redeemed View of Life* was the first paper I did that incited the desire to write a book. This book speaks to a systematic approach to Christian living.

5 *The Two Sides of The Cross* was my second vision for a book. I may still write this to deal with technical issues of redeemed distinctions between mercy and grace to provoke a redeemed definition of grace that supports holiness and Christ-reflection. I push for a definition (what is it?) rather than a glorified description (what does it look like or do?) that requires adjectives to make sense. In my mind, the typical 'definition' adds confusion to a doctrine that requires clarity and consistency because this pleases God.

6 Jude 3

7 Ephesians 4:4-7

8 Hebrews 11

9 *Ligonier Ministries* is the ministry started by R.C. Sproul in the Ligonier Valley of Pennsylvania. The ministry is currently located in St. Mary, Florida.

10 *Renewing Your Mind* is the daily radio ministry of Ligonier Ministry. Check your Christian radio stations for broadcasting or call toll free at 1-800-435-4343.

11 *TableTalk* is the monthly devotional magazine distributed by Ligonier Ministry. Call their toll free number as they are known to offer 6-month trial subscriptions.

12 2 Corinthians 12:9. From what God taught Paul through the thorn in the flesh trial, Paul says he *learned* that Christ's Grace was sufficient.

13 In John 3:3, Jesus tells Nicodemus we must be born from above.

14 *The Two Sides of The Cross* is the title I gave a work that began 18 years ago. I saw a sharp distinction between grace and mercy throughout Scripture; therefore Two Sides. God unfolded a different definition of grace. Common Man demonstrates disregard for godliness or practical righteousness but Scripture presents a definite link to holiness. God gives us power to imitate Him; learn this power for yourself and you can please Him.

15 John Piper, *Living in the Power of Future Grace*. This was the first book to really grab my attention about the subject of grace.

16 John Calvin, *Institutes of the Christian Religion* (Philadelphia, PA.: The Westminster Press, 1950)

17 John Colquhoun, *A Treatise On The Law And The Gospel* (Morgan, PA.: Soli Deo Gloria Publications, 1999)

18 John Murray, *Principles of Conduct : Aspects of Biblical Ethics* (Grand Rapids, MI.: Eerdmans Publishing, 1957)

19 Jonathan Edwards, *Religious Affections: A Christian's Character Before God* (Minneapolis, MN.: Bethany House, 1996)

20 John H. Gerstner, *Primitive Theology: The Collected Primers of John H. Gerstner* (Morgan, PA.:Soli Deo Gloria Publications, 1996)

Part 1

Clearing the Land to Build
A Redeemed Foundation

We need to play...

In the hay
of God's Word

Chapter 1 – From the Haze to The Cross

It's not easy to approach a book like the Bible and claim to know God's main thrust. It's like finding that needle in the proverbial haystack. Written by men on different continents with a few original languages over several thousand years with 66 individual books, it can be difficult to discern accurately. But it can be done. I wish there was an easier way to see through the fog[1] but the tried-and-true method of diligent study stands as The Way God ordains and blesses. In this chapter I will explain that haze from a different vantage point.

If we profess His name, it's crucial to know His Will! My attempt is to help us get over some hurdles I faced in my growth. I don't want to burst any bubbles but I don't think any shortcuts exist to gain organic and practical Christian knowledge – and Christ-Imaging practice. From what I know, we can't short-change this process.

To search His Word, find His Will and discover His designed application is not easy; therefore seriously pursue these objectives. Scripture spans roughly 3,500 years with many stories and teachings. To properly understand God's Word, Will and Ways can seem a daunting task. As much as I believe Scripture is more than sufficient to lead us to know God and His Truth, variables like mental blocks, sin, arrogance, rebellion and faulty teaching can make it seem impossible to discern correctly. Be willing to lay these down at Jesus' feet to see through the haze and clearly see the salvation He offers in Christ.

When God invests everything He is to bring salvation, it is right that we owe Him our all to pursue His Will, learn His Word, and walk in His Ways. To help us understand the haze better, analogies depict our struggle to read and know God's Word and understand God's approach in the matter. With variables, we can see ever changing pictures as we go to His Word. We will see and live a magnificent picture if we look through haze-factors to find the Redeemed View of Life.

One seminary professor, Dr. Timothy Beougher,[2] often used the analogy of a box top to speak of our approach to Scripture. With a puzzle box top in mind, consider how we learn to put puzzles together. As youngsters, we learn to do puzzles with etched piece-outlines. After a while they are easy to do and we do more advanced puzzles on the table. Most put edge pieces together from the box top and fill in the middle to fit put-together-edge pieces – much the same way as a child.

I often expand Dr. Beougher's helpful box top analogy to ask people, "How well could you put a 1,500 piece puzzle together if you did not have edge piece or the puzzle box top that shows the completed puzzle?" It would seem impossible. Putting that puzzle together would require great time and probably many restarts.

Putting a 1,500 piece puzzle together without a border, edge pieces or a box top describes how many originally approach Scripture. Typically we start with simple stories and make progress. We may be taught about the birth, life, death, and ascension of Christ or we may read Scripture to discover these details ourselves. This may be likened to having edge pieces but we are still in a quandary without a box top. I was raised in a bible-believing home and loved to hear Bible stories. I enjoyed good preaching but didn't really study the Bible until after my new birth at age 20. I tell you not to waste another day looking for that box top; get busy putting God's puzzle together or walking in His Way.

In a passing comment some say we can see life with rose colored glasses. A colored-glasses idea relates to how we bring rose-colored vision to God, humanity, Scripture and redemption. The reason I emphasize these generalities is that more than we know, we add our elements to the haze of Scripture but this can be overcome. I want us to change rose-colored glasses for Cross-colored ones.

Everyone finds their view of 1) God, 2) humanity, 3) Scripture and 4) redemption within one of the following scenarios. From a mere human perspective, we can see <u>humanity</u> with or without various perspectives of necessary <u>Divine</u> intervention. Conversely, from a divine perspective or with God's eyes, we see varied human responses to divine initiatives in regards to their vision of redemption.

God wants us to see life and humanity from a Scriptural and Divine perspective. The closer we come, we see humanity's story with divine considerations. Actually the Bible is God's story with huge implications for humanity; therefore, how we view humanity and Scripture has significant implications for how we approach God's Will.

These perspectives flow into salvation and redemption. We can see salvation and redemption in <u>causal</u> mechanics of humanity – with or without divine help. Or we can see salvation and redemption as God's domain – with or without human participation in the new-birthing or regenerating part of salvation. These perspectives are presented and discussed throughout the book. Upfront, I unashamedly embrace a humanity that requires God's intervention to bring salvation.

My former truncated view saw the Bible as a mass of puzzle-pieces strewn on the kitchen table seeking someone to put them together for me. In reflection, I felt like I did not have the border, much less the box top. With years of searching and study I finally began to see the border of the puzzle; then God showed me the box top. Wow!

God unfolds His Story of redemptive history in Scripture even as we struggle to understand correctly. The box-top-view is much clearer today. As I teach, pastor and preach the box top view comes into still clearer focus. I passionately want those in my sphere of influence to live the box top picture – even my readers.

We can believe God and live in faith without a complete puzzle edge or box top. Our groping describes typical Old and early New Testament saints as they sought to understand without complete prophecy-fulfillment or the complete Scriptures we possess. This book can inflame us to pursue God's Word and Will toward a complete picture. Pursue this reality in your living until you arrive in heaven.

God's approach to unfold His Story shows how the details come together in one Story. Consider *The "A" TEAM* television show that I used to enjoy watching. Mr. T, Face and Murdoch were sidekicks of Hannibal – the spokesperson and leader of a renegade group of military men who were perpetually on the run. No matter how deep their dilemma, how much the odds were stacked against his team or how many devious plans were designed to thwart his plan, Hannibal's plan always won the day! He rightfully relished the outcome of every success and victory. After winning the perpetual victory, he would light a cigar to toast the victory. As he puffed away to celebrate the victory, he would say "I just love it when a plan comes together!"

Although it does not compare to Hannibal's victory, Jesus' victory on the Cross was God's Plan from the beginning.[3] We could say the odds were stacked against God – as Satan and angels rebelled, Adam and Eve sinned, revealed details could potentially unravel His Master Plan and devious plans were implemented. God's Plan often appeared that His effort failed because His people disobeyed but in the end God demonstrated His Plan won the day.

Like *The "A" TEAM TV* series, a series-ending show will come. An end will come with full exposure of ultimate victory and eternal unveiling. On the backside of His victory in Christ's death, I almost hear God say from heaven, "I just love it when My Plan comes together!" In His dying breath, this explains Jesus' words, "It is Finished!"

As we learn God's Plan, the Bible manifests differently because *knowing is living*; and *living is knowing*. To know His Plan impacts an essential relationship as we live in a pleasing way. One overarching event defines His Plan – the Cross – yet many get stuck in a quagmire of variables that skews His picture. Thankfully, as we see, God allows us to share the majesty and exultation of His victory in His puzzle. If we are to make spiritual progress, we need the right answers and must dig deeply with great care. Then we can walk in His truth.

As we approach the puzzle-haze, many headings can be used to differentiate points. I chose not to break up this chapter under headings because haze-points are presented throughout the book. Headings that vied for consideration were distinctions between the Old and New Covenants; law versus grace; the Genesis account of The Fall; the effects of sin; paralyzing paradigms; doctrinal differences; family divisions; contradicting variations; universal salvation and mystery-unpacking teachings that reveal New Covenant truth. Many reasons are untouched but these offer a helpful overview.

Misunderstanding family-trees in Scripture adds to the haze. First we struggle with Adam as Scripture contrasts him with the Second Adam; we might ask how sin entered a perfect environment? Second we struggle with contrasts between Cain and Abel – how could the first murder take place? Third, the dichotomy between Ishmael and Isaac adds to the haze – how does the slave woman/free woman come into play? Fourth, covenantal differences between twins Esau and Jacob are difficult to sort through – how can a Covenant-denier fall below a deceiver who is then regenerated in a struggle with God? In these four contrasts, the first name manifests those who reject God's Covenant and live in a gospel-forsaking way. The other four are types[4] with great redemptive significance. Only as we work through these issues and embrace biblical qualifiers can we clear the haze of family ties.

Other haze factors surround the attempt to create doctrines to explain biblical truth. Attempts are noble but not always accurate. John Calvin wrote extensively; he knew His God and said something like: 'I step to the ocean of God's truth and pull out my thimble full of explanation.' I love to read Calvin and appreciate his endeavor to protect God's doctrine in the face of heresy but also realize we can make unwarranted stretches. In all veins of Christianity, troublesome or stretched doctrines add to the haze. We must know enough to see through doctrines – but this would take a systematic theology book.

Rather than see seemingly disconnected stories in the Bible, it's helpful to see one overarching story from God's Eyes. With after-the-fact clarity, God willingly shared His plan although prior to the Cross this clarity was vague per 1 Corinthians 13:12. In crucial ways, God limited the unveiling of His Truth and revelation primarily to two things – the display of the Cross and the ripped Temple veil.

For majestic reasons, God shrouded truth from Satan and his cohorts until His plan fully came together. God's shrouding might be the greatest fog in Scripture and, primarily through Paul, God unpacked previously veiled mystery. God unveiled the fullness of His Plan in the Cross and this exposure is manifest in the Church during the last 2,000 years. Clearly, the Cross and Redemption was God's central plan!

I think the Cross Event – Christ's Crucifixion – is Christianity's greatest event and day. Bear with me in this assertion because I didn't always see it this way. Jesus wore many ministry-hats during His earth-time and it's hard to sort through His ministries to see His major ministry – to die on the Cross. Contrary to skeptical teachings by those who claim Jesus 'stumbled upon a workable plan' or 'got too far into a conspiracy to extricate himself before he was judiciously hung for his stupidity,'[5] Jesus came to earth with a clear plan – the God-head's Plan – and the Father, Son and Spirit worked that plan to perfection!

To see through the haze accurately, we must understand the evolution of the Covenants or Testaments. It's said "The Old Testament is the New Testament concealed; the New Testament is the Old Testament revealed."[6] Great truth is contained in these nutshell facts. The first point teaches that the New Testament or Covenant is concealed in the Old Testament. The haze of concealment is almost beyond our imagination and rarely examined for what it is.

The second point teaches that the New Testament reveals the Old Testament. The statement contains valid sentiment but falls short of redeemed understanding as the Mosaic Covenant is often contrasted with the Abrahamic/New Covenant. A brief look can't do justice here but God explodes Old Covenant haze with New Covenant majesty.[7] In many ways, the Old reveals the New; this is why the hermeneutic[8] that magnifies the Redeemed View of Life is crucial.

Correctly seeing through the haze might not essentially bear on regeneration but wrong seeing prevents individuals from crucial insight in salvation.[9] The negative impact is the inability to speak into the intellectual and moral fallen-ness of self and man to affect salvation and provoke a God-honoring perspective. It's not imperative to reach the intellect for regeneration but the mind is crucial in sanctification. Wrong seeing can mean questions go unasked and unanswered. To overcome the intellect, we must love God with our minds. Mere mental acceptance of God's Work and Word is unable to overcome moral rejection[10] and a spiritual link exists between the haze and unbelief.

Great debate surrounds the use of biblical proofs[11] to provoke faith in sinners. From my perspective, biblical proofs can become the fool's errand of unbelief but, at times, we need pre-evangelism. With that in mind, I offer proof-answers to provoke biblical faith. No matter the end of these debates, people want to know whether the Bible can stand on its own. It can and does but searching ones often put themselves in a position of truth arbiters. Without realizing what they do, they reject the notion that godly men could allow the Spirit to work perfectly through them to write God's complete sufficient Word. In this way, they tragically retain for themselves the right, authority and power to stand as judge *over* the validity and truthfulness of the Word.

How we view God's Word is crucial to our understanding and practice as our view can be a self-inflicted inhibitor to correct living. There is no way to briefly unpack all arguments or approaches to God's Word but let me dissect them into four loose generic categories to answer each category with a call to the Redeemed View of Life. If we can see God's Word through redeemed eyes, we will find God's Will.

First, <u>unbelievers</u> essentially reject the authority of God's Word and rarely seek to know its essence. Their ignorance is often assumed to be excused by God and others. Unbelievers can be those who have not heard God's Word and therefore need gospel preaching. Some believe not to believe – culpability is very present here. Unbelievers need to become Disciples of Christ to receive and live the gospel.

Second, <u>claimers</u> suggest a relationship with God through the Risen Christ yet in their practical approach they treat God's Word as a waxed nose. Maybe without malice or intention, they twist God's Word to match their opinionated whims – believing their perspective is God's Truth. In a crass way, they *stand over* the Word as they define what the Word means rather than seek God's intent in the matter.

Third are <u>professors</u> who may or may not actually possess Christ – but most profess possession of Christ. If 'may-not-ones' don't possess Christ, it's no wonder the world doesn't see much objective faith, but this assessment needs further details. 'May-ones' struggle to accept God's Word at face value as the unadulterated, authoritative and binding foundation for their life; this waffling must be corrected.

Fourth are <u>possessors</u> who accept God's Word as written by God's hand, similar to the Ten Commandments Written by God's finger – given to Moses and by extension, the universal Church. Possessors may struggle to willingly submit to the Written Word since **conversion is a life-long process** but its truth and authority is beyond debate. Possessors seek to <u>*stand under*</u> the Word in submission to His Will.

As we seek to live God's Will, we are somewhere in these four categories. Seek the fourth category that represents a redeemed view. Until we come to see God's Word as He intended through human writers, our belief and practice will be skewed. Worse, we might not be in true relationship with Him as God unpacks truth for possessors.

Possessors are empowered to manifest right relationship to God's Word. Possessors eventually *stand under* the Word where we acknowledge The Bible as the authoritative inerrant Word and allow the Word to preach to our souls to conform us to Christ's image. Gospel acceptance by true faith brings us into this fourth category.

Part of the problem, even after we come to faith, is overcoming the tendency to _stand over_ the Word. This is practical unbelief even as we might stand in faith. It sounds conflicted and inconsistent – and it is! At its root, conversion can eradicate conflictedness from our thinking and living but it's hard to lay down our pride to bow before God's Word. It's difficult to realize how we stand _over_ the Word rather than _under_ its penetrating transforming power. We should not judge the Word; the Word must judge and correct us! This is His Way!

Another statement Dr. Beougher used to say bears on this point, "It's SO NOT about us!"[12] Conversely this means "It's SO about Him!" As God Justifies and Sanctifies His people there's much to learn and do, if only we knew the way. Once the fog lifts we see clearer.

People say that many ways exist to know God's Way. Some are difficult; some easy. Some wind through history; others jump over Scripture to offer a cut version. Some get bogged down; others flow smoothly. Skeptics offer some; godly men offer others. Some are all-inclusive; others exclusive. Some are trivial; some deep. All in all, we must work through the haze to the point of victory through His Word. Paul hints at this in the Love Chapter of 1 Corinthians 13:8-13:

> Love never ends. As for prophecies, they will pass away; as for tongues, they will cease; as for knowledge, it will pass away. For we know in part and we prophesy in part, but when the perfect comes, the partial will pass away. When I was a child, I spoke like a child; I thought like a child, I reasoned like a child. When I became a man, I gave up childish ways. For now we see in a mirror dimly, but then face to face. Now I know in part; then I shall know fully, even as I have been fully known. So now faith, hope and love abide, these three; but the greatest of these is love.

Paul says a believer must change his approach to God's Word and we essentially learn a redeemed view of life. From the God-act of re-creation we learn what God requires; how God works redemption; the logistics of the sacrificial system; Old Testament prophecy, history, rebellion and sin-induced bondage; Messiah typology; the Incarnation of Jesus; and prophecy toward New Covenant understanding. The grandest points of biblical emphasis toward God's Will proceed directly from the ministry and Atoning Work of Jesus – and its application. This majesty is seen in the Garden of Gethsemane and the Cross. To consider the ministry of Jesus in light of what He said about His acceptance of God's Plan is crucial. Depending on our view, we can miss or misunderstand the main point He repeatedly proclaimed about His public ministry. God necessarily authenticated Christ's person, authority and ministry, but misunderstanding adds to our haze.

How we see Christ's ministry impacts many things. Let's put some meat on the bones of this skeleton to see the outcome; besides the few points here, the book helps explain the haze. Our view affects how we approach Church ministry and how we reflect Jesus, His commands, or works. Our perspective affects our approach to life and exposes whether we allow His life to be our imitation-model.

What I began to see clearly were distinctions between His primary and secondary ministry. Kevin DeYoung and Greg Gilbert filled in cracks[13] as Christian books and ministries can exalt various aspects of Christ's ministry. Mercy ministries live out their understanding but can be seen as *the* gospel rather than as manifestations of the gospel. Practical outworkings will be examined to help us work through this.

Misinterpreting Scripture always presents meaning that can't be supported from a full redeemed box-top-view. We are responsible for our teaching/preaching efforts as everyone must give an account for their understanding and conduct. My concern is not so much against noble desire or effort, because it can be huge, but against confused understandings of Christ's focus or the redeemed truth. This is why I am so passionate about teaching redeemed **grace**.

In a Good Friday-to-Easter preaching series, I showed that Jesus' works and ministry-reasons can cloud our eyes so we cannot accurately see His proclaimed mission. I'm not sure I accomplished my objective but God's Spirit continues to work this message in me. We can all gain benefit as we ponder these points. As The Spirit pushed me, each week I touched on a different reason. The questions below flowed from the main question: Was Christ's primary focus to:

1) Draw disciples to Himself?
2) Perform miracles and heal the sick?
3) Preach repentance and the Kingdom gospel?
4) Call Israel back to Himself to be witnesses?
5) Be the conquering King (as Jews expected) and provide salvation for all?
6) Reinstitute proper worship from the fulfilled Law and God's Word? Or
7) To be the Suffering Servant and go to the Cross to obtain Atonement for His sheep?

Jesus 'wore' each point as a mission-hat. This sounds crude but helps distinguish His ministry thrust. Only one hat signifies the mission He presents as primary: the last one. We should never miss or dismiss this. Without unduly treading on pet beliefs, keep questions or thoughts in mind as we seek to understand Jesus' ministry.

Scripture indicates that going to the Cross is the answer Jesus gave most often. As a boy, He knew His destination – the Cross. When He was baptized and tempted, He knew His destination – the Cross. When He was honored as a teacher, He kept sight of His mission – the Cross. When He was applauded as King, He knew His destination was the Cross. When He prayed in the Garden before His death, He knew His purpose and destination – the Cross. He never flinched from completing His Father's Plan until it came to drinking the cup of sin and understanding he would be rejected. Clearly, the Cross was His mission or objective and He willingly embraced God's plan.

Jesus proclaimed His purpose yet His disciples missed His point. Even if they saw Him as Savior, they expected Him to be King. Most Jews did not see Jesus as Savior, at least not as New Covenant saints should understand. Professed saints often miss this point too.

At His triumphant entry into Jerusalem, Jews were abuzz with the possibility of overthrowing the Romans. They could not fathom the Suffering Servant and Messiah in one package, so they missed reality right before their eyes. He failed their expectations. If Judas held this view, this might explain why he subsequently rejected Him. While His disciples, much of the Jewish nation and Jewish leaders misunderstood His purpose and ministry, this does not warrant slanderous arguments.

Some see Jesus as host of a *Let's Make a Deal* Show. They think He makes different offers, with a different choice behind each curtain. Satan offered different curtains from the beginning and people freely choose what they want. Know this – Satan's curtains lead away from what God desires for your life! What are a few Satan-curtains?

Curtain #1 – Approach God and His gospel from biblically-distorted positions like Jesus Seminar teachings, Quest writings, New Age material, the New Spirituality and other heretical positions.

Curtain #2 – Imagine that Jesus stumbled into the right choice – and therefore reject His Work as substitutionary atonement and/or sufficient unto perfect salvation.

Curtain #3 – He was rightly crucified as an insurrectionist; therefore, His crucifixion is 'just condemnation' for a rebellious citizen of the Roman world.

Many distortions and enticing curtains are offered. Satan's curtains lead to faulty views but Jesus boldly proclaimed His curtain – He was going to the Cross to effect salvation for His sheep. Part of our problem is that natural thinking 'puts pressure' on a perfect God that is able to pull off a plan without a hitch in light of sin and evil. Man likes to blame God for his failures. We should be embarrassed to think like this but most do until after they are redeemed. If we would look deeply enough, He pulled off His plan with odds stacked against Him. Satan always seemed to be around the corner and in the face of Jewish rejection and Roman intimidation, Jesus held firm and accomplished His purpose. At the Cross, God's Plan won the day!

Even His disciples missed His main thrust until the resurrected Jesus taught more. Jesus gave compacted teaching before ascending into heaven because now they saw with redeemed eyes. Later the Holy Spirit unpacked truth for them and they wrote Scripture. Like us, they also learned throughout their lives as they proclaimed the gospel.

We often miss the magnitude of their earlier oversight. At least three times Jesus told them plainly He had to go to the Cross and die, yet they missed His clear words. They missed it so bad that two disciples on the Emmaus road (Luke 24) were down in the mouth about the events of the crucifixion – totally missing the thrust of prophecy, Jesus' mission or the recent Cross-victory.

His 11 disciples (minus Judas) missed it so bad they did not wait at the tomb to see Him come out. They missed it so bad that some went back fishing. In many ways, they deserted the mission Jesus gave them. Whatever happened – they thought – they were done! Whatever hope and vision they held before, at this point it was gone. If you asked His disciples *then* whether God's Plan came together at the Cross, they would vehemently deny the possibility. Many today do the same.

Jesus' disciples required the breath of God before they could understand and perform the mission He commissioned them to do. John 20:21-22 says, "Jesus said to them again, 'Peace be with you. As the Father has sent me, even so I am sending you.' And when He had said this, He breathed on them and said to them, 'Receive the Holy Spirit.'" This was like an 'inner-circle-Pentecost' where Jesus taught them – the just – to live by faith. We too need this serious education and transformation if we hope to do what God desires. After this Spirit-education related to His Power, they turned their world upside down.

Jesus instituted the promised New Covenant as His disciples were the first-actualizers. It took time to grow on them but they understood the <u>necessity of new birth to image Christ and understand His Will</u>. If we come alive to Christ, the Spirit works regeneration in us per John 3 & 4 and Ephesians 2:4-5. We need to see what His disciples needed – before they could properly see and do His Will.

In the Upper Room Discourse, Jesus began to unpack His truth plainly and His disciples still did not understand – as they would later. In His High Priestly prayer recorded in John 17, Jesus said "Father, the hour has come; glorify your Son that the Son may glorify you, since <u>you have given Him authority over all flesh, to give eternal life to all whom you have given Him</u>." As the 1) New Adam, 2) Abraham's seed and 3) God, Jesus breathed the Holy Spirit on them but they still needed Pentecost and more instruction from His soon-to-be-newly-finished Word. Even His disciples needed the fog removed to practice His Will.

All saints enter through Jesus the Door.[14] His God-breathed teaching allowed His disciples to begin to properly understand what was cloudy before – *after the resurrection*. Jesus gave the Spirit and more teaching to lift the fog a bit. Without this, they did not understand the Cross properly and the Spirit taught them *after* the resurrection.

Jesus boldly proclaimed His intentions in the majesty of the Cross in His Upper Room teaching. He was cautious about what He said at times but boldly proclaimed His plan. We may not think God would flout His plan but Jesus often used an in-your-face-manner. The greatest in-your-face teaching was the Cross – God's greatest plan!

Since his insurrection to produce heaven's first outcast, Satan has warred against or rebelled against God. Ever since, Satan is out to get God, yet God shows time and again He will win the victory. Satan could never win but he keeps trying. In the face of Satan and evil rebellious men, God proclaimed His intentions – working toward His great fog-clearing at the Cross and subsequent Resurrection.

Throughout Bible history, Satan seeks to thwart God's Plan. His desire to unseat God causes a perpetual running battle and, in his mind, Satan is never going to give up. His first victory over Adam and Eve heightened his taste for more blood and libelous influence. If we did not know that God wins and redeemed sinners win as a result, we could easily see or fret over another outcome. Distorted outcomes provoke some to stand on arrogance, blindness and rebellion to slander God and His fulfilled Plan, even as they claim to believe Him.

Scoffers say "Satan won many skirmishes and appeared to win the war at the Cross." By mere outward appearances, they are right. Somehow they think – as one yells into the television screen to correct an official's call that decides a baseball, football, hockey or basketball game – they have the ability to decide who won that day at the Cross. Similar to a political straw poll, they imagine their vote can determine the outcome. As arm-chair quarterbacks, they think they know better but their opinion-poll has no bearing on God's plan. It does however have great bearing on their eternal destiny and those they lead into error as Jesus accused the Pharisees in Matthew 23:15.

A different perspective may change scoffers' choices; in the meantime, let's humor them a bit. After all, the Messiah died as an outcast. Jesus died with God's curse upon Him. After claiming to be King, He died a naked beaten prisoner. After claiming to be Messiah, He could not extract himself from the torture leading to his death – so they thought. After claiming the ability to rebuild a destroyed Temple, He died as an impotent man – so they thought. After claiming to be God's Son and equal with God, He died as anything but – so they thought. Praise God, they had it wrong! They knew what they saw and this is often how we ascertain truth – but their foundation was skewed.

Along with the fickle scoffing crowd, we hear communication that transpired between the Cross *occupants*. Luke 23:39-43 says,

> One of the criminals who were hanged railed at him, saying, "Are you not the Christ? Save yourself and us!" But the other rebuked him, saying, "Do you not fear God, since you are under the same sentence of condemnation? And we indeed justly, for we are receiving the due reward of our deeds; but this man has done nothing wrong." And he said, "Jesus, remember me when you come into your kingdom." And he said to him, "Truly, I say to you, today you will be with me in Paradise."

Before one of Jesus' dying-partners died, we could say he 'saw the light.' He saw what and who Jesus was – and <u>believed Him</u>. Because of what this thief knew about himself and saw, he trusted Jesus and asked to be mercifully and gracefully remembered. Near as I can tell he *stood around* Christ's Cross and understood the Cross correctly. His *standing around* is not how we would usually speak but in the end, he won an eternal victory with Christ's victory. Now he had a story to tell; and through Scripture he's still telling it – Wow!

Discussions about this thief-turned-saint who was blessed by Christ to receive eternal life often start with the thought that he did not exhibit repentance or conversion. A few qualifiers are needed here. I have heard or been involved in discussions that debate the nature of this man's salvation granted by Jesus from the Cross. The cursory view is often distorted; let me attempt to explain why.

This snapshot-salvation is not the norm – although some want a truncated experience to be normative. In this death-bed conversion, we must be careful to think we can get someone to make a viable <u>profession</u> on their deathbed that adequately resembles the Cross communication that manifests a true <u>possessor</u>. This sometimes occurs and is more than sufficient as Jesus demonstrates. While this point is true, we must remember that **life-long discipleship is still the design**! In light of this, Christ called this man and he followed! This is the thrust of discipleship even though he was unable to follow as we imagine.

I have heard teaching suggest this repentant thief never had opportunity to experience real conversion. This suggestion posits one of two extremes – either conversion is unnecessary or his supposed 'non-conversion' experience is normative. These common positions evidence faulty logic and lead to twisted practices of 'christianity' that I want to correct. If we look beyond the obvious, the forgiven thief-turned-saint experienced true conversion but it manifests differently than we often judge and we must interpret and apply carefully.

Salvation paradigms should be 'formed' after the Gospels with post-Acts-eyes. The normative Scriptural paradigm is true conversion. This sentiment may be tough for some to process here, so salvation experience is explained later. The point here is *this man* showed true repentance, faith and conversion but we often do not look hard enough.

Salvation happened so fast to this man through a divine intervention of regeneration, similar to the women at the well in John 4, that we can accept spurious teaching that confuses the biblical reality. Salvation – especially in the Cross-picture – occurs immediately even though Scripture also speaks of an ongoing salvation process. The immediate reality always coincides with ongoing lifelong reality.

When we misunderstand salvation and conversion, we wrongly judge the reality that occurred that day. For many years, I did. Without a scriptural doubt, conversion must always be manifested in sinners-turned-saints! As breath always manifests life in a newborn baby, conversion always manifests life in a newborn saint. Newborn-saint-life always manifests the breathing of faith – this is Christ's Way.

Jesus shows us that it's never the wrong time to bring people into the kingdom. It's always the right time to boldly proclaim gospel promises and New Covenant reality. We know this because **the regenerating gospel produces eternal life in those who believe and follow the Lord in His Way**. This man followed even though he could not take visible steps that we often use to judge right belief.

Scripture gives another account of one who saw the Cross correctly. Please remember here that even His disciples did not see the Cross correctly yet. The centurion was the second believer to see the Cross correctly. Luke 23:47 says, "Now when the centurion saw what had taken place he praised God, saying, 'Certainly, this man was innocent!'" **When we see Jesus for who He is, it's a beautiful day**!

Some saw what Jesus was in prophecy. At His Incarnation, a few saw. In Luke 2, lowly shepherds saw a spontaneous heavenly celebration that no one has ever seen; they heard and saw. In Luke 1, John the Baptist's parents Zechariah and Elizabeth saw. In Matthew 1, Mary and Joseph knew. In Luke 2, Simeon was promised he would not see death until he saw the Lord's Christ; he waited and saw. In Luke 2, Anna the prophetess waited, saw and told. She proclaimed the good news of His birth to those who listened. In Matthew 2, wise men came, saw and gave gifts. Even after His birth, only a few saw Jesus for who He was before God fully opened His revelation after the Cross event.

Only a few correctly saw the Cross before the apostolic mystery-unfolding explanations of the New Testament. God's truth was forever exposed when Jesus victoriously declared in His dying breath, "It is finished!" in John 19:30. But we often misconstrue His point.

Let me take what might seem like a small detour. It might seem like a 'Duh! Moment' but it's a crucial point because Jesus had not died yet or been resurrected. Many do not correctly see the Cross without the organic relationship *from* the Cross. We struggle to see prior to the disciples' resurrection-epiphany to see the Cross for what it was. Many therefore frame the Cross through the eyes of the Resurrection rather than through the Cross – adding to our haze.

If not for His dying breath, I'm convinced Jesus' statement "It is Finished!" would have screamed His triumphant declaration. Since His final statement is not heard in exuberant victorious celebration, His whimper adds to our confusion and haze. God wants us to see the

Cross for what it was and evermore shall be! The Cross was God's victory over Satan, sin and death. The Way of salvation was complete!

The Cross **finished** God's eternal plan of Redemption. Eternity may be required to unpack and manifest the totality of God's successful plan; redeemed vision can really challenge us here![15] God displayed revelation-fulfillment on the Cross but continued to unpack revelation through the Resurrection, His Apostles, the Written Word and church. **The Way of salvation was complete on the Cross** and we are sure that His New Covenant prevailed in the face of all opposing factors.

His "I Am The Way!" statement is highlighted in the words of *The Way of the Cross leads Home* song, published by Jessie B. Pounds in 1906. It's printed below for our consideration:

1. I must needs go home by the way of the cross,
   There's no other way but this;
   I shall ne'er get sight of the Gates of Light,
   If the way of the cross I miss.

   > Refrain:
   > The way of the cross leads home,
   > The way of the cross leads home;
   > It is sweet to know, as I onward go,
   > **The way of the cross leads home**.

2. **I must needs go on in the blood-sprinkled way,**
   The path that the Savior trod,
   If I ever climb to the heights sublime,
   Where the soul is at home with God.

3. **Then I bid farewell to the way of the world,**
   To walk in it nevermore;
   For my Lord says, "Come," and I seek my home,
   Where He waits at the open door.

Put the Cross in its right place and you will be on your way to rightly discovering God's Will. The Cross and its majesty is why Paul proclaims in Galatians 6:14, "But **far be it from me to boast except in**

the cross of our Lord Jesus Christ, by which the world has been crucified to me, and I to the world." All Scripture comes full circle to the Cross – either before or after, or all the way back into eternity past and into eternity future. It's that majestic and it's that important!

Primarily the Cross deals eternally with sin and holiness for His sheep. In addition to sovereignty, because Jesus fulfilled atonement requirements, **God has authority to transform sinners into saints**. Without succumbing to sinner/saint discussions,[16] our sin produces a big part of our personal haze. When sin and knowledge of sin enters cognitive reality, we can literally say we have been *hazed*! Learning from the split Temple veil, Jesus saves us from sin.[17] Saint-status allows us to walk in converting faith as His victory brings haze-healing. Also, the more we reflect Christ, the more the haze is removed.

Strange as it sounds, the Resurrection can add to our haze. Because the disciples missed the Cross so bad, the Resurrection was their epiphany or key paradigm change; they saw it as the power of their transformation; therefore it's easy for us to hang doctrinal spurs on the Resurrection and Easter without re-examining the Cross in light of Christ's declaration or Paul's teaching. Even as God highlights the Resurrection's power,[18] Jesus and Paul highlight the Cross more.

Christ hardly mentions the Resurrection when He reveals Himself after the Cross and Resurrection; **Jesus focused on the Cross**. I think we should too! The Resurrection confirms His power and His revelation but **the Cross is God's haze-removing salvation-completing ingredient**; search this out. Especially as we hear Paul's mystery-unpacking teaching and his after-the-fact focus on the Cross, we can gain a greater appreciation for the Crux-nature of the Cross.

Your thinking and life may be changed when you see the Cross as the Crux of Scripture. Seeing the Cross as the crux of Scripture is a huge step toward living its mystery-unpacking power. Seeing the Cross as paramount will pay huge dividends. Seeing the Cross as the New

Covenant door – that Jesus was – opens understanding. **Cross-vision is complete and compelling**; this is partly why God tore the Temple curtain to demonstrate that He would no longer keep His revelation in mystery form, even as we still see through a dim glass.[19] There's much to unpack or unveil through the split veil – regeneration, salvation, Covenant, Gospel, Law, salvation encampments, repentance, faith, conversion, redeemed living and more; I trust you're ready for the trip.

Maybe you say, "I never thought about those things before!" Maybe you never thought about overcoming a vast frustrating haze. Maybe you never thought about a Dot-to-Dot approach to understand Scripture and salvation. Maybe you never saw the Cross as central to the Christian message or knew the Cross was Christ's central ministry. Maybe you never thought about salvation too deeply before. As the song says, the way of the Cross will lead you home.

Similar to the final scenes of *The Wizard of Oz* with a smoke-filled room, as the dog pulls the curtain back so the terrified seekers see the impotent man behind their terror, God pulls the curtain back for you at the Cross. God is not like the impotent man but the comparison to the pulled curtain is real. I do not know if *The Wizard of Oz* is a satire to mock the God of the Bible but many parallels exist between the revealed man in the climax versus the Cross Event and torn Temple curtain. God's plan is exposed to those who diligently seek Him and follow His Will. To them, He is not a Wizard but a loving saving God.

The torn curtain reveals more than we realize. Our challenge is to study the haze and torn curtain to learn significant things. You might be amazed at how much haze is removed as we study the curtain and what God revealed through this historic Cross event. Like pea-soup fog, most of the haze is impenetrable only to those who refuse to follow. Seek God's Will and, once He births us into His Covenant, He gives graceful liberty in our following. Then, you will find that the Cross leads you home – as the song says – to glory rather than to Kansas.

---

1 I use haze and fog to refer to fuzzy thinking and seeing until we obtain redeemed eyes. God's Spirit confirms that a redeemed lifeview can lead to great illumination.

2 I had Dr. Timothy Beougher for five seminary classes. He graciously critiqued my *Two Sides of the Cross* writings. He kindly gave permission to use two of his sayings.

3 Ephesians 1:3-14

4 Type is the root word of typology, showing that some figures are – in addition to their usage or personhood – God's analogy of higher meaning by pre-figuring Christ.

5 This type of saying is heard in Quest, Jesus Seminar, and Postmodern writings to suggest Jesus did not follow God's sovereign plan or understand His mission until it was thrust upon him by his stupidity. The lower case refers to liberal designations.

6 In the church that I cut my theological teeth on, I often heard this phrase. Sadly I don't know its origins but it gives helpful haze qualifiers. I love to give more.

7 I am convinced Paul lays this mystery wide open for our viewing if we can get beyond typical historic or truncated teaching. Paul contrasts the Old Covenant with the New Covenant to the point that in 2 Corinthians 5:17, I'm convinced his greater point is the change that occurs because the New Covenant *comes to* the person in regeneration rather than the oft-thought idea of a miraculous change, although this is surely in view.

8 Hermeneutic is the word used to describe the rules or practice of interpreting. In a broader view, we might see a hermeneutic as the presupposition of how we view the overall picture of Scripture. The closer we get to God's sight, the more glorious it is!

9 Scripture demonstrates a clear distinction between regeneration and salvation, although they are necessarily linked. What we know at new birth, unlike an infant's birth, is the seed of maturity yet what we know in new birth is crucial to the outcome.

10 Whereas God is required to regenerate a soul, Scripture passages like Romans 1 suggest that <u>moral rebellion rather than an intellectual rebellion is the bigger issue</u> that prevents a person from properly coming to Christ. Surely the intellect is important but the importance is accentuated after regeneration. The moral predicament is the biggest hurdle because this prevents people from willingly coming to Christ – with supposed Free Will no less. This also confirms the rejection of the rich young ruler when Jesus presents him with salvation requirements in Luke 18:18-27. Many are unwilling to follow!

11 The subject of biblical proofs is a hotly debated item that often flows from or into the Inclusivist/Exclusivist debates. Personally I fall somewhere between R.C. Sproul's and Robert Reymond's positions. Sproul's is published in Classical Apologetics and Reymond's in his Systematic Theology. Romans 1 has much to say on this topic as we ponder whether or how we can help people come to Christ, and the degree to which the verbal profession of faith is necessary in the reality of salvation.

12 I often heard Dr. Beougher relate this directly to how we approach worship, church and redeemed living. This is one statement we should keep on our rear view mirror, fridge, eyelets or any place that will cause us to think with a redeemed focus.

13 Kevin DeYoung and Greg Gilbert, *What Is the Mission of the Church: Making Sense of Social Justice, Shalom, and the Great Commission* (Wheaton, Ill.: Crossway, 2011). Excellent biblical positions for each topic give the church fodder to chew.

14 John 10:9

15 Every year as I study and preach through a Good Friday-to-Easter series, I see more and more of why Good Friday is the greatest day of Christianity. Redeemed vision allows more looking-back at events and New Covenant reality that we take for granted.

16 Great discussion surrounds the debate of whether we are sinners (and stay that way) or saints who occasionally sin (yet should seek perfection). I favor the second label because it better-represents regeneration reality and New Covenant language.

17 When we say Jesus saves us from sin, we mean original sin or the condition of being a sinner. Practice of sin is something that is overcome (**grace**d) in sanctification.

18 Somewhat ironically, Paul teaches much about the Resurrection – more than other writers – but his unpacking of the Cross is significant. Even Paul saw dimly but he demonstrates the power of the Cross in stark New Covenant teaching.

19 1 Corinthians 13:12

Chapter 2 – Approaching God's Will

How we approach the reality of God, humanity, the Fall, Scripture and redemption is pivotal to how we approach God's Will. With the generalities in mind from chapter one, we need to think about changing our perspective to God's perspective. From the Bible's paradigm, this is the hardest transition humans can make. Seeing and living life from God's view will be the greatest step of your life. If you start today, this might be your greatest day ever! Let's unpack these ingredients to establish a rubric to approach God's Will.

How God designed man is crucial to understand when we think about pursuing God's Will. I'm not looking so much at <u>how</u> as <u>design</u>. Genesis 1:26 says, "Then God said, 'Let us make man in our image, after our likeness.'" We can perform gymnastics trying to figure out what this verse means but one grand design is toward Holiness. This verse might expose the foundation behind God's command, "Be ye holy as I am Holy!" We unpack this later but it's important to keep this Holiness Design in mind as we start our journey.

Many people today can't look deeply into God's salvation because of three primary reasons. First, wrong teaching and belief lead many to UN-believe in God and Jesus; we call them atheists but often it's un-believing. This book answers faulty premises and challenges toward a pleasing response. Second, some are bitter about their past – bitter at God, self or others. Overcoming those barriers helps us see God's perspective and salvation as necessary missing ingredients. Third is a faulty perspective – seeing the trees but not the forest.

To declare that "Some people think wrongly" might lead to disjointed thinking about this author – the one doing the provoking. It was said, "If you make people think they are thinking they will love you. But if you really make people think, they will hate you."[1] If we see things from a different perspective, our understanding-world will change. We all think our perspective is the right one. Whether you're a seeker or experienced believer, I humbly challenge thinking at all levels. As a scientist keeps 'upping' the magnification of his microscope to see better, I keep upping the ante of provocation and teaching.

Some are bitter toward God or their past and this 'prevents' them from taking an honest look at God, His Ways or His Word. It could be a death, glaring life-style contradiction, a divorce, tragedy, crippling effects of disease or perceived judgmentalism to provoke, "I can't follow *that* God or Christianity!" God-denying wounds can be a lie from our enemy. God overcame our enemy and can bring healing. Work to see beyond Satan's lies as God's Will and salvation can be real for you!

Some ask, "Does it really matter how we approach God and His Word?" Humanity offers myriad answers to God and Scripture without much consideration of the implications of their beliefs. Even within the church, various approaches to these matters play out in different doctrine and approaches to man's responsibility before God.

Scripture teaches us to see that God's Plan was fulfilled in Jesus Christ on the Cross. To purchase Redemption through His Cross Atonement was Jesus' main ministry. Everything else was secondary, subsequential or subordinate to The Plan. Cross-Redemption exposes the New Covenant so let me share how some points flow into the book:

1) Redemption is subsumed in The Cross as the pinnacle of God's eternal Plan; these two themes are organically connected. The Cross is seen in Old Covenant shadows whereas in the New Covenant, the Cross stands out-front in key characteristics.

2) We work through biblical haze in mind and life. God veiled His truth until a time in history when He opened things up – when the Temple veil was torn from top to bottom. This tearing signified He would primarily unpack mysteries and secondarily replace the Mercy Seat so priest-believers could gain mercy and **grace** through Christ their High Priest. Cross-fulfillment clears up the haze.

3) A flip-flop of vivid **grace**/mercy teachings is evident. In the Old Testament blood was explicit, smeared in Passover and flowed abundantly in sacrifice as evidence that God offers forgiveness to His people. Blood parallels Mercy, Supper-wine and where we fall short of God's glory.[2] On the other side, **grace** parallels the body or bread, demonstrating where God works empowerment in and thru saints. **Grace** is *implicit* in the Old Testament except for Genesis 3:21 and the Sacrificial System. New Testament teachings of grace or body often miss the <u>necessary sacrificial flesh</u>. We must not miss the significance of Christ's body or bread in the *translation* between Testaments. New Covenant flip-flops are: grace becomes explicit and mercy becomes implicit; and after the Cross, the Mercy Seat is replaced by The Throne of **Grace**[3] verified in Hebrews 4:16.

4) I push for a **Grace** Hermeneutic,[4] the foundational starting point for overarching biblical interpretation to see the Bible from a redeemed view learned from The Cross and Christ's substitutionary atoning Redemption. Those who correctly say we must see Scripture from a Cross-view don't push for a **grace** hermeneutic. With a **grace** hermeneutic, the whole Scriptures takes on a redeemed focus and troubling issues are resolved almost immediately. I will not argue this point here but will keep unpacking **grace**.

5) God's Will and Way are found in the Cross in a paramount way.

Let me explain what I mean by the term lifeview; this skeleton will be clothed with meat and skin in Chapter 4. *Lifeview* has no dictionary definition, so I understand a term-struggle for many. For me, the word <u>lifeview</u> came from one R. C. Sproul book with that title but I have rarely seen it since. A worldview unpacks someone's view of the world but a lifeview unpacks someone's view of life. Sproul says:

> Some people believe that there is no God. Others say that there are many gods. Some folks believe that man is supreme.

Others believe that man is worthless. Many people believe there is a God, but they live as if there were no God. Still others ask, "What difference does it make?" Where Christ is invisible, people perish. Where His reign is ignored, people are exploited. They are demeaned, enslaved, butchered, aborted, raped, casualties of war, robbed, slandered, oppressed, cheated in marriage and in their wages, left to go hungry, naked, and unsheltered, consigned to loneliness, ridiculed, and frightened – that and a whole lot more is what difference it makes.[5]

I build further on R.C.'s foundation, but Sproul adds:

Socrates said that the unexamined life is not worth living. To examine one's life is to think about it. It is to evaluate. To evaluate requires examining values and value systems. We all have values. We all have some viewpoint about what life is all about. We all have some perspective on the world we live in. We are not all philosophers but we all have a philosophy. Perhaps we haven't thought much about that philosophy, but one thing is certain – we live it out. How we live reveals our deepest convictions about life. Our lives say much more about how we think than our books do. The theories we preach are not always the ones we actually believe. **The theories we live are the ones we really believe.**[6]

God declares His intentions for us to know how to obtain and live from a biblical lifeview. For now, realize that a deficient lifeview and worldview are part of the haze. Without a biblical lifeview, we cannot live as God desires but discovery and implementation of a redeemed lifeview is a work-in-process so be patient as progression is made.

We can approach God and His Will in different ways; some think it's all a matter of different paths to the mountain top. It takes time and commitment to develop a Christian lifeview and it's my pleasure to share my journey. My life experience may not be normative but it can be instructive.[7] If we get on board with a godly lifeview, the Spirit walks with us on this life-long journey so be patient if you are on the journey. If not, jump on the wagon and join this pursuit.

Before we get after the task of approaching God's Will, consider qualifiers about approaching the Trinitarian God. It will do little good to explain how to approach God's Will if we approach God in the wrong manner – outside of His Image. We must approach God through Scripture, particularly through Christ's Person and Work. If we cannot do that, it's impossible to embrace the person and work of Jesus Christ! The best questions we can ask deal with our approach to God.

Since God invests Himself in the redemption of a particular people – His sheep – my convictions are confirmed. It's correct to say that God's Will is seen in the salvation of His people as we seek answers to how this is accomplished, applied, known and lived out in a believer's life. The essence of God's Will for us is to pursue this salvation in redemptive living. From this reality and understanding, we will seek to build this reality in others with whom we share the Gospel.

Putting a Christian lifeview together can be like doing dot-to-dot pictures; it's only scary if you have never done it before. Remember doing dot-to-dot pictures? As a child, I remember my first picture in a doctor's office. I remember being caught up in moving from one number to the next. For me, that was victory. At the time, I could not see the forest for the trees. Never mind that I could not see beyond my maiden voyage in dot-to-dot pictures to see the unfolding picture as I connected the dots. That ability took a while but I remember it was fun; in a similar fashion working His Lifeview will be fun too.

Approaching God's Will and seeing through the haze is similar to the evolution we go through in dot-to-dot pictures. The more mature we are, the easier it is to see beyond our childish paradigms to see the big picture. Essentially we must unpack Scripture with the dot-to-dot method and The Spirit is pleased to show us the big picture. Great study and application are required to see His Story. Until we know better, keep moving from dot to dot – the picture will come into view. As our paradigms evolve higher,[8] we see the picture quicker and clearer.

It's said that God seems to hide His face from non-believers although He is plainly manifest through nature, the Word and Christ. God tells us to seek Him if we desire to know Him. At times He hides

His face per Luke 8:9-10; therefore, many struggle to seriously seek His Truth and **grace**. At minimum believers must be God-seekers per Hebrews 11:6. Connecting the dots is crucial; seek the big picture. With that in mind, let's take a Creation-story fly-over regarding salvation.

God's overview of salvation is expressed and unpacked in an ongoing way throughout this work. My desire is not to get too deep into theological terminology but when I get close, I seek to explain terms. Please grant charity as you consider the details. For some, it will be routine. For others who've never heard, it might be difficult; if so, plod along, and open Scripture to study and see for yourself.

Adam was formed by God and implanted with a living soul in the Garden of Eden. He was commanded to work and tend the garden. God communicated His Will and intentions to Adam; however, the first recorded communication is in Genesis 2:16:

> And the LORD God commanded the man, "You may surely eat of every tree of the garden, but of the tree of the knowledge of good and evil you shall not eat, for in the day that you eat of it, you shall surely die."

Simply, Adam had unbridled freedom to perform God's Will. Besides his tasks, Adam had one stipulation, "Do not eat of the tree of the knowledge of good and evil." From this stipulation and qualifiers, we extract helpful understanding of God's required perfect obedience!

Although He created Adam in a state of sinless innocence, God commanded perpetual obedience through His power of **grace**. Since Adam failed this stipulation, deadly consequences occurred. As a result of eating forbidden fruit and rejecting God's perfect **grace**, Adam died as a result. Adam's freewill – unbridled from God's power to do righteously – got him into big trouble; in fact, eternal trouble.

How the Garden scenario plays out is heavily debated. These debates are often driven by atheistic, unbelieving and skeptical people who cloud right understanding. Even in-house debates within the

Christian family can get heated. Nevertheless truth becomes clear once we see the Garden scenario as the microcosm of the whole fulfilled Scripture and work to see God's Will in the midst of faulty opinions. No matter modern denial, Adam sinned, died, and we suffer consequences as a result. With this in mind, we will examine The Fall – with man's sin and spiritual death, and God's redemptive activity on his behalf.

As we learn God's Will from the Garden scenario, three crucial requirements are understood. 1) God requires perfect obedience. 2) God requires perpetual obedience. Back to the violated stipulation – once Adam sins, 3) God requires perfect sacrificial atonement to remove the holiness void and sin, and restore right relationship through mercy and **grace**.[9] These scripturally-evident but oft-denied points are taken from *The Treatise on the Law and Gospel* by John Colquhoun.[10] To seriously grab hold of these requirements might seem like grabbing a tiger's tail but I encourage you to "Grab hold to see where God's truth takes you." God calls mankind to reasonable search and subsequent right action, and responds to their sinful life in Isaiah 1:16-20:

> Wash yourselves; **make yourselves clean**; remove the evil of your deeds from before my eyes; cease to do evil, learn to do good; seek justice, correct oppression; bring justice to the fatherless, plead the widow's cause. "**Come now, let us reason together**," says the LORD: though your sins are like scarlet, they shall be as white as snow; though they are red like crimson, they shall become like wool. **If you are willing and obedient**, you shall eat the good of the land; but **if you refuse and rebel**, you shall be eaten by the sword; for the mouth of the LORD has spoken.

God is always concerned with how people act – especially those who claim His name. It's sad to see many in the church think God isn't really concerned with how they live. Contrary to this distorted thinking, Christ-imitation or reflection has always been God's agenda – especially for those who claim His name. Once we realize this, we can understand that sin never reflects Christ's Holiness. Man needs his 'needs' fulfilled – so God performs crucial offices for His people.

God demonstrates an office before He commands His people to follow. Before reading about a father, leader, mediator, judge, prophet, king, priest, apostle, disciple, pastor, teacher or evangelist in Scripture, God performs them. God is the complete perfect role model. Because sin destroyed fellowship, God restored fellowship through applied redemption or personal salvation.

Salvation can mean many things but the greatest salvation is from the eternal damnation we deserve for violating **grace** and sinning against a Holy God. Salvation is seen through the doctrines of justification, sanctification and glorification. Some find it difficult to process the divisions and out-workings of salvation doctrine so look for God's upward moving concepts as these doctrines show that:

God saves us by justifying us – accounting us righteous by Christ's Atoning work on the Cross. Justification is the eternal basis for all sanctification that follows in the Christian life. Scripture often shows Justification as a one-time God-act in the past tense but ever-working. Justification can be seen in a positional manner where our position in Christ is already secured through judicial action on His part. This legal or forensic judgment shows that we have no part in this.

God continues to save us by sanctifying us – setting us apart unto holiness and working in us so that, through the power of Grace, Spirit and Word we are set apart for His service. Scripture often shows Sanctification as a joint effort in the present tense because it's current and ever-working! Sanctification can be seen in a progressive manner where our practical outworking is produced by the Holy Spirit through **grace**. This is a joint effort that requires our diligence in living by faith.

God continues His work of redemption by later glorifying us to bring us to glory with the Beatific Vision and to cause us to mature more in our imitation of His Son per 2 Corinthians 3:18. For our benefit, glorification is a God-act in the future tense. Glorification can be seen in a paramount[11] way where our faith, produced by God alone in

44

justification, and lived out in pro-active synergy in sanctification is rewarded with life in glory or heaven.

Paul speaks of these three salvific realities in Romans. My coming Thread of Continuity is built on God's principles and realities. At first blush they seem out of order but when we look deeper, they are promised in this same order. Consider Romans 8:28-30:

> And we know that for those who love God all things work together for good, for those who are **called according to His purpose** [the Us and We]. For those whom He foreknew [through election and justification] He also predestined to be conformed to the image of His Son [through <u>sanctification</u>], in order that He might be the firstborn of many brothers. And those whom He predestined He also <u>called</u>, and those whom He called He also <u>justified</u>, and those whom He justified He also <u>glorified</u> [through glorification].

Once salvation comes to our souls, we possess salvation in the past, present, and future tenses. Once God works redemption in our lives, we can say "*we were saved, are being saved and will be saved*." Each sense is proper and helpful even as it may be difficult to sort through Scriptural qualifiers and practical dynamics. We must grab hold of God's truth to understand redemption – as there is no greater joy than when we realize He works **grace** and redemption in us!

Getting back to the Garden scenario, Adam sinned and died. How he died is debated but a whole-Scripture-understanding confirms God spoke of this death as spiritual death that terminated his innocence and perfect image/likeness/relationship with God.[12] God spoke of spiritual/physical death to contrast eternal life He possesses, gave to Adam in creation and gives to redeemed sinners. Practically, spiritual death brings subsequent all-inclusive dysfunction.

Adam died in myriad ways yet, in judgment, God prophesied a future Redeemer to the serpent in Genesis 3:15. Many look long into the future for fulfillment of <u>God's redemption</u> promise but it comes to Adam in Genesis 3:21 – just six verses later! I only know of one theologian who posits what I just presented[13] but now you can look deeper. Genesis 3:21 packs a wallop of truth regarding man's attempt to obtain self-salvation – showing that God's salvation, gospel, **grace**, mercy and redemption are the things man needs to be redeemed. In their death, Adam and Eve need God to bring realized salvation.

In their sinful hiding, Adam and Eve attempt to clothe their sin to *become* presentable to God. By itself, this manifests a great irony of sin and its condition. God creates them without sin, righteous and presentable. But after sin they are unpresentable and they know it. How? The knowledge of good and evil is already at work, and they seek covering. The best they can do is fashion fig-leaf clothes.

Some see the knowledge of good and evil as a good thing but if we examine the results of this – never mind that it brought spiritual death – Adam and Eve seek to hide from God and further deceive themselves. The tragic results demonstrate why the hoped-for-gaining of equality with God are the epitome of Satan's lie. If we *only* had knowledge of Holiness – as God created – life would be much different!

After Adam and Eve model their fig-leaf attire, Scripture says "And the LORD God made for Adam and for his wife garments of skin and clothed them." God quietly but emphatically rejected their designer clothes and dysfunctional cover-up. He does this so quietly that we often miss His explicit action and redemptive teaching that screams to me! God applies the future-accomplished-atonement of the promised Savior to Adam and Eve and thereby restores them to right fellowship through a new birth or regeneration. God's redemptive clothing allows them to once again image God through grace. The consequence of lost Holiness – we see it as sin – means they are cast from the Garden.

Being cast out is more than a negative repercussion; man is outside of God's salvation in that condition. When a person is in bondage to sin and its nature – our heritage and *gift* from the Fall – Scripture says we are dead in trespasses and sin, unable to come to God for right relationship unless God does something in our soul per

John 3 and Ephesians 2:1-10. If we are spiritually dead, God – and God alone – must make us alive again! This point addresses a major denominational/theological question that is admittedly difficult to process – "How do we become born again?"

How one is born again is greatly debated in the church. One divide is over whether man can *bring about* his own salvation, with or without God's help, or whether God's-work-alone is required to accomplish new birth. In this debate there can be more emotional smoke than substance. Scripture provokes me to hold the view that God's work alone is required to accomplish new birth; I acknowledge different positions – I once held one – and will explain my position.

Other divides surround the doctrines of Justification, gospel and Paul's understanding of salvation. You might see why my primary emphasis points to these doctrines. Some differences are huge but great strides can be made when we see Scripture through God's eyes. We can overcome faulty views because, after the torn veil, God was pleased to put up sufficient markers for His sheep to follow.

Jesus was often berated for His Signs; John's Gospel presents seven.[14] We struggle to differentiate miracles and Signs but John helps. As Interstate highway signs tell us destination and how many miles to a given city, Bible Signs point beyond the event to the reality. The greatest Sign is God's Son crucified on the Cross for His sheep's Atonement. Jesus's Signs demonstrate that God – as God's Son – accomplishes salvation for His Sheep. John's emphatic presentation starts with his thesis statement in John 1:11-13 and concludes in 20:30-31. From beginning to end, John demonstrates that God's Son is the Only One who can accomplish salvation as God demands. Look with new eyes to see the majesty that John clearly proclaims.[15]

The seventh Sign that John presents is Lazarus' resurrection in John 11 where Jesus demonstrates significant realities. First, He is the Resurrection and the Life. Jesus teaches the reality of His pending death and resurrection with a living visual aid. Second, to complement His teaching in John 3 and amplify the God-alone necessity of salvation, He teaches rebirth through a visual aid that blows us all out of the water. Third, He clearly demonstrates that He holds the keys to life and death as God's Son lays His life down and picks it up again. The Cross IS THE EVENT! The Resurrection is proof of The Event.

Expanding on God-alone new birth in John 3 and Ephesians 2 Jesus shows through this Sign – that dead people can't resuscitate their selves. If we think man has the ability to effect rebirth in himself, we posit a form of self-salvation denied in Scripture. This is why I use the word effect rather than affect in rebirth. In light of our inability through spiritual deadness, self-salvation is impossible. We understand the biological sense but struggle to 'come alive' to God on our own.

The new birth is a mystery that Jesus taught to Nicodemus and the Samaritan woman at the well per John 3 & 4. When we are spiritually dead, we need to be redeemed by the Redeemer. We need to be saved from God's holy wrath – actually by God Himself! As God, Jesus often claimed and demonstrated this ability and power. Per our wreck scenario, the remedy we need is restored Holiness! If we think sinful man can restore Holiness – think again! Only God – through Jesus Christ's Cross – can perform this necessary remedy.

A great example of proper response to God's work that results in redemption through repentance, faith and conversion is Acts 16:25-34. After exorcising a demon from a girl who was being exploited, Paul and Silas are thrown in prison because her owners cause a riot. In jail, Paul and Silas pray and sing praises to God. Other prisoners and the jailor hear; then an earthquake occurs. Prisoner's shackles are broken and they could escape. If a Roman soldier loses a prisoner, it is considered his fault and he is subject to immediate death. This is why the jailor pulls his sword and is ready to kill himself "But Paul cried out with a loud voice, 'Do not harm yourself, for we are all here.'"

What occurs next contains the classic words that disciple-makers want to hear – a proper response to God's Gospel. The jailer's response acknowledges God's wrath, his need of salvation, a grateful response to evangelistic effort, baptism, house-hold salvation, rejoicing in what God did, rejoicing that he believed in Christ's Work and was being converted. A quick view allows us to miss logistical ingredients of the text, so studiously look again. Hear the words of Acts 16:29-34,

> And the jailor called for lights and rushed in, and trembling with fear he fell down before Paul and Silas. Then he brought them out and said, "Sirs, what must I do to be saved?" And they said, "Believe in the Lord Jesus, and you will be saved, you and your household." And they spoke the word of the Lord to him and to all who were in his house. And he took them the same hour of the night and washed their wounds; and he was baptized at once, he and all his family. Then he brought them up into his house and set food before them. And he rejoiced along with his entire household that he had believed in God.

"What must I do to be saved?" are words a disciple-maker or evangelist loves to hear. This question might indicate the hearer is ready to make the commitment to Christ's gospel. When the sinner believes in Christ, it is a great day! What we often forget is the spade work that prompts the decision of the heart revealed in this question. For reasons we don't know from the text of Matthew 13, other than that God prepared him to sprout and come alive, the jailor was made ready for the gospel to take root and grow to the point of bearing fruit.

"What must I do to be saved?" does not always indicate a person is ready to repent and believe in faith. We often quickly present the "Believe in the Lord Jesus, and you will be saved" comeback with the idea that we bring a soul into God's kingdom. If we rush the 'acceptance' without spade work or repentance, we often manipulate a false profession. Pre-empting pressure leads to many problems that border on fraudulence and credulity, and we must guard against manipulation, even as some think there is no other way. My concern is that stillbirths exist in the church from misguided salvation logic and this pressure; let's not add to that tragic number. I'm convinced a better way exists; therefore I seek to explain and show that way.

In making disciples, we can truncate or cut off a vital part of the biblical gospel. We must realize that Acts capsulizes history and terms as Luke crams history into short segments. We should look deeper at textual emphasis to guard against betraying the biblical gospel no matter how many biblical terms are used or how sincere our effort. In noble zeal to see people saved we must know that all good-sounding responses or positive-looking actions are not legitimate.

As the Great Evangelist and Savior, Jesus was not quick to unduly bless a decision or good-sounding question. Consider the rich ruler who came to Jesus with a similar question. Jesus did not jump to sign him up! Rather, the gravity of His message and this man's honest evaluation made this man go away empty. Matthew 19:16-26 says:

> Behold a man came up to him saying, "Teacher, what good deed must I do to have eternal life?" And he said to him, "Why do you ask me about what is good? There is only one who is good. If you would enter life, keep the commandments." He said to him, "Which ones?" And Jesus said, "You shall not murder; You shall not commit adultery; You shall not steal; You shall not bear false witness; Honor your father and mother; and, You shall love you neighbor as yourself." The young man said to him, "All these I have kept. What do I still lack?" Jesus said to him, "If you would be perfect, go, sell what you possess and give to the poor, and you will have treasure in heaven; and come, follow me." When the young man heard this, he went away sorrowful for he had great possessions. And Jesus said to his disciples "Truly, I say to you, only with difficulty will a rich person enter the kingdom of heaven. Again I tell you, it is easier for a camel to go through the eye of a needle than for a rich person to enter the kingdom of God." When the disciples heard this, they were greatly astonished, saying, "Who then can be saved?" But Jesus looked at them and said, "With man this is impossible, but with God all things are possible."

Like Paul and Silas – believers, pastors and evangelists love to see people 'get saved.' We cannot control the work of regeneration as

Jesus did but we can work to make sure the tilling or ground work is sufficient to receive the seed of faith that grows into new life. Repentance, conversion and obedience must follow the Believe-on-the-Lord-Jesus-decision; otherwise, something is very wrong! Toward this truth, I build toward a Gospel corrective in the Gospel chapter.

Seek true disciples who bear the fruit of Christ's salvation through regeneration, as personal experience of regeneration provokes great joy. If God plants new birth in your soul,[16] marvel that God redeemed you from the clutch of sin and death – and plants you in Christ. To be brought into right relationship with God and possess eternal life brings a desire to reflect God's glory through **grace**ful living. God chases after His sheep per Psalm 23:6,[17] but reflecting His Image requires diligence and discipline. Let's consider how this can be done.

In order to grow in Christ-likeness, we need instruction from His Word, Spirit and saints. Before His ascension when He went to heaven, Jesus told and instructed His disciples to teach His commands to new believers.[18] sadly, confusion exists over what Jesus meant by His Great Commission to make disciples and instruct new believers to obey His commands. I think it's only difficult to understand when we twist meaning like a waxed nose – as Jesus spoke clearly. Follow it clearly!

We should wonder why some don't grow in Christ-likeness. When we rightly judge the anemic results of modern evangelism, it's no wonder many don't grow in their faith or Christ-likeness. This point is expanded later but let me offer brief comments for consideration.

First, it could be they are not instructed well. This may be true but this often becomes an escape hatch for _professing_ believers. Remember, only _possessors_ have eternal life so we can't expect people to manifest faith without conversion and proper teaching.

Second, _professors_ may not possess regeneration or new birth that Scripture presents. If we expect people to _possess_ new birth without the God-alone act of regeneration, we expect the impossible. It is impossible for people to act like regenerated ones if no God-alone reality is present within. They may act the part for a while but it cannot last unless it's real. Some might ask, "What are we missing?"

Some preach the reality of salvation without conversion; this betrays the Gospel the apostles preached. In His last recorded words before He went to heaven, Jesus gave significant direction for His fledging church. Just before He was taken up to sit on the Throne of Grace, with key words highlighted Jesus said in Matthew 28:18-20:

> All authority in heaven and on earth has been given to me. *Go therefore and make disciples* of all nations, baptizing them in the name of the Father and of the Son and of the Holy Spirit, *teaching them to observe all that I have commanded you*. And behold, I am with you always, to the end of the age.

Believers are commanded to make disciples in their every-day business and travels. In our going, we teach disciples to obey God's commands if granted time and influence. His Command sounds simple but in the Great Commission outworking many are unwilling or untrained to practice His obedience-teaching command. This should be second nature to those who *profess* to be transformed by His power.

Many don't make Great-Commission-obedience a high priority; therefore, it's impossible to gain wide consensus to fix this problem. Churches give to foreign missions but some do little for home missions or vice versa. As churches and individuals are responsible for the lack of proper teaching and mentoring, my focus here is on individuals so we can speak to this void by proclaiming answers from God's Word.

Many struggle at foundational levels of salvation-knowledge yet training, mentoring and the power of His Word and The Holy Spirit can get faithful believers on the right track. Faulty teaching and cultural worldviews bombard our minds and life. This bombardment typically comes without our acknowledgment or understanding and leaves many confused in the resulting quagmire. Know that we can do God's Will because He gives direction and power to perform it. That's real liberty!

52

Sadly doctrine and faith confessions are avoided and denied in some churches today. If teaching occurs, its depth is often shallow. In contrast to this reality, Scripture indicates the study of correct doctrine is paramount to godly living. Practical doctrinal implications are greater than some imagine. Tragically many professing believers think doctrine is not practical and unnecessary but we can affect correction.

Scripture provokes maturity and true obedience and 2 Timothy 2:15 gives God's challenging remedy, "Do your best to present yourself to God as one approved, a worker who has no need to be ashamed, rightly handling the word of truth." Doctrinal teaching runs the gamut of difficulty. Some is easy to assimilate while others are difficult to grasp. Some teaching is clearly evident whereas some requires development and critical thinking. Since Scripture can be explicit or implicit and therefore unknown until brought to light, my desire is to make points fairly evident and easy to assimilate or understand. As we seriously pursue God's Word to learn His Will and reflect Christ, we can get beyond theological fears.

Some of my personal journey is shared to encourage and challenge others in their walk. Thanks to the *Blueprint For Thinking*[19] series by R.C. Sproul, my approach to a biblical lifeview still reframes my thinking. Adjustments affect essential life-changes and we need to be conformed to His image more each day. As I was encouraged, taught and mentored, I seek to encourage you.

In ignorance, some think "I don't have a worldview!" The stark reality is that everyone has a worldview. Being ignorant of or in denial of your worldview does not exclude its reality and impact. The principle of a biblical lifeview, while easy to understand, is not often taught. I hope the progressive nature of this study makes a biblical lifeview easier to understand and practice as you bring it into focus.

Once the biblical lifeview is taught, realized and embraced, we see it as very practical. If we come to a new understanding of God's grace in salvation and live His Will, our wreck remedy will be realized. Actually, a biblical lifeview is realized as we practice the Redeemed View of Life and reflect God's grace through Christ's gospel.

Personally, I bumped into my own worldview in Ethics class in seminary. I was amazed at how little I knew even though I learned much from Francis Schaeffer, R.C. Sproul and what God taught me through my *Redeemed View of Life* writings. I wrote about this concept but it was a semi-non-labeled entity in my mind. It took time to get a handle on this label. *The Universe Next Door*[20] by Jim Sire helped.

A shocking statistic from *The Truth Project*[21] by *Focus On The Family* is that fewer than 10% of professing believers live with a Christian worldview. This point helps explain the anemic Western church. We may ask, "Why is a Christian worldview important? Isn't it enough to be saved?" Yes and No. When the Spirit makes us new in Christ, we obtain complete salvation in Christ. But Scripture teaches that we must put off the old man and stinking thinking so that we retrain our actions and thinking to His perspective. The goal of this book is to, as Paul did, compel us to bow to His Will per Romans 12:1-2.

Competing worldviews include Christian theism, Naturalism, Deism, Nihilism, Existentialism, Eastern Pantheistic Monism, New Age, Postmodernism, Bobble-headism, Secularism, Secular Humanism, Materialism, Hedonism and Edenism. Edenism[22] is the dysfunctional lifeview from the Garden of Eden that affects everyone and flows into other worldviews. Uncorrected, Edenism manifests a perverted life. No shortcuts exist so, from the ashes of Edenism, we must work diligently to build a redeemed view. Charles Malik said,

> We find on the whole and for the most part: materialism and hedonism; naturalism and rationalism; relativism and Freudianism; a great deal of cynicism and nihilism; indifferentism and atheism; linguistic analysis and radical obfuscation; immanentism and the absence of any sense of mystery, any sense of wonder, any sense of tragedy; humanism and self-sufficiency; the worship of the future, not of something above and outside and judging past,

present and future; the relative decay of the classics; the uncritical worship of everything new and modern and different; a prevailing false conception of progress; an uncritical and almost childish optimism; an uncritical and morbid pessimism; the will to power and domination. All of which are essentially so many modes of self-worship. Any wonder there is so much disorder in the world![23]

Besides myriad worldviews that compete against right belief and action, denominational divisions can confuse the picture of God's Will. Some can't comprehend why teachings lead to divisions. It's a shame that so many divisions occur, even as we understand that doctrine must be protected, sometimes to the point of division. Ideally, God desires us to seek faith-unity even as this is difficult to define, qualify in a redeemed way, and maintain with Upper-Room-thoughts.

I'm thankful God planted me in various denominational settings because this provoked an eclectic mind – trying to find common ground without compromising fundamental truths. Many cannot intelligently speak outside of their box but my mind is pushed to seek clarity and unity through redeemed teaching. I seek to overcome inconsistency when I can see it. My wide base helps me grant charity to others but my gifting causes me to be guardedly suspicious of faulty lifeviews.

Faulty lifeviews appear everywhere but obedience to good teaching can bring correction. With the spirit of a prophet and heart of a pastor, I struggle to patiently endure blatant ignorance and contradictions that flow from lack of biblical knowledge. We need mercy to stand firm for truth yet speak toward clarity in thinking.

When David passed the baton to Solomon in 1 Chronicles 28:9, he said, "Know the God of your father and serve him with a whole heart and a willing mind, for the LORD searches all hearts and understands every plan and thought. If you seek Him, he will be found by you." Proverbs 12:5 says, "The thoughts of the righteous are just." More than we realize, how we think determines how we live and how we search for His Truth in His Will determines what we find.

As the girls play in the hay with hope of stumbling across God's needle (cover & p.13), play till God brings us to **grace**ful obedience. If we play sufficiently, we will learn what the prophets of old knew – **the just shall live by His Faith** – put into words by the prophet Habakkuk.

Habakkuk's words reflect what Christ taught His disciples before He left earth. Jesus taught His disciples to walk by faith and not by sight – even though *their* sight was of the risen Christ!   When Thomas finally saw the risen Christ in John 20:28, he said "My Lord and my God!" Jesus wanted His disciples, not just Thomas, to learn that walking by faith – even without physical sight of Him – is the model that pleases God. Jesus responded with, "Have you believed because you have seen me? Blessed are those who have not seen and yet have believed." They learned and turned their world upside down; this will lead us home too – not to Kansas but to a Redeemed lifeview.

If we understand Paul's teaching through something less than New Covenant eyes, we might frame his teaching with revisionist theories. I reject many theories because, rather than being correctives they distort essential foundations of Christianity. If we uphold God's revealed Will, we will discover coherent redeemed truth.

God's Will is found in obedience to Jesus' command, "Follow Me." It's true He said these words to His disciples but it's also true He gives this command to every disciple today. From the New Testament record, He called disciples. From Matthew 28, He commands us – His disciples – to make more disciples. By extension, those disciples are called to make more disciples to continue the cycle.

Our tendency is to frame the scope of obedience. Sometimes we make the gospel into disciple-making-denial rather than doing God's Will. Stepping into His yoke requires submission to follow where He takes us; this attitude reflects the heart of a believer. Say with His disciples, "What do you want me to do Lord?" Consider *A Student's Prayer* to provoke your study of God's Will:

1. God, the all-wise, and Creator of the human intellect,
   Guide our search for truth and knowledge, all our thoughts and
        ways direct.
   Help us build the towers of learning that would make us wise,
        astute,
   On the rock of Holy Scripture: Truth revealed and absolute.

2. O how vast the shores of learning – there are still uncharted
        seas
   And they call to bold adventure those who turn from sloth and
        ease.
   But we need thy hand to guide us in the studies we pursue,
   And the presence of Thy Spirit to illumine all we do.

3. May the things we learn, so meager, never lift our hearts in
        pride
   Till in foolish self-reliance we would wander from Thy side.
   Let them only bind us closer, Lord, to Thee, in whom we find
   Very fountain-head of wisdom, Light and Life of all mankind.

John W. Peterson's words provide a lattice to hang crucial doctrines and grace-provoked activity upon. As God directs, seek wisdom and obedience to new truths.

A one-page book synopsis is offered below as a contemplation template. Knowing that myriad beliefs exist, slide over things until they are unpacked. Don't get 'quagmired' in any one teaching. The Holy Spirit may continue this unpacking long after you finish reading so approach this book's teaching as the 'Hide the Thimble' game we played as children. Someone would hide a sewing thimble. We went around the room to find the hidden thimble. We might hear "You're cold! You're lukewarm! You're getting warm! or You're really hot!" to indicate our proximity to the hidden object. We were never offended to hear "You're cold!" We turned and tried again. Learning from God is sometimes like that; make corrections until we get hot and find the thimble or needle! Find out that Jesus is God and you're on the Way!

One-Page Book Synopsis

Before man's creation, God (the Father, Son and Spirit) agreed to redeem sinful man; this resolution is called the <u>Redemption Covenant</u> as Scripture gives clues of this agreement. The <u>Covenant of</u> **Grace** flows directly from the Covenant of Redemption. Through 1) the Father's direction, 2) the 'sending' and substitutionary Atonement of Jesus on the Cross, and 3) application of redemption by the Spirit, God redeems sinners so that they are empowered to **grace**fully **likeness** Him. The Son agreed to perfectly do what man would fail to do, with promise of reward. This reward is Christ's bride – His sheep.

Man was created to **image God** in Holiness, more specifically to **imitate Jesus** through God's power. The Trinity created man for *that* specific purpose! In the Garden and thereafter, God accurately declared the essence of relationship – giving His Gospel-Word, quite a few specifics and commands (Law) and consequences for rejecting His provisions. The eternal moral Law was declared as binding and man radically messed up that design. By forsaking Holiness, Law and *grace* – Adam and Eve destroyed a pristine relationship. They died a radical death, meaning every facet of their being was perverted. Being found naked, Adam and Eve fashioned <u>fig-leaf clothes</u> to redeem themselves. Man concocted his own plan – <u>the Covenant of Works</u>; an impossible plan. In Holy Mercy and **Grace**, God clothed them in animal skins – redemption through Christ's applied blood and righteousness.

The time between man's creation and now, we call history. As God laid out His plan in full view of Satan, man often plays Satan's harlot by perverting the **grace**ful relationship that God designed. This perversion continues today as we struggle to see God's eternal moral Law, God's Holiness and the Covenant of **Grace** lived out in His people – Christ followers or reflectors. **Grace**ful living leads us to **grace**ful evangelism to make disciples who follow God in His design. His stated plan will not be accomplished until all His Sheep are brought home!

As His last revelation, God sent the Son into the world (Incarnation) to do what Adam failed to do. **The title Son has more to do with being sent** than many imagine. The Son finished salvation – realized in the Spirit's redemption application, giving effective new birth to make His Sheep holy after Christ through **grace**ful obedience.

With the unveiling of finished Redemption, the Old Covenant of Works gives way to the New Covenant of Grace – pictured in the Garden. God's salvation is the only thing that will save us from the two car wrecks in our mortal and eternal lives. The old saying is true, "Born Once; Die Twice. Born Twice; Die Once." If we are birthed into His Holiness, Law and **grace**, our life will forever be redeemed – even as we struggle to understand the fullness of this ongoing truth!

As a student of God's Word, we can connect the dots to become a Christ-reflector. I don't expect you to say, "Now it's all clear to me!" so I will unpack details so it might become clear. His Word must be the foundation; feed on it because it's our spiritual lifeblood! Our oxygen is **grace**; ask for and breathe in all He gives, as life IN Christ requires **grace**! Join the Triune God in proactive sanctification to demonstrate you are Justified to be glorified with a heavenly home.

---

1 I could not put my hand on the source of this great quote, but I use it often.

2 Romans 3:23

3 The reality of the *Throne of Grace* in Hebrews 4:16 indicates the Mercy Seat was replaced by the Throne of Grace to confirm the explicit/implicit flip-flop between grace a n d mercy in the Two Covenants. The Mercy Seat isn't mentioned again until Revelation to concur with the redeemed switch. The Throne of Grace magnifies the two sides of the Cross – making the Cross the crucial dividing line between the Old and New Covenant.

4 I don't claim to be a top-notch theologian but I argue for a grace hermeneutic that more-consistently explains the whole Scripture and helps unpack the haze of the Garden scenario better. My thoughts bump into common understanding but I would like to provoke serious discussion of this matter as a redeemed view has huge ramifications for historic divisions. May God provoke serious consideration and helpful change.

5 R.C. Sproul. *Lifeviews: Make a Christian impact on culture and society* (Old Tappan, NJ; Power Books, 1986), 19-20. This excellent little book lays a foundation for understanding the worldviews that ultimately control our lives – despite what we think. I wish R.C. had defined a lifeview more concretely, so I filled in some holes.

6 Sproul, *Lifeviews*, 25-26.

7 Briefly and comprehensively, I present my experience in Appendix 1 to provoke some to consider the magnitude of conversion and the study that is needed.

8 2 Corinthians 3:18 speaks of this ever higher maturity as we go from glory to glory. If you're not maturing to higher levels, do an evaluation before God's face.

9 The typical view of the Garden is the perspective of Law and Love but this view does theological cart wheels to explain the appearance of sin. I empathize with the struggle but seek to explain my perspective through a consistent definition of grace.

10 John Colquhoun, *A Treatise On The Law and The Gospel* (Morgan, PA.: Soli Deo Gloria Publications, 1999). I greatly appreciate Colquhoun's three points; they helped me see the Garden experience for what it is – the denial of grace that led to sin. We often think sin leads to the denial of grace but I would argue for the former position.

11 The term paramount was used in a Habakkuk sermon by Pastor Chidduck of Bethesda Baptist Church, Allen Park, MI many years ago. I borrowed his term.

12 This image/likeness/relationship topic impacts how we see God's power of grace in our lives. The supposition and reality of image-bearing brings regeneration into the discussion. I'm convinced regeneration is necessary for likeness ability per Psalm 1. Historic Catholic/Reformed debates can be influenced with a redress as common grace is often co-opted to become a grace-denying reality that besmirches the gospel.

13 Michael Horton is the only theologian I know who says that Genesis 3:21 is the type of Christ application that occurs in New Covenant Justification. Seeing this truth helps us understand of the reality and application of salvation that reflects the redeemed position – especially the later-explained Two Sides of explicit **Grace** and implicit mercy.

14 The seven **Signs** before His death are #1) Jesus turns the water into wine in John 2:1-11. #2) Jesus cleans the Temple in John 2:13-24. #3) Jesus heals the official's son in 4:43-54. #4) Jesus heals the man at the Pool of Bethesda in 5:1-17. #5) Jesus feeds the 5,000 in John 6. #6) Jesus heals the man born blind in John 9. #7) Jesus raises Lazarus from the dead in John 11. John's teaching shows His death and Resurrection are signs #8 and #9 but he doesn't say this. Jesus shows He is God – evermore *hazed* as God's Son – who deserves all praise for the salvation He merits and accomplishes. The fact that Jesus is God is one of our greatest haze-hurdles within the mystery of the Trinity. John helps us overcome this haze-factor if we look again.

15 Appendix 3 gives a list of John's explicit or implicit presentations of Jesus being God (God's Son) who brings salvation to those who believe in Him through following.

16 A decision that 'causes' salvation is typically represented by a semi-Pelagian or Arminian belief versus a God-alone-act taught in reformed and Ephesians 2 perspectives. I originally believed the former position but God corrected my conviction. This issue plays significantly into the points of biblical proofs and the Exclusivist/Inclusivist question. For now, try to take confused concerns off the table to realize that Scripture says that God's Work is **effective** in regeneration – while it denies man is effective to bring regeneration.

17 In Psalm 23:6, The Good Shepherd declares that His Spirit will chase after us like a police car with its red lights on. In Spurgeon's words, God is the great hound of heaven who follows after His own. This is a comforting reality when it occurs.

18 The *Great Commission* as it's called is found in Matthew 28:18-20.

19 R.C. Sproul's *Blueprint for Thinking: Reforming the Christian Worldview* tape series was possibly the most foundational teachings I ever consumed. Charles Spurgeon read John Bunyan's *The Pilgrim's Progress* close to 100 times. I've listened to Sproul's series at least 20 times and it was very instrumental in my biblical thinking development.

20 James W. Sire, *The Universe Next Door: A Basic Worldview Catalog* (Downers Grove, IL.: InterVarsity Press, 2004).

21 *The Truth Project* by Focus On The Family is an excellent source of teaching toward a Christian Worldview. If you can, please watch this series.

22 *Edenism* is a word I coined to describe the lifeview that from the Garden of Eden because of the denial of grace and the first human sin. This lifeview likely undergirds every faulty worldview. This is why a Redeemed View of Life is crucial.

23 William Lane Craig, Paul M. Gould (Eds.). *The Two Tasks Of The Christian Scholar: Redeeming the Soul; Redeeming the Mind* (Wheaton, IL.: Crossway Books, 2007), 61.

Chapter 3 – In Pursuit of God's Will

An intriguing thought heard in the sales environment, but a relatively true philosophy for life is, "If you fail to plan, you plan to fail!" Whether you save for retirement or develop a life plan, we need a plan. This statement suggests that necessary planning is required to successfully accomplish a goal. The prophetic implication is that, without planning, failure of the vision will naturally occur. This small statement has a powerful message. It especially applies to our life with a Christian lifeview – seeing life through God's eyes.

Do we need a plan to pursue God's ways? The resounding answer is "Yes!" In a general sense, we have plans for most anything. We use a plan to obtain employment, take a trip, get married, buy a home, plan a budget, raise a family, get a degree, put a kit together, go to the corner store or write a book. Without a plan, it's unlikely we will accomplish our goals or worthwhile endeavors. This truism shows why believers need a plan to accurately pursue and honor God.

A pursuit is a great way to speak of finding God's Will. At the least, we need to be intentional and diligent in our seeking Him and His Ways. We are intentional and purposeful about many things in life – even some things we give little thought to – and we should be intentionally purposeful about our relationship with God and His truth.

Many rarely think about a plan when they pursue God and His Ways. Without a plan or intentionality, it's no wonder so few find THE WAY to which Jesus pointed. Few seem to know His plan or work the plan; without this, we deny or forsake God's Way without really knowing the nature of God's plan. In Matthew 7:13-14, Jesus speaks to this Gospel key when He talks about the two roads of life. He said:

> Enter by the narrow gate. For the gate is wide and the way is easy that leads to destruction, and those who enter by it are many. For the gate is narrow and the way is hard that leads to eternal life, and those who find it are few.

If we are honest, we realize those who enter the wide and easy way embrace nominal Christianity. This is expanded later but a brief synopsis is offered here for reflection. In John 14:6 Jesus says, "I AM The Way, The Truth, and The Life." He and His Gospel is THE ONLY WAY to the Father; He is THE ONLY TRUTH that matters eternally; and He is THE ONLY ETERNAL LIFE. He unequivocally proves His statement through His Mission, Work, Words and Gospel; therefore we must deeply consider how we approach our relationship with Christ. Against nominal Christianity, consider a few points that some believe:

- Do we profess belief in God or as a god among many?
- Do we think and live with objective or subjective faith?
- Are you a CINO – Christian-In-Name-Only?
- Are you a vampire Christian – believe only in His blood?
- Do you hold subjective faith with you as the object?
- Do we know God as Knowable Revealer or vague hider?
- Is God the Supreme Father or a waxed-nose deity?
- Is God the Moral Standard or your Good Suggester?

Many declare, "There are myriad ways to get to heaven." It's said, "If I try to be good, no matter the path, God will accept me and my approach to heaven." Scripture declares these beliefs are false. Sadly many don't walk the Way of Jesus[1] - the hard narrow way or His Way – as this requires them to repent of their sin, believe in and follow Him.[2] Refusal to follow Jesus is moral, intellectual and volitional unbelief.

The New Covenant gospel requires a complete following but sin gets in the way. Adam and Eve committed the first human act of cosmic treason.[3] Lucifer committed the first angelic act of treason to earn eternal separation from God and glorified existence. For a reason God never explains, He chose not to redeem fallen angels and they were eternally denied renewed relationship with God. But God chose to redeem some of mankind for the glory of His Son's Work and **grace**.

As a result of Satan's judgment, he was sent to earth where he sought to get mankind to join his rebellious fate. His effort worked and sin plunged mankind into spiritual death. We could examine unbelief, rebellion or rejection of **grace** but let's focus on the independent spirit and man's dysfunctional desire for autonomy. Autonomy creates self-law or makes one a law unto self, and Adam and Eve chose autonomy. In too many ways, we choose autonomy but **grace** can overcome.

At its root, autonomy is an anti-law stance towards God's Laws. Even professed Christ-followers fall into this pit at times without realizing what they do – until they discover their rut-driving. Satan's Lie causes us to imagine we can obtain God's best by rejecting God's Will in His Law. Autonomy always *leaves* us naked or 'rutted' before God because we strip ourselves of God's remedy. When we are exposed in our autonomy, the nakedness and futility are eternally lacking.

At its deluded worst, autonomy believes practical knowledge of good and evil – walking in sin – is God's Will. Autonomy might be 'coming to Christ' on own terms, with our rules. Actually the desire for autonomy is behind every sin. Autonomy occurred when Adam and Eve rejected God's Word and decided to pursue the knowledge of good and evil instead. When we seek life outside of God's Word, as Adam and Eve discovered, we live in the self-ordered clutches of autonomy and rebellion. If we are to find life, integration and healthy relationship, we must reject autonomy and depend on God's provision in Christ.

Sin is defined in different ways. Common definitions are: miss the mark or violate God's Rules or Ways. With Math, we can't come to right answers by using faulty methods or signs. Likewise, when we do not follow God's rules and Ways we get the wrong answer – sin with a displeasing life. In Romans 3:23, God says sin falls short of His Glory.

At its root, sin violates God's declared Will. God reveals His Will and Design for mankind – to be Christ reflectors. David Wells adds, "Sin is defying God, disobeying his law, rejecting his Word, and refusing his Christ."[4] This is why walking boldly into disobedience will never stand at the bar of God's justice. James 4:17 shatters the common excuse about not knowing what God commands, "So whoever knows the right thing to do and fails to do it, for him it is sin."

From the beginning, God designed Christ-imitation for His creatures – and the mirror of His Character is shattering. Paul offers a tough definition in Romans 3:23; "For all have sinned and come short of the glory of God." Anything that fails to glorify God is sin. More specifically, sin is any deviance from God's Character. Rather than throw out the foil of God's Character, embrace it to find God's Will.

Some struggle to wrap their minds around contrary actions that describe sin. When we consider pure solution, it only takes one drop of poison to pollute the solution. It's the same with innocence, as sin pollutes and kills. When we don't see our sinful thoughts as God does, we struggle to realize how much divine help is required to correct, destroy and overcome God-contrary thoughts and actions.

In a recent *TableTalk*[5] article by R.C. Sproul Jr., he speaks of how God works worship through believers. From a different perspective, another qualifier for sin is exposed. A sin-point says,

> It was Augustine who argued that every sin is a failure to love ordinately. Sin is the result of either loving something more than we ought or the result of loving something less than we ought. . . . All of us fail to love the Lord as we ought. We are commanded to love Him with all our heart, mind, soul and strength. We are commanded to have no other gods before Him. **He is to be our singular holy passion**, and every other passion ought only to serve this one passion. We fail, however, not only in loving too little, but in loving [other things] too much.

Sin takes many faces. After God regenerates us, however, He gives us power to overcome every facet of sin even though we often fail. Through repentance, faith and conversion, God makes us into reflectors or 'Imagers' of His Son Jesus Christ; this is sanctification.

God commands man to obey or follow His plan but man rejects this life-giving way because he imagines Satan's plan is better. Before its time, Adam and Eve used Frank Sinatra's famous song, "I did it my way!" This might have been the first duet in Scripture (Adam and Eve) but that song's sentiment is the problem – then and now! In reality, this trio sinfully reflected God's Trinity that could only work destruction.

My terminology or labels are not important but a holy foundation of thinking and living is crucial. If you believe your thinking and living pleases God, lay your foundations before His inspection. If our thinking needs a makeover, give serious contemplation and ask God to do His work in you. In 2 Corinthians 10:1-6, Paul gives words of wisdom as we approach this necessary mental makeover:

> I, Paul, myself entreat you, by the meekness and gentleness of Christ – I who am humble when face to face with you, but bold toward you when I am away! – I beg of you that when I am present I may not have to show boldness with such confidence as I count on showing against some who suspect us of walking according to the flesh. For though we walk in the flesh, we are not waging war according to the flesh. For the weapons of our warfare are not of the flesh but have divine power to destroy strongholds. We destroy arguments and every lofty opinion raised against the knowledge of God, and take every thought captive to obey Christ, being ready to punish every disobedience, when your obedience is complete.

In firm words, Paul begged his readers (us too!) to use God's divine power to correct our thinking and living. A stronghold indicates a mental fortress that Satan uses in our mind. Like the Tower of Babel, Satan builds fortresses in our minds to fight against the knowledge and Will of God. By God's power, we can tear them down. <u>The correcting-effort of conversion requires the piece-by-piece dismantling of our prior thought structure</u>. God's power helps us root out and punish wrong beliefs that stand against God but this only comes through **grace**ful obedience. Faulty arguments, false opinions, wrong thoughts and ungodly actions are put forward from our mind against God's Truth and

Grace. Only when we handcuff these thoughts for interrogation can we submit to Christ's authority, mind, Faith, glory, Law and obedience.

God calls saints to imitate Him, so elemental foundations must change. God the Father, Son and Holy Spirit all call us to imitate Him – with the perfect visual aid or Divine analogy presented in the life and person of Jesus Christ. Like a weight lifter who trains by continual exercise, resistance-training, and ability-stretching, God commands this at the spiritual level. Consider 1 Timothy 4: 7-10.

> Train yourself for godliness; for while bodily training is of some value, godliness is of value in every way, as it holds promise for the present life and also for the life to come. The saying is trustworthy and deserving of full acceptance. For to this end we toil and strive, because we have our hope set on the living God.

Some imagine a quandary in finding God's Will, but Jesus said there is only one Way. As Jesus prepared to go the Cross, a discussion occurred among Him and His disciples that bears significantly on our topic. In John 14:4, Jesus talked about preparing a place and said, "You know the way to where I am going." Jesus implies that His disciples knew The Way but, like them, we often fail to properly understand and follow – especially when we are still in a fog.

After the resurrection and Spirit's direction, His disciples learn what He was talking about. Lest we be too hard on the 11 Apostles for not knowing *beforehand*, Jesus said, "These things I have spoken to you while I am still with you. But the Helper, the Holy Spirit, whom the Father will send in my name, He will teach you all things and bring to your remembrance all that I have said to you."[6] Jesus spoke specifically of New Testament writings – declaring they will later write God's Word. With the Spirit's illumination, they would teach New Covenant mystery as the Spirit-teaching foundation for what we believe. Despite God's Scriptural revelation and regeneration-encounter, some still wonder "How can we know God's Way or Will?"

In Thomas' words from John 14:5, the cry of many hearts is heard, "Lord, we do not know where you are going. How can we know The Way?" Without understanding, it can seem impossible to know God's Will or Ways. Walking in God's Ways takes **grace**ful fortitude. Learning to "observe what I have commanded you" takes diligent study and obedience. This is for our benefit as it strikes at the root of autonomy. Loosing autonomy allows us to pursue His Will. Thomas learned by sight but Christ later taught them to live by faith.

Jesus' command-statement should cause people to struggle with their sinful motives, thoughts, actions and lack of obedience. In the midst of Spirit-inspired struggle, we should ask, "What can I do to close the gap between my conduct and God's Will?" One major premise is:

Believers cannot imitate God without using His ordained plans or methods!

Put another way, we cannot accomplish something Right, Good or Holy with the use of wrong, evil, or profane methods. Sadly, few think in these terms but a Christian lifeview requires this ongoing adjustment. Because of that oversight, many try to do 'pleasing' things with wrong, evil or profane methods. Associated thoughts to the above premise are motivation behind my attempt to challenge believers.

We cannot afford to go our own way after Jesus clearly points out The Way. In *The Jesus Who Never Lived*[7] by H. Wayne House, false approaches to the Biblical Jesus and His gospel are exposed. In answer to false messiahs, religions, 'christianities,' varied Quests for the Historical Jesus, Existentialism and Jesus of media and popular religion, the Biblical Jesus boldly declared that Only One Way exists. *This* Jesus is The Way, The Truth, and The Life per John 14.6.

At some point, we struggle with Mathematics with a range from minor to perpetual problems. As a corrective, we must learn that Math has perpetual, specific, objective rules to follow to consistently obtain the correct answer. We cannot use wrong methods or signs to correctly solve math problems. I recently saw a *Ten Commandments of Math* poster that loosely reflects God's Ten Commandments. Sadly some honor Math rules but not God's rules. We can't violate Math rules if we expect to get right answers. We can lazily short-circuit the process but adhering to the rules is the only way to get the correct answer. This is the same way to honestly pursue redeemed reality in our spiritual lives.

God's economy works the same way. **God has rules and principles to follow – always**! If we could burn that into our minds, we would be closer to living God's Will. Life cannot work as God designed if we use autonomous methods and principles that violate His rules as this brings dysfunction. In a broader extension, another premise is:

Methods that violate God's design, Character and Ways will not work toward His glory!

Because of Satan's delusion, we can be confused about the impact and reality of sin. Sin always denies or rejects God's glory as we seek our own will rather than God's. While sin always destroys, God's sovereignty and grace are able to work around sin, dysfunction and suffering – this is the beauty of His gospel and power. He promises to do so[8] but we must never imagine that God is pleased with our sin or unholy living.[9] In teaching that future glory is fulfilled in redemption, Paul explains the dichotomy of the created-man/redeemed-man scenario. His teachings are often co-opted to mean things Paul did not intend.

In the following passage, Paul presents qualifiers where God promises to work through and in spite of our struggles and sin to bring glory to His grace. Hear the words of Romans 8:26-30:

> Likewise the Spirit helps us in our weakness. For we do not know what to pray for as we ought, but the Spirit himself intercedes for us with groaning too deep for words. And he who searches hearts knows what is the mind of the Spirit, because the Spirit intercedes for the saints according to the will of God. And we know that for those who love God all things work together for good, for those who are called according to his purpose. For those whom he foreknew he also predestined to be conformed to the image of his

Son, in order that he might be the firstborn among many brothers. And those whom he predestined he also called, and those whom he called he also justified, and those whom he justified he also glorified.

We make disciples to see them redeemed by a Holy God but we don't wait to see God redeem sinners before we attempt to make disciples. We make disciples to teach them what God commands so they glorify His grace through faithful obedience per Matthew 28:16-20. Thereafter, God continues redemption toward imitating His Son in their lives. In God-imitation, we learn more about what redemption means.

As God-imitators or reflectors, we can shine Christ's light through our life. Provoke yourself and others to be Christ-reflectors. Science says the moon only reflects the light of the sun, as it has no inherent light. This has great implications for those who are supposed to reflect the Holiness, Image and Likeness of God. A reflector stands in front of a culvert, bridge or curve to shine for oblivious needy folks without inherent light. If no light shines on the reflector, it's ineffective. If it's dirty or smudged, its shine is minimized. Sit at the feet of a reflector to learn valuable lessons about Imaging Christ. There is no greater way to reflect Christ than through Moral-Law-obedience – as He did!

Reflectors need outside light to shine or to be effective as designed. This reflective ability is the same with believers; we must put ourselves in God's Way to shine for Him. **We shine for Him when our life reflects His perfect Righteousness**. If our slate is muddied with things He wants removed, our shine is minimized. Jesus tells us to clean up our reflection, "In the same way, let your light shine before others, so that they may see your good works and give glory to your Father who is in heaven" (Matthew 5:16). In 1 Corinthians 11:1 Paul tells us "Be imitators of me, as I am of Christ." Being a Christ-imitator is a great hope and goal for life; and **knowing God's Will provokes and leads us to be the cleanest Christ-imitators we can be**.

The following premises relate directly to the upcoming *God's Thread of Continuity*. While they may initially seem somewhat vague or general, they are given to encourage contemplation:

You cannot perform God's Will until you fulfill God's Word.

You cannot reflect God's Holiness without knowing His Law.

You cannot reflect Christ without knowing Atonement dynamics.

Our holiness performs God's Will, Ways, Word and Law through His grace.

Only *by* and *through* Law and gospel will we *know* God's Ways.

For believers, it's necessary to practice God's Will and Ways. It can be encouraging to learn and know that graceful efforts please Him. Faulty teaching on Law *leaves* believers thinking they cannot really please God in their efforts. As a result some take a "Why bother!" stance. Some take an "I guess it doesn't matter what I do!" stance even though God applies Christ's righteousness to saint's account.

So, what is the crux of the matter? The crux of the matter is found in the Crucifixion. It may seem quaint because we hear it many times but Jesus' words in John 14:6 provide the crux of the matter, "I am The Way, and The Truth, and The Life. No one comes to the Father except through Me!" Very bold words! His words provoke the accurate charge of Christianity's 'narrowness and arrogance.' Based on God's declaration and the objective work of the Cross applied to lives in justification and sanctification, we can stand firm on the Only Way of Jesus Christ and His gospel through faith and **grace**.

In addition to His applied work, God requires personal righteousness despite the fact that we sin and come short of His **grace**. Some take a "That's not what I signed up for!" stance and back out of what they imagine to be Christianity. Others take a "That sounds good but I can never do it!" stance that manifests the difficulty of trying to do God's Will in our own power. Both positions need **grace**!

Paul challenges us to develop and live from a Christian lifeview. From Paul's words, it's a tough job and somebody's got to do it. That somebody is you! Don't argue with God or me about this. He gives the power to perform this task and we find joy as we glorify His gospel of **grace**. Get going and live a Redeemed View of Life.

To understand the lifeview God desires for saints, we must realize how a worldview relates. A lifeview falls under a worldview umbrella as the essential foundation. A house is only as good as its foundation; in this way, a worldview is only as good as its lifeview. A Christian worldview must be built upon a Christ-reflecting redeemed lifeview so let's parse this out a bit. *The Universe Next Door* by James Sire provides an unabashed Christian perspective. Deeply consider each phrase to ponder his brief but coherent definition of worldview:

> A worldview is a commitment, a fundamental orientation of the heart that can be expressed as a story or in a set of propositions (assumptions which may be true, partially true, or entirely false) which we hold (consciously or subconsciously; consistently or inconsistently) about the basic constitution of reality that provides the foundation on which we live and move and have our being.[10]

Sire provokes us to meditate on each phrase to glean examination from his worldview/lifeview teaching. If we do, the impact can be heavy! Sire says, "If we want clarity about our own worldview, we must reflect and profoundly consider how we actually behave in reference to our worldview."[11] Sire gives seven questions that can be asked of any worldview.[12] These questions prime the thinking-pump:

1) What is prime reality – the really real?

2) What is the nature of external reality – the world around us?

3) What is a human being?

4) What happens to a person at death?

5) Why is it possible to know anything at all?

6) How do we know what is right and wrong? and

7) What is the meaning of human history?

Different things limit our submission to God's desires and sometimes we need stark questions to shake us from our lethargy. Sire's questions spoke to me! Great work is needed to gain a viable lifeview that pleases the Father – but the Spirit promises to lead us. Those born anew to His Holiness and Gospel have no right to violate His thoughts and Ways. Sadly we violate His Gospel with **grace**-denying thoughts, attitudes and actions. According to 2 Corinthians 10:4-5, they can be captured, handcuffed and executed by God's truth.

Ironically, the subject of personal righteousness, holiness or godliness can get strange looks. Speaking *Christianese* can be a turn-off for those who don't know biblical lingo but I don't understand a few things. In a television series, Detective Columbo's favorite line was, "There's just one thing I don't understand," and then he would ask the case-unfolding question. In the same way, I don't understand why, for some, discussing holiness is like talking about leprosy. When I attempt to provoke or teach sanctification – the upward growth of personal righteousness, holiness and godliness – it often seems like I talk a foreign language. Let me shift gears to approach holiness.

Consider the development of a healthy job search. To approach the job market, some imagine that jobs will 'seek them out.' It's a shock for some to realize their looks, attitudes and approach actually have a great bearing on employment possibilities. It might sound basic and crass but making this link is crucial. Job-needing-teens need to know and consistently do a few things like work hard; take a shower; get a haircut and shave; don't wear gaudy things; learn how to speak well; portray respect and honor; dress for success; and go prepared. The list could go on but to find a job that we want to pursue to get hired, there's essentially a protocol to follow.

It's not too different as we approach God and His Will in regards to holiness. I draw a comparison without speaking of moralism or behaviorism where we clean ourselves up before God will accept or use us. That's exactly *not* what I present. When people claim they don't know, a valid comparison to ignorance exists. If we don't know that holiness is foundational to Christianity, we will be confused.

Since our culture bombards us with contrary thinking and pushes to conform us into its mold, serious mind-change takes great commitment and work. Twenty years ago Southern Baptist Theological Seminary endured a major transition. Liberal theology and apathy had changed the culture of the seminary away from orthodox beliefs. God's Word was seen as less than inerrant. A new president, R. Albert Mohler, Jr. was elected to bring a correction. As Mohler speaks of the institution, consider how your thinking might need a similar correction:

> The only way to reform an academic institution and bring it back to a clear affirmation of biblical orthodoxy was to make clear that we were a confessional institution that held to those doctrinal parameters. It was a very difficult time. The controversy and conflict were, in human terms, almost unbearable, but it was clear to those who love biblical truth that it would be far better for the institution to die than for it to continue in the direction it had been headed for several decades. . . we also understood that it simply had to be done. Institutions move left progressively, inch by inch. They move in a more liberal direction compromise by compromise. But you cannot correct an institution the same way. Confessional integrity is not something that can be accommodated to a progressive timeline. There is no way to say, "We are tolerating less and less heresy and false teaching." If **confessional integrity** is to mean anything, it **must stand as an absolute standard**.[13]

Rather than a progressive move left, we <u>*are left*</u> <u>when we come to faith</u>. Remember the car wreck? We are in a dead condition when God calls us from spiritual death. From God's view – in our dead state – there's nothing in us that imitates Christ; this is why He must rebirth us unto Himself. As a car-wreck survivor, He calls us through **Grace** to His Holiness and Law – to imitate His perfectly-obedient essence.

For a new believer, the rightward movement may be more severe. God calls us to work repentance, faith and conversion as we learn to exercise ourselves in godliness. This explains our great joy and zeal when we are rebirthed and begin the majestic transformation. As we come alive by God's **grace** per Ephesians 2:4, we find great joy in walking in good works He has prepared for us per Ephesians 2:10.

Every believer must go rightward as Heaven will be eternally Right. After God rebirths us, He works for us, within and with us to correct our attitudes, thoughts and actions. This rightward movement is what Paul describes in 2 Corinthians 3:18, "being transformed into the same image from one degree of glory to another." God always wants us to take it to a higher level. He ensures that it works!

Some words incite consternation quicker than others. The first word is provoke or to stir up as used in Hebrews 10:24. It's my hope that we are provoked in a redeemed way to see differently. The second word and biblical concept is duty. Duty is inherent in a redeemed believer but many treat this as the 'four-letter-curse-word' of Christianity. When we see duty as submitting to His light and easy yoke – through the hard and narrow road – we will freely embrace this reality.

The last thing many consider is filtering their life and mind through God's Word. We can *think without thinking* but our minds need filtered or sifted to become pure as He intends. The question we might have is, "What should our thinking be sifted through?"

Back in my sand-box playing days, one thing I remember doing at the beginning of our playing year was sifting the sand. We would sift the sand in the whole box quite often to get the purest softest sand we could get. We sifted out garbage, rocks and sticks. It was fun to play in clean sifted sand. I hope you remember something like that in your life.

We need this sifting or filtering in our minds. **We are called to imitate God and think God's thoughts after Him** – the foundation of the redeemed lifeview. One statement 'fences' my lifeview-thinking better than others. Years ago the following statement burned a hole in my soul and applies to whole-life thought patterns. It still challenges me today as I challenge others. If you like it, claim it as your own.

Rather than 1) filter God's Word through our perspective, we must 2) filter our culture, motives, belief, experience, actions, opinion, tradition, doctrine, assumption, thought, perspective, perception, disposition, feelings, knowledge, temperament, personality, reasoning, and attitudes through God's Word, Truth, Design, Will, Character and Christ's Cross with New Covenant understanding![14]

This life-pattern can firmly plant us on the path of finding God's Will in the Redeemed View of Life. May this foundational statement burn a tattoo into your soul. By practicing this foundational saying that reflects what God's Word commands, our minds and souls can be redeemed. In a book that honors Charles Malik's life, thinking and practice he gave a great synopsis to provoke us to right thinking:

> I speak to you as a Christian. Jesus Christ is my Lord and God and Savior and Song day and night. I can live without food, without drink, without sleep, without air; but I cannot live without Jesus. Without him I would have perished long ago. Without him and his church reconciling man to God, the world would have perished long ago. I live in and on the Bible for long hours every day. **The Bible is the source of every good thought and impulse I have**. In the Bible God himself, the Creator of everything from nothing, speaks to me and to the world directly, about himself, about ourselves, and about his will for the course of events and for the consummation of history. And believe me, not a day passes without me crying from the bottom of my heart, "Come, Lord Jesus!" I know he is coming with glory to judge the living and the dead, but in my impatience I sometimes cannot wait.[15]

Charles Malik, born in the Ottoman Empire in modern Lebanon, was once President of the United Nations. He challenged the church to embrace university education, calling teachers to boldly declare their faith to win students to Christ – redeeming the mind and soul. If you are a teacher, this is a great book for insightful encouragement.

This is a good place to define and unpack the word Redeem. Webster's New World Dictionary defines Redeem as: to buy back; to get back; recover, as by paying a fee; to set free by paying a ransom;

to deliver from sin and its penalties as by a sacrifice made for a sinner (the whole-Bible Redeemed view); and to make amends or atone for a sin. Jesus is our Kinsman Redeemer[16] and His substitutionary sacrifice on the Cross bought us back or redeemed us from our dead state.

God's redemption leads to the work that transforms us from our sinful anti-law and anti-God positions into forgiven sinners who pursue Righteousness. We can only live from the redeemed position after Jesus actually redeems us and applies that redemption. Without regeneration and redemption, we cannot live a Redeemed View of Life. Here's an old saying that speaks to how we approach God's Will,

> Sow a thought; reap an action
> Sow an action; reap a habit
> Sow a habit; reap a character
> Sow a character; reap a destiny

God is serious about Redemption; this should be our focus too. God works **grace** through every aspect of our life as He Redeems our soul and life. Redemption must be our evangelistic focus as we make disciples according to Christ's last command before His home-going.

Redemption should be our teaching focus as we mentor others to become Christ-reflectors and disciple-producers. Per the car wreck, we are all in the dilemma of Romans 3:23-24, "For all have sinned and fall short of the glory of God;" redeemed ones "are justified by his grace as a gift, through the redemption that is in Christ Jesus." When we do God's Will, we are God-glorifiers who do our best to shine for Jesus.

I would love to sit across the table from you to discuss book sections. Face-to-face time helps people more-quickly-grasp what I mean. Sometimes I say it better than write it. If you struggle with a point, contact the author or take it to the Lord, His Word and Spirit.

Typically we take a systematic approach to important decisions. We seriously approach careers, homes, marital relationships and friendships; it should be no different for Christian faith! Get on track with a serious systematic approach to Christianity but do not work *your* plan! Work His Plan – the key to peace, joy and pleasure.

As we put things together from God's perspective, we will be amazed at what we see and learn. From His view, the picture is more glorious all the time as it moves upward.[17] Without redeemed **grace**, our faith and sight is insufficient. His Lifeview can be obtained when we live by His Faith, His sight and His power of **grace** through the Word.

This nutshell synopsis is my attempt to sufficiently explain or describe a redeemed lifeview. The rest of the book puts more skin on the skeleton. May God challenge us every day to fall under His plan and work it by His design through His Word and **grace**.

I want you to come up from the haystack with the needle in your hand. A Finding-His-Will paradigm can inflame Christ-reflection in thought and action. Rethink foundational thoughts and pursue Him as the following song says: *Have Thine Own Way, Lord!*

1. Have Thine own way, Lord! Have Thine own way! Thou are the Potter, I am the clay; Mold me and make me after Thy will, while I am waiting, yielded and still.

2. Have Thine own way, Lord! Have Thine own way! Search me and try me, Master today! Whiter than snow, Lord, wash me just now, as in Thy presence humbly I bow.

3. Have Thine own way, Lord! Have Thine own way! Wounded and weary, help me I pray! Power, all power, surely is Thine! Touch me and heal me, Savior Divine!

4. Have Thine own way, Lord! Have Thine own way! Hold o'er my being absolute sway! Fill with Thy Spirit till all shall see Christ only, always, living in me!

As the song says, we know His plan works when others see the majesty of His gospel in us, or when we boldly proclaim His powerful salvation that overcomes nominal Christianity. When His

Will holds prominence in our **grace**ful thinking, it becomes lovely to submit to His Law. The reason it's lovely to submit to His Law is because He builds obedience into saints to glorify His **grace**. At the point of submission, this reality gives the blessing Jesus mentions in the Beatitudes. This realization prompted David to say his Christ-reflecting famous words, "Oh how I love thy Law!" If you aren't here yet, be patient and seek that <u>rightward lifeview correction</u>.

---

1 In Matthew 6:13-14, Jesus says that many find and walk the broad way that denies the Way of God and rejects the Gospel Way of Christ.

2 In Matthew 19:16-22, the rich young ruler asks Jesus, "What must I do to inherit eternal life?" without moral willingness to follow. While some focus on *what* Jesus said, many fail to acknowledge that obedience to God's commands is required.

3 <u>Cosmic treason</u> are words attributed to R.C. Sproul that refer to Adam and Eve's sin that plunged them and the human race into the clutches of sin and death. Cosmic treason is a great qualifier for what was done, provoked, and impacted in the Garden.

4 David F. Wells, *Losing Our Virtue: Why the church must recover its moral vision* (Grand Rapids, MI.: Eerdmans Publishing, 1998) 36.

5 *TableTalk* is the Devotional from Ligonier Ministries located in St. Mary, FL. In the July 2010 TableTalk was the *Right Now Counts Forever* article.

6 John 14:25-26

7 H. Wayne House, *The Jesus Who Never Lived: Exposing False Christs and Finding the Real Jesus* (Eugene, OR.: Harvest House Publishers, 2008).

8 Romans 8:28-30

9 Scripture teaches this qualifier. Many are familiar with Micah 6:8 but often fail to consider the whole book as God's plea to worship Him correctly through obedience. In the verses prior to 6:8, Micah says God is not pleased with offerings and sacrifices apart from a holy life. Rather than merely give forgiveness, God is pleased with holiness. Realizing this point can help us adopt a necessary, Christ-reflecting paradigm.

10 James W. Sire, *The Universe Next Door: A Basic Worldview Catalog* (Downers Grove, IL.: InterVarsity Press, 2004), 17.

11 Sire, *The Universe Next Door,* 19.

12 Sire, 20.

13 TableTalk interview in *Holding the Line* article, April 2011, page 76.

14 This was the foundational statement that originally framed the whole paper of the Redeemed View of Life. This statement essentially burned its tattoo into my soul. I cannot say it made me a perfect Christ-reflector but it radically pushed my thinking in a Godward direction like never before and I've never looked back.

15 William Lane Craig, Paul M. Gould (Eds.). *The Two Tasks Of The Christian Scholar: Redeeming the Soul; Redeeming the Mind* (Wheaton, IL.: Crossway Books, 2007), 55.

16 The book of Ruth mentions kinsman 12 times. In the form of type, Jesus is our Kinsman Redeemer – possibly the greatest message from the book of Ruth.

17 2 Corinthians 3:18. My 'Kentucky buddy' as I call him has a personalized plate with this verse on his study wall. I first met Shaun Golden in Israel on a Southern trip and we became fast friends. God has used him often to mentor my pastoral sentiments. He could have been one of my dedications but I'm grateful that he humbly models a mentoring pastor and is a provoking fellow undershepherd.

Chapter 4 – God's Thread of Continuity

God's majestic **Grace** and Truth are so vast that I think God will take eternity to unpack doctrine for heaven-dwellers as suggested in Ephesians 2:7. With many intricate details to learn about Scripture and biblical culture, I wish I had 10 lifetimes to learn God's Word but I only have one lifetime to learn, with no time to waste. Pursue an eternal perspective to make your life count for the glory of His grace.

To inflame right thinking on top of my major premise, I present my foundational rubric – *God's Thread Of Continuity*[1] – like a lattice upon which a vine grows. My purpose is to show aspects of God and Truth from a different perspective to provoke transformation. Webster's New World College Dictionary defines <u>continuity</u> as the state or quality of continuous; connectedness; and coherence within a coherent whole. My goal is to demonstrate a correction to humanity's fragmentation due to his sin and radical death by showing that God's continuity can bring coherent integration to our souls, minds and lives.

My coming presentation shows a thread that ties God's doctrines together in our lives as we submit to His lifeview. I desire to effectively communicate but, more than I can hope to perform, I want each of you to pursue God-designed life from a redeemed lifeview. I don't believe there's another approach that pleases God. My hope for God's Thread of Continuity is that we will pursue a transformed mind to think, see and live His **grace** and Gospel from His perspective – the redeemed fulfillment of the major premise.

As thread moves through each eye, remember that each eye is interchangeable without significantly changing meaning. In a literal sense this picture is a lifeview stitched together by God. Think of God skipping a stone that touches the water of our life 12 times – making concentric circles of reverberation every time it skips off the water. My thread touches key aspects of God's truth to provoke contemplation.

This stitched entity is intended to reveal His thoughts and Will in saints – to the praise of His **grace** taught particularly in Ephesians1:6 and 2:7.

I don't remember reading Homer's *The Odyssey*[2] in school. It may take a long time to assess the magnitude of this story and I wish I had more history with this story because great parallels exist with my book and Thread of Continuity. I knew little about Homer's work until a few months ago as I watched the last DVD scenes during a substitute teaching job. I was impressed with the storyline and details of *The Odyssey*. One particular segment of this epic provides an excellent backdrop and illustration for God's matrix. My segment is longer than I'd first choose but it sets up the rest of the book well.

The Odyssey provides a snapshot analogy for *God's Thread of Continuity*. In a roundabout way, let me tell you how. Excuse my ignorance if I distort details, as my intention is noble. As the television story goes, the kingly character Odysseus goes off to fight in what became a ten-year Trojan War.[3] He played a vital role with the Trojan Horse of Greek lore, but his return home to Ithaca was a nightmare!

After the war, it takes another ten years for Odysseus to get back to his home and family. He endures a 10-year hair-raising return trip because of Poseidon's curse – making his 20-year absence more amazing. Upon his return, the goddess Athena *helps* Odysseus by disguising him as a wandering beggar to allow him to take stock of the situation. In his beggarly disguise, he discovers a whole band of suitors vying for the hand of his wife, Penelope. Odysseus is disgusted with the condition of his estate as suitors live presumptuously off his wealth and essentially misuse everything he built and cherished.

Odysseus also wants to discover the intentions, heart and purity of his wife to make sure he can approach a renewed marital union from his pure heart that kept him going for the past 20 years. He returns to the love of his life and family with no thought of having to fight so that he can assume his former position as husband, lover and king. Nevertheless, he wants to win the heart of his wife and properly deal with the audacious suitors. They imagine him to be dead and, without knowing for certain, they disregard him out of their picture.

His son Telemachus, a baby when he left, struggles to maintain his father's legacy by attempting to fight off the suitors – at least for the sake of Odysseus' legacy and his manhood! He soon discovers that his father still lives so now he fights for renewed family relationship. In his beggar-disguise, Odysseus talks with his son who plays the part of a heat-seeking missile to evaluate the heart of his mother. Odysseus is able to assess the situation without the suitors knowing who he is.

Against all hope, Penelope has begrudgingly given in to the idea of taking another husband. She is tormented with the thought of moving on but deems it necessary after 20 years. In the course of the story, the goddess Athena moves Penelope to propose a test to decide who is worthy to take her hand. The test, designed to center around the integrity and majesty of her husband, will take place the following day. Great excitement mounts as a new leader and husband is anticipated.

News of the test allows Odysseus to hatch a plan with his son Telemachus to destroy the unwanted suitors who disrespect yet live off his wealth and seek to marry his wife! Having fought valiantly for his father's character and legacy, Telemachus looks forward to his father's honor being maintained. The death of the devious suitors would bring him pleasure, yet his father tempers his wrath for the moment.

The next day, all viable suitors file into a miniature Coliseum of sorts to discover details of the test. The doors are locked and, like a cage fight, at best only one entity will emerge. The suitors are ready for any test – so they think. The test is two-fold and the test-criteria sound simple. If anyone can 1) string Odysseus' bow and 2) shoot one arrow through all 12 rings at once on strategically placed axe handles they will win Penelope's hand in marriage. As easy as it sounds however, it was a tough test – indeed almost impossible.

To begin with, no one is able to string his bow. Surely the suitors had strung bows before but no one accomplishes stringing *this* bow! After several attempts, the suitors deem the test to be impossible! They can't string the bow much less shoot the arrow through 12 axe handles! At this time the wandering beggar – the disguised Odysseus – limps up to the bow. All eyes are on this despicable character, with no thought that he can accomplish the already-deemed impossible task.

Almost as an afterthought, to their amazement he strings the bow, nocks an arrow and shoots it through the twelve axe handles – in one shot, the first time. After his shot, his disguise lifts and everyone sees him for who he is or was. Then all hell breaks loose and all suitors are killed at the hands of Telemachus and Odysseus. Another view might say that all heavenly wrath broke loose and justice was served. The king returned to vindicate himself and take what was his!

The point of this Odyssey story-rehearsing is two-fold – similar to Penelope's test. First, while everyone thought others could easily perform the test, only Odysseus could fulfill the test. Second, shooting the arrow through the eyes of the axe handles parallels the threading of the needle through the eyes of God's continuity. Before we move into the pictorial presentation of *God's Thread of Continuity*, let's consider the story of *The Odyssey* a bit further.

I am amazed at the worldly critiques of *The Odyssey* that do not see a majestic story of God's story of redemption in this classic. I can't yet speak to Homer's intent but it seems that he describes the picture of God's story in humanity and His relationship with sinful humanity through His redemption. I need more research but I see a huge connection between *The Odyssey* and The Bible's Story.

From the beginning, God made it plain what He built and intended for humanity. While He went away for many years – such that other suitors came to steal away His wife or bride – His Son held the fort until the crux of the story could be manifest. His people tried to hold out but the struggle seemed to be overwhelming. The haze of his return and story was too nebulous to imagine a victorious ending. As Odysseus was the only one who could string the bow and shoot the arrow through the axe handles, Jesus was the only Worthy One who could open the book, told in Revelation 4, 5, 19:1-10 and 21:1-8.

As in The Odyssey, many live as though God will not return to His rightful place. But God did come again to set things in order. Not only did He return in Christ, He will come again to finally set things in order as time comes to a close. God returned to earth 'after many years' – so many that some never imagined it could actually be Him. For many, he was a has-been and they treated his servants as such per the Parable of the Tenants in Matthew 21:33-46. As God was 'changed' to Jesus Christ, Jesus won the correcting victory.

The magnitude of Odysseus' wrath and vengeance will pale in comparison to the certain justice and judgment brought by God at His final return. Christians bank on His return and justice. Our search is for that needle in the haystack to help us understand and properly deal with God who sits on the Kingly seat of authority. It's not just that He came back to His country to take what was His because of Re-creation – but He comes to eternally rule in redeemed minds and lives.

The book cover shows a hand coming forth from the hay holding the proverbial needle in a hay stack.[4] When we first contemplate finding God's Will, it seems a daunting task. Finding the needle is Key, allowing us to stitch God's truth together to transform our lives. Don't run from the search. Embrace the search because this is God's Will for you – to find the needle to enable the stitching.

This search is God's process for every believer – actually every person – even as you might sometimes feel you are in over your head. Even if our search 'finds' God, we spend our lifetime in pursuit of Him; this is why we need a redeemed lifeview. Keep seeking Him. Spend time in God's haystack so that you can burst forth with the needle in your hand too. If you don't desire to frolic in the hay – the Bible – do some evaluation; lack of desire does not speak well of someone who is supposed to seek Him with their life. Like David, God's children enjoy playing in the hay. In the midst of the fun, you will find the lost needle.

As we evaluate this pictorial continuity or coherence, remember that we can exchange eyes without changing intent. We are not really looking for a needle in a haystack but the needle you find goes through God-venues. It's not Dot-to-Dot per se but the thread goes through each eye. Imagine a thread woven through the eyes (O's) to guide the process – as these doctrines are woven or stitched together.

God's Thread of Continuity

O	God's Will ...	must ALWAYS be accomplished through
O	God's Ways . .	that are ALWAYS understood through
O	God's Word . .	that Essentially flows from His
O	Holiness . . .	that is summarized and reflected in His
O	Character . .	that leads to guidance and power through His
O	Law...	that functions as a regenerative mirror to His
O	Grace...	that provokes Christ-conformity through the
O	Gospel	that transforms us by Christ's atonement by
O	Faith	that provokes proper response to
O	Repentance...	that leads to our sanctification and leads to
O	Conversion ...	that transforms us into Christ-reflectors.

As thread continues through varied eyes, dwell on how these points fit together into one stitched piece of practice. These points work in conjunction to accomplish God's Will for our life. We cannot violate one without violating another. Conversely our respect and practice of each point leads into the next point. We could examine His glory, Kingdom, Wisdom, Name, Being, Mission, Love and other valuable points but these 'eyes' are given to offer a workable approach to His salvation and our conversion. Other doctrines are acknowledged as necessary although not presented in the above chart.

Some needle-eyes may seem vague or mysterious. When we see them clearly, we can develop them into thoughts, attitudes and practice. A complete study would be great for each topic but it does not occur here. My aim is to present an overview so readers can make helpful connections to the whole picture. My hope is that qualifiers answer questions before they are asked. We could examine these topics from God's view but remember the primary focus is on God's desire for saints to live out what God designed per Romans 12:1-2. The focus is purposely kept on what we do in His power. Be willing to learn as you progress through the Thread of Continuity follow-up chapters.

Biblically, the presented points are indisputable but erroneous teachings abound in the church today. Surely some will disagree with my premises even as I attempt to explain my positions through Scripture and experience. Erroneous teachings in the church make a consensus of belief difficult and I understand that; this is why I try to offer cogent understanding that stands up under pressure. Please evaluate your heart and belief by the overall teaching of Scripture and when you discover discrepancy, embrace biblical change.

While change is a certainty in life, we struggle with change. Biblical change might be a new phrase but don't let it intimidate you. It simply means to make life-corrections that glorify the thinking and actions that please God the Father, Son and Holy Spirit. It might sound simple – like shooting an arrow through 12 axe handles – but doing it may seem an insurmountable task. Without **grace**, it is impossible!

My design in this presentation toward a biblical lifeview and holy living is to share what God illumined to my mind and practice years ago as the reverberations are still ongoing today. I share to provoke us to offer ourselves – mind and all – to the Spirits' conversion on a continual upward-moving basis. Like learning to swim, we can be overwhelmed at first until we learn the basics and get past our fears.

Biblical change comes from biblical thinking – what I present as seeing with Redeemed eyes. This flows back into understanding **grace**, faith and the Gospel as a reciprocating-gospel-energy.[5] My eyelet subjects are practical prerequisites explored later through the biblical 3-Step Process of change presented in Chapter 11. The three points are 1) put off the old man through repentance, 2) correct our thinking through God-honoring faith and 3) put on the new man through ongoing conversion. These steps encompass redeemed biblical change.

The 'eye'-order was considered for clarity of main points rather than for explicit teaching of additional reality. Realize that God's Will, Ways, Word, Law, Holiness and Character all flow into a redeemed view of Gospel, **Grace** and the collective gospel-results of faith, repentance and conversion. Allow *God's Thread of Continuity* to help you see the need for a systematic approach. See these 11 eyes as 12 axe handles that God must shoot through to remove any doubt of who He is – the One who claims the Throne over all things!

Although I didn't make regeneration[6] an 'eye' in the Continuity list, this crucial doctrine is taught throughout. As I often dialogue with authors in margins of books I read, ask questions for clarification or additional input. The Spirit is pleased to unpack His Word about regeneration or 'being made alive' for those who diligently seek answers and wisdom. Creating regeneration and a biblical lifeview in you is beyond my ability but my attempt is meant to foster mental and practical changes toward Christ being created or formed in you. This is partly what Paul intends when he says in Galatians 4:12-19,

> Brothers, I entreat you, become as I am, for I also have become as you are. You did me no wrong. You know it was because of a bodily aliment that I preached the gospel to you at first, and though my condition was a trial to you, you did not scorn or despise me, but received me as an angel of God, as Christ Jesus. What then

has become of the blessing you felt? For I testify to you that, if possible, you would have gouged out your eyes and given them to me. Have I then become your enemy by telling you the truth? They make much of you, but for no good purpose. They want to shut you out that you may make much of them. It is always good to be made much of for a good purpose, and not only when I am present with you, my little children, for whom I am again in the anguish of childbirth **until Christ is formed in you**.

Paul sought to see Christ birthed and manifested in those he evangelized, discipled and worked with – especially in churches he started. God's passion is still ongoing through the very Scripture Paul penned. Ultimately Paul's passion to see Christ birthed and manifest in people speaks to the reality of regeneration rather than the gospel we often hear and propagate today. I wish we were more like Paul!

Paul speaks further of a biblical lifeview that is only obtained as our mind and actions become like Christ's. **Grace** leads to a changed soul leading to a redeemed mind and biblical lifeview. A biblical lifeview leads to gospel-reflecting Holy Spirit-inspired action that allows us to demonstrate His Life as people see real Christianity in us.

In reflection, writing this book holds several purposes for me. First I share my experience to challenge my flock and readers. Second, I put meat on crucial teaching-skeletons – this might be an epiphany for some. Third, I present a systematic approach to the Christian Faith lived on the anvil of His Word. These purposes encourage me to think God will use redeemed **grace** to bring corrections to how we view personal holiness, Law-keeping and the majestic doctrine of **grace**.

I trust you pursue God's Will. If not, there is no better time to start this blessed pursuit. I trust you are working His Plan that He has unfolded at great cost. If not, there is no better time to start! As we consider other qualifiers from *God's Thread of Continuity* realize that God calls saints to exercise godliness per 1 Timothy 4:7. Following God's Will takes great effort that only you can give. Give your best to the Master and you will never be sorry – He will make sure of that!

As we begin Part 2, consider the thread that runs through the Continuity eyes. As Odysseus was the only one who could shoot one arrow through axe rings, Jesus is the only One to finish the necessary Cross Work. Through His Work and the Spirit's application of effective **Grace**, we are empowered to shoot a needle through God's eyes of Continuity to gain salvation that wins the eternal prize. Seek His ability to shoot straight and pursue the needle-prize with all your might.

---

1 *God's Thread of Continuity* is the thought that came to mind as I drew this section in my mind and put it to paper. I always felt it was a God-thing through me.

2 *The Odyssey* is one of two major ancient Greek classic poems attributed to Homer. In part, it is a sequel to the *Iliad*, another poem attributed to Homer.

3 In Greek Mythology, the Trojan War was waged against the city of Troy by the Greek Achaeans after Paris of Troy took Helen from her husband Menelaus who was king of Sparta. The Trojan Horse that allowed the Greeks inside the city – leading to final victory – was the brainchild of Odysseus who was there to give honor to and fight for Helen as a former suitor

4 Finding the needle in the haystack is a good analogy for finding God's Will through the haze of Scripture. My prayer is that this book might help you find that needle in the haystack of God's truth – even though you keep seeking.

5 Until we get to give a grace chapter, I try to give a preliminary look at how God has pushed me to define **grace**. I see **grace** as a reciprocating gospel energy that continues to cycle upward per 2 Corinthians 3:18. The more we do by His **grace**, the more it reciprocates to redound to His Glory. The more we glorify **grace**, the more **grace** He gives; this is a crude way to describe reciprocating gospel energy that I believe flows from **grace** as Bible-writers describe – especially for evangelism and proclaiming.

6 Regeneration is an oft misunderstood word. It's a word I like to use in regards to salvation because I think it better reflects the biblical understanding of right relationship with God through Christ 's Atonement – especially as it manifests the birthing reality that Jesus teaches in John 3, 4 &11. People often talk about 'coming to Christ,' 'accepting Jesus,' 'being saved,' 'being born again,' 'being baptized' or 'joining a church' but many are clueless to the reality and results of biblical Justification and salvation. When I ask about regeneration, despite their previous claim, I often find confused looks and a glaring lack of practical knowledge. Lack of knowledge doesn't necessarily mean regeneration hasn't occurred but this is something that needs to be reconsidered and redemptively evaluated. There are many distortions of this biblical concept and I unpack and challenge views of regeneration and salvation later. For now, understand regeneration as the God-alone-effecting-working in the soul of the spiritually dead sinner to make them alive to Christ and His righteousness as Paul teaches in Ephesians 2. Many draw an equation between various responses to the Gospel and the reality of New Birth that Jesus tells Nicodemus and the Samaritan woman in John 3 and 4 that are often faulty or come up short in New Covenant reality. With this in mind I'm provoked by God's Spirit to challenge these assumptions to the glory of His **grace**. By an equation, I mean something like 1+1 = 2. As to gospel presentations, many say that personal faith (1) added to (+) the facts of the gospel (1) equals (=) new birth or salvation. I don't challenge biblical logic or the biblical Gospel per se but rather conclusions we easily draw from cut-in-stone teachings that may come from truncated understandings of what Scripture presents. Many confuse the Good News of the Gospels (Matthew, Mark, Luke and John) with The Gospel of salvation and its results although overlaps exist. Many thoughts are unpacked later.

Part 2

Claiming a Literal and Objective Divine Foundation

God's Thread of Continuity

God's Will...   Must ALWAYS be accomplished through

God's Ways... that are ALWAYS understood through

God's Word... that is basically synonymous with

The Law...   that manifests, reflects, or mirrors His

Holiness...   that is summarized and reflected in His

Character...   that leads to regeneration provided through the

Gospel...   that transforms us by Christ's atonement by

Grace...   that provokes Christ-conformity through

Faith...   that provokes proper response to

Repentance... that leads to our sanctification and leads to

Conversion... that transformers us into Christ-reflectors.

Chapter 5 – God's Will

The subject of God's Will should be clearer now but redeemed examination of His Word gives clarity. God's Will probably seemed a little ambiguous at first. As we put puzzle pieces together or connect the dots, we find God's Will is concrete and progressive in nature. Keep in mind that the total picture requires a working understanding of the *Eyes* of Continuity, so be encouraged to work these out in your life. Be sincere in graceful effort and you will find God's Will!

It took many years for me to stumble over a teaching that provoked a Christian lifeview in my mind – with God's Will as the central focus. I studied God's Word for years and, like many, I stumbled to find God's Will. It took years of diligent study to see what I later called the edges of the picture or box top picture. I'm still amazed at how long it took me to gain a biblical lifeview but it's ever growing.

Discovery has much to do with practical holiness related to God's Will for fundamental thinking, attitudes and actions. St. Augustine of Hippo once said, "**I believe in order to understand**." St. Anselm of Canterbury said, "I do not seek to understand in order that I may believe, but I believe in order to understand." Believing God is the only way to find God's Will as it leads to practical following. Without walking in God's Will, we have no valid right to claim to know His Will.

God's Will is a broad subject and some might think, "I'm finally going to get my nagging question answered." To find God's Will, people ask questions like, "Does God want me to take this job? Buy this house or car? Marry this person? or Write this book?" We can fill in the blank with our choice of life-options to make the question personal but that is not what I drive to uncover. Because God's Will is clearly presented, it behooves us to know His Will personally but don't be disappointed if you want the focus to be on these types of life-questions; as important as they may be, this is not my focus here.

Rather my focus is on God's Will for and in saints – on sanctification through obedience to God's <u>directives</u> even as this flows into life-option answers. Everyone who seeks God might claim a desire to know God's Will so let me qualify other aspects. It's not my intent to focus on God's Will inherent in Himself. We sometimes ask about God's Will to use the answers for selfish desires unlinked from His purpose; this is wrong, but not my focus. Know that a redeemed focus on God's Will for and in saints changes the questions and foundations.

The scope of God's Will as framed demonstrates its necessity and importance for our life. God's Will in respect to the Redeemed View of Life might be the most important factor for us to know. This truth, before explanation, may leave some in a fog. Scripture's haze easily comes to the fore in this discovery and we will speak to this more deeply. As much as we like to grab hold of God's Truth and run with it, it's not as easy to do properly or biblically as we like to think.

Years after adopting a Christian lifeview that radically changed my life I'm amazed and saddened to discover that fewer than 10% of <u>professing</u> believers have and live from a Christian worldview.[1] This statistic comes from *The Truth Project* by *Focus On The Family*. The 10% statistic indicates a huge problem in the church – many tied directly to questions related to my emphasis that some deem narrow.

God partners with us to develop a Christian lifeview. Much of the Old Testament speaks of God's desire for His saints to discover and walk in His Will. Old Testament saints often claimed their lineage from Abraham without realizing that faith and faithful living are essential results of regeneration. We struggle with this issue as we approach salvation; this is partly why some reject Old Testament sanctifying teaching and the godly pursuit it compels. Proverbs 1:7 says, "The Fear of the Lord is the beginning of Wisdom." Scripture speaks of hard work that many dismiss. It seems they say, "Hard work? That's not for me!" Please repent if you use this **grace**-denying response.

The 10% statistic suggests that people 'come to faith' and never have their soul and mind converted to a Christian paradigm. This may be much worse than a grave concern. It's one thing if people really come to faith; it's another thing if they assume they come to faith with no biblical faith in their being. It's one thing to merely 'believe in God' (nominal Christianity) and another to believe God and His Gospel![2]

The tragic 10% number manifests three glaring ingredients. Many merely 1) believe in God, 2) have a bobble head mentality and 3) live in a way that denies their profession. Let me expose what true belief in God looks like because many hide behind this façade. Mere belief in God produces a bobble head mentality. We know what a bobble head does; they stand there shaking their head up and down in a "Yes!" response at the slightest provocation – with no follow-through.

When Moses presented the Law in Egypt after the Exodus, many Israelites gave a bobble-head-response. Exodus 24:2 tells us, "Moses came and told the people all the words of the LORD and all the rules. And all the people answered with one voice and said, 'All the words that the LORD has spoken we will do.'" I'm sure good intentions existed but the bobble head mentality possessed many. Throughout their history they often gave bobble head responses; this eventually led to them being sent into captivity and losing their national rights.

The bobble head mentality is alive today in nominal Christianity. I offer two questions with answers from David Wells to expose this reality. "Do you know what sin is?" What is our response?

> In America today only 17% of people understand sin in relation to God. **What in the Bible makes sin to be sin has disappeared for the great majority of Americans**, and the consequence is a massive trivialization of our moral life. This happens because moral offenses against God are reduced simply into bad feelings about ourselves.[3]

Most Americans profess belief in God. Conformity to God's Will should be higher in the church, but the churched-mentality is not too different from those outside. It's no wonder people outside the church reject God's Will when people inside manifest a bobble-head mentality.

> While the great majority of Americans believe that they actually keep the Ten Commandments, only 13% think that each of these commandments has moral validity. It is no surprise to learn that 74% say that they will steal without compunction; 64% say that they will lie if there is an advantage to be had in doing so; 53% say that, given a chance, they will commit adultery; 41% say that they intend to use recreational drugs; and 30% say that they will cheat on their taxes. What may be the clearest indicator of the disappearance of a moral texture to society is the loss of guilt and embarrassment over moral lapses. While 86% admit to lying regularly to their parents, 75% to a friend, 73% to a sibling, and 73% to a lover, only 11% cited lying as having produced a serious level of guilt or embarrassment. While 74% will steal without compunction, only 9% register any moral disquiet. While pornography has blossomed into a 4 billion dollar industry that accounts for a quarter of all the videos rented in shops, seen in the thriving hotel business or on cable, only 2% experience guilt about watching. And, not surprisingly, at the center of this slide into license and moral relativism is the disappearance of God. Only 17% define sin as a violation of God's Will.[4]

As a citizen, father, teacher and pastor, I see this bobble-head mentality every day. "Do you know why fornication is wrong?" "Yes!" "Do you know why truth is critical?" "Yes!" "Do you know why drinking and driving is taboo?" "Yes" On and on the bobble heads go with no real connection to <u>believing God</u>. I do not deny a vital connection, but belief in God comes short of believing God! Do not settle for belief in God. We must **believe** God! When we compare a bobble head mentality to believing God and His Will, there is a huge difference.

The book of James shows this difference by demonstrating that 'naked' belief in God is not sufficient! Do not hang your spiritual spurs on a <u>belief in God</u>. James says that <u>believing God</u> shows substantiating obedience and works – a living working pro-active faith. James also clearly shows that without works of sanctification, we should not claim salvation. Hear his words in James 2:14-26:

> What good is it my brothers, if someone says he has faith but does not have works? Can that faith save him? . . . So also faith by itself, if it does not have works, is dead. . . You believe that God is one; you do well. Even the demons believe – and shudder! Do you want to be shown, you foolish person, that faith apart from works is useless? . . . And the Scripture was fulfilled that says, "Abraham believed God, and it was counted to him as righteousness" – and he was called a friend of God. . . For as the body apart from the spirit is dead, so also faith apart from works is dead.

It's true that believing God manifests belief in God but the converse may not be true. Believing in God typically does not manifest actions to demonstrate believing God. Bobble heads claim to believe God but their actions show otherwise. Belief in God with a dead faith manifests demonic belief (James 2:19) – even as it's an emotionally charged belief. Believing God occurs in regenerate ones; thereafter they confirm this by following. Belief in God could get Abraham to go look at the mountain; believing God caused Abraham to take his son Isaac and lay him on the altar. An eternal difference exists between these two points; the first gets you to hell, the second gets you to glory.

The number of stillbirths[5] in the church today seems to confirm the bobble head mentality of nominal ones who believe in God. Some say stillbirths possess eternal life without new life – by itself, a glaring contradiction. Trying to provoke professing believers to develop a Christian lifeview can expose the reality of spiritual life or death! We must move past a naked belief in God and believe God. We must challenge marginal Christianity with the **grace in** the biblical Gospel.

Those who cannot manifest a Christian lifeview may have dead faith; they may 'correctly' believe in God but exhibit no living working pro-active faith. I'd rather not make this judgment but this conclusion might bring some to face stark reality. As stillbirths mock God's Gospel, we might need to rethink our foundations. For this intent, a Redeemed lifeview is examined in Romans 12:1-2, Philippians 2:5-13, 2 Corinthians 10:4-6 and 1 Peter 4:1-2. Let's look at Romans 12:1-2 first:

I appeal to you therefore, brothers, by the mercies of God, to **present your bodies as a living sacrifice**, holy and acceptable to God, **which is your spiritual worship**. Do not be conformed to this world but **be transformed by the renewal of your mind that by testing you may discern what is the will of God**, what is good and acceptable and perfect.

Very few verses burned a hole in my soul and challenged my lifeview like Romans 12:1-2. To know that God's mercy forgave my sins and grace 1) regenerated my soul, 2) adopted me as a son, 3) established me in Christ to present my thoughts, attitudes, studies and actions, and 4) transforms me into a living rather than a dead sacrifice on His altar is a life-long continuous challenge. Paul confirms this is a vital part of a biblical lifeview. I pray these keys live in you.

To have my mind transformed through diligent study helped me understand God's Will; I know this does not come through osmosis but through God and diligent labor. It's still an ongoing process. Seek to 1) present yourself as a living sacrifice in practical worship and 2) transform your mind into a Christ-reflecting machine – two essentials of sanctification. With new birth and graceful effort, we might provoke believe-in-God-professors to develop a Christian lifeview.

Throughout Scripture, **God's Will for us is to see, understand and live all things from His perspective**. If this is the first time you heard this it may not be an easy thing to chew on but it's God's Will for saints. This is why He reveals His intentions and purposes – essentially only to those who believe Him. God's eyes see this: **God-reflection is seen through Christ-reflection as The Great Pursuit of Christianity**. Sadly, many misunderstand this call. God commands us to be like Him and sanctification calls us to holiness. **God works sanctification in our lives as we practice God's Will**.

As we connect the dots to see the box top, we can begin to realize how God commands us to imitate Christ – the essence of God creating us in His Image and Likeness.[6] Philippians unpacks truths

96

about Jesus and His Incarnation – where God bridged the human/divine chasm without sacrificing His requirements.

In light of the coming majestic Cross work by the Incarnated Savior, Jesus tells followers in Matthew 16:24 "Take up your cross and follow Me." At times saints give their life as martyrs – His witnesses. No matter how it *fleshes out*, we are true witnesses as we believe God. Even with obedience to the Cross, in a little different way, saints can imitate Christ in all His ways for us. Philippians 2:5-13 says:

> **Have this mind among yourselves, which is yours in Christ Jesus** who, though he was in the form of God, did not count equality with God a thing to be grasped, but made himself nothing, taking the form of a servant, being born in the likeness of men. And being found in human form, **he humbled himself by becoming obedient to the point of death,** even death on a cross. Therefore God has highly exalted him and bestowed on him the name that is above every name, so that at the name of Jesus every knee should bow, in heaven and on earth and under the earth, and every tongue confess that Jesus Christ is Lord, to the glory of God the Father. Therefore, my beloved, as you have always obeyed, so now, not only as in my presence but much more in my absence, work out your own salvation with fear and trembling, for **it is God who works in you, both to will and to work for his good pleasure**.

The Will of God for us is that we possess the mind and actions of Christ – and Paul speaks of Jesus' mind toward the Cross. Jesus – though He was God – believed God and was obedient to God at every point! We cannot do what Jesus did at the point of making redemption but we can follow Christ in incarnational and redeemed ways. **Living by Jesus' Faith and Sight can only occur if we believe God**. If we believe God, we will take up our cross and follow Him. Have you?

Obedience is displayed in The Fear of the Lord by working-out our salvation. If we do not see God working His Will in our life through our willing and working for His pleasure, speaking to the overcoming power of **grace**, we should be alarmed. God's working includes our proactive response – thinking with the same mind as Christ.

Paul encourages us to develop <u>Christ's mind and lifeview</u>. In view of secularism, pluralism, materialism, spiritualism, postmodernism, Eastern thinking, Edenism, and faulty religious views of pride and unbelief we must consider how to extricate ourselves from thinking that keeps us in bondage to sin and self. All entrapments are due to faulty thinking, and saints may not consider how much bondage is self-induced. Without Christ's mind, we fail to live God's Will.

Faulty thinking makes it impossible to live as God desires yet we might wonder why things don't work right. Don't deceive yourself by imagining you live as a Christ-reflector without a Christian lifeview; this is delusional thinking! Get after right thinking because it's crucial to your life! To find His Will, God helps us transform our minds by His power to work-out His Lifeview that this book provokes.

Let me explain where our confounded thinking got its start in humanity. Just as Adam and Eve stood before the serpent that tempted them to eat the forbidden fruit – and they failed – the insight we gain by evaluating the result of their disobedience can be valuable. And we can win by rejecting their way – the Covenant of Works. Man was created to depend on God as life's <u>Source</u> – as God is the Source![7] The first Commandment is to love God with our whole being; anything less is sin! As The Source, everything or everyone else is a <u>resource</u>.[8]

Charles Hodge said, "The duty to which we are directed by this commandment is the highest duty of man." In *Why The Ten Commandments Matter*, D. James Kennedy said,

> God demands first place in our lives, and it's only right that He should do so. He is the Author of our being, the One on whom we are absolutely dependent, the rightful Possessor of our souls and bodies. He is God, the Creator of everything we see, and those He created must worship and revere Him. I believe we find peace and fulfillment only when we give God His rightful place in our lives.[9]

Rather than be dependent upon The Source, the serpent tempted Eve to make her own way of sustenance and thereby circumvent the only true BEING in the universe. Since God has eternal life within Himself,[10] no one can possess eternal life – independent of God! Yet, Adam and Eve believed they could make a life independent from God – and we do too at times. Learn from His Being as it relates to our derived life; this knowledge can lead us to seek Life in Him.

Derived life means that we possess life from another. As Creator, we are given life by God. Humans depend on One with Life to live biologically, relationally, spiritually, incarnationally and missionally. Humans are dependent upon God but those who live in rebellion reject eternal life by refusing to believe Him. God wants us to move beyond derived life to **grace**-dependent re-created life. Seek this reality.

Satan's temptation was to get Adam and Eve, the creatures to become equal with God, the Creator but the result was that they ended up hiding in creation bushes. This tragedy speaks to a great futility and irony, maybe the greatest I know. In the attempt to be like the Creator, the Creature hides in the Creation. Talk about futility!

This decline occurs every time man imagines he can dethrone God and sit in His place. Or it occurs when pride or unbelief stands supreme. We can assume Eve's posture in conduct – to be God in His place. Most world religions stand here too – attempting to think and act like God without His power and means. It's no wonder many things do not work as they should. Go figure! Actually it's not a mystery!

We may struggle to sort through many instructions but there should be no real confusion. 2 Corinthians 10:4-6 says:

> For the weapons of our warfare are not of the flesh but have divine power to destroy strongholds. We destroy arguments and every lofty opinion raised against the knowledge of God, and **take every thought captive to obey Christ**, being ready to punish every disobedience, when your obedience is complete.

Peter agrees with Paul's teaching. Peter also speaks of Christ's suffering and how we should live in the face of suffering. Peter is the one who rebukes Christ for His statement about going to Jerusalem to die on the Cross – right after God the Father reveals through his mouth the redeemed reality of Jesus the Christ. Peter's letters are chock full of great instruction but in 1 Peter 4:1-2 we are given a synopsis:

> Since therefore Christ suffered in the flesh, **arm yourselves with the same way of thinking**, for whoever has suffered in the flesh has ceased from sin, **so as to live** for the rest of the time in the flesh no longer for human passions but **for the will of God**.

Peter makes the connection plain: Christ's thinking – that we should possess – translates into living for God's Will. The mystery is gone; the only thing left is how we live the claimed reality in our soul.

As we examine Scripture, some verses speak of God's Will for His people but don't use the explicit word. A few explicit ones are considered that reveal snippets of His Will for us:

Matthew 7:21 – "Not everyone who says to Me, 'Lord, Lord,' will enter the kingdom of heaven; but *he who does the Will of my Father*, who is in heaven."

John 17:7 – "*If any man is willing to do His Will*, he shall know of the teaching, or whether I speak from myself."

Colossians 1:9 – "For this reason also, . . . , we have not ceased to pray for you and to ask *that you may be filled with the knowledge of His Will in all spiritual wisdom and understanding*."

1Thessalonians 4:3a – "For *this is the Will of God* for you brethren, *even your sanctification*."

Hebrews 13: 20-21 – "Now may the God of peace,… make you perfect in every good work to do His Will, *working in you that which is well-pleasing in his sight*, through Jesus Christ."

From these verses we can extract qualifiers of God's Will for believers. If vagueness permeates your perspective, realize three explicit generalities exist in the verses above. Salvation, obedience and sanctification are all linked to holiness – God's desire for you. The more I learn about His Word, the more I realize all three points fall under

Grace – His empowerment to save and sanctify me. **Grace** eternally effects salvation, obedience and sanctification. I use the word <u>effect</u> rather than <u>affect</u> because Scripture says God effectually works in saint's lives so we can live from its affect-reality.

The biblical fact of this *effecting* is why I argue elsewhere for a **Grace** hermeneutic,[11] an ultimate perspective to interpret Scripture. Holiness is the essence of **grace. Godliness or Christ-Imitation is God's major emphasis throughout His revelation**. **Grace** is unpacked in subsequent chapters as God's path that leads to a redeemed focus. If we are on God's path, Christ will be in us – working for us by working His **grace**ful pleasure within us.

Holiness is God's Will for His saints. Part of heaven's majesty is that God ensures that it's filled with Holiness. No sin will pollute the new heaven. With that in mind, why do some imagine that holiness is no longer required of saints – otherwise known as 'holy ones?' I think this is a bobble head response that manifests rampant confusion.

No command regarding God's Will is repeated more than "Be holy as I am holy!" By sheer numbers, we should never misunderstand this point! Ponder the questions below that God used to drive my passion for a discovery of redeemed **grace**. May these questions spark serious inquiry and practical out-working toward Christ-reflection.

- Do we easily miss the necessary point of holiness in our salvation?
- Do we disregard this full-Scripture command and essence?
- Has teaching so deluded our minds that we blatantly deny holiness?
- Do we focus so much on the blood and 'forget' the burning flesh
    that God said was a sweet smelling savor to His nostrils?

- Can we recover right understanding? If so, how?
- Do we honor God's **grace** as He exalts in the reality of Holiness?
- Do we seriously ponder our duty before God?

When I speak of <u>necessary holiness</u>, I see many blank faces. While holiness is an indisputable point of Scripture, tragically many do not understand its necessity or nuances; therefore many dismiss or reject this reality especially when common teachings encourage or espouse holiness-rejection. Many do not have holiness on their radar screens and if this applies to you, put holiness back on your radar screen because the pursuit of Holiness matters to God!

Holiness leads us to please the Father and magnify His **grace** yet anemic teaching clearly deludes many. Some fail to imitate Christ in righteousness. Some fail to honor **grace** despite the fact that He exalts **grace** in a higher way than many imagine per Ephesians 2:7. The pursuit of holiness-maturity and Christ-reflection is crucial to our walk in **Grace**. When we truly understand how high God exalts holiness and realize that He gives power to perform it, what are we waiting for?

We can highlight mercy to the practical exclusion of **grace** and empowerment. If so, we live with what I call a <u>half-cross-theology</u> and present a <u>half-cross-gospel</u> that leads to myriad still-births and satisfied-unregenerated-ones. Broad-brush assessments are unpacked later but if my assessment is half-correct, many deluded or deceived souls attend church and believe they have life in Christ. This may explain why people in the world don't see too much real Christianity.

There is a glaring reason for many oversights listed above. Like the *Pin the Tail on the Donkey* game, people pin tails in strange and wrong places. If it wasn't so sad, we could laugh at where people pin some doctrinal or spiritual tails. Some pin them on wrong doctrine – such as deficient definitions of grace that lead to sloppy thinking and confused sinful living. If you know better, help confused ones put the tail in the right place; as the Good Samaritan with the beast of burden, Jesus narrows our search to Him and His Work – the tail belongs here! Take the tail off personal confusion and wrong thinking to put the tail in the right place and God's success will find you!

As we close this chapter, listen to the words of a prayer from *The Valley of Vision*.[12] With prayers for many occasions, *Heart Corruptions* puts a redeemed tail on our journey to this point:

O God, May thy Spirit speak in me that I may speak to Thee.
I have no merit; let the merit of Jesus stand for me.
I am undeserving, but I look to thy tender mercy.
I am full of infirmities, wants, sin; thou art full of grace.
I confess my sin, my frequent sin, my willful sin;
All my powers of body and soul are defiled:
A fountain of pollution is deep within my nature.
There are chambers of foul images within my being;
I have gone from one odious room to another, walked in a no-man's
      land of dangerous imaginations, pried into the secrets of my
      fallen nature.
I am utterly ashamed that I am what I am in myself;
I have no green shoot in me nor fruit, but thorns and thistles;
I am a fading leaf that the wind drives away;
I live bare and barren as a winter tree, unprofitable, fit to be hewn down
      and burnt.
Lord, dost thou have mercy on me? Thou hast struck a heavy blow at
      my pride, at the false god of self, and I lie in pieces before thee.
But thou hast given me another Master and Lord, thy Son, Jesus, and
      now my heart is turned toward holiness, my life speeds as an
      arrow from a bow towards complete obedience to thee.
Help me in all my doings to put down sin and to humble pride.
Save me from the love of the world and the pride of life, from
      everything that is natural to fallen man, and let Christ's nature
      be seen in me day by day.
Grant me grace to bear thy will without repining, and delight to be not
      only chiseled, squared or fashioned, but separated from the old
      rock where I have been embedded so long, and lifted from the
      quarry to the upper air, where I may be built in Christ forever.
      Amen

As we transition between God's Will to God's Ways, consider Moses' prayer after the children of Israel abdicated their relationship with God and worshipped the golden calf. In his intercession of Exodus 33:13, he prayed "Now therefore, if I have found favor in your sight, **please show me now your ways, that I may know you** in order to find favor in your sight." I trust that is our prayer and we are ready to obediently follow His Ways as He clearly shows us His Ways.

1 There is a difference between worldview and lifeview even as they relate. Simply, a worldview is an extension of a lifeview. Both should be studied and pursued as they significantly play into foundational thinking. For my purpose, a redeemed lifeview is on a higher plane because of its implied **grace**-empowered livability. A biblical worldview can be 'embraced' without Christ-reflection whereas the Redeemed View of Life necessitates Christ-reflective-living. No matter which concept is referred to in *The Truth Project* from *Focus on the Family*, the 10% figure is intriguingly instructive and revealing.

2 Many claim to believe God but what they often mean is that they believe in God. Belief in God is good, in and of itself. At another level, a huge difference exists between believing in God and believing God. On one level, believing God is demonstrated by our following – this is the essence of Abraham's faith. Some 'believe in God' but refuse to believe God as demonstrated in their lack of following. On another level, Scripture says demons believe God and tremble (James 2:19). While they don't come to faith, their belief is accurate as they tremble because of what they know and believe. Possessing saints tremble before God out of a godly fear and through a redeemed view of life!

3 David F. Wells, *Losing Our Virtue: Why the church must recover its moral vision* (Grand Rapids, MI.: Eerdmans Publishing, 1998) 29.

4 Wells, *Losing Our Virtue*, 59.

5 The word stillbirth is used to put this tragic reality into a light that many can understand. A human stillbirth is when a woman delivers a baby that has already died; no life comes from the womb. It's a shattering human reality that compares to the spiritual. Many talk around this sad reality of spiritual stillbirth by pointing to ingredients that further confuse the reality but I take this issue head-on to answer this conundrum biblically. I cannot rest until truth is lived out in biblical reality; for me, this reflects my life search. Great pain surrounds this reality, just like in human life. When we believe a new spiritual person is born and the spiritual baby comes from the womb without life (speaking pejoratively), I will speak of stillbirths to give my readers time to chew on this point. We might speak this way as a form of denial or deflection but life provokes us to move into **grace**ful reality; this is my challenge. So preach and disciple to prevent stillbirths.

6 Many draw a sharp distinction between Image and Likeness. I realize there is a sense that everyone – even in their unregenerate sinful state – can 'image' God but there's a fundamental point that many never consider. I focus on the necessity of regeneration to Image or Likeness God in Christ. Without spiritual re-creation, that only God can bring, man cannot Likeness God in Christ reflection!

7 The source of this teaching came from a couple books by Jeff VanVonderen. He wrote an excellent book - *The Subtle Power of Spiritual Abuse* - with Dave Johnson that I highly recommend. While everyone wants to avoid spiritual abuse, we must not abandon the church – God's bride and family-house. This 'well-intended fleeing' – so common today – can be worse than what we accuse others of perpetrating. People rationalize this excuse but the Church is the storehouse of Gospel, salvation, **Grace** and sanctification.

8 I first heard this designation from Dave Johnson and Jeff VanVonderan in their excellent book *The Subtle Power of Spiritual Abuse*.

9 D. James Kennedy, *Why The Ten Commandments Matter* (New York, NY.: Warner Faith, 2005) 21. To my knowledge, this is the last book he wrote before graduating to glory. As a fine apologist, Kennedy was a great inspiration to me with his political focus to redeem the church and redeem the culture in the process. I know there's a balance between saving individuals and culture but they are significantly interrelated.

10 Taught in 1 Timothy 6:13-16 and other places.

11 Outside of local pastors, friends and seminary classmates and professors, I have been unable to obtain a hearing to discuss this matter to my satisfaction. In many Systematic Theologies, I read of different hermeneutical approaches that don't sit well with the whole Scripture. I argue that a hermeneutic of **grace** is consistent with the whole canon and properly addresses significant points in a New Covenant manner.

12 Arthur Bennett, *The Valley of Vision: A Collection of Puritan Prayers and Devotions* (Carlisle, PA.: The Banner Of Truth Trust, 2003), 130-1.

Chapter 6 – God's Ways

When I first studied God's Ways as they apply to how we use His Word in life qualifiers, I was mildly surprised at how little I knew. It was not that I wanted to keep the idea of God's Ways outside my consideration and practice but the study really opened my eyes. Some of what I present, I had never considered before! You may find yourself in a similar position. If so, accept the challenge that can flow into pleasing action as we discover and follow God's Ways. To do this, we must know God's Ways before we can walk in them.

God intervened on behalf of fallen humanity and said, "Hear my Son!"[1] In His Sent-One-authority, Jesus said, "I am the Way, Truth and Life."[2] Jesus basically said, "This is The Way; walk in it!" This might seem simplistic but as we proclaim New Covenant **grace**ful obedience, we will be much closer to a redeemed Gospel. As we think of walking in God's Ways, think about how Jesus performed this pro-active doing.

If we could ask Jesus to summarize God's Ways for us, in light of God's commands to imitate Him, what do you think He would answer? We could speculate on acceptable answers. He might speak of release from bondage, becoming a servant, taking up a Cross, a dying-unto-Him-mentality, or a master-with-an-apprentice. All these sound good; it's also what He answered in Matthew 11:28-30,

> Come to me, all who labor and are heavy laden, and I will give you rest. **Take my yoke upon you, and learn from me**, for I am gentle and lowly in heart, and you will find rest for your souls. For my yoke is easy, and my burden is light.

In light of this illustration from the Master, we learn significant things about how He views our learning. He does not tell us to pull ourselves up by our bootstraps to perform His Will. He does not tell us to earn our salvation or necessarily follow the church. He does not tell us to be baptized. He tells us to step into the ox yoke with Him – just you and Him and no more – to learn from Him. As the Chief Shepherd, He narrows our focus of the yoke to the Word, Church and **grace**.

As the lead ox, if you will, He expects us to learn under His care. His Yoke likely had more to do with Him being a recognized Rabbi where He called and people dropped everything to follow – per His 12 disciples – but the Rabbi/disciple motif is comparable to a two-sided yoke where we are the ox that needs instruction. He tells us the straight truth. **He still calls, "Step in; Learn to follow me step-by-step!"**

Years ago, I struggled with the subject of God's Will because I somewhat felt I wrongly intruded into God's domain, and many feel this dilemma. We are taught not to enter God's knowledge that He does not sufficiently reveal to avoid speculation; this warning contains wisdom. Like unwarranted entry into the Holy of Holies, where one was struck dead, we think we tread on dangerous ground by intruding into God's domain. This leads some to think God and Holiness are unattainable and unapproachable. With a valid fear in mind, I understand the apprehension but this guard needs healthy qualification.

Let me speak to how easily we skew right understanding when we wrongly interpret a biblical text. The principle can carry over into any biblical passage that we wrongly interpret. We may not believe that we skew Scripture but we might be surprised. Skewed thoughts 'come from' the Bible easily; therefore two passages are examined to show what I mean. Noble good intentions never trump wrong interpretation.

The first deals with worshipful existence from a negative light yet we often sing or quote Isaiah 55:8-12 in a joyful manner. When verses are taken out of context, distorted doctrine flows from this defective form of exegesis. Exegesis is the effort to pull out God's meaning from the text; but we typically and wrongly put our meaning into God's text. This latter method distorts Scripture albeit not always through flagrant design or knowingly intentional. Many do this but we never have the right to distort God's Word with faulty interpretation. Isaiah 55:8-9 comes after God speaks to wayward sinners, calling them to repent. Pay attention to the text; carefully hear verses 8-9:

> For my thoughts are not your thoughts, neither are your ways my Ways, declares the Lord. For as the heavens are higher than the earth, so are my Ways higher than your ways, and my thoughts higher than your thoughts.

Isaiah 55:10-12 is familiar because of popular songs and teaching. By failing to put these verses in the greater text, distorted beliefs emphasize rejoicing isolated from repentance. The design of God's Word going out is to bring redeemed results. The godly outcome of repentance brings rejoicing, as suggested in songs but God never isolates rejoicing from repentance, as we often do.

Believers get repentance-blessings by walking in God's Ways. This is why believers can trust His Ways even when they are difficult and seem wrong to our carnality. People actually do evil things, yet God is sovereign and can work these to our good so He gives the power to perform His Will in His Ways. Because God is the Great Planner who creates results, God has plans for His outgoing Word. In Isaiah 55:10-11, God says His Word will not return to Him void without effectually fulfilling the purpose He designed or sent it to perform:

> For as the rain and snow come down from heaven and do not return there, but water the earth, making it bring forth and sprout, giving seed to the sower and bread to the eater, so shall my Word be that goes out from my mouth; it shall not return to me empty, but it shall accomplish that which I purpose, and shall succeed in the things for which I sent it.

Knowing God has a plan for His Word and people, let us return to consider whether we shortsightedly joyously sing and practice the wrong message. Verse 12 says, "For you will go out with joy, and be led forth with peace; the mountains and the hills will break forth into shouts of joy before you, and all the trees of the field will clap their hands." The text reveals this clapping isn't for what many sing and live.

The greater context of Chapter 55 demonstrates God's compassionate pleading. He calls His people back to Himself. Listen to His list of pleadings with the associated verses:

1) He compels them to give up their bankrupt living (v.1).

2) He pleads with them *not* to spend dysfunctional energy on resources or gods that do not fulfill – and calls them to faithfully depend on the only Source that fulfills (v.2).

3) He calls them to forsake their deafness and open their ear-cheese to hear and do His Word and Ways with the promise of regeneration in eternal covenant (v.3).

4) God gives a back-handed slap against their lack of following David, the "man after God's own heart" that He sent. God rebukes them for not listening to His King who held the throne until His eternal replacement arrived to take His seat (v.4).

5) He rebukes them for forgetting their roots. He made them a nation out of nothing and confirms that revolting nations will submit when they do as God desires (v.5).

6) God threatens them in their flagrant disobedience. Many object when they are rebuked with threatened wrath for disobedience, but, if the shoe fits, wear it or change it (v.6).

7) God begs them to repent and live righteously, a promise if they return in repentance and obedience (v.7).

God pleads for contrition and true repentance. Verse 12 speaks of how joy flows after repentance – but more clearly emphasizes how nature rejoices when God's people repent. If the message stays in context, it's a beautiful picture of God-glorifying nature clapping its hands at His people's repentance. Believers should clap their hands as we repent but the text says nature rejoices – suggesting His people didn't. Jesus makes this point before His triumphal entry into Jerusalem when He says nature will cry out if His people don't.[3] If *this* is what we sing it's okay, but that's doubtful.

God is serious about repentance but the message does not get through stubborn unrepentant minds. It's not that God's Ways and thoughts are above our understanding – even though they are, at an eternal level – but when people are unrepentant, God's Ways – at that point – are beyond their practical grasp. This passage screams of God's desire for people to forsake dysfunction, know His Ways and walk in His Ways! Rather than a warning "Don't enter!" God invites, "Please reverently enter my domain, as this is your life!"

This powerful teaching from God through Isaiah parallels what Paul often taught. Paul teaches what I call his **1-2-3 Method of Conversion**. This method is seen in 1) Put off your stinking thinking and evil deeds, 2) Get your thinking right and 3) Put on holy living. Several passages are very succinct, others less obvious, but we see this process throughout Scripture in both Covenants.[4]

From these passages, we readily see that God is serious about 1) Repentance or putting off, 2) Faith or getting our thinking straight and 3) Conversion or putting on holy living. The Bible's Three Step Method of God's Ways is expanded later. God is serious about Holiness because it's His Nature. Holiness is the foundation of Justification, Sanctification and Glorification. In the Parable of the Lost Sheep in Luke 15, God in Christ is the Great Shepherd. Jesus says, "Just so, I tell you, there will be more joy in heaven over one sinner who repents than over ninety-nine righteous persons who need no repentance."[5]

Since heaven rejoices over repentance, know that God is concerned that people follow His Way. Despite many who reject God's Way, the glories of mercy and **grace** are exalted when people repent. Please know that anyone can repent and follow Christ. To add flavor, Scripture paints a picture of unregenerate ones – showing that some follow God's Ways and are therefore regarded as God-fearers.

God is in the business of finding and saving lost souls. Two God-fearing individuals from the Old and New Testament are Rahab, the prostitute from Jericho who helped the spies escape in Joshua 2, and Cornelius in Acts 10. Being a God-fearer also depicts Abraham's action and faith. As a pagan, Abraham <u>believed</u> God! His believing pictures repentance by leaving sin, and conversion by following God.

Abram's faith, by believing and following God was counted as righteousness. We will return to this point later, but when God rebirths one, He changes their name.[6] God changed Abram's name to mean *Father of the faithful.* Abraham's faith foreshadows his spiritual children walking into the Promised Land of Holy Living. God counted Abraham's faith as righteousness, the doctrine many Jews stumble over in considering God's Ways. Today, <u>Imputed Righteousness</u> is a major hurdle[7] but when God makes people come alive per Ephesians 2, He accounts His Righteousness, **Grace** and Life to their soul.

When new life comes, God's sheep follow His Ways. This is not a mystery but an outflow of regeneration. Sheep are led or pursued in Righteousness taught partially in Psalm 23:6, "Surely goodness and mercy <u>shall follow me</u> all the days of my life." God is the 'Hound of Heaven' who hunts his own.[8] As the Good Shepherd, Jesus <u>follows after</u> His sheep who find joy in obedience – the beauty of green grass.

To chew on deep succulent grass, if you will, listen to a man who greatly challenged me. Spiritually I salivate over the writings of men like John Owen, John Colquhoun and John Murray. They speak of a biblical ethic in the same way that I speak of a Christian lifeview. In his first chapter in *Principles of Conduct*[9] John Murray writes,

> If ethics is concerned with manner of life and behavior, biblical ethics is concerned with the manner of life and behavior which the Bible requires and which the faith of the Bible produces. When we say, 'manner of life' or 'behavior' we must also take into account the correlative considerations.
> 1) While we may use the word 'conduct' or 'behavior' to denote the sum-total of actions which constitute the pattern of life, yet behind all overt action is the dispositional complex or character which is the psychological determinate of action. Hence ethics must take into account the dispositional complex of which the

overt act is an expression. This is to say, biblical ethics has paramount concern with the heart out of which are issues of life.

2) The conduct in view in ethics, even when conduct is considered in terms of overt action, is not simply the aggregate of actions. Ethics views actions in their organic relations to one another. There is a certain unity and coherence of pattern; each action stands related to others and cannot be understood or assessed except in that relationship [Thread of Continuity?].

3) The behavior with which biblical ethics is concerned is not simply the behavior of individuals; the principle of society bears intimately upon all ethical studies and it bears also upon biblical ethics. The biblical ethic takes account, not only of individuals as individuals and of their behavior as such, but of individuals in their corporate relationships. There's corporate responsibility and there's corporate action.

4) The behavior in which we are interested when we seek to determine the biblical ethic is not the sum-total of the behavior of a particular believer, not even of a peculiarly exemplary believer, nor the sum-total of the behavior of a believing society. We have to reckon with the imperfection of every saint in this world and with the imperfection that attaches to the most highly developed Christian society. There is still sin, oftentimes grievous sin; and therefore we find inconsistency and contradiction in the holiest of men and in the most sanctified society. The sum-total of behavior cannot show the unity and coherence which the biblical ethic would require – there is no perfect pattern of behavior exemplified in the individual believer or in the organism of believers. . . and,

Since there is so much sin and inconsistency in the behavior of believers at their best, whether they are viewed individually or in their corporate relations, we could not by any such empirical method delineate the biblical ethic. The biblical ethic is that manner of life which is consonant with, and demanded by, the biblical revelation. Our attention must be focused upon divine demand, not upon human achievement, upon the revelation of God's Will for man, not upon human behavior. In the biblical ethic we are concerned with the norms, canons or standards of behavior which are enunciated in the Bible for the creation, direction and regulation of thought, life and behavior consonant with the Will of God.

I trust you can hear Murray's passion as he seeks to establish a biblical ethic. He helped frame my understanding; **standing on the eternality of God's Will strips confusion of its destructive power**. The unwilling, unregenerate man's 'grain' goes against Scripture's overarching message. God's Ways are never found in <u>sinful attempts</u> to mimic God or His truth – but are only found in true godliness!

To show a box top view of redeemed salvation, I unpack common erroneous teachings in faulty gospels. Some claim salvation is different in the Old Testament but this position is faulty; Paul shows no essential difference in Abraham's life and salvation. In Galatians, Paul relates the gift of the Spirit back to Abraham. Believing God through Faith and obedience is the epitome of salvation in the whole Bible. One is hard-pressed to show biblical faith disconnected from God's Ways and Law; this is why common teaching leads to tragic results.

Faulty conclusions are possible anytime; knowing that, I highlight two passages. The second passage that can lead to faulty conclusions is Romans 11:33, "Oh the depths of the riches both of the wisdom and knowledge of God! How unsearchable are His judgments and unfathomable His Ways!" Misunderstanding suggests that investigation into God's Ways should not be pursued, but look again.

We can jump to wrong conclusions if we take Romans 11:33 out of context. God uses Chapters 9-11 to rebuke His chosen people toward repentance. Many think that when Scripture calls Hebrews 'God's people,' they are inherently 'in' with God, but this is not so! Paul rebukes fellow-Jews just as God in Isaiah 55, where He calls them to repent. It takes about an hour to read Romans in one sitting; as the Spirit opens our mind, consider a one-sitting-read-method.

Paul writes to encourage and strengthen believers in Rome but we can see this as Paul's evangelism tract. He lays all men open to God's Truth, Will and Ways. As an equal-opportunity evangelist, Paul leaves no man with an excuse *not* to submit to God in faith. Paul was the Apostle to the Gentiles yet always devoted his first attention to Jews – his blood brothers. This priority reflects the ministry of Jesus that we fail to understand correctly. In this way, Paul gives his harshest rebukes to Jews and men (women too) who do not come to Christ.

Paul teaches that salvation is because of Christ, by **grace** and through faith in Ephesians 2:7-10 – no matter your ethnic or societal heritage. As Paul declared, Jews have blood heritage to 'show' they are Abraham's sons but many have hearts to show they are Satan's sons.[10] Paul didn't tolerate misguided thinking or blatant disobedience; therefore, he confronted their belief that blood, circumcision or baptism was sufficient.[11] This salvation-warning is needed today as many rely on faulty salvation-understandings without proof!

Paul's warning relates to us today, especially as we seek to understand biblical salvation. Just like Jews, people today can bank on wrong foundations. They find comfort in being a member of the church, being baptized, going through confirmation, finding solace in the blood-line or circumcision of denominations, or church teachings that lead to wrong conclusions. Often we cling to 21st century 'Jewish-blood-or-circumcision' and don't ask necessary questions about biblical reality.

I'm afraid that too many stand on salvation-assumptions without tangible subjective proof; therefore I beg you not to stand on faulty assumption. We should hesitate to claim assurance of salvation for anything less than regeneration-reality and associated holy living! Scripture's warnings are clear and Paul shattered the faulty Jewish argument by presenting God's Way of faith through Christ. To assume that 'God's people' (speaking without qualifiers) corresponds to those rebirthed by God's Spirit presents a possible problem.

Paul says everyone who is <u>of</u> Israel through bloodline is not necessarily part of <u>Israel in Christ</u>. Similarly we can say everyone who 'accepts' or 'believes in' Christ is not His. Paul distinguishes between Abraham's physical and faith bloodlines as salvation is by faith in our Messiah's rather than Abraham's blood. Only those found in Christ's blood will see Heaven, and Scripture says these are described by holiness. God demonstrates that only those who come to Christ by **grace** through faith, seen in conversion, are part of His family.

Though we often practically claim Christ's blood, we rarely claim His Holiness. It would be right to say that only those in Christ's Holiness are Christ's. God's Ways refers to properly understood directives, commands and laws. Consider a few verses:

> Deuteronomy 5:33: "You shall walk in all the Way which the Lord your God has commanded you, that you may live, and that it may be well with you, and that you may prolong your days in the land which you shall possess."

> Psalms 25:4: "Make me know Thy Ways, O Lord; teach me Thy paths."

> Psalm 51:13: "Then I will teach transgressors Thy Ways, and sinners will be converted to Thee."

> Isaiah 2:3: "And many people will come and say, 'Come, let us go up to the mountain of the Lord, to the house of the God of Jacob; that He may teach us concerning His Ways, and that we may walk in His paths, for the law will go forth from Jerusalem."

We can reflect God's glory only if we practice His Ways. He is not pleased when we use methods that violate His Ways. If we claim a 'desire' to honor Him, it really does matter what we do because God says we cannot honor Him with faulty sacrifice. If asked to define God's Ways, I trust our behavior demonstrates redeemed answers.

Experience shows that life-confusion follows those who violate God's Ways, due to several things. Maybe they never thought about or were never taught God's Ways. Maybe they live in willing violation and fall into autonomy and rebellion. They may gullibly believe doctrine that leads to deception. Maybe they are just duped. Many have no spiritual knowledge of Covenants, unpacked later, or how they apply to us. Some realize their violation and want to change but do not know how.

We need to be encouraged to think God will cause an Exodus in our lives. We learn the most with Redeemed eyes[12] as the Spirit leads our instruction through the Word. I use the term Redeemed eyes to indicate the vision we gain when we are redeemed by the application of Christ's Cross Work and realize New Covenant distinctions that live strongly in our life due to experiential knowledge. This distinction acknowledges some regenerated and converted ones do not yet see with Redeemed eyes as Jesus taught His disciples to see. The greatest learning comes from correct understanding of the whole Cross, the Covenant of **Grace** and seeing the New Covenant in its fullness.

Jesus declared our Emancipation Proclamation from the Cross so we <u>can</u> walk in this freedom but the Proclamation – by itself – does not guarantee our assumption of walking in His freedom as many erroneously believe. **Ultimately, God delivers us through His two Words**. <u>#1 – Jesus Christ the Living Word</u> purchased our Atonement and <u>#2 – The Written Word</u> is sufficient for salvation and sanctification. In a spiritual sense, God firmly plants us in the Promised Land to overcome enemies through the two-sided Word's direction and power.

Our knowledge of God's Ways impacts our presented gospel. If asked to tell how salvation is viewed in the Old and New Testaments it's easy to say, "God's people need salvation through the finished work of Christ in both Testaments." But it's not easy for many of us to give a sufficient explanation. Granted, many Covenants are mentioned in Scripture and one is declared obsolete. We must ask which one, why, and what necessary qualifiers honor God's Word and Ways.

If there is One faith, Lord and salvation per Ephesians 4:4-6, **salvation must be by grace alone through faith alone throughout the history of redemption** (Ephesians 2:1-10). Redemption and salvation goes back to the Garden of Eden when Adam and Eve sinned and God clothed them in animal skins to apply the significant work of Christ's Atonement – but it was not finished until the Cross. While it's not easy to properly reflect on Old Testament haze in view of New Covenant reality, looking back upon redemption history through the <u>corrective lens of the Cross</u> helps us see Old Testament salvation understanding through the Way of the Lord picture, described next.

Jesus said John the Baptist was the greatest Old Testament prophet. When we fail to properly distinguish this designation in biblical history or in a biblical timeline, we misunderstand this New Testament passage about John the Baptist. We can gain perspective as we realize the Old Covenant was not officially terminated until Jesus' death as the Passover Lamb on the Cross.[13] In another sense, since Jesus said His blood was the promised New Covenant reality, Jesus was the first or primary New Covenant prophet.

John the Baptist functioned as the harbinger of Christ's birth and the New Covenant. A harbinger is a sign that precedes a coming event or reality. Robins are the harbinger of spring. Hunters know that first light comes in early morning as a harbinger of daylight. In contrast to first-glance-perceptions, the New Covenant dawns with the reality of the Cross. Per the Lord's Supper, Jesus said "For this is my blood of the covenant, which is poured out for many for the forgiveness of sins." He made a particular distinction between the Old and New Covenant that would start at His fast-approaching death on the Cross.

John the Baptist was the herald of Christ's ministry. In what may seem a denial of his mission through couched language, Jesus provides positive explanation for those with ears to hear. To support this, John the Baptist declares "I am the voice of one crying in the wilderness: Make straight the Way of the Lord." John spoke of repentance and holiness. John the Baptist, the last Old Covenant prophet, spoke of the coming Messiah and New Covenant – only possible if the Old Covenant was still in effect at this time.

Before first being labeled Christians in Antioch in Acts 11:26, Christ-followers were known as *People of the Way* as taught in Acts 9:2; 19:9, 23; 22:4; 24:14 & 22. Acts tells of Apollos, possibly the writer of Hebrews, an Alexandrian Jew who was "eloquent and mighty in the Scriptures, and instructed in the Way of the Lord" per Acts 18:24-28. We too must be people of the Way! If not, who are we following?

When we follow this theme throughout Scripture, *The Way of the Lord* theme accurately reflects Old and New Testament salvation doctrines. We must carefully listen to the Apostles' New Covenant exposition to correctly understand these implications. Their observation speaks of no essential difference and greater focus results from their qualifiers. Old Testament salvation-terms are greatly enhanced by New Testament understanding when we look beyond flawed presentations.

Many 21st century Western people embrace an idea that being baptized into a church or making a decision for Christ necessarily equates to new birth. Some know no other way of one 'coming to faith' outside of these formulas – what I like to call recipes. Those who embrace baptism for entrance into Christ's church may never look for necessary realities that flow from rebirth. Those who embrace an 'accepting' decision see new birth like a decision to make a cake. I often challenge these premises, not least because of *The Way of the Lord* passages. No matter how you understand Old and New Testament salvation or attempt to assimilate the Way of the Lord passages into infant-baptism-for-salvation or salvation-by-a-decision teachings, be willing to consider another paradigm. This is specifically where redeemed eyes can truly give a different picture.[14]

The overarching biblical message is clear – there is a Way of Salvation! Jesus declared this boldly in public and behind the closed private doors of the Upper Room to highlight the message that would shine in New Covenant writings. In John 14:5-6, Thomas asks, "Lord, we do not know where you are going. How can we know the way?" Jesus said to him, I am The Way, and The Truth, and The Life. No one comes to the Father except through me."

We can quote John 14:6 and forget The Way of Salvation – to truncate the Gospel. Christ followers should be ever-reforming per 2 Corinthians 3:18; if anything, we must reform our modern gospel. A refocus on The Way of the Lord passages shows a d i r e c t relationship between Old and New Testament salvation. Positive and negative factors show necessary emphasis on crucial ingredients often lacking today. To help us see better, consider *The Way of the Lord*:

1) is entrenched in covenant;
2) leads to blameless living;
3) provokes justice and righteousness;
4) provokes obedience;
5) culminates in walking in the Lord's pleasure;
6) provokes repentance of sin;
7) finds fulfillment in serving the Lord with a pure heart;
8) pursues profitable things that bring blessing;
9) acknowledges the Law as perfect;
10) delights in and meditates on the Law;
11) finds instruction in the Way;
12) acknowledges the Retribution Principle;
13) pursues covenant obedience;
14) avoids idols of any kind;
15) is courageous for the Lord in all ways;
16) pursues humility before the Lord;
17) sees His Way as our glory road;
18) realizes that obedience is our protection;
19) overcomes foolishness and ignorance;
20) acknowledges and pursues His Ways;
21) discovers that repentance leads to holiness;
22) walks in the Lord's ways continually; and
23) reflects Christ-likeness through a regenerated heart.

All these ingredients reflect the realities of new birth that are often lacking in those who assume or profess a relationship with Christ. God draws sinners out of deadness to give new life per Ephesians 2. When new life doesn't manifest in above ingredients, something is seriously wrong! We should examine and challenge those who claim to possess Christ or faith without associated evidences.

Conflicting teachings about how we obtain salvation exist. While I cannot correct anyone's belief, I explain my position with the belief that God's Spirit will provoke new understanding in some.

Subsequent holiness is the *result* of regeneration and not the *cause* of regeneration. If we were Justified, we will be Sanctified – set apart unto His desires and Will. Certain following-realities correctly qualify or give assurance of new birth whereas mere believers qualify as seed that fell on bad ground per Matthew 13. This is similar to Old Covenant 'believers' who qualify as generic Gentiles – separated from God.

I can't make seeds grow but the farmer is responsible to make the ground seed-receptive, if you will. Tilling and fertilization is often needed but some forget this dynamic in evangelism and living – to our individual and collective hurt. When we ponder *God's Way of Salvation*, rather than see actions as causal factors unto salvation, we can correctly see resultant assurance-factors of repentance, faith, belief, conversion and good works for results or out-workings. To manifest salvation, we must work out what God works into saints.

The Spirit can help us find the Way. As we walk the narrow and hard Way rather than the broad and easy way, per Matthew 7:13-14, we will be gloriously surprised at where He takes us. Are you shocked at the lack of **grace**-works in yourself or those you know? Do you evangelize? Do you bring the above factors to bear in evangelism? What gospel do you share? Does the gospel you share include necessary holiness? Do you incite people to walk in God's Ways? Does your life shine for Jesus? Do your good works cause people to ask about Jesus? Do you call people to believe in Christ and His Gospel? Some need to go back to God's drawing board.

Many believe in Jesus and His Work on the Cross and might affirm their belief in Christ to their dying day – without inward essence. In a similar way, many believe in Santa Claus and the Easter Bunny. From a socio-cultural level, we can embrace a 'truth' without believing in the reality but that's not the point I stress. The child who grows up believing in Santa Claus may believe in Jesus in the same way. Then, when they discover that faulty childhood notions of the Easter Bunny and Santa Claus must be discarded or re-qualified, they easily dismiss Jesus too. Sadly this is often true and I'm not sure we challenge this faulty notion – especially when it comes to Jesus.

Many voices tell listening ears that the Bible is little more than a fairy tale. They clamor for people to <u>not believe</u> that Jesus is God as Scripture presents. Sadly many listen as if these voices were cosmic authorities. My great concern in this is that children, even grown ones, reject Jesus as a myth or fairy tale because they are told Jesus is not what they once thought. I wonder how many put belief in Jesus, Santa or the Easter Bunny in the same rejection-basket after we 'discover' a better way? An honest search of God's Word and Way finds that Jesus is a reputable reality – exactly who He claimed to be!

Ask yourself "Does your belief in Jesus go beyond a simple unchallenged belief in Santa Claus?" If so, how so? We can 'believe' in Santa or the Easter Bunny but we should not follow *them*. My concern is that we believe in the historic atoning Jesus who is God and follow Him with our lives. Regeneration moves us quickly beyond an infantile faith in Santa Claus into a reality from which we will praise God forever.

Apart from Scripture, let's consider regeneration in literature. Consider the second-chance rebirth message contained in *The Christmas Carol*. It's a great picture of the Gospel's call on a life in bondage to depravity. As we watch the movie, we can picture Jesus standing outside of Lazarus's grave as spirits ultimately present Scrooge with two clear choices. The spirits present the reality of hell in vivid color and show Scrooge new possibilities if he changes – totally against the bitter nature he developed. They show him the reality of his chosen destiny if he doesn't change – and it's not a pretty sight. Who wants an eternal destiny in the pit? What an awful thought!

Like the Prodigal Son in the pigpen, Scrooge comes to his senses to realize a new direction. He is transformed and *now* loves life – the **grace**-empowered life God gives through regeneration. He sings in the streets, "I love Life!" He comes alive to God's Will and lives a vividly transformed life. There is no mistaking the holy change! In joyful praise, Scrooge proclaims the majesty of his redeemed life. Scrooge found God's Will in his newly adopted Redeemed View of Life!

Life can be fun as we walk in God's Ways, even as that life may be full of suffering for the Gospel's sake. The Spirit gives all the impetus to be encouraged and strengthened through the Word. **Grace** emboldens saints to share His redeeming transforming Gospel. God will eternally reward us – for what He invests and incites in us.

Like Scrooge, we enjoy the pursuit of **grace**ful living. *The Christmas Carol* depicts the transformed life we gain by following God's Ways and Word. Once God brings us to new life, we can walk like Scrooge after his transformation. The change is fun to watch – even within ourselves. I can almost hear Scrooge holler, "I love life!" I hope you sing the same words. Let's close with another Valley of Vision prayer that speaks to the Cross-result in us: *Calvary's Anthem,*

Heavenly Father,
Thou hast led me singing to the cross where I fling down all my
    burdens and see them vanish, where my mountains of guilt are
    leveled to a plain, where my sins disappear, though they are the
    greatest that exist, and are more in number than the grains of fine
    sand;
For there is power in the blood of Calvary to destroy sins more than
    can be counted even by one from the choir of heaven.
Thou hast given me a hill-side spring that washes clear and white, and
    I go as a sinner to its waters, bathing without hindrance in its
    crystal streams.
At the cross there is free forgiveness for poor and meek ones, and
    ample blessings that last forever;
The blood of the Lamb is like a great river of infinite grace with
    never any diminishing of its fullness as thirsty ones without
    number drink of it.
O Lord, forever will thy free forgiveness live that was gained on the
    Mount of blood;

In the midst of a world of pain it is a subject for praise in every place, a
song on earth, an anthem in heaven, its love and virtue knowing
no end.

I have a longing for the world above where multitudes sing the great
song, for my soul was never created to love the dust of earth.

Though here my spiritual state is frail and poor, I shall go on
singing Calvary's anthem.

**May I always know that a clean heart full of goodness is more
beautiful than the lily; that only a clean heart can sing by
night and by day, and that such a heart is mine when I abide
at Calvary.**

---

1 Matthew 17:5. At the *Transfiguration* God calls from heaven, "This is my beloved
Son, with whom I am pleased; listen to Him." See Hebrews 1:2.

2 John 14:6. Sent-One-Authority reflects what Jesus possessed. My attempt rightly
shifts the focus to being Sent rather than His being 'Son' – that too often provokes confusion.
He is Son because He is Sent rather than being a 'divine offspring' as many wrongly imagine.

3 Luke 19:40

4 See Ephesians 4:17-24; Colossians 3:1-17; and 1 Thessalonians 1:9-10. This
Three Step Process is variously found in Romans 12:1-2; 1 Corinthians 6:9-11; 10:31-
11:1; 15:9-11; 2 Cor. 4:5-12; 6:14-7:1; 10:1-6; 13:4-9; Gal. 2:19-21; 5:16-25; Eph. 2:11-
22; 3:14-21; 4:17-5:20; Philippians 2:1-13; 3:8-4:1; 1 Thes. 4:1-8; 2 Thes. 2:13-17;
1 Timothy 1:15-17; 6:11-15; 2 Timothy 1:8-14; 3:10-17; Titus 1:10-2:15; and 3:1-8.

5 Luke 15:7

6 We see this in Abraham, Sarah, Jacob, Peter and Paul. While these are key
figures in redemption's story, the point of a changed name is significant in regeneration.

7 *Imputed righteousness* is particularly rejected by the Islam faith. Most unbelievers
reject the Atoning Work of Christ on their behalf for many reasons. At the root of their
unbelief, they think their righteousness is sufficient.

8 I think this phrase was coined by Charles Spurgeon to denote the following-after
or pursuing His sheep. Rejoice in the fact that Christ is this serious!

9 John Murray, *Principles of Conduct: Aspects of Biblical Ethics* (Grand Rapids,
MI,: Eerdmans Publishing, 1957) 12-14.

10 Matthew 7:21-27

11 The whole book of Galatians refutes the inferior Jewish claim of life in Christ
through Abraham because they did not manifest his faith. We should take heed here too.

12 I often use this term to reflect the paradigm gained after we see the mechanics
and reality of New Covenant truth. A book that provoked some of my thinking is by David
Powlison, *Seeing With New Eyes: Counseling and the Human Condition Through the
Lens of Scripture (Phillipsburg, NJ.:* P&R Publishing, 2003).

13 In Matthew 11:7-19, Jesus says John the Baptist is the last Old Covenant
prophet. When Jesus compares the Old Covenant to the kingdom of heaven, this hazy
teaching confuses us until we see that the New Covenant begins at His death on the
Cross. This helps us properly evaluate many New Covenant truths.

14 For further study or clarification of the Way of the Lord, consider a partial list of
Way of the Lord passages: Genesis 17:1; 18:19; Judges 2:22; I Samuel 12:19-24; 2
Samuel 22:22-25; 2 Kings 21:19-22; 2 Chronicles 17:6; Psalms 18:20-24, 25:8-10, 138:5,
Psalms 1; 19:1-11; 119; Proverbs 1-3; 10:29; Jeremiah 5:4-5; Ezekiel 18:19-32; 33:17-
20; and Hosea 14:9. Similar references of the Way are Matthew 21:32; 22:16; 2 Peter
2:2; 2:21; Acts 13:10; 16:17; Luke 1:79; and Romans 3:17.

Chapter 7 – God's Word

When Jesus was led into the wilderness to be tempted by Satan, what He said is crucial for us to know. After the first temptation to turn stones into bread, Jesus said, "Man shall not live by bread alone, but by every word that comes from the mouth of God." After the next two temptations, Jesus began His answers with, "Again it is written" and "Be gone, Satan! For it is written."[1] If God's Word is critical for Jesus, we must not forget its foundation in our life.

What Jesus said in the face of Satan's temptation is the foundation of our salvation and essence of a Christian lifeview. In regards to the fundamental response of Jesus, Russell Moore says,

> God provided his people with bread from the sky and with water from the rock <u>for the purpose of whetting an appetite for the gospel</u>. . . God's provision for our appetites is tied up completely in that Skull Place execution, which itself is tied up in those wilderness temptations. <u>Our salvation hinged on Jesus' mouth</u>.[2]

Whereas Adam and Eve failed, Jesus overcame; therefore The <u>Living and Written Words</u> must be our foundation and lifeblood! It can be said that God's Word does not require any discussion since orthodox believers believe His Word is without error, concise, eternal, open to life-long study, sufficient for salvation, effective for life and practice, and comes with an Illuminator – the Holy Spirit. Many <u>professing</u> believers say they hold to *this* Word of God – but their word is much less than His Word. This gap needs to be filled; this is why we need His Word living powerfully within us. If we <u>believe Him</u> and His Word – our repentance, faith and conversion proves it!

If Scripture is Written by less than a Holy God, our soul, life and practice never finds rest. Sadly we can treat God's Word like a waxed nose to shape it to please our taste. If we don't like something, we tend to cut it out of consideration. We can acknowledge God's Word with our mind but then violate His Word like a practical atheist.

Believers should never treat God's Word as a flexible standard. God's Living and Written Words are firm throughout eternity![3] I'm not bashful about belief in God's Word as revelation that God gave so His people can understand Him, His Gospel, salvation and our mission. For those who find it hard to believe God and His Word as God's salvation revelation without error, let me present something to chew on.

I had an experience as a young child where I felt I was going to drown. Maybe it was my imagination but it scared the life out of me as it scarred me to the thought of swimming. Our family was at a favorite beach. My sister and I were playing in medium-depth water. I never got in over my head but I had a floating ring for safety. As I walked to shore, I stepped into a hole and was over my head instantly. I lost my ring and couldn't touch bottom. As I cried out "Help!" people stood around watching. I thought, "Won't you help?" No one did! My father came in from deep water to pluck his flailing son out of the water. I later learned to swim, but a huge comparison exists between learning to swim and learning God's Word.

Classical Apologetics[4] remains in my top ten books all-time and laid great foundations in my life. This book offers points to counteract the thinking-destruction perpetrated by Immanuel Kant and others. The authors demonstrate classical biblical thinking as redeemed change flows from biblical thinking. Ever since I read their teachings, my mind was irrevocably changed. The title says Apologetics, and this book **effectively teaches a Christian worldview with redeemed eyes**. You might need a floaty to get through but it's highly recommended.

From a teacher's or pastor's perspective, we walk a tight rope between giving saints the milk of the Word versus drowning them in deep water. I say this with a little tongue-in-cheek reminder that several methods exist to teach people to swim. Emotionally I like the newer method of teaching children to swim. I've heard of the old way; it sounds like an old wives' tale and cruel but maybe effective – throw a person in deep water until they learn to swim. This is something like parent eagles who throw their youngsters out of the nest when they are ready and observingly monitor and assist them in flying until they actually *learn* how to fly. Sometimes I think we need to do this in a tongue-in-cheek way to get 'saints' beyond a perpetual infantile stage. There's something wrong with perpetual infancy – yet growth in the faith occurs as we swim in the deep water of God's Word.

Some liken theology to swimming in deep water. For some, this book might make you feel as though you walked into that hole that leaves you without a floating ring and unable to swim. You might feel like you're in over your head. That is a scary proposition but God wants us to learn to swim in His Word, if you will – or play in the hay. He does not want us to flounder or keep holding onto the security ring.

Through His power of **grace**, we can learn to swim in deep water. Indeed His Spirit acts like the parent eagle that flies below us to teach us to fly. We can't 'fly' without the Spirit or **grace** but a healthy comparison exists. My desire is to do what the parent eagles does – push some out of the nest to learn to fly and then soar on the eagles wings of His majestic Word. Look beyond awkward feelings to fly in greater heights or swim in greater depths. In the soaring or swimming, we learn to praise Him for His mighty works. Once it's second nature, we then lead others into spiritual swimming.

If you learn to swim in God's Word, *successful* sessions provoke progressively better swimming. In linear fashion the authors of *Classical Apologetics* demonstrate the plausibility of natural theology that many reject. Consider their valuable presentation of Romans 1:

#1) There is a general or natural revelation;

#2) There is content to natural revelation;

#3) Natural revelation is clear, not obscure;

#4) Natural revelation has been continuous since creation;

#5) Natural theology proceeds from the visible to the invisible;

#6) Natural revelation leaves humans morally responsible for their
response to it;

#7) Natural revelation "gets through;" it is subjectively appropriated;

#8) People respond negatively to natural revelation, refusing to
acknowledge the knowledge they should have; and

#9) General revelation yields a knowledge of God from nature – a
natural theology.

Natural revelation and natural theology point us to the viability of Scripture and Special Revelation - against erroneous positions. Scripture does not make a defense for itself because it is presented as all truth. If we can offer plausible linear reasons to accept this necessary foundation, we can work through common doubts to believe God's Word. A logical linear flow of seeing God's Word without circular reasoning is refreshing. Circular reasoning occurs when we use part of our conclusion as reasons for our logical argument; therefore we establish the conclusion in our premise. If we struggle with the practice of using circular reasoning, notice the authors do not reason from the possible to the actual but rather from the actual to the plausible:

The Six-Step Classical Argument for a Divinely Inspired Bible[5]

#1) It is virtually granted that the Bible (not assumed to be inspired at
this point) contains generally reliable history.

#2) The Bible records miracles as part of its generally reliable history.

#3) These miracles authenticate the Bible's messengers and their
message.

#4) The Bible message therefore ought to be received as divine.

#5) The Bible message includes the doctrine of its own inspiration.

#6) The Bible therefore is more than a generally reliable record; it is a
Divinely inspired record.

Liberal writings and arguments provoke many to refuse to accept the Bible as God's Word. They think Jesus did not know about His Father's business or His mission on earth from the beginning. In *I Don't Have Enough Faith to be an Atheist*[6], Norm Geisler and Frank Turek present Jesus' points concerning God's Word. God's Word is:

1) **Authoritative** – 92 times Jesus or the Apostles confirm this by saying, "It is written." This is contrasted against rabbinic teaching and "You have heard it said" (Matthew 4:4, 7, &10).

2) **Imperishable** – Jesus could not have expressed this concept more forcefully. He said, "Do not think that I have come to abolish the Law or the Prophets; I have not come to abolish them but to fulfill them" (Matthew 5:17).

3) **Infallible** – Jesus demonstrates both the infallibility of the Written and Living Word of God (Himself), "Jesus answered them, 'Is it not written in your Law, "I said you are gods?" If he called them gods to whom the Word of God came – and Scripture cannot be broken – do you say of Him whom the Father consecrated and sent into the world, "You are blaspheming," because I said, "I am the Son of God? (John 10:34-36; 17:17).

4) **Inerrant** – God cannot err; therefore, His Word cannot err! (Matthew 22:29)

5) **Historically reliable** – Matthew 12:40 is a *larger* passage than we often acknowledge pertaining to eschatology; it reads, "For just as Jonah was three days and three nights in the belly of the great fish, so will the Son of Man be three days and three nights in the heart of the earth." (Matthew 7:6-7; 12:40; 13:14-15; 24:15; 37-38; Luke 4:17-19)

6) **Scientifically accurate** – Speaking of the origin and nature of wind, Jesus said to Nicodemus in John 3, "Truly, truly I say to you, *we* speak of what *we* know, and bear witness to what *we* have seen, but you do not receive *our* testimony. If I have told you earthly things and you do not believe, how can you believe if I tell you heavenly things?" (Matthew 19:4-6; John 3:11-12)

7) **Ultimately supreme** – In a day when parents are not honored, obedience from redeemed thinking is crucial; Matthew 15: 3-9:

He answered them, "And why do you break the commandment of God for the sake of your tradition? For God commanded, 'Honor your father and mother,' and 'Whoever reviles father or mother must surely die.' But you say, 'If anyone tells his father or his mother, "What you would have gained from me is given to God," he need not honor his father.' So **for the sake of your tradition you have made void the Word of God**. You hypocrites! Well did Isaiah prophesy of you, when he said: "**This people honor me with their lips, but their heart is far from me**; in vain do they worship me, teaching as doctrines the commandments of men."

Sadly God's Written and Living Word is under attack from many fronts today. This attack has been ongoing since the beginning of time. Aquinas said God and His Word "Cannot not be!" Yet Lucifer attacked God's Word and attempts to get humans to deny it in its entirety or, at least, to the point of subtle rebellion. It only takes a simple twist!

When God's Law (Word) is forgotten, people and society are in trouble. A Bible search can show the recorded times when God's Law was recovered (see p.307). Why do we think we can forget God's Law and not be in serious trouble? In early 1963, during my fourth grade, the Bible was taken out of our schools. Many don't know the Bible was the first textbook authorized by Congress, yet we continue to chip away at His Law – and wonder why society does not work well. Go figure!

Many don't know apologetic arguments that confirm a cogent reasonable faith; therefore we 'buy' relativism, secularism, liberalism, and other faulty systems yet claim to believe God's Word. How can this be? When we reject the authority, inerrancy and sufficiency of God's breathed-out Word, we have a dilemma in the world and church.

God's Word and Law must be recovered! In Genesis 3, the serpent speaks to Eve with Adam at her side – not doing as he was commanded. The serpent questions God's unambiguous Word in Law form and questions God's clear command. We can abolish, deny or talk around them and slander God by saying He didn't mean what He commanded to thereby give lip-service – while claiming obedience.

Satan contradicts God's Word by suggesting that disobedience to God's Word will produce a desirable outcome (v.5). Right! When Satan speaks, he deceives. Rather than rebellion producing death as God promised – which it did – the serpent says the outcome will be an autonomous god-likening result (v.6), akin to New Age teaching. I trust you see why god-likening lies must be rejected – and quickly.

Tragically Adam and Eve pursue this god-likening result, causing **The Fall** after the example of Lucifer's fall. In a great irony, in their effort to likeness the Creator, the creatures end up hiding in the creation (v.7). Imagine that! Something's very wrong here!

Talk about a downward Fall! This is the biblical version of Humpty Dumpty where all the king's horses and men could not put Humpty together again. It takes God Himself to perform this re-creation and we cannot forget this! What occurs as a result of their disobedient fling is the epitome of absurdity. People often argue that hiding in the bushes is akin to sitting on God's throne. Imagine that again! Sitting on 'God's throne' brings rebellious ones nothing but confusion and death.

The Fall exposes the Big Lie and the fatal switch introduced earlier.[7] Rejecting, denying, or twisting God's Word always leads to deadly and dysfunctional results. The only way to reverse the Big Lie is to believe The Truth and walk in the Way. Re-creation is required by God but Scripture suggests that man can put himself in a salvation position by being a God fearer. The only way to reverse the fatal switch is to believe God's Word, embrace the Atonement's dual imputation, be converted to think with Christ's mind and act in a Christ-reflecting way. Our diligence in the matter of conversion is required 24/7.

It's crucial to understand the double-switch of Imputation to recover a biblical lifeview. Basically Satan gives them a lie in exchange for their life. Adam and Eve trade life for a lie and death! This is the evil double switch offered by Satan – not a good curtain-choice! Sin produces spiritual, physical, emotional, relational, and mental death.

When you replace God's Word with sinful autonomous actions, the result is always death of some kind. This outcome should be beyond dispute, but many reject the truthfulness and consequence of this reality to their own hurt and possible eternal destruction.

Once Adam and Eve *swallow* and act upon the serpent's deception in a psychological, figurative, literal and willful way they are plunged into sin and death – along with the whole human race. This is the reality of original sin. Without debating this issue here, I do not know a person who does not sin or who has not died at the end of so many years. I know a man who is 105 but that is rare. Beginning with The Fall, humanity consistently questions God's Word and believes violation is somehow desirable, god-reflecting and god-likening. What a distortion! And Adam and Eve soon find out. They were duped!

The whirlwind tour of the first human sin in the Garden of Eden provides crucial insight into the sinful inclination to reject the <u>clearness</u> of God's Word. Scripture says the first two humans were created without sin. Some think this was sinless perfection. I agree as far as the generality goes; however, Scripture provokes a different position. Many wonder how sin entered the human race and how humanity in a perfect state can reject and violate God's Word. We ask, "If man was created without sin, how can this be?" Adam and Eve rejected **grace** and Holiness, and therefore sinned. I know this perspective is different than most acknowledge but there is much to learn about our car wrecks.

The following is a brief defense of my positions on humanity, **grace** and an overview of terms that describe Christ's divinity in laymen's terms. Be encouraged to delve theology's depths to jump-start a redeemed understanding of Garden teaching. Adam and Eve were created without sin but not to the degree that Jesus was without sin. I affirm Jesus was born with a holy divine nature (one of two natures He possessed) and His divine nature – part of *His* humanity – was incapable of sinning. This was part of His perfect Holiness.

Two huge differences exist between the First and Second Adams. The first is *created-Adam*; the second is *birthed-Christ.* It's not that Jesus didn't have a humanity that was able to sin except for **grace** – because He did – but He had an element Adam and Eve didn't possess. As 'humanized' God, He is the epitome of humanity and the fullness of **grace**. He is Divine; they were not! He is Truth and **Grace**; they were dependent on Truth and **grace** for salvation and holy living. Specific qualifiers are presented here rather than broad implications. The first Adam was created human-becoming with derived life. The second Adam, Jesus was birthed human-existence with Eternal Life. Jesus tabernacled in human flesh; He was literally God with us!

Without detracting from His divinity that was mostly veiled while He lived on earth or unnecessarily positing a different humanity, **New Covenant understanding informs us that the human Jesus as the second Adam was the man-model God intended from the beginning**. We tend to focus on the first Adam as the model but this unqualified error distorts our Incarnation and salvation understandings.

To the degree that Adam was in a state of innocence and probation, we see him as the model without realizing that **Jesus Christ is the ultimate picture of humanity as God desired and ordained**. If we misunderstand this point, we come up with distorted thinking about Creation, The Fall, mankind and salvation. Rather than attempt to be like the first Adam, **Scripture tells us to imitate Jesus** – the second Adam. This is why **we must be re-modeled after Christ through regeneration to likeness and image Our Flesh-God** in a pleasing way. This also explains why the implicit assumption that 'we are all in Adam' skews our understanding of regeneration and redeemed living.

Second, as an eternal **BEING** Jesus **IS** eternal life and therefore can't be created. He was **BORN** human **LIFE** but He **IS** and 'was' eternal life; therefore, He fully possessed eternal life even though He died. This is why He could honestly offer Eternal Life to all who believe in Him. He actually **IS** Eternal Life with authority to give eternal life – no mere human has this ability! This explains why He entrusted his spirit into the Father's hand as He submitted to death on the Cross. Because of veiled Divinity, His form of life manifests huge differences but *never doubt His Divinity*. We know these differences were mostly veiled and typically rejected or slandered by religious leaders of His day and today; therefore, a further expansion is offered.

As God's Living Word, Jesus demonstrates who He Is when He spoke healing into existence. When He heals a 38-year invalid man at the Pool of Bethesda in John 5:1-17 as LORD of the Sabbath, He demonstrates this difference. He authoritatively interchanges the words "Take up your bed and walk" with blasphemous-sounding words "Your sins are forgiven." **His words are only blasphemous if He is not who He claims to be!** Jesus poignantly and purposely speaks this difference so no confusion exists as to who He Is. Even though skeptics argue otherwise, the Jews pick up stones to stone Him for His claim to be God. He proved His claim – we too must know this!

Believing is faith's job as declared in the Faith Chapter. Hebrews 11:6 says, "And without faith it is impossible to please him, for **whoever would draw near to God must believe that he exists** and that he rewards those who seek him." From a different angle, this partially explains why Christian proofs don't produce faith.[8] Without knowing **that God exists in Jesus** and rewards those who diligently seek Him, to support a God-fearer approach, it's impossible to convince someone that Jesus exists to save them through His Gospel.

A private conversation with His disciples demonstrates this pregnant truth. Revealed truth, by itself, has no power to produce right belief. In Luke 10:21-24 Jesus teaches 1) The Holy Spirit ushers in 2) general belief in God, required for 3) proper belief in Jesus as God in flesh! Then 4) Jesus – **through this necessary belief and understanding** – leads to proper belief of the Trinity-God.

A simple study examines Jesus' "I AM" statements. John's Gospel presents them with Signs so we can learn about God's Living Word. Jesus didn't waffle. He IS God in the flesh but **in His veiled reality – <u>short of the Cross</u> - we struggle with the haze**. Against contrary voices that say we can't know, Jesus boldly claims divinity:

1) **"I AM the Lamb of God"** – John 1:29 & 36. This indirect I AM saying comes from John the Baptist when he refers to Jesus. Scripture teaches this truth through the Passover and sacrificial system, "The next day he saw Jesus coming toward him, and said, "Behold! The Lamb of God who takes away the sin of the world!" The next day John stood with two of his disciples, "And looking at Jesus as He walked, he said, 'Behold the Lamb of God!" This prophetic declaration was part of why John the Baptist was the greatest Old Covenant prophet in New Testament times.

2) **"I AM Jacob's Ladder"** – John 1:51. This is another implicit I AM saying. From Genesis 28:12, Jacob wrestled with God, "He dreamed, and behold, there was a ladder set up on the earth, and the top of it reached to heaven. And behold, the angels of God were ascending and descending on it!" As Jesus called His disciple Nathanael, "He said to him, 'Truly, truly, I say to you, you will see heaven opened, and the angels of God ascending and descending on the Son of Man;" therefore (implicitly), "I am Jacob's Ladder!"

3) **"I AM the Gift of God"** – John 4:10. This was said to the Samaritan woman at the well, "Jesus answered her, 'If you knew the gift of God, and who it is that is saying to you, 'Give me a drink,' you would have asked Him, and He would have given you living water;" therefore (implicitly), "I AM God's Gift to humanity!"

4) **"I AM the Living Water"**– John 4:13-14. In this third implicit saying, "Jesus said to her, 'Everyone who drinks of this water will be thirsty again, but whoever drinks of the water that I will give him will never be thirsty forever. The water that I will give him will become in him a spring of living water welling up to eternal life."

5) **"I AM the Bread of Life"** – John 6:35. Jesus went to the other side of the Sea of Galilee after feeding the 5,000. The people made their way around the Sea of Galilee looking for another sign, "Jesus said to them, 'I AM the Bread of Life; whoever comes to Me shall not hunger, and whoever believes in Me shall never thirst." In this statement He literally 'types' the Lord's Supper 'elements.'

6) **"I AM the Light of the World"** – John 8:12; 9:5. This passage occurs after the Feast of Booths or Tabernacles where candles hearken back to the wilderness water-providing-rock and pillar of fire that provided light and guidance – both point to Jesus. A woman caught in sin's darkness experiences *illumination and sees the Light*, "Again Jesus spoke to them, saying, "I AM the Light of the World. Whoever follows Me will not walk in darkness, but will have the Light of Life." This is also a 'private' Sign.

7) **"Before Abraham was, I AM**!" – John 8:58. In speaking of the contrast between the sons of God and Satan, Jesus is in a heated debate about who He is. The slander is brought to an end when "Jesus said to them, 'Truly, truly, I say to you, before Abraham was, I AM!" Lest there be any misunderstanding of what Jesus claimed, "So they picked up stones to throw at Him (they thought it was blasphemy); but Jesus hid Himself and went out of the temple."

8) **"I AM the Door of the Sheepfold"** – John 10:7, 9. Speaking of the True Shepherd, Jesus says in 10:2 "But he who enters by the door is the shepherd of the sheep." The people did not understand His illustration "So Jesus again said to them, 'Truly, truly, I say to you, I AM the Door of the Sheep (7)." "I AM the Door. If anyone enters by Me, he will be saved and will go in and out and find pasture (9)."

9) **"I AM the Good Shepherd"** – John 10:11. As the Good Shepherd, He lays down His life for the sheep.

10) **"I AM the Giver of Eternal Life"** – John 10:27-28& 10:10. "My sheep hear my voice, and I know them, and they follow Me. I give them eternal life, and they will never perish; and no one will snatch them out of My hand."

11) **"I AM God!"** – John 10:30. This statement cannot be any clearer about Jesus' claim as part of the Trinity despite the absurd rejections of many, "I and the Father are One!" After this the Jews took up stones to kill him for blasphemy; they knew exactly what He claimed! We should too!

12) **"I AM the Son of God"** – John 10:36-38. After speaking of Scripture's infallibility Jesus asks "Do you say of Him whom the Father consecrated, 'You are blaspheming,' because I said, 'I AM the Son of God'? If I am not doing the works of My Father, then do not believe Me; but if I do them, believe the works that you may know and understand that the Father is in Me, and I am in the Father." Clear enough?

13) **"I AM the Resurrection and the Life"** – John 11:25. After Lazarus' death, when Jesus purposely comes late, "Jesus said to her (Martha), I AM the Resurrection and the Life. Whoever believes in Me, though he die, yet shall he live."

14) **"I AM the Serpent on the Pole"** – John 12:30-33. This speaks to the crucifixion by hearkening back to the serpent lifted on a pole for salvation of believers in the wilderness; all who looked upon it were healed! It speaks of Satan's destruction from the reality of the Cross (John 16:8-11); "Jesus answered, 'This voice has come for your sake, not mine. Now is the judgment of this world; now will the ruler of this world be cast out. And I, when I am lifted up from the earth, will draw all people to Myself.' He said this to show by what kind of death He was going to die."

15) **"I AM The Way, The Truth, and The Life"** – John 14:6. From the Upper Room, Jesus spoke to Thomas about the Way, "Jesus said to him, 'I AM The Way, The Truth, and The Life. No one comes to the Father except through Me."

16) **"I AM the True Vine"** – John 15:1, 5. In a clear statement that dispels any doubt about the Life Jesus possessed and was able to give in regeneration, Jesus said, "I AM the True Vine, and My Father is he vinedresser."

Many deny His divinity in the face of bold statements but Jesus declares who He IS. With these 16 sayings, **Jesus makes plain He IS the Living Word**. In Appendix 2, **John posits Jesus in his Gospel as God so people will believe and find life in Him**. This is the thrust of His powerful Gospel – the clear message of who the unveiled Christ is!

Because of who Jesus IS, He makes promises to His sheep that no one else can fulfill. As The Gift of God, Jesus can create faith. As the epitome of **Grace**, Jesus can grant **grace** and regeneration. As the Resurrection and Life, Jesus can bring spiritually dead ones back to life – as only God has the power to rebirth sinners into saints!

If we imagine Jesus had God's power without being God, our teaching is futile and we have no biblical Gospel. We see this power in the Father, Son and Holy Spirit. If you study and believe the "I AM" statements alone, with Appendix 2 as help, the Living and Written Word reaches into our soul to change us into a Christ reflector by His Life and power that God gives. His holiness can be formed in you!

Adam was a lump of clay before God formed his body and made him a living soul. God put a living soul into Adam's body. With poor English, Jesus IS LIFE before God put Christ's Spirit into a body – birthing Him into humanity. The Incarnation is a great mystery of Life and highlights my point. When some Jews question His existence and where He was going as He spoke of the Cross, He said to them "You are of this world; I am not of this world" – here's the thrust of that second difference. Jesus IS ETERNAL LIFE despite the fact that He was tented or tabernacled in a human body per John 1:14. As such, the mystery of the Incarnation is a great stumbling block for many.

In another irony against those who imagine He was not human, in an eternal display of God's power to show His humanity, Jesus will eternally inhabit His human body to the glory of **grace**. Chew on this for a while. What this means is that Jesus' resurrected body went with Him to sit on God's Throne. By itself, this is huge but there's more.

According to Hebrews, we might say Jesus took the curtain with Him to heaven. We know the curtain in front of the Holy of Holies was torn from top to bottom when Jesus died. But Hebrews 10:19-20 says, "Therefore brothers, since we have confidence to enter the holy places by the blood of Jesus, **by the new and living way that He opened for us through the curtain, that is, <u>through His flesh</u>**." Three points here; first, His body is the pinnacle of the new and living way of New Covenant. Second, His flesh or body is the reality of the curtain. Third, this is why His body – rather than His blood – is the ultimate essence of our salvation. Think about those points a bit.

As His divinity is encased in humanity, Jesus displays God's power through 1) regenerated life: re-created existence by His Spirit and 2) **grace:** God's empowerment in humanity to cause us to reflect Him. Here's the practical breakdown I drive toward: Adam and Eve were created in a pure state of innocence – rather than perfection as is often taught and believed[9] – fully dependent upon God's power to do what He designed. **The Second Adam Jesus was Holy, lived without sin, and His Holiness was actually perfect and savingly necessary**.

On one hand, Adam and Eve could only fail without **grace** – something they didn't possess.[10] On the other hand, as the epitome of **grace** Jesus fully possessed God's power of **grace**. This is a helpful tautology to demonstrate this truth. As these differences are eternal and significant, God is willing to invest organic **grace** in believing humanity to renew relationship with Him and His Word! Amen!

When I extensively evaluated Adam and Eve in the Garden environment years ago, many truths opened up in my understanding. This book is driven by material that originally prompted my study of God's Will. Any position that rejects any facet of Christ, His Atonement or God's Word depicts man's autonomous attempt to reach the same desire Satan proposed to Adam and Eve. This autonomous attempt will never 'work' for us either! As Adam and Eve bought into a damning proposition, Christ's saving work reverses the results by application.

Claim often doesn't represent reality. Many claim homage to God through His Word yet seldom open the Word and rarely reflect Christ. I fear that some are vaccinated against the real thing so it does not organically infect them.[11] It really does matter how we live when we claim to be a Christ follower! Scripture gives a fundamental ought-factor that significantly correlates to holy living according to the Word. Many claim to look but don't have eyes to see. Some claim to hear without spiritual ears. We can be deceived by professors who don't possess Christ, yet God and Christ see through false claims.

It's my hope that this idea of the switch is clear in our minds. God can reverse Satan's evil switch with the double-Imputation of

Christ's Cross when it's applied to our account. He doesn't do this for every person and doesn't reveal why He particularly chooses some and not others. **While it's not causative, a necessary vital link exists between personal believing, acceptance and following**. For Christ's Sheep, God imputes sin and death to Christ in exchange for His Holiness and Life. When God reverses spiritual death in our soul, our mind and actions will be conformed to God's Will and Way.

God applies the necessary switch but we are involved in its out-working manifestation. Without this necessary switch, people continue to use ungodly thinking and methods to 'follow' God's Word. Seek first to become a God fearer and see what God does. Then as a regenerated one, be a Christ reflector through **grace** as **God's Word must be followed – Jesus too – to accomplish His Will**. If we do not know this, our efforts will be frustrated without knowing why. If we pursue His Way through a Redeemed View of Life, we can know He performs the double switch in us to live like the converted Scrooge!

In another Classic, *Moby Dick* by Herman Melville, Ahab the ship captain pursues the white whale. The white whale is analogous to God. We might think this is a good thing; after all, pursuing God or some concept of God is seen as the goal of many religions. In a TableTalk article *The Unholy Pursuit Of God, In Moby Dick*, R.C. Sproul puts this common belief in serious doubt.[12] He says, "Ahab's pursuit of the whale is not a righteous pursuit of God but natural man's futile attempt in his hatred of God to destroy the omnipotent deity." This is Satan's desire and he infects humanity with this many-headed desire.

Many claim to follow God and His Word but do so wrongly. Scripture clearly demonstrates Jesus and God's Word are infallible, authoritative, inerrant, eternal, and binding. The Bible is God's perfect error-free revelation of salvation through the Trinity and **Grace**. Embrace the Word for what it is and declares – salvation to believing sinners as they follow Jesus through His Truth, Plan, and Way. As

God's Word is pivotal to our eternal welfare and sufficient for salvation, pursue It and Jesus with all your soul and might. Has His voice called you out of death? If so, like Scrooge, you have a mission. With the mouth of Jesus, salvation comes but must flow from our mouth too.

---

1 Matthew 4:1-11

2 Russell D. Moore, *Tempted and Tried: Temptation and the Triumph of Christ* (Wheaton, IL.: Crossway, 2011), pp.73-75. Moore's book presents excellent qualifiers, explanations and encouragements for the contrasts between the temptations of Adam and Eve in relationship to what Christ endured, with practical implications for our lives.

3 His Word and His Law never changes – never! – per Matthew 5:17-20.

4 R.C. Sproul, John Gerstner, Arthur Lindsley *Classical Apologetics: A Rational Defense of the Christian Faith and a Critique of Presuppositional Apologetics* (Grand Rapids, MI.: Zondervan Publishing, 1984), 62. This book was huge in my life.

5 *Classical Apologetics*, 141.

6 Norman L. Geisler, Frank Turek, *I Don't Have Enough Faith to Be an Atheist* (Wheaton, Ill.: Crossway, 2004), 357-9.

7 *The Big Lie* is the lie Satan told Adam and Eve from the beginning. We like to blame Eve but Adam was present and silent. The lie basically said that whatever God tells us to do is not important; in fact, we are free to make of it whatever we want to suit our needs at the time. *The Big Switch* goes two ways from two sources - from Satan's end, he switched life for death. The Switch from God's end is what we call Double Imputation where God can take our sin and death and replace it with Christ's holiness and life. The switch everyone needs is the one God offers but rebellion runs deep.

8 Christian proofs or apologetics are often posited as creating faith but this is a misnomer. For many, this is an attempt to make someone believe who has chosen not to believe; humanly this effort can't work unless God changes a mind through regeneration. If this attempt seeks to accomplish pre-evangelism to make a disciple, I acknowledge benefit; otherwise, I think this is the fool's errand or throwing pearls before swine.

9 At this very point grace is most-often interjected into the picture and teaching of The Fall. If Adam and Eve were created perfect, they could never have sinned; however, if they were created innocent and lost the holiness of grace as I contend, they could and did indeed sin. For many, what I present goes against what they always believed but I think redeemed eyes shows a more-consistent **grace**ful picture.

10 Many theologians speak of grace as an entity that comes along after the Fall, even if this is presented in an inconsistent manner. This is intimated in the *Dispensation of Grace* that 'starts' with The Fall. With the idea of perfection that is typically posited for Adam and Eve, the origin and idea of **redeemed grace** is confused in many minds. This confusion lives supreme in the teaching of common grace that is anything but **grace**ful, although the need is common. As the being and life of humanity are described as being derived existence and life, this same thinking applies to **grace** as well. As man has not one ounce of eternal redeemed life in his being without the **grace** of God in regeneration, so man has not an ounce of **grace** in his being without its application by God. I think many would agree if they could see **grace** with redeemed eyes. No matter your position, at the least Adam and Eve did not possess **grace** as Christ does.

11 Matt Chandler, *The Explicit Gospel* (Wheaton, IL. Crossway, 2012) Matt does an excellent job of describing those who look the part but fail to produce the fruit of regeneration. I heard Matt at the 2012 *Together For The Gospel* Conference and loved his sermon while I still love his book. I refer to his book later in the gospel chapter; I highly recommended this book.

12 R.C. Sproul, *TableTalk: The Ungodly Pursuit of God In Moby Dick* (Lake Mary, FL.: Ligonier Ministry, August 2011) 6-7. TableTalk is Ligonier's devotional.

Chapter 8 – God's Holiness

Holiness stands behind every doctrine about God and we need to see how Holiness is fleshed out in humanity. Other books look directly at God's Holiness in Himself but my desire is to focus on how it is lived out in those regenerated by His Word of rebirth. God's Holiness is lived out in Christ-reflectors only because God is Holy and applies and manifests His Character in saints through His Holy Spirit.

We were designed and commanded to image or perfectly reflect our God/Redeemer Jesus Christ. Shirt manufacturers place emblems or verbiage on shirts through a screening process that vaguely reflects the regeneration process God works in those He Redeems through Christ. To Image and Likeness God as He designed from the beginning – in the Image and Likeness of Christ in His Holy **Grace**, Truth, Faith, Mind, Sight, and Power – we must be 'printed,' 'screened,' or manufactured anew into God's Holiness.

This reprinting or remanufacturing is what the Gospel is about – making sinners into saints who reflect our Holy Christ. From the beginning, Satan was at work to destroy this Image-reflection. When Adam and Eve forsook God's Holiness in their presence and rejected His **grace** in their soul, they sinned and shattered that Image-reality – this was the essence of their spiritual death. The sooner saints realize that God's Holiness is behind everything He wants us to become, the sooner we can submit to this **grace**ful process in reverence and worship. **By Holiness, God re-screens sinners**.

When we see God's Holiness as foundational to His Works, it's easier to see the biblical progressions to help us understand qualifiers pertaining to necessary practical holiness. After all, we can't reflect something in a crude pejorative sense if we can't accurately see or understand what it is we were designed to reflect. This is the problem with the residual effects of our spiritual death in Adam – our sight and experience of Holiness is skewed. Redeemed eyes begin to see the Law as God does – as a mirror to reflect His Holiness through **Grace**.

To prime the pump, Holiness can refer to what God is in Himself and what we do because of His Word for, in and through us. I'm sorry for negative pictures of practical holiness but don't throw out an eternal concept because of faulty representation. All aspects of His Holiness bear on His Work in us – as we live to the glory of His **grace**.

I was born into The Holiness Movement with John Wesley's Methodism. As a child, I thought I was saved. In a later rebellious state, I didn't appreciate Holiness teachings and realized I wasn't regenerated by God's Spirit. Now I can look back with admiration for where I was originally planted. At the least, this holiness teaching laid an essential foundation in me that many seem to miss today.

After hundreds of trips down the aisle to be saved or 'saved again,' there came a time where I knew God regenerated my soul. From that point on, I never looked back. I could say "I knew beyond a shadow of doubt." Yea right, but I'll use that terminology because many know what I'm talking about. Those in different denominational camps may not know experientially what I'm talking about but the point is between wish and certainty. More basically I came alive to God's Word and Holiness when it once-and-for-all grabbed my soul. The point of regeneration is this – God imprints souls with His Holiness and His Life.

Let me speak briefly to how God's Holiness got hold of my soul. Two books greatly influenced me. God significantly put Holiness on my radar screen through R. C. Sproul's classic book, *The Holiness of God*.[1] God used this book to significantly speak to my soul. Sproul's teaching provoked serious reflection in my mind and life. This was my introduction to Ligonier Ministries. God continues to use their reformed influence in my growth. Ligonier primarily teaches saints about God's Holiness – this learning cascaded into every facet of my being. This would be a great start for anyone.

About that same time I read *The Pursuit of Holiness*[2] by Jerry Bridges. God used this small book in my life to cause me to answer questions similar to those I like to pose. Bridges provoked me to question why I did things – in light of God's demands for holiness. He made a clarion call to the reality of holy living, similar to the church foundation I was raised in. I highly recommend either book for any who want to seriously examine their life in light of God's design.

God continues to provoke me to heightened thinking. The habits I learned from these books still function today; therefore I often ask people a question like, "I'm not so much interested in *what* you believe or *that* you believe, but *why* do you believe *what* you believe as it relates to Holiness?" This is still a necessary question for all today.

I challenge people to offer a personal definition for Holiness. Knowing God's definition is a better place to start but, for your benefit, take the time to do this. It's important to know <u>what</u> we believe and <u>why</u> we believe what we profess. I'm concerned to get to the heart of the matter. Many beliefs are mere head knowledge but **redeemed beliefs boil down to convictions – where we live what we profess**. Most beliefs are subjective in form and foundation; redeemed beliefs are built on objective reality. Convictions based on God's Holiness and His work of regeneration last; subjective ones often fall or waste away.

Consider God's Holiness and saint's practical holiness. Holiness is God's <u>attribute</u> that can describe His totality of Character. In this divine sense, Holiness can't be our attribute. We can be described as holy because His Character lives in us by **grace**. Don't pass over the concept of Holiness and pretend it doesn't exist. Some do this with Holiness but God wants to move us past spiritual paralysis. Consider:

Can you offer a practical definition for Holiness?

Is Holiness an objective reality or a relative, nebulous concept?

Are believers really supposed to be concerned about holiness?

When God commands saints to be holy, do we *know* what He desires?

Does God clearly define holiness, or does He leave us to our own
subjective interpretation and application?
If pressed for biblical responses, can we offer God-reflecting answers?
God commands everyone to be holy; does this change our thoughts?
Can we describe holiness to our neighbor or a child?
Do we, with conviction, know what holiness means?

Consider what you deem the important element of holiness at a personal level and how it's formed in saints. Many <u>professors</u> are void of any understanding of personal holiness and are not frustrated by this lack. Some just 'leave the faith because it didn't work;' it could be they didn't put forth holy effort but that's another point. My hope is to provoke you to a diligent pursuit of holiness. **If you are <u>re-created</u> to reflect His Holiness, knowing holiness should be second nature**.

Charles Colson said, "If we really understand what being a Christian means – that this Christ, the living God, actually comes in to rule one's life – then everything must change: values, goals, priorities, desires and habits."[3] Holiness is serious business and takes great effort but God offers His power when we submit to His Ways. Holiness-producing **grace** is unpacked in later chapters for our assimilation.

Sadly many professors do not seem to make holiness a serious issue nor do they apply great effort. In this vein, Kevin DeYoung says:

> There is a gap between our love for the gospel and our love for godliness. This must change. **It's not pietism, legalism, or fundamentalism to take holiness seriously. It's the way of all those who have been called to a holy calling by a holy God**.[4]

I do not claim a life verse but Hebrews 10:21-25 is significant in my knowing God's Will for holiness in my Redeemed View of Life. Possibly the greatest phrase God burned into my soul is "consider how to <u>stir up or provoke</u> one another to love and <u>good works</u>." What would happen if we took this seriously? I do! It often brings trouble for me but that does not mean we should not perform this burr-in-the-saddle duty especially when we understand **grace**. Ponder His Word as it speaks to drawing near with a true heart, clean hearts and pure bodies.

> And since we have a great priest over the house of God, let us draw near with a true heart in full assurance of faith, **with our hearts sprinkled clean from an evil conscience and our bodies washed with pure water**. Let us hold fast the confession of our hope without wavering, for he who promised is faithful. And **let us consider how to stir up one another to love and good works**, not neglecting to meet together, as is the habit of some, but encouraging one another, and all the more as you see the Day drawing near.

To ponder the pursuit of holiness we must acknowledge that many struggle with this necessary godly pursuit because of wrong thinking. I attempt to correct this distortion and put us on the path of a healthy pursuit of God's Will in the Redeemed View of Life. We can move past distortion to find God's Will. Kevin DeYoung says:

> The truth is [that] **God's people can be righteous – not perfectly, but truly**, and in a way that genuinely pleases God. With all the best intentions, **we tend to flatten the biblical view on holiness until we squeeze out the dynamic nature of life with God**. In an effort to own up to our own abiding sinfulness and highlight the gospel of free grace, we remove any notion that we *can* obey God or that he can delight in our good works.[5]

Lately I've read several Kevin DeYoung works. As a gifted orthodox reformed writer, he concisely presents a synopsis of biblical truth. As we pursue holiness, listen to his warning and encouragement,

> **The Christian should no longer be trapped in habitual lawlessness** (1 John 3:4). "By this it is evident who are the children of God, and who are the children of the devil: whoever does not practice righteousness is not of God, nor is the one who does not love his brother" (1 John 3:10). **God expects us to be holy and gives us the grace to be holy**. After all, he created us for good works (Eph. 2:10), and he works in us to will and to work for his good pleasure (Phil. 2:13). Christians *can* be rich in good works (1 Tim. 6:18: Acts 9:36). We *can* walk in a way worthy of our calling (Eph. 4:1). **We *can* be trained to live in a way that is holy and acceptable to God** (Rom. 12:1-2).[6]

Back to our mini quest; consider a diagram that visualizes critical biblical concepts. Think of a continuum with Holiness on one side and utter depravity on the other. Where does your definition fall?

Utter depravity ←--------------→Holiness

God's Holiness exists on this continuum, but where? Speaking of humans, does holiness begin with our will, soul, mind, actions or a combination thereof? Does it begin with us; if so, how? Does it start with someone else; if so, who and how? Is holiness possible without God? Some think so. If we could divide this continuum into a biblical distinction, how would we do this? Place a point on the continuum where you can differentiate a move toward or away from holiness.

Here?   Here?   Here?
Away from Holiness ←--------------------------------→Toward Holiness

In my factory days, I often heard, "Can't we just all get along?" to mute any resistance. Discussions of holiness often provoke a similar response. In a recent book by the Dalai Lama, *Beyond Religion: Ethics for a Whole World,*[7] he posits a neutral notion of goodness in mankind. He suggests man can be good or ethical without any belief in God – an impossibility in orthodox Christian belief. He says man can forgive without any foundation for *this* forgiveness. Muslims claim this thought as they struggle with Christianity's claims.[8] Most agree that generic goodness – if it's possible – would improve this evil world, but in inherited and actual sin, man cannot perform God-pleasing activity without an objective foundation and divine intervention.

True believers agree that moving toward Holiness is pleasing to God. Conversely, most agree that moving away from Holiness displeases God and should be avoided by professing believers. Saints agree in principle even if they deny it in theology and practice. We need a consistent practical definition with a holy hatred for sin and diligent pursuit of holiness. God's power in our life through regeneration and Christ-reflecting **grace** changes this conflict.

Some imagine that God grades on the *Bell Curve of Life*[9] but this demonstrates faulty thinking that should never describe a Christian. God does not use a floating scale to judge holiness. Rather, He uses the absolute, objective, and eternal criteria of His Holiness as the Standard of our holiness. Believers must realize the objective eternal dividing line for our continuum – even as our imperfect holiness is accepted as pleasing through the Work of our mediator Jesus Christ.

The Thread of Continuity suggests an eternal dividing line. For now, look past the notion that we cannot use the term Holiness in our criteria for holiness; thereby creating a mini tautology. A tautology occurs when we use an unnecessary modifier that adds nothing to the fact. Actually Holiness related to holiness does not constitute a tautology because the first is divine; the second is human. I will not use this heading so our choices include: God's Will, Ways, Word, Law, Character, or something else. I chose God's Character.

I have plenty to say and teach about holiness but other voices provide stability. J. Sidlow Baxter defines holiness in *A New Call To Holiness; A Restudy and Restatement of New Testament Teaching concerning Christian Sanctification* published in 1967; Baxter says,

> What is holiness? Or, more importantly, what is the holiness to which the New Testament calls Christian believers? **Holiness**, however, like many other intangibles, is not easy to define so as to bring a vivid image of it before the eyes of the mind. It **is easier to describe than define**. Some, perhaps, might define it negatively as absence of sin, or positively as absolute virtue. Or maybe some would define it ethically as impeccable righteousness, or more spiritually as moral perfection. Yet all such definitions are abstract and unpictorial and therefore elusive. **We need somehow to apprehend holiness photographically**; and with this in mind I do not hesitate to affirm that the truest preliminary description is **HOLINESS IS LIKENESS TO GOD, or more precisely likeness to the moral character of God**. This, so I believe, in both Old and

New Testaments is the centric idea in the call to holiness. Away back in Leviticus, there we see it, gleaming over the vestibule of the Israel theocracy, as the first and supreme requirement: "Ye shall be holy; for I JEHOVAH YOUR GOD AM HOLY!" (Lev.19:2). It was this which first gave coherence and sanction to all the Levitical enjoinments and prohibitions, ceremonial, sacrificial, hygienic, social, moral and spiritual. The Ten Commandments are simply an amplification of it in ten aspects: "Ye shall be holy, for I JEHOVAH YOUR GOD AM HOLY." This challenge: "Ye shall be holy, for I JEHOVAH YOUR GOD AM HOLY," surely rebuts those teachings which would persuade us that in most of the Old Testament the idea of holiness does not have an ethical content.[10]

Baxter provides an excellent foundation. For many, holiness is intangible and not applicable to daily life. Many never consider what holiness is; much less that God commands this of every human – especially holy ones. My desire is to remove abstractness to something we must **grace**fully pursue. **There is coherence in Holiness – and this is exactly why a biblical lifeview is crucial to our lives**.

I'm not sure I ever heard the word photographically before as Baxter used but I've used the concept in my teaching for years. I do this with *God's Thread of Continuity*, the *Character of God dividing-line* in the next chapter, and biblical repentance in chapter 13. I trust the photographic approach helps us live and proclaim the call to holiness.

To satisfy the absolute, objective and eternal criteria Scripture uses, let's insert the *Character of God* as the dividing line with numbers 0 - 100 for varying degrees within each side. The thickness of the line houses the letters, so our diagram now looks like this:

100 ←—Away From —<0   Character   0>—Toward Holiness —→100
                       Of God

When God commands Laws for us to obey, it's in our best interest to follow precisely, despite what our flesh desires. Some argue that saint's flesh is not yet redeemed but I quibble with this understanding, believing it is redeemed to the degree that conversion occurs in our mind and life. Is it perfect? No! Paul speaks of this battle in Romans 7 and we are in a continual battle for conversion on this side of glory. 2 Corinthians 3:18 says we increase from glory to glory – one faith to a higher faith – especially when we live in His Faith with His power. God gives victory attested in Romans 8:13-17 and 2 Corinthians 12:9-10 through **grace** rather than mere motivation or gratitude.

Christ-reflectors should hotly pursue His Holiness in their whole life; if we do not, consider a new practical paradigm. I read a small powerful book that did not speak directly of holiness but it applies. As you think about upward movement of holiness in your life, consider:

> At 211 degrees, water is hot. At 212 degrees, it boils. And with boiling water, comes steam. And steam can power a locomotive. It's your life. You are responsible for the results. It's time to turn up the heat. **From this day forward, commit to operating at 212 degrees in everything you do. Etch it into your thinking – into your being. Apply it to your actions**. It guarantees to increase your results positively and, in so many cases, increase your results exponentially.[11]

Seek to boil for Christ; live your holiness at the 212 degree mark – 24/7 – the Master deserves nothing less. Our joy requires nothing less.

Without solving common debates, we need **grace** because our *unconverted* flesh compels us to deny His Laws, rules and methods. Accordingly, our flesh desires to keep us on the 'violation side of the continuum' in practice of disfunction,[12] contrary to God's Holiness. The term disfunction is used to denote activity and methods of the flesh and world – opposite of holy or healthy – almost like <u>dis</u>-function.[13] Disobey is to obey like <u>disfunction</u> is to healthy. Even in psychology, <u>dysfunction</u> denotes ways that do not reflect God's Ways – even though they deny this in the current DSM-IV-TR – leading directly to another premise:

The use of disfunctional methods cannot work God's Will!

The fact that God chooses to work in us despite our faulty methods should not cause us to believe these faulty methods or rules are acceptable to Him; it's critical to see this line of differentiation! The fact that God sometimes works favorably in spite of faulty methods leads some to imagine it's okay to use methods that don't reflect God's Character, Design or Holiness. This favorable working in spite of sin has to do with His Character – ours by application and practice.

In speaking to necessary law-keeping in the practice of holiness in his classic book *Holiness*,[14] J.C. Ryle says,

> There is no greater mistake than to suppose that a Christian has nothing to do with the law and Ten Commandments, because he cannot be justified by keeping them. **The same Holy Ghost** who convinces the believer of sin by the law, and leads him to Christ for justification, **will always lead him to a spiritual use of the law**, as a friendly guide, in the pursuit of sanctification.

One modern-day quote I love comes from Dallas Willard who recently graduated to heaven. Against those who have a polluted understanding of holiness related to law-keeping, he says,

> **As apprentices of Christ, we are** not **learning** how to do some special religious activity, but **how to live every moment of our lives from the reality of God's kingdom**. I am learning how to live my actual life as Jesus would if He were me. Jesus stands beside me and teaches me in all I do to live in God's world. This enables me to find the reality of God's world everywhere I may be, and thereby to escape enslavement to sin and evil. **We become able to do what we know to be good and right**, even when it is humanly impossible. Until we are clear on this, we will have missed Jesus' connection between life and God and will automatically exclude most of our everyday lives from the domain of faith and discipleship. In His presence, I learn the goodness of His instructions and how to carry them out. It is not a matter of meriting life from above, but of receiving that life concretely in my circumstances. **Grace, we must learn, is opposed to earning, not to effort**.[15]

In dependency treatment, people find healing only when they discontinue methods that keep them in bondage to the addiction and walk in a healthy direction. True healing to overcome dysfunction in 12-Step programs comes when people embrace Christ's Holiness. This is not a mystery. God glorifies His **grace** with transformed lives as healthy living displaces disfunctional living. Redeemed vision creates **grace**-habits of holy, healthy and pleasing living of Romans 12:1-2.

Sinful humanity's nature is to sin and violate God's Ways. Remember the switch? If we transform our minds through the creation of a biblical lifeview – the necessary-reality-of-conversion-as-a-result-of-salvation – we please God when we **grace**fully follow James 4:5-10:

> Or do you suppose it is to no purpose that the Scripture says, "He yearns jealously over the spirit that he has made to dwell in us?" But he gives more grace. Therefore it says, "God opposes the proud, but gives grace to the humble." Submit yourselves therefore to God. Resist the devil, and he will flee from you. Draw near to God, and he will draw near to you. **Cleanse your hands, you sinners, and purify your hearts, you double-minded. Be wretched and mourn and weep.** Let your laughter be turned to mourning and your joy to gloom. **Humble yourselves before the Lord, and he will exalt you.**

Only by God's **grace** in glory are we free from our bondage to sin. In this life, our freedom only goes as far as our practical holiness although it is protected by our Justification. And, **only as our life is transformed can we reflect Holiness.** Consider 1 Peter 1:13-16:

> Therefore, preparing your minds for action, and being sober-minded, **set your hope fully on the grace that will be brought to you at the revelation of Jesus Christ.** As obedient children, do not be conformed to the passions of your former ignorance, but as he who called you is holy, **you also be holy in all your conduct**, since it is written, "You shall be holy, for I am holy." And if you call on Him as Father who judges impartially according to each one's deeds, **conduct yourselves with fear throughout the time of your exile**, knowing that you were ransomed from the futile ways inherited from your forefathers, not with perishable things such as silver or gold, but with the precious blood of Christ, like that of a lamb without blemish or spot.

Peter tells us how to conduct our life in 2 Peter 2:15-16:

> **For this is the Will of God**, that by **doing good** you should put to silence the ignorance of foolish people. **Live** as people who are free, not using your freedom as a cover-up for evil, but living **as servants of God**.

As bond-servants, we never get time off from holiness. Hebrews talks about our Father's desire to discipline us by putting this desire into the context of fatherly discipline in Hebrews 12: 10-11:

> For they disciplined us for a short time as it seemed best to them, but he disciplines us for our good, **that we may share his holiness**. For the moment all discipline seems painful rather than pleasant, but later **it yields the peaceful fruit of righteousness to those who have been trained by it**.

Every world religion has a notion of moral goodness. Many ignorantly lump Christianity with other religions. If we think Christianity is just another approach to morality and everyone is okay because of universal salvation, we miss whole-Scripture points.

First, Holiness is critical to the Trinity. To me, the Trinity is beyond dispute but some disagree. We must understand how their Holiness plays into essential truths and doctrines to help our Imaging.

God's Holiness and Justice are not compromised by Christ's Atoning work or its application. We often 'apply' details of Christ's Atonement to our own ideas of salvation. Granted, details of the Atonement utterly slap our sensibilities but redeemed eyes allow us to see another picture. Without a perfectly Holy requirement for salvation, the crucifixion of God's Son for believing sinners doesn't make sense.

It doesn't make sense to have a perfectly Holy Savior who perfectly keeps God's Law for the salvation of His Sheep – who believe Him and are supposed to imitate Him – without a necessary holiness element as part of *that* salvation. I offer a complete redeemed view of salvation as God demands and the Word describes with a holiness additive. This redeemed picture of holiness is what most struggle with when they wrongly lump Christianity in with other world religions.

If His death was merely to atone for sin – and not to perfectly fulfill and meet the Holy requirements of a Holy Father to restore the once-lost Holiness factor that reflects the Trinity – His death compromises several biblical doctrines. To His glory, God's Holiness is exalted in the death of Christ on the grounds of double Imputation where God replaces the believing sinner's sin with the perfect righteousness of Christ. This replacement is mercy applied with **grace**. God also replaces the sinful state of deadness with the empowering state of holiness; this is **grace** applied. New Covenant teaching helps us see and rejoice in the Trinity's eternal plan.

Second – Holiness, as the foundation of salvation, flows from the first point of the Trinity. If man merely sinned against a Holy God, we might imagine that God could extend mercy and man's attempts to appease God might actually restore the ruptured relationship. Most people bank their eternal destiny on this distorted belief but Scripture tells us otherwise. In Genesis through the whole Bible, especially in redeemed New Covenant truth, Holiness rather than mercy is the foundation of salvation. Man lost Holiness through a rejection of **grace** and lost spiritual life in his rebellious action; we need restored holiness.

This Holiness-factor can't be replaced by sinful man, no matter the attempt! Mere mercy or forgiveness, that Muslims and others claim won't work – as this compromises God's Holiness. In order for salvation to be extended and applied to spiritually-dead man, God's Holiness must be honored and vindicated! This is why Christ's Atonement on the Cross is the crucial event to vindicate God's Holiness. If sin, spiritual death, and a Holiness-void are replaced with a perfectly Holy Atonement – it must be replaced with a Living, Holy Ingredient. The death of Jesus on the Cross vindicates God's Holiness and secures salvation as *that* ingredient to restore Holiness.

It's true that Christianity has a moral element but it's not a mere subjective one that other world religions are built upon. In context, God can't look on sin, condone it, or merely dismiss it – especially not in Jesus as He hung on the Cross. **God's forgiveness is built upon the Holiness and perfect Justice of God in Christ** rather than upon a generic mercy that flaps in the breeze of popular opinion.

Sin must be judged either in Jesus as the substitute or in the sinner through eternal judgment! One of only two things will occur. Sin will be judged by a Holy Just God 1) in the sinner who stands condemned in his sin or 2) in Christ – in the stead of believing sinners. This is why Christianity is built on God's objective perfect Holiness. There is no other sufficient foundation! Salvation is built on the perfect Holiness of Christ shed on the Cross as a substitutionary Atonement for believers – this is the unmistakable reality of the biblical Gospel.

Third – **a Christ reflector is dutifully free to be gracefully holy by Law-keeping and Gospel proclaiming**. Peter boldly confirms this by teaching that new life in Christ is manifested at a basic level. Jesus declared our Emancipation Proclamation on the Cross with the words "It is Finished!" but **freedom is gained only when we walk in holiness**! The Cross gains positional Holiness – being clothed in Christ's righteousness that was willingly laid on the altar – and practical holiness is gained in sanctification. The call to holiness is not legalism; **holiness is the essential source of our life in Christ**. "To be gracefully holy is to be Free!" does not contain an ounce of legalism. Seek to favorably hear the encouragement of J. Sidlow Baxter,

> **Can we now commit ourselves to** the following definition? **Holiness is moral likeness to God, as required by His Written Word, as revealed in His Incarnate Son, and as inwrought by His Holy Spirit**. It is inwrought in suchwise as to penetrate and purify our whole moral and spiritual nature, without excluding any part as being imperviously and irrecoverably corrupt – such as that phantom 'old Adam' of the usual holiness theories. This **inwrought holiness transforms the whole man**. It may operate in differing degree, but its extent is always the entire moral being.[16]

Submit yourself to Holiness as God's Will in joyful **obedience**. Remember, **Grace** is not opposed to effort; therefore, strengthen godly muscles. For some, this might be new but Scripture declares this often. I like to interchange godliness with holiness because godliness may seem more-attached to God-and-Christ-reflection than holiness. Many use holiness pejoratively easier than godliness so **we need to put effort back into our spiritual vocabulary and strive for godliness – as the essence of Christ reflection**. **Grace** provokes Christ-glorifying sanctification – the ongoing reality of becoming practically holy through God's power. Remember, this is God's Will for you!

Mere Christ professors don't know holiness at the practical level but this can be changed if we discover freedom in godliness. Years ago, especially growing up in a Holiness environment, I thought holiness was on the radar screen of every believer. Today it's almost a foreign word. At minimum, it seems to be an anomaly if you hear it taught and see it lived out in vivid color. Rather than the rule of faith as Scripture posits, holiness seems to be the exception of faith today.

Since God gave the faith once for all-time, diligently seek the faith. He gives His Faith for our temporal and eternal benefit. The Faith given once has not changed! God's command to "Be holy as I am Holy" was never rescinded! Thinking and living can change upwardly when we keep the world's thinking out of our spiritual foundations.

At times, God evaluates life as "everyone did what was evil in the sight of God" per Genesis 6:5. Another synopsis is the tragic commentary, "everyone did what was right in his own eyes" per Judges 17:6 and 21:25. Still again He said, "Woe to those who call evil good and good evil" per Isaiah 5:20. Too often today, people in our society are governed by sin rather than righteousness. God sees differently than we do, and this can't please God as some suggest.

When we allow sinful behavior rather than godliness to be the potential norm when obedience is not necessary, we fall into the mire of calling evil good and good evil. We must wake up to the reality of our confusion and call a spade a spade. Without this correction, we cannot expect good things from God's hands. God calls people back in repentance and faith, so if we profess Christ yet live in sin and autonomy, expect discipline. Get back on God's page and pursue His

Righteousness as Matthew 6:33 tells us. May God give us redeemed eyes to see life through godliness and live out the Ephesians 2:10-life.

John Charles (J.C.) Ryle wrote a classic on *Holiness*. He starts his Holiness chapter with Hebrews 12:14, "Strive for . . . holiness, without which no one will see the Lord" and asks, "Are we holy?" He says, "That question can never be out of season. . . **there is no time, no, not a day, in which man ought not to be holy**."[17] He then gives a "poor imperfect outline at the best" to describe practical holiness:

> **Holiness is the habit of being of one mind with God**; **a holy man will endeavor to shun every sin and keep every known commandment**; will strive to be like our Lord Jesus Christ; follow after the Spirit-fruits of Galatians 5:22-23; temperance and self-denial; charity and brotherly kindness; a spirit and benevolence toward others; purity of heart; the fear of God; humility; faithfulness in all the duties and relations in life; and spiritual mindedness.[18]

Later in that chapter, Ryle explains the importance of practical holiness:

> Our purest works are not better than filthy rags, when tried by the light of God's holy law. The white robe, which Jesus offers and faith puts on, must be our only righteousness, the name of Christ our only confidence, the Lamb's book of life our only title to heaven. With all our holiness we are no better than sinners. Our best things are stained and tainted with imperfection. They are all more or less incomplete, wrong in the motive or defective in the performance. By the deeds of the law shall no child of Adam ever be justified. . . Why then is holiness so important? . . . Let me set out in order a few reasons. . . **we must be holy, because the voice in Scripture plainly commands it; this is one grand end and purpose for which Christ came**; this is the only sound evidence that we have a saving faith in Christ; this is the only proof that we love the Lord in sincerity; this is the only sound evidence that we are true children of God; this is the most likely way to do good to others; our present comfort depends upon it; and without holiness on earth we shall never be prepared to enjoy heaven.[19]

Let me shift gears a bit to prevent misunderstanding. Wrong Law teaching says that sincere obedience to the Moral Law is unnecessary and maybe wrong. I've heard people imply that if perfect Law-Keeping is required, "We don't want to follow *that* Christ!" It's like,

"I believed in a forgiving God, not one who wants Righteousness." It's almost like, "If that's what He expects, count me out;" therefore the question of Holiness is valid. **To hear that Law-keeping is necessary might turn someone's world upside down**. But, if that's what's needed, embrace it – even if it turns our doctrinal world upside down.

In 1972, *The Poseidon Adventure* hit the movie screens. In the story, an ocean liner is capsized by a tsunami wave. Those who survive the initial topsy-turvy turmoil realize if they want to live, drastic measures are necessary – as they try to piece tidbits together in an upside reality. A preacher, Reverend Scott (Gene Hackman), leads a small group to the engine room which is on top of the water – so they hope. At one point, they meet a larger group heading in another direction; Scott is unable to convince them they are wrong and need to join his group. Undeterred, Scott's group heads in the chosen direction. Progress is not without dissension or loss; several die in the process. As steam prevents the last steps, the preacher risks his life to make the escape possible and dies in the process. Rescuers finally burn through to save only six survivors. No others are rescued – something like Noah's Ark. **In the end, the right path is essential to survival**.

What does this movie have to do with our approach to God? My research indicates no intention of biblical truth but parallels exist. The tsunami of sin turns our world upside down. Those who survive the first wreck seek escape from final death. In the topsy-turvy haze, it's hard to find the right path. A tree is their Way. Some think it's a crap-shoot; yet only one way leads to Life. A preacher leads the way. A Redeemer makes final passage effectively workable and dies to ensure salvation. The wrong-direction-crowd walks into the second death.

Connections with the Law exist in this movie. The popular-guided crowd often goes in the wrong direction – against the right path. Many hang their eternal hats on two foundations – being baptized into a specific church or 'accepting' Jesus as Savior. What if the eternal litmus test of Life-in-Christ or salvation is actually obedience to the Law? After all, Jesus Christ won salvation through perfect obedience.

The first recorded communication between God and man concerns Law and promise. Genesis 2:16-17 – "And the LORD God commanded the man, saying, 'You may surely eat of every tree of the garden, but of the tree of the knowledge of good and evil, <u>you shall not eat</u>, for in the day that you eat of it you shall surely die.'" We know what happened; Adam and Eve rejected **grace**, ate, died spiritually, and were kicked out of the Garden. Humans #1 & 2 disobeyed Law.

Enter Cain and Abel – humans #3 & 4. We don't read of God's instruction but apparently Cain didn't obey blood requirements for sacrifice. We can surmise they sinned and brought sacrifice. Rather than bring what God required, Cain's sacrifice was rejected. As a result he killed Abel in violation of Command #6, "<u>You shall not murder</u>." Violation of Law went from bad to worse – culminating in the flood.

The first dry-ground communication after the flood began with right sacrifice and God smells the pleasing aroma (symbolic of **grace**) yet declares in Genesis 8:21, "the intention of man's heart is evil from his youth." What a convergence of two diametrically opposed thoughts! The first recorded act after God makes Covenant with the surviving men is a despicable sexual act between Ham (son) and Noah (father), a gross violation of Command #7 – "Thou shall not commit adultery."

The legacy and lineage of Ham is sin and God-rejection. Is it any wonder they were thorns-in-the-side to God's children? Cain's sons were <u>Cush</u>, <u>Egypt</u>, Put and <u>Canaan</u> – and we know much about three of the four. Behind them we see Babel, Nineveh, Philistines, Jebusites, Amorites, Girgashites, Hivites and others that God wanted destroyed as the children of Israel went into the Promised Land. Descendants of these families still persecute and kill Christians today.

On the other hand, Abram (Abraham) came out of the loins of Shem. It's not so much about bloodline although it's significant, but it's more to do with Law-keeping. God-rejecters ultimately disobey God's commands and God **blessed** families of the world through Abraham's obedient faith. His seed was the perfect Law-Keeper Jesus Christ.

Law-keeping or Command-keeping is basic to Covenant. There is no better picture of Law-Keeping than the Founder and Initiator of the New Covenant – Jesus Christ. We see this true reality in Isaac and Jacob (Israel). Conversely, in the life of Esau (Edom) – the Covenant rejecter – we again see the sinful outcome as he takes wives from the Canaanites (Ham's offspring) and settles in Canaan.

Against this Covenant-rejecting backdrop of Ham and Esau, God shows His Gospel power through the lives of Joseph, Moses (The Law Mediator), Joshua, and other Covenant-keeping Christ-followers. In light of New Covenant reality, we see Law-keeping in a powerful way through the eyes of effective empowerment but let's get back to our Law-Keeping overview to see its validity in the scope of redemption.

We could look at Gideon, Samson, Ruth and Boaz but let's get to Samuel. Samuel's mother was Hannah, who asks God for a son and dedicates him to God's purpose, "I will bring him, so that he may appear in the presence of the Lord and dwell there forever" per 1 Samuel 1:22. What a Covenant theme! Samuel was the young boy who heard God's call and, per 2:12 'replaced' Eli's wicked sons, "Now the sons of Eli were worthless men. They did not know the LORD." Samuel sanctioned Israel's first two kings – as David typifies Christ.

David's first words in Psalm 1 are, "Blessed is the man . . . whose delight is in the Law of the LORD, and on His Law he meditates day and night." **David saw the Law as the pinnacle of His life in Christ**; this is why he said, "Oh how I love thy Law!" Sadly this perspective has changed in the church today and some think David did not know the power of grace. Think again! In Psalm 18:1-2 he says, "I love you, O LORD, my strength. The LORD is my rock and my fortress and my deliverer, my God, my rock, in whom I take refuge, my shield, and the horn of my salvation, my stronghold." We look at Psalms 19 and 119 later but the Law – for Christ too! – is David's premier focus.

Let's take a brief look at how the prophet Micah cycles between judgment and salvation. In 4:1 he says the mountain of Jerusalem is established as the pinnacle of faith (per John 4:20-22) pointing to the shining mountain of Christ and His Gospel. Micah 4:2-5 presents God's Ways, Path and Law or Word as the means to properly call Jesus Lord – per Matthew 7:21-23 where lawless or disobedient ones are unknown to the Lord at His Judgment Seat.

Let's fast-forward to The Ultimate Prophet, Jesus Christ. One Beatitude, Matthew 5:6 is "Blessed are those who hunger and thirst for righteousness, for they shall be filled." Later in this sermon, He says "(Obey) so that you may be sons of your Father who is in heaven" per 5:45 and "You therefore must be perfect as your heavenly Father is perfect" per 5:48. After a reference to Gentiles in Matthew 6:33, He says, "But seek first (primarily) the kingdom of God and His Righteousness, and all these things will be added to you."

Should we imagine being perfect and seeking righteousness – to be Sons of God – does not mean pursing God's Law with His power? I think the church today needs a paradigm adjustment in regards to the Law. Even if this thought causes a Poseidon Adventure of sorts, **if we want Eternal Life we must take this Law adventure seriously because it's serious to Christ, Paul and Scripture**. Some argue it's not salvation's litmus test but I believe it is! **We must seriously consider our approach to God's Law and Law-keeping**. Some already do; others need a tsunami wave to hit them.

God exalts in Holiness and the Trinity is glorified when saints live in godliness. **Holiness is the foundation of our life in Christ as the essence of Christ reflection**. Read the words of *Holiness Unto the Lord*, a fabulous song by Lelia N. Morris. May the words challenge us to put holiness or godliness high on our agenda. According to

Scripture, holiness actually defines our Life In Christ! **Making holiness our watchword and song will surely change our world!**

1. "Called unto holiness," Church of our God, Purchase of Jesus, redeemed by His blood; Called from the world and its idols to flee, Called from the bondage of sin to be free.

   Refrain:
   "Holiness unto the Lord," is our watchword and song, "Holiness unto the Lord," as we're marching along; **Sing it, shout it, loud and long, "Holiness unto the Lord," now and forever**.

2. "Called unto holiness," Children of light, **Walking with Jesus in garments of white**; Raiment unsullied, nor tarnished with sin, God's Holy Spirit abiding within.

3. "Called unto holiness," praise His dear name! **This blessed secret to faith now made plain**. Not our own righteousness, but Christ within, Living and reigning, and saving from sin.

4. **"Called unto holiness," glorious thought**! Up from its wilderness wanderings brought, Out from the shadows and darkness of night, Into the Canaan of perfect delight.

5. "Called unto holiness," Bride of the Lamb, Waiting the bridegroom's returning again; Lift up your heads for the day draweth near when in His beauty the King shall appear.

Every phrase is theologically correct as a clarion call to saints to live in godliness. **We were purchased by Jesus for holiness, and freedom in righteousness is our heritage in Christ**. His Finished Work is our license to keep God's Laws as godliness by His **grace**. He gives saints His Righteousness, Faith and Power to walk in godliness. **The haze was overcome and revealed in the Cross; walk like it!** If you are His saint, walk in the freedom He bought. The goal of **grace** is to be practically holy. Find and never leave that camp! **Make holiness your watchword and you will be close to living in God's Will!**

1 R.C. Sproul, *The Holiness of God* (Carol Stream, IL.: Tyndale, 1998). The newer version is referenced since I cannot find my older copy. R.C. unabashedly declares God's Holiness as the pinnacle doctrine of the Faith – and I wholeheartedly agree!

2 Jerry Bridges, *The Pursuit of Holiness* (Colorado Springs, CO.: NavPress, 1978).

3 Cited in Carol J. Ruvulo, *Grace To Stand Firm, Grace To Grow* (Phillipsburg, NJ.: P&R Publishing, 2003), 91.

4 Kevin DeYoung, *The Hole In Our Holiness: Filling the Gap between Gospel Passion and the Pursuit of Godliness* (Wheaton, IL.: Crossway), 21.

5 DeYoung, *The Hole In Our Holiness*, 64.

6 DeYoung, *The Hole In Our Holiness*, 66.

7 His Holiness the Dalai Lama, *Beyond Religion: Ethics for a Whole World* (NY, NY.: Mariner Books, 2011). From a general baseless perspective, his book can satisfy and challenge the mind that is unconnected. Can you tell he approaches ethics from a postmodern warrantless approach? The absurdity is that he speaks of a neutral ethic but wants to be called His Holiness? Go figure.

8 Biblical forgiveness is not a baseless forgiveness like generic love. Man cannot assume an implicit belief that God will forgive because they ask for forgiveness as often taught. God's forgiveness is built on the foundation of the crucifixion of Christ on the Cross – the perfect Atonement that accomplishes the dual Imputation purchased through the blood and body of Christ. Even animal sacrifices couldn't take away the people's sins; these looked forward to Christ's ultimate sacrifice. Jesus perfectly meets the three requirements of God – the only way of forgiveness. Forgiveness is obtainable only through the finished work of Christ. This Once-for-all-time worthy sacrifice is the only one that counts.

9 *The Bell Curve* is a tool teachers use, even if it's at an implicit level. What the Bell Curve demonstrates is that most students fall under the umbrella of the bell with few on the weak and strong sides. If they grade on the Bell Curve, they often downgrade to meet weaker students. With this in mind, God never downgrades His requirements to meet sinners; He maintains His holiness as He makes a way to redeem sinners!

10 J. Sidlow Baxter, *A New Call To Holiness; A Restudy and Restatement of New Testament Teaching concerning Christian Sanctification* (Grand Rapids, MI.: Zondervan Publishing House, 1967) 107.

11 Sam Parker, Mac Anderson, *212 Degrees – the Extra Degree* (Aurora, IL.: Simple Truths, 2006) 22-23

12 Since sin entered the human race, we can correctly use the word dysfunction to describe actions that violate God's design; however, I like to use the word disfunction because the prefix correctly highlights the opposite of functionality through Christ.

13 I am not sure about the etymology of the word dysfunction because the prefix 'dis' is typically used to speak of the negative factor of a valid characteristic. I would argue that the negative of functional is disfunctional rather than dysfunctional but I didn't write any Dictionary. God created us to function as He designed but sin distorts this functionality.

14 John Charles Ryle, *Holiness* (Webster, NY.: Evangelical Press, 1979) 26. This book was originally published in 1879. It should be a current book on your shelf after you read its wisdom.

15 Dallas Willard, cited in J.P. Moreland, *Love Your God With All Your Mind: The Role of Reason in the Life of the Soul* (Colorado Springs, CO.: NavPress, 1997) 11-12. Willard gives an excellent qualifier for redeemed **grace**. This book, in my top ten, speaks to how God particularly gifted me. Sadly those gifted to love God particularly with their minds are often ostracized or pushed to the periphery of the church.

16 Baxter, *A New Call To Holiness*, 126.

17 J.C. Ryle, *Holiness*, 33

18 Ryle, Holiness, 33-37

19 Ryle, Holiness, 39-42

Chapter 9 – God's Character

With God's Character as our dividing line of action, let's build on this reality. My goal in this chapter is not so much to display God's Character in Himself but to highlight His Character-input into our lives. Few verses say it better than Galatians 2:20, "I have been crucified with Christ. It is no longer I who live, but Christ who lives in me. And the life I now live in the flesh I live by faith in the Son of God, who loved me and gave Himself for me." God made this verse huge in my life. Holiness can live strong in us as we seek to reflect His Character.

Some say God does not put His divinity in us. I understand the point and partially agree because we are 100% human, but there is a sense that God organically invests Himself in His Sheep. God invests Himself in us from an outward sense but I gather from Scripture that God invests Himself in us from an inward sense. Some argue against this <u>organic deposit</u> of Christ's life in individual saints, but what do they posit? Paul often speaks of this organic reality and Peter does too.

Maybe this organic sense is what Peter means when he talks of a nature-input that compels Character-driving-ability in us. Consider his words as he talks about grace in 2 Peter 1:3-8; emphasis mine:

> **His divine power has granted to us all things that pertain to life and godliness**, through the knowledge of Him who called us to his own glory and excellence, by which he has granted to us his precious and very great promises, **so that through them you may <u>become partakers of the divine nature</u>**, having escaped from the corruption that is in the world because of sinful desire. For this very reason, **make every effort to supplement your faith** with virtue, and virtue with knowledge, and knowledge with self-control, and self-control with steadfastness, and steadfastness with godliness, and godliness with brotherly affection, and brotherly affection with love. For **if these qualities are yours and are increasing they keep you from being ineffective or unfruitful in the knowledge of our Lord Jesus Christ**.

We will forever be human, though someday with glorified bodies. I understand all that, but God invests in us beyond the ongoing process of being conformed to His image and likeness by His Christ, **grace**, Holy Spirit and Word – although that's enough. I may tread on salvation/sanctification doctrines but I hope to provoke consideration as I guard against slipping into a full mystical sense of salvation.

When I suggest that God invests an organic deposit in us at the point of regeneration, I often speak of this as an <u>essential or ontological</u> aspect of God's work. Ontology is the study of essence, essentials, or is-ness of an entity so let's ponder ontology from a salvation reality. **When God clothes us in Christ's Righteousness, Scripture teaches that something occurs at an ontological, essential or organic level – the essence of regeneration and new Life in Christ.** We are not mysteriously absorbed into God or divinity and we can't become divine but there's a biblical sense that God invests Himself in His sheep beyond an outward sense. I will further clarify my position.

In salvation we are freed from the reign of sin so that we can live in the power of His **Grace** and Character. Unpacked later, I see **grace** as Christ's Effective Righteousness in saints to be saved and righteous. To this end, I teach Holiness as the ontological essence of **Grace**. My understanding of **grace**'s ontological essence is a tautology – where essence gives no assistance or added meaning – as ontology and essence address the same thing. An intended tautology helps accentuate my point to overcome inconsistent views that betray the biblical picture and reality of <u>effective empowering redeemed **grace**.</u>

God loves to live strong through His saints! In the practical realm, we all battle with residual sin in our flesh. John Owen provides a short statement that helps us realize how we must approach sin, "Be killing sin or it will be killing you!"[1] **As we depend on the Spirit and grace to put off sin and transform us into His Holy Image and Likeness, we are on God's path to imitate His Character in Christ.**

To accomplish a redeemed understanding we need to highlight the Character-dividing-line. Some professors seem unable to follow God's methods and Ways; sadly, the dividing line is fundamentally missing in their lifeview. It's no wonder. Disjointed thinking and behavior occurs in this mental, logical and moral void to cause the gospel to become skewed. When we fail to reflect Christ, it's no wonder our 'good works' fail to lead people to Christ per Matthew 5:13-16.

This deficiency can be corrected with thinking and actions that reflect God's Character. This is how the Spirit provoked an atmosphere in my life years ago. May God help us translate His essence into our being to manifest His Holy Character. As we are saved by **grace**, His Character must be worked out in us. As God provoked Christ-reflection in me, I learned that I could imitate God in Christ through **grace**.

This is partly why humanity needs a flesh-God so we can photographically or visibly understand God; hence the sending of Jesus Christ in human flesh. With His photographic teaching, how can some claim to believe in God but reject a flesh-God? **If we do not believe this flesh-God, we slander God and reject His Gospel!** We must believe that He rewards those who diligently seek Him per Hebrews 11:6. This is God's perfect plan. Many don't get this point and may not want to understand. In unbelief, they mock and slander God's Character in His Law and Gospel. Conversely, and the natural desire of **called-ones emulate His Character as a Holy pursuit** His true Abrahamic offspring who possess God's Character-driving-ability.

The reality of being IN Christ[2] will be manifest most by our desire to please The Father by emulating His Character through **grace**. John Piper says, "He is most satisfied in us when we are most satisfied in Him!"[3] To truly delve the practical application of His Character, we **must** have eternal life that only God can give. Many know this as being saved, being born again, being born from above or becoming a new creation but many are confused with the term **regenerated**.

Personal experience makes it obvious that two keys are often missing from common doctrine: 1) the reality of regenerated ones and 2) **grace**. Scripture often speaks about "we, us, and you" and it's imperative to know who the Bible addresses when it uses these terms. If not, we typically fall into error. The whole concept of 'The brotherhood of man and Fatherhood of God' is not found in Scripture other than in our Adamic creatureliness that flows from the Creator. This Brotherhood/Fatherhood teaching creates false impressions about Scripture regarding who the "we, us, and you" are in salvation terms.

If we address this Brotherhood/Fatherhood scenario from the perspective of being regenerated in Christ – the second Adam rather than the first Adam – I could agree with this teaching but most do not use this perspective when speaking of this point. The Christ-perspective of brotherhood would change the discussion to one of being Covenant keepers rather than Covenant breakers. Every person relates to God through Covenant – as a Covenant keeper or Covenant breaker. There is nothing in between! This is why every person will stand before God and give an account for their life.[4] If we teach regeneration, people might give greater heed to God's Will for their life.

Every person is _created_ by God in a physical or biological sense but not every person is _re-created_ by God in a spiritual eternal sense after the model of Christ. In an evangelistic discussion with Nicodemus, Jesus proclaims powerful truths about regeneration. In John 3:3, "Jesus answered him, 'Truly, truly, I say to you, unless one is born again he cannot see the kingdom of God." Nicodemus could not comprehend so "Jesus answered, 'Truly, truly, I say to you, unless one is born of water and the Spirit, he cannot enter the kingdom of God. That which is born of the flesh is flesh, and that which is born of the Spirit is spirit. Do not marvel that I said to you, 'You must be born again." Jesus freely proclaimed necessary new birth; we should do no less as regeneration is the ontological foundation of our faith.

Many teach that God loves every person. This is true in a sense per John 3:16 but God specifically wrote Scripture to His people, elect ones, called ones, sheep, saints, born-from-above-ones, etc. Once we see that God distinguishes between <u>created ones</u> versus <u>re-created ones</u>; blessed vs. wicked; wise vs. unwise; saved vs. unsaved, and regenerate vs. unregenerate ones, we begin to see love passages through God's eyes. Our view of love must be the love depicted in Scripture so as to not slander God. **In love, God gave the Gospel – but He does not necessarily regenerate everyone!**

As one called out of due time by his own testimony, Paul had a 'Come-to-Jesus meeting.' Christ appeared to Paul to bring new birth to his soul on the Damascus road in Acts 9. It's easy to do, but we should not think Paul's conversion experience is the norm; however, it's instructive. <u>The typical entity is new birth</u> – what I prefer to emphasize as regeneration. Paul experienced new birth on the Damascus Road. In 2 Corinthians 5:17 he says, "Therefore if anyone is in Christ, he is a new creation. The old has passed away; behold, the new has come."

The practical implication – besides regeneration – is that **when the Spirit puts you *into* Christ, you are in New Covenant reality**. At that point, the Old Covenant passed away as obsolete. Behold the New Covenant truth and its **grace**ful reality is come! I'm convinced this is Paul's biggest point. His Old/New Covenant distinction of passing away or becoming obsolete has more to do with New Covenant superiority in fulfillment. Fulfillment essentially outshines promise. This 2 Corinthians 5:17 **grace**-driven reality allows redeemed-ones to walk in the reality of the New Covenant when regeneration occurs.

The Fall, in the wrong light, can give a false sense of security to fallen man from a romanticized perspective. Fallen man can see God as the Creator and Father of mankind with no regard for our culpability toward sin. Fallen man imagines his 'inherent goodness' – with hell-driving rebelliousness – is acceptable to God. Fallen man is in love with his sinfulness; therefore, why change? Fallen man does not even know he's spiritually dead so he cannot look for missing spiritual life. Fallen man imagines his sinful offerings are accepted by God without knowing God requires Perfection – even when we cannot give it. The predicament of sinful man is really bleak! Remember the car wrecks?

But God commands us to speak His Gospel into deadness. Through preaching, God called dead bones back to life in Ezekiel 37. In reality, the Gospel calls dead ones to resurrected life like Jesus did with Lazarus. Evangelicals believe God calls some – not all – to spiritual life as He called Lazarus from the grave in John 11. Others think, "If He doesn't call me, there's nothing I can do!" But this stance creates a self-inflicted fatalism that we blame on God yet God calls us to proclaim His message to see people come alive in Him – this is His Love!

Prophets often spoke Gospel into deadness. Isaiah was called to preach to those who would not see or hear. Isaiah 6:8-10 appears in several New Testament texts and, without God's intervention, depicts a bleak picture of humanity. Hear the Trinity speak in the midst of the prophet's commitment toward the inherent futility in his mission:

> And I heard the voice of the Lord saying, "Whom shall I send, and who will go for us?" Then I said, "Here am I! Send me." And he said, "Go, and say to this people: "Keep on hearing, but do not understand; keep on seeing, but do not perceive." **Make the heart of this people dull, and their ears heavy, and blind their eyes; lest they see with their eyes, and hear with their ears, and understand with their hearts, and turn and be healed**.

Jeremiah was called to preach to those who would not respond. God requires us to faithfully tell His story and invite people to discipleship. The results are God's domain even as we passionately try to convert sinners. We sometimes confuse our responsibility with God's but I would rather error on the side of too much Gospel-proclaiming.

Because God redeems fallen sinners through New Covenant re-creation per Ephesians 2:4-10, we can boldly share the Gospel. With

God-generated horizons, God allows the genuine titles of Re-Creator and Father to be used by His faith-children – those who are found in Christ. God speaks directly and specifically to saints when using terms like "we, us, and you" – and often collectively.

To accomplish correct thinking that reflects God's Character, let's create a list to provide a workable understanding of God's Holiness. In the following two-sided list, moving toward the right side indicates movement toward God's Design, Will, Law, and Holiness by starting at His Character. Conversely, moving left indicates movement away from God's Design, Will, Law, and Holiness from His Character. Only two categories ultimately reflect mankind – those who believe and follow, and those who reject Him. We quibble over variations but it's difficult to argue against Scripture. Man either follows or rejects God!

Ultimately, every person falls before God in one of these two classes. A practical foundation of regeneration and **grace**ful obedience appears when we understand this division. Either we are In Christ or outside of Christ; to my knowledge, few other categories adequately describe the condition of humanity. In Christ – repentance, faith and conversion follow as a result. Outside Christ – we reject His Ways and Character. This does not leave room for middle ground.

The quicker we address this New Covenant distinction, it's easier to differentiate between those who reflect God's Character by following Christ in holiness versus those who reject God's Character by not following Christ in holiness. A naked claim, as many profess, without confirmation of **grace**ful works manifests the car-wreck damage. To judge our lives by God's Character provokes us to Christ.

To consider whether our conduct pleases God or violates His Character can be a real eye-opener. The coming list can challenge us with a before-the-face-of-God honest assessment. Evaluate your thoughts, attitudes, speech and behavior against the Character of God and His command to imitate Jesus Christ in His Holiness. If we want to talk about biblical love, God lovingly calls us to Righteousness – right behavior in Christ. **Grace**ful living must exude before our testimony holds value for the Gospel per 1 Timothy 1:16.

Mankind's Character Distinctions

Evil or Wicked Ways <Away From<		GODLY WAYS >Toward >
Sin or Dysfunction	C	Righteousness
Subjectivity		Objectivity
Autonomy or a law unto self	H	Submission
Disobedience/Rebellion		Obedience
Unbelief/Pride	A	Faith
Bondage/Slavery		Redemption
Dysfunctional Systems of:	R	Healthy Systems of:
Behavior		Behavior
Communication	A	Communication
Attitudes		Attitudes
	C	
Estrangement		Reconciliation
Illogical thinking	T	Logical thinking
Disorder/Chance		Order/Design
Chaos	E	Cosmos
Ungodliness		Godliness
Anarchy/tyranny	R	Systems of Authority
Inconsistent/Contradiction		Eternal/Unchangeable
Deception/Distorted thinking		Truth
Misunderstanding	O	Understanding
Broken commitments		Covenant/Commitment
Skewed/unhealthy relationships	F	Ordained relationships
Ignorance (intentional)		Knowledge
Unforgiveness/bitterness		Repentance
Vengeance/Barbarianism	G	Mercy/Compassion
Denial/Suppression		Acceptance of reality
Obstinate/rebellious	O	Confession of truth
Dishonor		Honor
Appearance/assumptions	D	Exclusive reality
Selfishness and passive "love"		Proactive love

Left-side living violates God's Holiness; if you are on the left side, seek God's help for regeneration and/or redeemed sanctification. Right-side living reflects God's Holiness – pursue right side thoughts and behaviors. Christ-reflecting paradigms must provoke our actions and methods. Through the power of **grace**, reject left-side behaviors. Seek **grace** to walk in right-side behaviors that brings soul-integration.

Some distinctions are quite obvious, others are not. On the backside of the list, the following points are offered to weight our response toward God's Character.

#1   Nothing on the left side of the dividing line will produce the Will of God in believers.

#2   Anything in violation of the Design, Will, Ways, Word, Law, Holiness and Character of God produces destruction and death, even in the life of a believer, at least to some degree.

#3   Movement toward God will not be effective or acceptable until we cross over into the right side of the dividing line and practice right-side behaviors and methods (conversion).

#4   Believers can never produce the Will of God or reflect His Holiness or image by using a dysfunctional, perverted, or ungodly method. God's Ways must be employed!

#5   To the degree that we break the bondage of sin or render dysfunction powerless is the degree to which we can pursue God's Holiness and relate effectively with others.

#6   Counsel that encourages, promotes, duplicates, or practices left-side items fall short of God's Will and must be seen as unbiblical and ungodly, regardless of how many Christian labels are used or how widely it's accepted. God's psychology is truth and holiness – creating an integrated mind and life.

#7   The debilitating struggles of the Christian life typically result from not experiencing biblical repentance, not breaking free from left-side bondage and not walking with the Spirit and power of **Grace** into right-side methods and behaviors.

#8   God will never work through left-side methods or behaviors to produce His Will in His saints – except repentance! Through His mercy, forbearance and goodness He may work despite them but never through them or because of them. Therefore,

#9   By His **grace** we must eradicate left-side methods and behaviors from our life through biblical repentance and conversion if we are to reflect His image and Character.

As you might make a stew and put it on the back burner to simmer, let 'our' stew simmer for a while. Simmering on God's truth brings out the best flavors. David called it 'meditating on His Law day and night.'[5] Let me remind you, it's your stew; I may only help a bit.

Allow me to tell a story of by-gone days so we can relate better to regeneration and spiritual stew. Years ago, before better vehicles and smoothed-out-mountaintops, a trip over the Smokey Mountains was risky business. Vehicles were not built with the physical capability to endure the grind. Radiators blew. Transmissions burned up. Air conditioning overtaxed the system. A nice trip could be destroyed if even one of these conditions 'caught up' to your vehicle.

We all go through a painful process of learning about vehicles. We've probably seen someone tear up a tire because they didn't know it was flat. Some only need to go a bit further so when the engine starts smoking, they don't heed the message and a motor is burnt. The climb up God's truth-mountain might tax our vehicle, so shift into a lower gear. Maybe you already burnt your engine or created another self-induced disaster? God is able to take our broken vehicle and give us a new one – this is the essence of His mercy and **grace** exchange.

In God's remaking us, we learn about thinking. Subjectivity is part of our journey but if we put our relationship on the foundation of objectivity – God's effort, Christ's work and the Spirit's application and empowerment – our relationship significantly changes. Examine your relationship with Christ to see if it's defined by an implicit or explicit foundation. Implicit faith can be seen in infant-baptism or 'accepting Christ' campgrounds. Implicit faith says, "Because I was baptized as a child or accepted Christ, that's all I have to do to make it to heaven!" or "I'm covered and that's good enough!" If we move our relationship to an objective, applied and explicit level – significant redeemed things occur!

Generic-individualism or an all-inclusive mentality permeates many. They rarely question the validity of their assumptions with God's

Word. These assumptions appear in general sentiments of "Jesus-died-for-everyone" and "I'm part of the 'everyone,' right?" It can appear in the "I've been baptized in the church, so I must be okay with God" mentality. It can appear in the "I accepted Christ as my Savior" thinking. No good thing comes out of assumptions if regeneration is not the foundational reality of these subjective convictions.

A redeemed view of Scripture shows that Jesus only died for His sheep, not for everyone. Let me be clear, I truly wish Christ died for all and everyone will join God in eternal relationship[6] but I cannot find that pie-in-the-sky reality in Scripture. If Christ died for everyone, as many inconsistently claim, and God sends some to hell as declared in Scripture, God would be guilty of legal double jeopardy. This would make God guilty of violating His own Law and would destroy His Holiness. On the flipside, an all-forgiving position makes His justice spurious, again slandering His Character. Only in the Atonement of Christ do we see His Holiness and Justice upheld and exalted, and this is done through the regeneration of His sheep through Christ's Work.

We can talk about <u>elect ones</u> but this is 'too vague' for some by creating unsettling but necessary questions. In picture form, we could say that Jesus only died for those on the right side of God's Character-line since only those who faithfully obey prove to be elect ones. That is why the result of <u>Christ-reflecting obedience manifests right relationship displayed in the Character of God's dividing line</u>. This is why **grace**ful actions demonstrate regeneration per Ephesians 2:7-10.

We struggle with the scope of salvation – especially when we initially hear that Christ didn't die for everyone. I remember my reaction the first time I heard this. I thought it was totally blasphemous and initially rejected this teaching. This consternation exposes different preconceived ideas, perspectives of biblical belief and salvation paradigms that either bind us or give redeemed freedom. The binding or freedom is determined by the paradigm or validity of new birth.

A <u>paradigm</u> is a way of thinking or perspective that locks us into a certain picture of reality. Webster's defines paradigm as "an overall concept accepted by most people in an intellectual community because of its effectiveness in explaining a complex process, idea or set of data." I remember an instructional video that explained paradigm in the story of wrist watch evolution. Years ago, all watches were the wind-up variety. When the electronic watch was proposed, it was declared 'it' would not work yet famous watch companies went out of business because they did not change their paradigm. From this simple history, we see it's difficult to let go of our favorite paradigms.

It's a real jolt to our system when our first paradigm is shattered. The more we understand this necessary reality of life, the more we can allow God's Spirit and Word to change our paradigms. I like to imagine my paradigms all fall on the right side of our Character chart – that would be naïve – but I would much rather have God and His truth define my paradigms, especially as applied to salvation.

Many imagine salvation as a scope or frame – a salvation paradigm, if you will. My teaching bumps against paradigms – seeking to move us toward God's paradigm of the Redeemed View of Life. God's salvation can apply to a collective group but Scripture suggests a better view is an individual <u>salvation-scope</u>. **Jesus died for the collective church but the Spirit applies His Work to individuals**. The Gospel goes to individuals but individualism doesn't trump the need to be planted and proactively participate in church. God designed us to live in the **grace**ful structure of His Word and church. Within the church however, we must examine our view or scope of salvation.

Common errors abound in how people relate to Jesus. Many assume Jesus is there for our personal welfare as the divine genie given for personal needs rather than <u>approach Him on His terms</u>. Satan failingly enticed Jesus to use His powers for personal gain and he uses this enticement with us too. How we approach God in Christ is serious business; in a related way, to seriously approach how God works His Will in us for His glory, we must ask how we view salvation.

As we contemplate biblical salvation, let's address salvation scopes. By this term, I mean particular paradigms that people believe for salvation. It's easy to adopt an unbiblical salvation-scope without realizing we use misguided interpretation. Salvation scopes go hand-in-hand with Atonement Theories. We may think our view of salvation is biblical but how do you view salvation? Do you see salvation as a(n). .

Life-long commitment to a regimen like a weight lifter?

Anecdotal "An apple a day keeps the doctor away" remedy?

Antibiotic shot to cure a disease?

Intellectual assent to in-the-know knowledge like Gnostics?

Vaccination to prevent an infectious disease like small pox?

Once-a-day pill for a condition that requires regular check-ups?

Compact to embrace an ideology like moralism?

Pull-myself-up-by-my-bootstraps-transformation?

Monogamous marriage of a loving commitment?

Voluntary social service job that dedicates you to service?

Joining a club like the Boy Scouts to earn the top prize?

Paradigm shift where we gain a new perspective?

Military enlistment, going to boot camp and lifelong service?

Joining a Country Club where you pay weekly dues?

Practicing a little Jesus and a few Christian principles in your life?

Life insurance policy with monthly payments to collect when dead?

Rebirth by the Re-Creating, Redeeming, Enabling Savior?

I'm sure other questions could be offered to depict how some view 'biblical salvation' – but our view might betray the Redeemed view of New Covenant Scripture. To add to this haze, let's consider a few Atonement theories – as faulty ones lead many astray even as they imagine their understanding of the Cross reflects what Scripture presents. Considering my main premise in Chapter 3 we must submit our Atonement and salvation views to the truth of Scripture. Consider various theories that people believe. It might not be as simple as a pick-and-choose method but few give serious thought to the origin of what they believe and how they live in regards to salvation theory.

This brief look as Atonement theories or Christ's Cross-Work shows historical and contemporary schemes of salvation. My hope is that increased knowledge will drive a greater commitment to the Gospel and Faith once-delivered-for-all. Mix-and-match views in theory and practice – weighed against what God presents in the New Covenant – might show our view is lacking, maybe eternally so.

Most laypeople have little idea how many theories 'float around' to impact denominational and/or practical understanding. We may reject one view mentally but hold it practically. Conflicted thinking provokes inconsistency, schismatic beliefs and behaviors to drive our theological notions. In this way, we allow understanding to adversely affect our behavior – sometimes without knowledge of this negative ongoing relationship – and we may be unaware of doctrinal hedging related to theological uncertainty. I trust this list helps bring clarity so that we can align our views with God's view.

The following summary by Gregg Allison[7] can help us evaluate our view. Don't judge yourself harshly, but seek to honestly correctly unfold doctrine. Also don't unfairly judge godly men who unpack and explain 'evolving' theology. Seek to understand the logical, mechanical and ontological realities as <u>Atonement theories</u> relate directly to our subsequent understanding of the gospel and salvation.

1. **Recapitulation theory**
   <u>Irenaeus</u> offered this well-developed view to say that what we lost in Adam can be regained in Christ through curse-reversing correctives through Christ's blood and obedience. This is a good early one but some voids are evident though unintended.

2. Ransom-to-Satan theory

Origen developed this popular view, still postulated today. It may proceed from erroneous exegesis of the passage 'suggesting' Satan has the power to take life. Naturally, spiritually and eternally only God has the power of life, and a ransom to Satan would suggest that Satan is the ultimate power rather than God.

3. Godly Deception theory

Gregory of Nyssa reworked Origen's theory to suggest that God fooled Satan with atonement actions. God veiled details in prophecy, and Jesus' answers to the wilderness temptation confused Satan. Deception is valid in war but God did not need to 'work His atonement through deception' although the haze works similarly. After-the-fact-teaching provides a redeemed corrective, so Gregory was not far off.

4. Christ paid the ransom to the Father theory

John of Damascus modified Origen's theory to suggest Christ paid a ransom to the Father to redeem His sheep. Christ's sacrifice purchased redemption for His sheep, but it's not biblically seen as a ransom.

5. Christ's death is a sin-atonement theory

Tertullian presents this popular view embraced at face value by much of the church. I call this the half-cross view with a missing holiness-corrective. Without blaming Tertullian, his view tends to divide the church over whether atonement is limited or unlimited, universal or particular, generally or specifically applied, etc. – without giving answers. By itself, it's not wrong.

6. Christ's death as sin-atonement through substitution

Athanasius expands Tertullian's theory with necessary substitution. Power and sufficiency were probably intended; if so, Athanasius offered excellent qualifiers. Skewed thinking can distort what Athanasius intended and it's doubtful he taught universal application.

7. Christ was priest and sacrifice in atonement substitution

Augustine's noble focus, gleaned from Hebrews, adds little to previous atonement theories. Augustine contributed greatly to early church theology and his input on Atonement theory highlights the complexity and majesty of Christ's work.

8. **Satisfaction theory**

> Anselm suggests Christ's sacrifice reinstitutes God's honor. The feudal system of Anselm's day influenced his position as he offered plausible options to wrong teaching. God's honor was never broken! Misguided application 'opens the door' for the 'blame God for sin' sentiment prevalent today. I don't think Anselm posited that notion because he was a great Bible thinker.

9. **Moral-Influence theory**

> Abelard taught that Christ *demonstrates* love to the extent that he prompts people to love God through gratitude – a popular view. This 'love' 1) truncates the atonement's objectivity, 2) skews the necessary holiness foundation and 3) 'posits' subjective salvation. The typical danger is in seeing Christ's life and sacrifice as *suggesting* but not demanding holiness.

10. **Supererogation requiring appropriation by willing ones**

> Aquinas modified Anselm's view to suggest necessary human cooperation to gain salvation. Aquinas posited regeneration through ontological and imparted **grace** – what I teach as the holiness-corrective. He taught the application of salvation into willing souls (a valid qualifier) through supererogatory works ('extra-holy' works – that Evangelicals rightly deny. He correctly emphasizes necessary holiness in justification and sanctification. He posited an imparted-grace-qualifier that needs to be evaluated and possibly embraced.

11. **The Penal Substitutionary theory**

> Modifying Anselm's focus to God's justice, Reformers shifted the focus to sin. Double imputation is correctly posited, and their intended meaning is broader than their inconsistent presentation, as holiness appears peripheral and subsequential rather than objective and ontologically necessary to Christ's actual atonement.

12. **The Example theory**

> Socinus rejects God's standard of Law and judgment. Justice and mercy are seen as contradictory. Christ's Atonement is stripped from its historic sacrificial root as God requires perfect obedience perfect sin-atonement. Sadly, the idea that salvation is mere 'acceptance' of God's forgiveness is prevalent.

13. The Governmental theory

Grotius 'rejected' both Reformed and Socinian views, and posited God as Universe-Governor who could relax his holy standards and forgive through mere mercy. The Muslim view teaches that God's mercy and forgiveness hangs on no objective foundation. Grotius strips the atonement of necessary biblical warrant – and this fits today's subjective relativity of God's rule.

14. Dependence-on-God theory

Against penal substitution, Schleiermacher posits a valid-sounding subjective theory. The God he posits is a pantheistic god who 'saves' into God-consciousness (co-opted by New Agers) rather than objective salvation applied by the Spirit.

15. Christ-as-Victor theory

Aulen rehabilitated earlier theories to posit that Christ merely gained victory against the evils that plague humanity – again stripping the atonement from its biblical context. He disallows salvation and life from the Law's demands – *the foundation of salvation*.

Did you find your Atonement view in the 15 or a combination of several? Does your view match the redeemed view of Scripture? Most put our views of Covenant, salvation and Atonement in one package, so we ask, "Where does this leave us?" I believe the combination of 6, 7, 8 and 11 depict the New Covenant Gospel. What we think and live matters. What God has done, declared and whether His salvation is applied and lived out in us is the thing that really matters!

It looks like the stew is ready; as we dip some, our approach to godliness says more about our claimed relationship than we realize. Make sure you are In Christ – firmly planted on Christ's terms, His Covenant, His salvation and His Atoning Cross-Work. A Royalheirs song, *So Glad He Knows Me*[8] speaks of regeneration.

1) Forsake this world of sin and sorrow; Leave it all behind;
   Kneel at the precious feet of Jesus; Oh what joy you'll find.
   Don't be late for I can promise; you will not regret
   For He is the dearest friend that I have ever met.

Chorus:
What joy I found in Jesus, how it fills my heart.
What peace the Lord has given since my brand new start,
My hope is everlasting; this He's given to me.
I'm so glad that I know Jesus, so glad He knows me.

2)   There is nothing in this world that can take the place
     Of the blessed Rose of Sharon and amazing grace.
     He's never failed me in the fight, God has stood for me;
     I'll keep holding to His hand, He'll take good care of me.

Next we evaluate how God's Holiness and Character flow into **Grace**. A bit after that, we will see how these three doctrines flow into His Law. Many see a discussion of Law as unnecessary; however, I declare we must learn the majesty of Law within Gospel **grace**.

My **Grace**-presentation is different from many teachings and I'm not bashful to make my case. It's amazing what we find about **Grace** and Law when we approach salvation with Redeemed eyes. God often challenges me to 'take things back to His drawing board' to explain what we should know; my desire is to be faithful. Look again with a fresh perspective; you might be surprised by what you find.

---

1 John Owen, *Overcoming Sin & Temptation: Three Classic Works by John Owen* (Wheaton, IL.: Crossway Books) 23. This was originally found in *The Works of John Owen*. Owen is one writer I could say that I 'drool at the spiritual mouth' to read.

2 *Being "In Christ"* is likely Paul's favorite saying. In addition to his teaching about the God-alone work of re-creation or new birth, being In Christ speaks to being inserted into the organic relationship mentioned earlier.

3 John Piper, *Living in the Power of Future Grace* (Colorado Springs, CO.: Multnomah Books, 1995) xvi. This proceeds from Piper's idea of a Christian Hedonist in *Desiring God,* "The chief end of man is to glorify God BY enjoying Him forever."

4 Some will give an account before the Great White Throne before they are cast i n t o Hell while God's saints will give an account of how they used or stewarded His grace. Sadly, many throw out accounting-teachings because of wrong teaching but Scripture says we will all give an accounting before God – without detracting from Salvation.

5 Psalm 1:2 but also read Psalm 19 and 119.

6 The greatest book I ever read on this subject is John Owen's *The Death of Death in the Death of Jesus Christ.* J.I. Packer's introduction alone is worth the cost. This tough read is well worth the effort if you can get past the author's writing quirks.

7 Gregg Allison, *A History of the Doctrine of the Atonement* (Louisville, KY.: Southern Baptist Theological Seminary; Volume 11, No. 2). This article was in *The Southern Baptist Journal of Theology* and is presented in abbreviated fashion.

8 Royalheirs, *God's Been Good* CD; used by permission.

Part 3

Clinging to a Redeemed
Grace-Full Salvation

Chapter 10 – God's Grace
Contrasted with Mercy

My spiritual eyes see the Bible divided between **grace** and mercy from Genesis through Revelation. This topic requires a whole book and if God grants enough life I plan to write a follow-up *The Two Sides of the Cross* to unpack this doctrinal divide. I do however present qualifiers to help us see that God makes **Grace** His greatest emphasis.

This chapter contains a great challenge because I'm convinced **grace** is God's biggest 'doctrine.' God passioned my soul to provoke a reformed definition as I teach what His Spirit taught me through His Word. As I stand on the orthodox faith once-delivered-for-all, I present what God revealed without thinking it's a private interpretation. Please pull up a chair with a Bible in hand and take a Berean approach.

Redeemed **grace** covers many biblical doctrines. Let me offer one crucial aspect of **grace** that I address implicitly but clearly. I believe the whole gamut of Holy-Spirit-teaching is subsumed under **Grace-application**. By this I mean that Regeneration, the Baptism and filling of the Holy Spirit, the empowerment to witness and preach, anointing and the Spirit's leading all fall under **grace**. In other words, the function-ability of **Grace** falls under the Spirit's Work. Whatever I say of **Grace**, I say of the Holy Spirit – maybe just not in this book.

I love to stand on the shoulders of faith-giants as theology can get deep. Pointedly I seek to glorify God's **Grace** as I share my theological **grace**-travels. Some of this has taken years to say correctly so my readers don't get lost on the journey; and God keeps tweaking.

Four faith-giants – all named John – provoked much **grace** thinking. John Piper is a modern one. John Murray is recent. John Calvin and Colquhoun are historic ones. At least one their books fall into my top-ten all-time books-list. Collectively these men paved the way for how I understand **grace** through redeemed eyes.

John Calvin first wrote *The Institutes* at 26 years old as a primer for laypeople; this amazes me! In my early days of pondering the Redeemed View of Life, I read The Institutes. It took over a year to wade through the first volume; trust me, I used spiritual waders! It was a slow read because the Holy Spirit did much work in my soul. I cried more tears over this book than any book but the Bible. No matter what one says about his theology, Calvin <u>knew</u> his God!

Because of Calvin's *Institutes*, I find it hard to tolerate the disrespect he receives but that's another story. 460 pages in Book Three discuss *The Way in Which We Receive the **Grace** of Christ: What Benefits Come to Us From It, and What Effects Follow*. I owe much to Calvin for what I learned about the message of **Grace.**

As we peer through the biblical haze, God highlights **grace** in a huge way. In my understanding of Ephesians 2:7, <u>God Himself exalts **grace** in heavenly neon lights for all the ages to see</u>. This is why I think Christianity would do better with a primary **grace** hermeneutic. I may be accused of a presupposition here but let me give a brief defense. Presupposition is when we suppose beforehand. The proverbial circular statement "Don't confuse me with the facts; I've already got my mind made up" is the practical reality of a presupposition. From what I learned, I'm convinced God presents a **grace** hermeneutic!

Circular reasoning needs support timbers to keep the straw standing up. What I say next does not diminish God's love, name, glory, Holiness or power. To my knowledge, Ephesians 2:7 is the only place where God is said to exalt in something He holds up for the ages to see. In this way, **Ephesians holds the greatest Bible-emphasis of how God sees grace** – and ultimately this divine-pointing shines on the greatest day and event in history – the Cross. **When God points to the Cross and grace in this way, we should do no less!**

It's necessary to establish a redeemed understanding of **grace** – not just to appreciate my major divisions between **grace** and mercy –

but to understand Scripture. Ultimately **grace** saves us according to Ephesians 2. Many believers agree, yet define **grace** as God's unmerited favor. Clearly God shows unmerited favor in salvation; this is where I posit God's **blessing** of regeneration. It's favor indeed; I don't doubt this for one theological second. But if we define **Grace** as that which leads God to unveil and display His heavenly neon-light-power, we ought to be as concise as we can be – as concise as He Is!

I do not quibble over the idea of unmerited favor but I quibble over favor as the foundational definition or essence. We must think deeply here. **When we define grace as essentially God's favor, we veil God's greatest giving – that He *just* unveiled in the Cross! – into a presupposition that shackles Grace into something that betrays God's spectacular neon-light-power exposure** in Law, Holiness, Atonement, Gospel, Imputation, Justification, Adoption, Salvation, repentance, forgiveness, the Lord's Supper, sanctification and glorification. For me, an insufficient definition is too costly!

No Christ-reflecting theologian or believer wants to shackle God's **grace** to betray God's intentional-Holy-effective-overcoming-power but I'm convinced that – as hard as we defend biblical truth against error or misunderstanding – we never stop long enough in our 'defending' to critique our common definition of grace with redeemed eyes. If anything, the church is guilty of a presupposition – and its health and advance of the regenerating Gospel is the cost. Let me explain how we shackle **grace** – mostly through a weak definition.

We shackle **grace** with an all-encompassing vague description in place of a precise redeemed definition. In our pursuit of doctrinal precision, a good and necessary thing, we offer an imprecise description that can apply to *any* blessing from God. What many call common grace I call common mercy because it flows into God's general blessings to all men. While **grace** and mercy meet in the Cross, we do a great disservice when we make them synonyms.

I wish it were easier to provoke a necessary re-evaluation of a critical definition. The weak definition <u>affects</u> the church as it <u>infects</u> the church and world – a costly oversight! Since my critique sounds harsh, let me 'explain' with a simple question. When we understand the magnitude of our sin and deadness because of lost Holiness and God-rejecting sin, do we receive anything from God's hand that does not qualify as unmerited favor? Most say "No!" so let me explain further.

No matter what we speak of – provisions of generic life, nature, oxygen, water, food, clothing, housing, marriage, reproduction, science, knowledge, communication, the giving of Law, the offer of salvation, government, responsibility, sacrifice for sin, love, atonement, justice, His presence, teaching, preaching, siblings and worship – it's all unmerited favor! If we define the greatest giving of God in terms that could apply to everything He gives, what's so magnificent about *that*? This self-inflicted oversight speaks loudly to stillbirths, godless living, ineffectiveness in Christ-professors and associated problems and we could realize a huge correction with a reformed definition of **grace**.

To that end, my simple definition of practical-living-**grace** is: **God's empowerment in us to do righteously toward redemption**. Primarily **Grace** is God's **active** power in sinners to become justified saints. We need **grace** to be regenerated, walk in God's Path, perform His Ways, live His Word, obey His Law, reflect His Holiness, image His Character and walk faithfully; therefore a **passive** element will not do. **Grace** relates directly to Christ's Holy sacrificed body. **Grace** flows from Christ's active obedience into the Spirit's application of regeneration and justification – and our active obedience. **Grace** is the basis of the bread or Passover lamb (body) in the Lord's Supper. **Grace** is specifically and organically linked with redemption realities – meaning those things that positively and obediently reflect Christ's Holiness. Favor or mercy can go to all men but **grace** is divinely restricted to justification, sanctification and glorification in saints.

I readily acknowledge that mercy can go to common man but in many doctrines, a two-sided giving exists. I speak to both sides but want to narrow my focus to the application of mercy to saints. In contrast to my definition of **Grace**, my simple definition of Mercy is **"God's longsuffering to His saints in the face of their sin**." As I understand, Mercy is always related to our coming short of God's glory per Romans 3:23 – always dealing with sinful responses. Mercy flows from Christ's passive obedience[1] into God's functional passing over of our sin. For His saints, this passing over or pardon is seen in Passover blood taught in Exodus 12. As Jesus taught, Passover blood is the basis of wine in the Lord's Supper. Mercy is practically seen in forgiveness and the repentance-reality displayed in Psalm 51.

With these simple qualifiers, let me unpack the division of **grace** and mercy more. The foundational biblical text is Genesis 3:21. These truths flow into the Passover of Exodus 12 and then into the Cross. From the Passover, let me demonstrate the *function-ability* of both **grace** and mercy. Applied blood caused the death angel to <u>pass over</u> homes. With modification for alliteration, this <u>passing over</u> means that blood and mercy **comes over** sin. In contrast, **grace** is seen in the Lamb – Christ's body or bread that **overcomes** sin through Holiness! Many focus on sin rather than the overcoming freedom of Holiness.

Let me offer an illustration of mercy and **grace**. Adam and Eve's sin left a bankrupt reality – they were spiritually dead, unable to pay their eternal debt or bring restoration. A check-book analogy helps us understand distinctions between mercy and **grace**. It's impossible to give a dollar amount to adequately express the debt we owe to God yet it's a helpful analogy. Sin manifests in us a negative balance of $50 billion that we can't pay. In Imputation, Christ's blood and forgiveness puts $50 billion into our bankrupt account to cover our debt and bring us back to an innocent state – this is <u>unmerited mercy</u>. This brings our checkbook tally to a $0 balance, similar to where humanity was in innocence; however, we can't write a legitimate check with a zero balance. We need a positive balance to legally write a check – this looks forward to a corrected Holiness void and **positive-giving-grace**.

Another perspective in the checking account analogy helps us understand how they could 'fall from grace' in the first place. It's this Fall from a Righteous innocent state (without sin) that befuddles even the best theologian and utterly confuses the layman. Some deny Adam and Eve could fall from grace but they do so without redeemed explanation. Yet this seems to be exactly what occurred! Adam and Eve 'depleted' their positive balance of right standing, if you will, before they could fall into sin or debt. This is why I suggest they lost holiness – the missing doctrinal element – before they could sin.

Grace is the positive factor we need for a positive balance. This isn't like optional oil additive. This **essential additive – only** supplied to saints – is Christ's sacrificed body and Righteousness. **His applied perfect Law-keeping, rather than inherent Holiness per se, gives us 'merit' with God**. Without outside confirmation I think **Grace** is propitiation. Except for a minor point, I won't argue that here.[2] More than any point, please realize the positive-adding factor.

With our check-book analogy, **right standing with God is only gained through the Righteousness of Christ being applied to our sinful account to the point of 'sufficient balance.'** This is why I contend common definitions of grace betray fundamental qualifiers as **grace** only applies to redemption in those who believe. God applies **grace** at some point in the life of His elect ones so it makes sense that He might 'apply **grace**' to those not-yet regenerated ones – knowing that at some point He will bring them to life IN Christ. This still means **grace** only applies to redemption – and this might explain where we 'get' the idea of common grace that 'pollutes' redeemed **grace**.

Only His Righteousness gives positive merit to make us acceptable to God. Scripture presents a direct relationship between

grace, the burned flesh of Passover, the burning flesh of sacrifice and Christ's Righteous body on the Cross – but many miss these vital points of connectivity. **We must remember that the burning flesh from sacrifice, rather than the blood, was a sweet-smelling savor to God's nostrils.**[3] If we miss this connectivity, we miss a crucial factor in our biblical understanding of **grace** and **grace**ful-living potential.

In our checkbook analogy mercy pays the debt but **grace** gives the positive balance. We need both mercy and **grace** for salvation but, **in a redeemed sense – as grace is the regenerating/overcoming power to perform righteously – grace is God's exalted 'entity.'** This is why Paul, the prophet of **grace** with his mystery-unpacking duty, is allowed to present **grace** as the essential doctrine of God's plan of redemption because God's heavenly neon-light exhibition was revealed to him. I hope you understand this <u>division</u> because *this* **grace** with associated mercy changes everything – according to Scripture!

As we briefly review the whole corpus of Scripture, **Grace** prompted God to refuse Adam and Eve's attempt to make their selves acceptable <u>after they lost holiness and sinned.</u> **Grace** explains why self-justification will not work even as God <u>explicitly</u> shows **grace** in the Garden through His replacement of their fig-leaf attire. From the beginning, God exalts **Grace**. When God applies New Covenant redemption, blood is <u>implicit</u> in God's <u>applied Righteousness</u>. Because blood is not 'present' in Genesis 3:21, this might be why most theologians miss this God-clothing as representing Salvation; blood is assumed. Let's go through the sequence and implications differently:

1) God pointedly implies through <u>His replacement</u> that fig-leaf attire does not meet His Holy standard of perfection; therefore God applies Jesus' perfect Law-keeping – and life – in our stead.

2) God teaches through <u>supplied substitution</u> that sin-stained hands cannot bring acceptable justification or perfect atonement. Only the perfect hands of Christ can bring a perfect atonement to the Father

by offering the elements God required – His Holy blood and body! As the perfect Lamb and Sacrifice, He took His blood and body once-for-all-time to the Father in heaven to stay with Him eternally.

3) God made sufficient fur/skin attire with blood-shed implied per Hebrews 9:27. I wonder what animal rights people would say about this Genesis 3:21 bloody-animal **mercy**-killing by the Creator with applied **grace** if they could get that far in reading Scripture.

4) God clothed them with the animal skins that He fashioned for them. He did not just take His Re-creative Unique attire and let them do as they pleased. He did not allow them to clothe themselves in the Only Atonement He would accept. God clothed them! This huge point indicates God does not allow self-application of His remedy! The Divine Re-Creator applies the remedy by clothing the sinners with Holiness – even as they watch.

5) God plainly emphasizes the explicit body/animal skins of **Grace** (New Covenant reality) over the implied blood of Mercy to demonstrate that the fragrant sacrificed body is more pleasing to His sensibilities than shed blood per Micah 6:6-8. Hebrews 9:23-28 gives insight into what God expects and what Christ performed:

> Thus it was necessary for the copies of the heavenly things to be purified with these rites, but the heavenly things themselves with better sacrifices than these. **For Christ has entered**, not into holy places made with hands, which are copies of the true things, but into heaven itself, **now to appear in the presence of God on our behalf**. Nor was it to offer himself repeatedly, as the high priest enters the holy places every year with blood not his own, for then he would have had to suffer repeatedly since the foundation of the worlds. But as it is, **he has appeared once for all at the end of the ages to put away sin by the sacrifice of himself**. And just as it is appointed for man to die once, and after that comes judgment, so **Christ, having been offered once to bear the sins of many, will appear a second time, not to deal with sin but to save those who are eagerly waiting for him**.

When God covers the nakedness of Adam and Eve with the skins of a substitute sacrifice that shed its implied blood – Christ who gave His body and blood on the Cross – God necessarily shows Himself as the Only One to effect rebirth and new life in Christ. This God-alone-act perfectly pictures the reality of **grace**, regeneration, Christ and His applied Atonement. In a later analogy, I demonstrate how this God-alone-act looks like the baking process of a cake.

In this God-alone-act, a direct parallel exists between the First Adam as God planted a living soul into his body with the eternal life given to those placed into the Second Adam by God Himself. In this God-alone-act of applying Christ, besides in His Written revelation and its teaching, **God teaches and applauds a Redeemed View**. There is so much to learn if we can look beyond what we were taught.

The presentation of this God-alone-act in the Old Testament at the earliest place possible is part of God's unveiling that is completed in the Cross. Between our sin and God's shrouding of truth, we can overlook or misinterpret these critical points. To miss the God-alone-act in Genesis 3 leads to faulty thinking about 1) the extent and reality of Adam's sin, 2) how sin occurred, 3) its correction, 4) what an inaccurate understanding of the Gospel looks like and 5) the Holiness-void-correction of **grace** that God supplies and exalts in.

Misunderstanding puts too much emphasis on mercy and the blood within the scope of salvation. It's not that blood and mercy cannot 'handle the pressure' but distortion comes when we skew redeemed **grace**. When blood is highlighted to the theological/practical exclusion or oversight of the Body and **grace**, this provokes a half-Cross gospel. This misunderstanding leaves us with a truncated mercy-gospel. If we could look beyond our imprecise definition of grace, there is much to chew on and change when we see God's truth in redeemed light.

This God-alone-act of covering with animal skins is as strong a theological point as the writing of the Tablets with His fingers. God vividly stamps His authority and action on a crucial element of **grace**, gospel, new birth and fulfilled salvation. This point is plain and more critical to biblical doctrine than we imagine. This is the impetus of Paul's teaching in Ephesians 2:4-5 when he says, "**But God ... made us alive!**" This point alone can redeem our thinking. Without this, we are shortchanged in our whole-Bible understanding and knowing how to access God's power for us to be holy or Christ-like.

This vivid and explicit God-alone-act of skin-covering is the foundation of my explicit-grace-understanding – in contrast to implicit mercy that deals with sin. Suffice it to say that this brief picture of salvation from Genesis 3 and Ephesians 2 summarizes the totality of the Gospel proper, both Accomplished and Applied. With this in mind, ask God to help you sort through the implications of a **grace**-induced Gospel that contains mercy without detracting from either.

FYI, my two *sides* of *the Cross* break down as follows. Mercy and Justice are on one side of the Cross through the blood and wine. **Grace** and Holiness are on the other side of the Cross through the body and bread. I was not the first one to picture the two sides of the Cross. God used this two-sided picture throughout Scripture to teach us about salvation – mostly in Covenants – but we must see through the haze until we get to the Cross and work to see it through God's paradigm. Jesus taught this explicitly in the Upper Room and in John 6 and there is much to learn from the redeemed or Cross-perspective.

Justice is placed with Mercy because Justice is ultimately applied to everyone, whereas **grace** is not! To the unrepentant sinner, God uses mercy to bring them to repentance. Redeemed sinners see Mercy as compassion, forgiveness and cleansing through Christ's blood and experienced passive grace. Redeemed sinners see mercy and forgiveness flow into **grace**-realities that produce sanctification realities but this is a somewhat distorted seeing similar to the disciple's epiphany of Resurrection that skews the majestic picture of the Cross.

From the Cross or redeemed perspective, **grace** freely flows into mercy. From the view of redemption – the default setting of **grace** is the *driver* of salvation – in regeneration and sanctification. Since lost Holiness provoked sin and death, correction of Holiness (**grace**) effects regenerated Life and advancement of becoming Christ-like. We see this in Ephesians if we look past misguided teaching and emphasis. Reformed **grace** shines in New Covenant teaching in the Bible.

At the judgment, Justice is applied either through God's wrath to unrepentant sinners or through Christ's blood and perfect life to His redeemed ones. Scripture teaches that everyone receives mercy and justice in this way, whereas it does not teach that everyone receives **grace** in a similar way – mercy is common rather than **grace**! This qualifier leads me to confirm that **Grace** is essentially applied only to believers; this may shock the average person but Scripture proves this out. For the redeemed sinner, the God-induced response of Ephesians 2:8 to new life causes a **grace**ful response to mercy that fully takes advantage of His Mercy and **Grace** supplied in the Cross.

Reformed writers often speak about the three uses of the Law; their valid teaching can help us here. The first two *uses* apply well to mercy while the third precisely attaches to **grace**. **First** is the civil use – the holding back of evil in society through common grace; there it is again; I'm convinced it's common mercy! **Second** is the pedagogical use – the schoolmaster or guardian function where the Law drives people to Christ for what Only Christ can do unto justification and salvation. **Third** is the normative use – the regulative function that only believers experience because **grace** removes the curse and God's empowerment causes us to love the Law for its Holiness-driving nature in our souls. The Law is a vehicle that **grace** uses to bring us to the promise-reality of Faith through mercy per Romans 12:1-2.

Grace is Christ's righteousness that overwhelms death in regeneration and Justification, and empowers saints to overcome sin.[4] This overcoming power is manifested in His overcoming saints – this is the function-ability of **grace**. When Paul says **grace** overcomes sin, he teaches that **grace** provokes saints to holiness because of the Spirit's empowerment – the third use of the Law in the hands of Christ. Because **grace**-empowered Law-keeping overcomes sin, Paul almost had a theological heart attack in writing Romans 6:1-4:

> What shall we say then? Are we to continue in sin that grace may abound? By no means! How can we who died to sin still live in it? Do you not know that all of us who have been baptized into Christ Jesus were baptized into his death? **We were buried therefore with him by baptism into death, in order that,** just as Christ was raised from the dead by the glory of the Father, **we too might walk in newness of life**.

Paul would say, "Sin always violates **grace**!" With the power God used to resurrect Christ, He works in us so that we walk in newness of life.[5]

Before Jesus died on the Cross, the Mercy Seat was functional and a vital part of Hebrew thinking. The Mercy Seat framed their understanding, and often ours too. If one object garnered huge Hebrew sentiment in their religious activity, it was the once-a-year activity that focused on the blood sprinkled on the Mercy Seat on the Day of Atonement. This Mercy-Seat-sprinkling-combined-with-Passover-blood provokes a Mercy-focus that carries over into the church.

In today's gospel, we often preach a half-cross gospel (or less) with explicit blood and implicit body – therefore truncated **grace**. **Forgiveness isn't the end of the Gospel but grace and holiness are!** This point comes back full-circle-force when Eternal **Grace** flows from heaven – with all Holiness and no sin – with no expressed need of mercy. Dallas Willard said, "Sin management produces vampire Christians who want Jesus for his blood and little else."[6] The half-cross-gospel does not work – not even for vampire 'Christians.'

Scripture tells us the Mercy Seat now resides in heaven and further indicates the Mercy Seat is not functional today although Jesus still offers mercy. Jesus makes intercession for the saints – but where? God tore the temple curtain from top to bottom to signify His Mercy

Seat is now open to the public and to demonstrate that He no longer veils His revelation. If the Mercy Seat is in heaven, why not ask people to come freely to the Mercy Seat? Instead, Hebrews 4:14-16 tells us that God significantly changed the paradigm or picture:

> Since then we have a great high priest who has passed through the heavens, Jesus, the Son of God, let us hold fast our confession. For we do not have a high priest who is unable to sympathize with our weaknesses, but one who in every respect has been tempted as we are, yet without sin. Let us then with confidence draw near to **The Throne Of Grace**, that we may **receive mercy and find grace** to help in time of need.

God pushes to redeem our salvation view – **after the Cross** – through Christ's Work and His Word! Remember, in many ways God veiled the truth and reality of the Cross until after the fact. As God acts in Genesis 3:21 – with no in-text commentary – He acts in Hebrews 4:16. **God does not explain this Mercy-Seat-to-Throne-of-Grace exchange** but in my estimation, it's a done deal that teaches.

Looking at the historical chronology of Scripture, I do not see the Mercy Seat mentioned again in Scripture after the Cross. **As God 'changed the menu' after the Cross, we can learn much**. From Hebrews 4:16, we can obtain mercy and **grace** at the Throne of Grace.

Let's take a look at how **grace** relates to Law as some teach that Law and Grace don't mix. Galatians 2:21 says, "I do not nullify the grace of God; for if justification were through the law [traditionalism built on Mosaic rather than Moral Law], then Christ died in vain." Salvation however comes through promises of fulfilled **grace** through Law.

From Ephesians 2:8-9 we are saved by **Grace**; therefore, we really are saved by and through the Law and Law-keeping. What a mixture! This speaks of Justification; then sanctification. Further, Law and **grace** must mix in sanctification to discover the freedom of an overcoming life. If we see **Grace** in a Redeemed Way, we live in this freedom – and paradigms will change. Let's see how this occurs.

1. Redeemed **grace** can change our understanding of sin, the Gospel, Justification, Salvation, Sanctification, and the believer's relationship with the Law.

2. Redeemed **grace** can help us see <u>necessary practical holiness</u> as an outflow of Christ and Word – to keep the Law.

3. Redeemed **grace** significantly impacts the presentation of the Gospel that is sufficient to bring sinners to salvation.

4. Redeemed **grace** can help us realize necessary reproduction as Jesus commanded in the Great Commission.

5. Redeemed **grace** can lead us into Christ-exalting missions and evangelism to the glory of God's **grace**.

6. Redeemed **grace** will lead us home in glorification.

More than a head knowledge of **grace**, real discovery starts when we 'put' God's power into Christ-glorifying activity. **Grace** shines in Gospel proclamation. This is the impetus of Paul's message of **grace** in 2 Corinthians 12. Paul is bombarded by criticism and he fights back. Paul boasts in God's sufficient **grace** especially as it's revealed and given during Gospel proclamation – and he proclaims it rightly!

In Romans 9, Paul talks about the stumbling stone of the Law. Moral Law is a stumbling stone when we whistle in the dark without culpability, when we do not properly bring it forward into New Covenant reality, or when we do not properly understand the reality and necessity of **grace**. Once we are born from above by **grace**, **it** empowers saints to obey the Law – never to condemn or deny Law. Scripture teaches that Law and redeemed **grace** do and must mix! This mixing is not like water and oil but as powdered milk is de-condensed or evaporated in water; **grace** and Law mix the same way in redemption.

Law and **grace** must mix if we are to be saved – God made this mixture eternally necessary in The Cross and Redemption. We can't have salvation without this mix, and we can't have sanctification without this **grace**ful Law-keeping either! The Law requires perfect obedience, perpetual obedience and perfect atonement for failure. Because we fall short, we need sufficient correction. Jesus provides all three components to satisfy God's Law in the life of His saints. In our Holiness void and sinfulness we could not do any of these but, in mercy and **grace**, He does all three in the stead of and IN His sheep.

When Paul speaks of the stumbling stone aspect of the Law, we tend to look too lightly at what he means. It's not just that Law makes us trip over ourselves to turn us to Christ; Christians stumble over the Law today as they did when Paul wrote Romans or Galatians. We throw the Law out of our path and shake the dust off our hands – thinking we solved Paul's dilemma – but this is similar to what the Pharisees did; we must rethink this! Rather than embrace a 'New Perspective of Paul' that I reject, we need to embrace what he taught about **grace**, regeneration and Law-keeping.

We must ask ourselves why Jesus never threw out the Law. Against contrary thoughts, **Jesus heightens the Law by fully obeying the Law as our Model**. We know His obedience earned salvation for His sheep but many stop thinking here – to stand on doctrine without necessary imitating-practice. Wrong! **His obedience demonstrates proper approach to Law through Grace.** Jesus fully fulfills the Old Covenant toward New Covenant **Grace** reality as the primary example for saints. If we want to stand on example – here's THE EXAMPLE! Imitate Christ in truth, **grace** and obedience!

This is a great place to unpack the realities of the change from the Old Covenant to the New Covenant. It might seem a little strange to unwrap Covenants in a **Grace**-versus-Mercy chapter but let me explain. Many see Mercy and Grace as God's favor, in light of sin. Glaring sin abounded in the Old Testament with vivid details. It's glaring in the New Testament with New Covenant correction. With implicit/explicit and Law/**Grace** contrasts, we can unfold the Covenants.

A Covenant is a binding agreement, a compact or promise. The associated and peripheral teachings of different Covenants can make it difficult to sort through this haze-factor. Correct Covenant answers may be the most difficult Scriptural answers to obtain; most hurdles and wrong thinking in the church surround this issue. In the search for correctness, our position must reflect a redeemed understanding. Redeemed eyes bring unveiled or exploded **grace** to the table but we must be willing to see and believe what **Grace** unpacks.

It's not easy to initially understand Covenant distinctions. To appreciate this real difficulty, consider a true statement and riddle. "**Blueberries are red when they are green**." Do you know the meaning of this riddle? Our mind first hears this as a contradiction, absurdity or stupid statement; if we leave it here, we will never understand. If we only think of colors – blue, red and green – it does not make sense, but all the words apply. At least three relationships flow into the whole riddle – species/fruit, color, and condition. Blueberries are a specific fruit. When they are not ripe, they are the color red. When blueberries are in the condition of being unripe, they are said to be green. "Blueberries (fruit) are red (in color) when they are green (condition)" is a perfectly true statement but we must know and/or learn the qualifiers to understand the riddle.

The confusion related to the above riddle reflects the difficulty of properly understanding biblical-Covenant qualifiers. We can magnify the difficulty about 10 X's and we wouldn't be close to the riddle-factor of learning redeemed Covenant distinctions. But, once we know the context of relationships mentioned, it's easier to see the beauty of the riddle. The riddle-factor is part of the haze we must work through – but God made the answer clear in the unpacked Cross as Paul explains. The torn or ripped veil, Christ's flesh according to Hebrews 10:20, opens the qualifiers of His majestic riddle, if you will. Once we literally and experientially see through the split veil, the picture is magnificent.

We do not need to know the intricacies of the riddle to enjoy eating blueberries! This type of logic – as true as it is – keeps some from pursuing a redeemed understanding of Covenants. Some types of Covenants seem to appear again and again in Scripture although in a different nature or context – making it difficult to ascertain correct application and understanding. Theologians and fellow Christ-followers attempt to work through the haze and do not always do this perfectly or at the same time – but our joy, fulfillment and Life are at stake.

Whether with math or riddles it's fun to understand how to work through qualifiers to get the right solution – especially if our Life depends on the outcome. The more Covenant intricacies we learn, the more fun and joy we find in walking in God's Will. Conversely, if we do not know why we do certain things, we could be confused and not know better. When contrary thoughts bump into our held-beliefs, we may resist what we should embrace. I see this dilemma often today and people do not think twice about their conclusions – even if they go against what God wants for Christ-reflectors. But we can wake up.

We may not talk about points that some think I should broach but at least two types of Covenant exist. Of the many Scriptural Covenants at the practical spiritual redeemed level, the two big ones are the Old and New Covenants. Directly related to these are the Covenant of Works and Covenant of Grace. Like our "Blueberries are red when they are green" riddle-statement, we must work through the various relationships to gain redeemed understanding.

Two huge qualifiers help. First, New Covenant reality is often found in the Old Testament, sometimes directly in Old Covenant contexts. Second, we must understand the Cross-reality in a backward sense to properly understand many Old Testament passages. Without these two qualifiers, we will always stumble over basic Covenant relationships. Be willing to lay down preconceived assumptions if we are to see God's truth and live in a God-pleasing way.

In the Old Testament, the Covenants include Redemption, Creation, Works, Old, Law, Promise and **Grace**. Major ones are listed under a person that speaks to another phase of redemptive history including those given to Adam, Noah, Abraham, (Sarah versus Hagar, and Isaac vs. Ishmael), Israel, Moses with Law as a peripheral attachment (creating great confusion) and David. By name or concept, many Covenants add to the haze but **grace** helps clear the haze.

Covenant in the New Testament is basically one – the New Covenant – but it's here that we see the mystery of the Old Covenant unpacked. In this unwrapping, qualifiers give understanding to the unknown or misunderstood details of the haze and riddle-relationships so that we can see and practice correctly. Like our Blueberry riddle, when we sort the species, colors and conditions of Covenants we can explain biblical 'riddles' that will take eternity to 'unravel' in fullness.

Scripture contrasts Law and Gospel. In the typical contrast, the Covenant of Works is closely related to the Law and the Gospel is closely related to the Covenant of **Grace**. Some say Law and Gospel are not contained in the same Covenant but they are kissing cousins in the New Covenant; this detail might surprise some of us.

It's crucial to know the timeline for when the New Covenant begins; it helps to put things in order. Some think a direct relationship exists between Old and New Covenants with Old and New Testaments but this is incorrect. Jesus says His Kingdom has come but the New Covenant did not begin until His Death on the Cross and Upper Room Discourse-verbiage unpacks this helpful qualifier. This is why the ripped veil screams more messages than we first imagine – a whole New Covenant has come and the Old Covenant is now obsolete for saints; but what this means is critical for our belief and practice.

The New Covenant is often misunderstood[7] because we jump to unwarranted conclusions. Let me list a few of our difficulties. The Old Covenant is rendered obsolete per Hebrews 8:13. As the New

Covenant comes, the schoolmaster or guardian is no longer needed per Galatians 3:24-27. We are released from law in Galatians 3 and Romans 7. The Covenant of death, written in stone, is passing away in fading glory per 2 Corinthians 3. Misunderstanding can lead to problems like stillbirths, doctrinal confusion related to salvation and sanctification, the bobble head mentality and **grace** to name a few. Sorting through Scriptural qualifiers is not always easy; therefore we need help so we don't throw out something vitally important.

We must ask and answer: To which Covenant does the New Testament refer when it speaks of the Old Covenant becoming obsolete or passing away? When it says we are under **grace** rather than law, what does this mean? Many accept easy answers that deny overarching or eternal truths without digging into the implications. Scripture 'supplies' answers but the answers must be gathered in a conglomerate overarching form like our Blueberry riddle. The scopes of salvation and Covenant are great biblical riddles and are all unpacked or unveiled in the Cross and His Finished Work – if we see correctly.

The more-difficult Covenants to recognize are the Covenants of Redemption, Creation and Grace. The Covenant of Redemption per Ephesians 1:4, made between the three persons of the Trinity, basically flows into the Covenant of Grace. The Covenant of Creation is the agreement to make man in God's image from Genesis 1:26, from which we understand the necessity of regeneration and Christ-likeness. In my understanding, the Covenant of **Grace** is the New Covenant!

Satan's perversion of Covenant provoked The Fall and our car wrecks; these must be overcome for salvation to occur. God must perform Justification and regeneration and, with proactive working, we overcome in conversion. This is accomplished when the New Covenant is applied to our souls and we walk in this practicality per 2 Corinthians 5:17. The following list qualifies the New Covenant rather than dissect its technical teaching. Grant charity as it's offered in loose form.

Old/New Covenant Contrasts

Old Covenant	New Covenant
Covenant of Redemption (in haze forms)	Covenant of Redemption (in unveiled form)
Perverted Covenant of Creation	Covenant of Re-Creation
Covenant of Works (minus grace)	Covenant of Grace
Veiled haze (Promise)	Unveiled mystery (Fulfillment)
Law with self-justification	Gospel with Christ's Cross
Law with servile fear	Law with the power of grace
Adam's sinful lineage	Adam's regeneration lineage
First Adam	Second Adam
In Adam – sinful lifeview	In Christ – redeemed lifeview
Cain – covenant-breakers	Abel – covenant-keepers
Gentiles, as God deniers	Spiritual Jews; God acceptors
Assumed implicit salvation	Applied explicit salvation
Under Law unto salvation	Under Law from salvation
Hagar, the bondwoman	Sarah, the free woman
Ishmael, son of bondage	Isaac, son of promise
Abraham's sinful bloodline	Abraham's faith bloodline
Satanic sinful flesh	Spirit/Grace-provoked flesh
Deliverer in a basket	Deliverer through Incarnation
Administration of Moses	Administration of Christ
Law written on cold-stone	Law written on living hearts
God rejecters – pending death	God fearers – pending life
System worshippers	Christ worshippers
Covenant of Death	Covenant of Eternal Life
Glory in Moses' face	Glory in Christ's face
Moses the Mediator	Christ the Mediator
Human sinful priests	Divine sinless Priest
Limited in-waiting sacrifice	Sufficient complete sacrifice
Blood/mercy emphasis	Body/grace emphasis
Admission thru Mercy Seat	Throne of Grace Admission
Law as a schoolmaster	Law as the family rules
Mosaic Covenant as a guardian	New Covenant as leader
Servants and vassals	Sons and heirs
Pharisees – man's traditions	Ministers of graceful Law
National Israel	Universal Church
Vain philosophy of life	Living graceful sanctification
Brotherhood of man	Brotherhood in Christ
'Righteousness' through works	Righteousness through Christ

We must solve myriad biblical relationships in our Blueberries-are-red-when-they-are-green-**Covenant**-riddle if we expect to honor and practice God's New Covenant view. Each point in the above list may need additional qualifiers – it would require another book – yet most are addressed. I trust this list helps us work through the haze to see and practice the New Covenant in a Christ-reflecting **grace**ful way.

In New Covenant writing – Acts to Revelation, and maybe John's Gospel – we struggle to properly understand 1) the contrasts between different law contexts, 2) Law and **grace**, and 3) Old and New Covenant-contrasts in different settings and relationships. For some, extended thoughts can be clear as mud, and this gets us back to haze factors. We can be confused and susceptible to wrong teaching and/or conclusions without serious evaluation – leading to wrong living.

A Mathematical illustration might give insight into the teachings and beliefs that can flow from Scripture into our interpretations to explain the associated confusion. Each of the three points above contains at least 5 possible variations. With the above three doctrines, with five variables considered for each, the formula 5x5x5 manifests 125 different variations. With this in mind, it's easy to see why confused understanding brings confusion through wrong implications.

To see from God's view is necessary – especially as we see New Covenant reality in the midst of Old Covenant texts. With that in mind, let's briefly unpack the contrasts in the above three most-crucial points that I highlight. You might be surprised by the outcomes.

A – The Law

1) The Law can refer to a <u>Moral-Law code</u> established by direct revelation from God to direct His people in worship, relationship to Him, and social relationships with others. This eternal Moral Law comes from God, issues from His nature or Character and is Holy, Righteous and Good. The Ten Commandments summarize this Moral <u>Law</u>.

2) The law can refer to how the unregenerate man sees in his rebellious state. Even saints struggle to overcome this former yet residual view. The unregenerate soul must see that the Law drives him to Christ for Justification. Yes, it's a guide for Life but – without **grace** through regeneration – the Law breeds death without power.

3) The law can refer to Israel's national law code that is linked to the moral Law but should not be seen as organically the same. This erroneous connection is a huge error perpetuated by wrong teaching and rebellious hearts. The Israelite national law code may be part of the abrogated or obsolete Old Covenant but must not be confused with Moral Law. Obsoleteness must be seen through the eyes of **grace**.

4) The law rightly refers to the Law that forms the basis of the Covenant of Works – but this more-correctly refers to the perverted imagination or paradigm that sees obedience to the Law as gaining justification with God. Saints are free from *this* law but not from the Law! The gospel delivers us from *this* law but plants us in another or new Law that's essentially and eternally the same per Romans 6:12-14; 6:20-23; and 7:4-8:11. The Covenant of Works is part of the 'obsolete' Covenant, even as **the New Covenant puts us under the Moral Law in the hand of Christ through His graceful power**.

5) The law can refer to the law of the mind that perpetually drives us – either to follow self-law or Law in the power of the flesh versus obeying God's Law through the overcoming power of **grace**. This **grace**less flesh-law of conscience brings bondage and death but God's answer is **Grace** and **grace**ful obedience rather than to deny, reject or cast His Law out. A mind-law-acknowledgement caused Paul to cry out, "Wretched man that I am! Who will deliver me from this body of death?" This can refer to the tormented mind of duplicitous thinking in a regenerate person – where our mind wars against the residual sin in the flesh – but I think it applies better to Paul's unregenerate state from the Cross-view of a redeemed person. Varied views exist but the

Redeemed View of Life provoked by **Grace** solves most of the confusion. **Grace**-Law gives Paul's answer, "Thanks be to God through Jesus Christ our Lord! So <u>then</u> (in duplicitous thinking), I myself serve the Law of God with my mind but with my flesh I serve the law of sin."

If Paul is speaking about a regenerated person, he might refer to one who does not know the full power of **grace**ful obedience – like the man who does not know about the power of the chain saw. If this is the case, the verse means, "So <u>then</u> (in my regenerate state without the power of **grace)**, I myself serve the Law of God with my mind (meaning that I embrace the Law inconsistently – intellectually but not practically) but with my flesh I serve the law of sin (without grace, I fall into the merry-go-round cycle of forgiveness-sin-confession). This also may refer to Paul's **Grace**-progression, leading to doxology when he discovers the overcoming power of redeemed **grace**. **Grace saves us from the futility of a graceless approach to the Law**.

There really is freedom in the Moral Law through **Grace** as Paul teaches. Consider the next few verses in Romans 8:1-4:

> There is therefore now no condemnation for those who are in Christ Jesus. **For the law of the Spirit of life has set you free in Christ Jesus from the law of sin and death**. For God has done what the law, weakened by the flesh, could not do. By sending his own Son in the likeness of sinful flesh and for sin, **he condemned sin in the flesh, in order that the righteous requirement of the law might be fulfilled in us, who walk** not according to the flesh but **according to the Spirit**.

Against the unregenerate backdrop of bondage to sin and death, **once we are in Christ we no longer bear the condemnation of that 'lifeless' law**. By the application of Christ's Atoning sacrifice on the Cross by the Spirit, the <u>righteous requirement</u> of the Law is fulfilled in us. It's easy to think this righteous requirement is merely Christ's Righteousness applied to our account (the reality of regeneration) but **Paul drives at the redeemed reality of sanctification – graceful Law-keeping through Christ's Faith, Sight and Power**. What a plan!

Once we are adopted as sons, it makes perfect sense to offer righteousness like Jesus always did; in this way, we are well-pleasing to God. We do not keep the Law to earn Justification, but **once Justification is applied, we keep the Law in the freedom of the Spirit** – the freedom to **grace**fully obey. This is the logical outflow of one who walks according to the Holy Spirit's power – in God's favor.

B – The contrasts between Law versus Gospel, Law versus Spirit or Law versus Grace; (see Colquhoun and Herman Witsius.[8)]

1) These contrasts can refer to technical distinctions between either pairing. If however, we confuse the technical meanings, we confuse the practical reality. Worse, we slander God's Word in the process with faulty interpretation, teaching and living.

2) These contrasts can refer to practical distinctions between either pairing. As practice flows from our thinking, we must be careful not to twist God's Word at this point. The practical point is hugely different between perspectives of unregenerate (not rebirthed ones) and regenerate ones; this correction is one great worthwhile struggle.

3) These contrasts can refer to general labels that speak to differences between Old and New Testaments versus distinctions in Old and New Covenants. We must avoid lumping eternal facts or redeemed factors into the Old Covenant *because* they occur in the same context. Seek the brighter shine per 2 Corinthians 3:7-11.

4) These contrasts can refer to necessary distinctions between approaching God's Will through man's perspective versus God's perspective. This may distinguish condition and lifeview. As condition, man's perspective is always in need of God's **grace**-remedy. As lifeview, only a redeemed person can adopt a redeemed lifeview.

5) These contrasts can refer to how we see **grace** – this partially explains why I take great pains to explain these points through redeemed eyes. The common definition of grace leaves many in the

powerless state Paul describes in Romans 7; conversely, this is why many are confused by my redeemed definition of **grace** – thinking it's not possible. A redeemed definition of **grace** helps us know exactly where our power comes and why God gives it – to walk in His Holiness.

C – The Old Covenant/New Covenant distinction

1) This distinction can refer to God's-creation-mandate versus the perverted understanding that flows from Adam's-sinful-loins. It's crucial that we realize this necessary qualifier in our discussions.

2) This distinction often refers to the Israelite Covenant after they left Egypt but this view can be split several times. Colquhoun demonstrates a dual offering in the context of what many call the Old Covenant. First, God covenants with the nation of Israel – the collective (#1) civil use. Second, God covenants with unregenerate ones, calling them to Christ through the Law – the (#2) pedagogical (schoolmaster) use. Third, **God covenants with regenerate ones, calling them to Law-keeping through Christ's hand with His power – the (#3) normative use**. Especially in God's Exodus-giving, we must interpret Law carefully; otherwise we put ourselves in practical bondage.

Let me illustrate a humorous point relating to how some wrongly view the Law. We leave home intending to drive our vehicle to our place of employment. Our vehicle sufficiently takes us to our destination. We would not say to the teenager we pass as we walk into our office, "Here's the keys to my vehicle; it got me here and now it's obsolete! You can have it!" We would never dream of this, yet many do this with the 'obsolete' Law. It serves a purpose (#1) to bring us to Christ (#2). Its purpose at that point is finished or obsolete but now we need it for another purpose – **grace**ful Christ-reflection (#3). We need our vehicles for other purposes; so, we need the Moral Law!

3) This distinction can be the Levitical structure commanded to the nation of Israel; this view – though correct with proper qualifiers – is

often taken of out context and stretched beyond what Scripture warrants. The Levitical or Mosaic Administration *was* abrogated or declared obsolete for the church but is further distorted when we do not correctly split the Moral Law's prior giving from its 'Mosaic-giving.'

4) This Old/New distinction can be attached to what is described as the Covenant of Works that sees man 'create' salvation through good works or self-righteousness; but true sentiment exists.

5) This distinction can refer to the **grace**less approach of the Law that leads to futility and God-violating thoughts and behaviors. But our look at Romans suggests this **grace**less approach speaks more to the futility of unregenerated ones in bondage to sin and death.

With redeemed vision, New Covenant power is vivid. **We see Law for its <u>saintly purpose</u> – the normative use (#3)! God's written-on-heart-Law is the same as the written-on-stone-Law – but with The Spirit's grace-power to bring obedience**. When we realize Law speaks to regeneration, salvation and redeemed lifeview through Gospel Faith (normative use), we can embrace its fullness. This Law-message is essential for every disciple to know and live.

God's **grace** is also revealed in the course of suffering for the Gospel's sake. Paul learned this critical lesson – to sufficiently relay this powerful message to those in need of **grace**. In his 'private lesson' that contained God's commentary (who receives this?), Paul says,

> Therefore I will boast all the more gladly of my weaknesses, **so that the power of Christ [grace] may rest upon me**. For the sake of Christ, then, I am content with weaknesses, insults, hardships, persecutions and calamities. **For when I am weak** [spiritually/physically]**, then I am strong [in the power of grace]**.[9]

Through **grace**, Paul knew God would really be with him – it would be more-than-sufficient! Paul had the thorn-in-his-flesh answer. Speaking as if after-the-fact in the midst of ongoing commentary, Paul learns that **God especially gives grace in the midst of – and for the purpose of**

Gospel proclamation. Afterward, Paul knew **grace** was God's power to advance the Gospel. Paul's thrust was to teach THIS **grace** that he learned, so Paul said, "Imitate me as I imitate Christ." If we learn *this* **grace**, we can also teach this to those under our influence!

God gives grace for redemptive purposes – to Justify, Sanctify and proclaim the Gospel. Paul understands that **grace** applies to his special commission – to unpack historical haze through mystery-unveiling. He unpacks the majesty of New Covenant truth, the application of **grace only to believers**, Gospel boldness, spiritual warfare, the purpose of suffering, worship to God for electing **grace**, the limited scope of future heaven-dwellers, faith-living-**grace**, **grace**ful understanding and the narrow focus to regenerated ones through the church. Wow! His heartthrob is expressed magnificently in Ephesians 3. It's given in its escalating entirety; emphasis mine. **This grace** is given to all saints; does it possess you? If so, live its fullness.

> For this reason I, Paul, a prisoner for Christ Jesus on behalf of you Gentiles – assuming that you have heard of **the stewardship of God's grace that was given to me for you, how the mystery was made known to me by revelation**, as I have written briefly. When you read this, you can perceive my insight into the mystery of Christ, which was not made known to the sons of men in other generations **as it has now been revealed to his holy apostles and prophets by the Spirit**. This mystery is that the Gentiles are fellow heirs, members of the same body, and partakers of the same promise in Christ Jesus through the gospel. **Of this gospel I was made a minister according to the gift of God's grace, which was given me by the working of his power**. To me, though I am the very least of all the saints, **this grace was given**, to preach to the Gentiles the unsearchable riches of Christ, and **to bring to light for everyone what is the plan of the mystery hidden for ages in God who created all things, so that through the church the manifold wisdom of God might now be made known** to the rulers and authorities in heavenly places. **This was according to the eternal purpose that he has realized in Christ Jesus** our Lord, in whom we have boldness and access with confidence through our faith in him. So I ask you not to lose heart over what I am suffering for you, which is your glory. For this reason I bow my knees before the Father, from

whom every family in heaven and on earth is named, **that according to the riches of his glory he may grant you to be strengthened with power through his Spirit in your inner being, so that** Christ may dwell in your hearts through faith – that you, being rooted and grounded in love, may have strength to comprehend with all the saints what is the breadth and length and height and depth, and to know the love of Christ that surpasses knowledge, **that you may be filled with all the fullness of God.** Now to him who is able to do far more abundantly than all that we ask or think, **according to the power at work within us**, to him be glory in the church and in Christ Jesus throughout all generations, forever and ever. Amen.

I trust you begin to see why I cry out for a reformed definition of **grace** that will be unpacked further as we go along.

---

1 Theologians speak of a valid distinction between Christ's active and passive obedience. Active obedience speaks to what Christ lived in <u>Law-keeping action</u> versus passive obedience that highlights <u>what happened to Him in suffering</u> – though active in a real sense. Popular teaching wrongly suggests 'passive' obedience in sanctification that distorts necessary active obedience on our part. I make this link between doctrine and practice especially as it manifests a significant difference between grace and mercy.

2 I contend for an exegetical distinction between expiation and propitiation – more on grounds of English grammar in our Bible. The prefix 'ex' refers to a degree of coming out, as in exit, exhale, exile or Exodus. Expiation links well with how I define mercy - seen thru His passive obedience, as 'taking out sin.' On the other hand, the prefix 'pro' refers to putting in or a positive adding as in proton, prototype, or provision. Propitiation links well with how I define grace – as <u>the positive adding of merit through Christ's Atoning Work</u> and particularly through His body or flesh seen through His active obedience.

3 The first reference is Genesis 8:21. The second is Exodus 29:18 where blood is instructively useful but somewhat a throw-away item. <u>Burning flesh is a sweet smelling aroma to the Lord</u>. No matter the offering – food, grain or animal – the flesh was a sweet smelling aroma to the Lord. Primarily we see this in Leviticus and Numbers: Lev. 1:9; 2:2; 2:9; 2:12 (minus leaven as a sign of sin); 3:5, 16; 4:7, 31; 6:15, 21; 8:21, 28; 17:6; 23:13, 18; and 26:31. Leviticus 26:31 confirms that God will not shine His favor on blatant sin no matter that sacrifices are brought. There are almost as many references in Numbers.

4 Our overcoming occurs because Jesus overcame; this is grace-power seen in John 16:33, Romans 12:21, 1 John 2:13-14 & 4:4, and Revelation 17:14.

5 This is seen clearly in Ephesians 1:19-20 in the context of verses 15-23. This power is referenced in Romans 1:16, 9:17, 13:1, 1 Cor. 2:5, and 2 Cor. 12:9.

6 My friend Shaun Golden has this quote on a plaque on his study wall. I need to buy a few Dallas Willard books because I love his thinking and statements.

7 Many great books teach Covenants. Three I recommend highly are Michael Horton's *Introducing Covenant Theology*, O. Palmer Robertson's *The Christ of the Covenants*, and John Colquhoun's *A Treatise on The Law and The Gospel*.

8 Herman Witsius, *The Economy of the Covenants between God and Man Comprehending a Complete Body of Divinity* (London: Begg, 1837). This book is referenced in Henri Blocher's chapter *Old Covenant, New Covenant* in *Always Reforming: Explorations in Systematic Theology* (Downers Grove, IL.: IVP Academic, 2006) 241.

9 2 Corinthians 12:9b-10

Chapter 11 – God's Repentance, Faith and Conversion

In a day when repentance, conversion and even faith are questioned realities in the church, these necessary doctrines go together under a popular biblical motif. In many places, Scripture presents the Three Step Process of **grace**ful change known as sanctification – the practical process of becoming holy. A generalization suggests these three doctrines are the totality of biblical salvation.

Paul is directly attached to 13 of the 27 New Testament books; 14 if he authored Hebrews. He is 'responsible' for more than half of New Testament substance so he had great opportunity to teach this Three Step Process; he taught it often and well. **The Three Step Process is 1) Put off the old man; 2) Get your thinking right; and 3) Put On Christ.** In Paul's writings, these three elements seek us out.

In the same order, Repentance, Faith, and Conversion parallel these three steps; this is why I put them together! They are not always presented in this order but are present, even if not mentioned. This order-and-label-ambiguity can add to our haze-confusion but it can be easily overcome. These doctrines may not always have a 'label' to easily identify but their manifestation demonstrates their presence.

Teachings of necessary repentance, faith and conversion are taught throughout Scripture. Sadly some Christ professors deny the reality or necessity of any element but ambiguity disappears once we see these doctrines for what they are. As we consider God's Will, we must see these ingredients of God's salvation as necessary as a living person must have blood, oxygen and food. On top of Chapter Six, some technical teaching lays a foundation for a redeemed picture.

Each element has different connotations in various settings. This can lead to minor confusion but a whole-Bible view can provide correct understanding. Points are not hard and fast like cement but their structure and essence is typically the same throughout the Bible.

Repentance

Repentance is often seen as practical penance or contrition. This limited view somewhat skews the biblical meaning, as <u>sorrow</u> is present and sometimes demanded but may not lead to a correction. Sometimes forgiveness is 'withheld' until 'repentance' is complete and even a 'correction' may not manifest biblical repentance. It took years for the Spirit to correct my mind so I want to help others avoid pitfalls of erroneous teaching. Great confusion exists over what repentance is; it's typically taught that a 180 degree turn accurately pictures repentance. The diagram below shows this prevalent view.

Common View of Repentance Today

<Toward Wickedness ← Away From <----->Toward -→Holiness >

Repentance

Though this picture may look biblical, two faulty aspects are present. First, some see repentance as merely a change of mind. A change of mind is necessary, but repentance is much more. Second, some learn repentance as "Turn around and go in the opposite direction." Both are true but **grace**ful qualifiers are missing.

Let's unpack this view that is easily misconstrued. Some believe they repent yet stay in sinful behaviors. Is this possible, as their practice stays in left-side behavior? Some play on Satan's merry-go-round and keep going in circles. As they cycle to the right, they might feel flurries of repentance but the merry-go-round takes them back to left-side behavior without remorse or victory (see pg. 92).

Others talk as if God is almost pleased with their sin. Is this possible? They fool themselves because, as they cycle to the right, they plead 1 John 1:9, "If we confess our sins, He is faithful and just to forgive us our sins and to cleanse us from all unrighteousness." Then, as they cycle back toward left-side behavior, they imagine they have God's forgiveness and blessing in the midst of their sin. In this circular living, they are 'convinced' they practice God's truth because they quote and 'live' Scripture. Many do not want off this unbiblical ride.

When someone tells a merry-go-round-rider they need to get off this ride, they cry "Foul!" On their fun ride, they do not understand why using Scripture to 'do repentance' is not sufficient to please God – surely it's pleases their flesh! In a huge way we learn, "Be true to yourself! And don't let anyone take away your free will!"

Others are unwilling to see beyond their paradigm, so they cannot see a redeemed picture. They think, "Why should we do differently? We're doing okay without your input, thank you very much!" I wish I could break other's faulty spiritual paradigms but I don't have this ability – only the Spirit can do this as we learn overcoming **grace**.

The common teaching of repentance heard in many churches says, "Change your mind, and *do* a 180-degree turn." By itself, this is correct but not when people keep riding the merry-go-round with faulty assurance. It's correct to change our mind, turn around, and move in the direction of God's Holiness – "But how far must we go?" some ask.

I do not want to disrespect biblical teaching as such, so I focus on consistent teaching that accurately reflects the repentance picture of salvation. If we consider a biblical picture of repentance, what should it look like? Consider a chart to help us work through the implications.

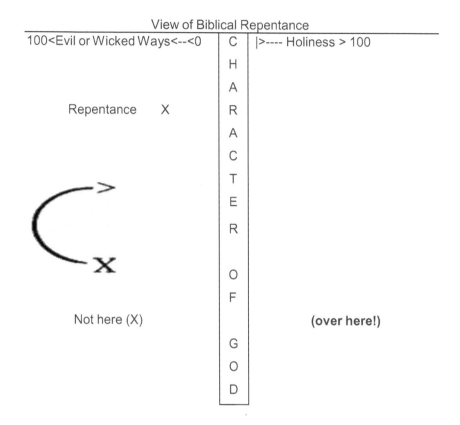

View of Biblical Repentance

| 100<Evil or Wicked Ways<--<0 | C | \|>---- Holiness > 100 |

Many agree with the common definition – *Change your mind and do a 180-degree turn* – but correcting qualifiers are needed. The problem with this generic definition is that it can excuse a life of sin with a 1 John 1:9 'blessing.' I contend the typical definition of grace adds to repentance-confusion. To the degree that our definition distorts truth, let's exclude error from consideration. Add God's Character to our dividing line to see God's point that rebellious ones don't hear or see.

A biblical corrective shows that a crucial key is 'missing.' Romans 6:1-2 provides repentance qualifiers, "What shall we say then? Are we to continue in sin that **grace** may abound? By no means! How can we who died to sin still live in it?" Merry-go-round-riders merely pick which verse they hang their actions on – without knowing that Scripture does not contradict itself. We cannot judge God's Law by our opinions, but many do. Others stay camped on their site – come hell or high water – and that might be what they will face if they do not run from that campsite and use Christ's real equipment to overcome.

There is no freedom in left-side living as it only brings bondage. Correction comes when repentance ultimately turns believers away from sin to be conformed to Christ's image. I once heard someone say ' Repentance is like a military about-face where we respectfully submit to the King of the Universe' – great definition! Repentance does not 'bring' forgiveness to leave us on the wrong side or in the wrong site. Repentance must be perpetual, but not the merry-go-round variety.

Many cling to a Free Will campsite – believing that, without this entity, our humanity is something less than God designed. Let's briefly examine free will to see its essence and where it comes from. Many confuse freedom of choice with free will – the dictionary puts them together but a redeemed distinction helps. Webster's New World College Dictionary defines free will as "the freedom of the will to choose a course of action without external coercion but in accordance with the ideals or moral outlook of the individual" – this is the problem! If our will is submitted to God's Will, we see free will **grace**fully and differently.

As the Father of Lies, Satan's goal is to distort and destroy God's Holiness and Works. In Adam's innocence, free will was fully submitted to God's Will. **Adam and Eve possessed free will *before* sin** – full-orbed willingness to follow God' Word – but as free agents they freely gave it away. After Satan's deception through the 'right' of autonomy, they lost Holiness and fell into sin. Thereafter, like every aspect of sinful humanity, free will is always perverted after Satan's design. In the pejorative sense, Free Will has more to do with man's sinful liberty to reject God's Will rather than pursue it with **grace**.

With a twisted will, man does not embrace or perform God's Will because of sinful motives and Satan's negative coercion. Now, free will is derived from Satan. Perverted free will – unattached to God's Law – destroyed man's **grace**-relationship with God. Think about its source if you cling to a personal right of free will. People who hang onto free will also hang onto Satan's evil autonomous ingredient.

In our sinful car-wreck-state, we cannot come to Christ with a free will. The person that hangs onto <u>free will</u> never submits to God's Will until they choose to – but choosing submission does not speak of <u>free will</u> but <u>free agency</u> – and gracefully so. The redeemed mind says, "To hell with *this* free will as it only leads away from God's Will. Since it originates with Satan it can go to the pit where it belongs." Only when God redeems us and grants new life with a changed will can we come close to a will that freely obeys. **Freedom is the power to do rightly** – this speaks of **grace**-provoked Law-obedience.

People are deceived about repentance when they merely 'change their mind' or 'confess sin.' Many professors and deluded sheep violate God's Law without remorse. Insufficient repentance leaves people entrenched in left-side behaviors, often with a smugness or arrogance that denies a valid profession. In Repentance we turn from sin to serve the living God. According to biblical writers, repentance requires <u>leaving</u> left-side behaviors and <u>cleaving</u> to right-side behaviors. A great definition for repentance is a **grace**ful about-face where – like Joshua – we submit to our commanding officer.

Faith

As faith is expanded in the closing chapters, I will give a few nuggets throughout this chapter. <u>Faith is the active manifestation of believing God</u>. Similar to Hebrews 11:1, true repentance demonstrates that salvation has occurred as Faith evidences itself by being firmly planted in right-behavior. **Faith always obeys God!** Faith never disobeys although His sheep can! Disobedience violates Faith. God gives Faith to His sheep in Justification (Ephesians 2:8-9); thereafter faith is always a proactive venture with the King of Kings. The just live by His Faith. Follow Jesus closely so others see His Faith in your faith!

Conversion

Conversion is emphasized in the closing chapters but a quick overview is given. Some see no need to be converted because they were taught "You are forgiven and saved!" Paul rebukes conversion-refusal as license in Romans 6:1. We all know one who thinks they repented and are 'saved' yet perpetually commit sin, with the belief of impunity or no culpability. Continued sin in the face of God's Word demonstrates lack of biblical repentance and faith. Consider how Paul presents all three elements in 1 Thessalonians 1:2-9, emphasis mine:

> We give thanks to God always for all of you, constantly mentioning you in our prayers, **remembering** before our God and Father **your work of faith** and labor of love and steadfastness of hope in our Lord Jesus Christ. **For we know**, brothers loved by God, that he has chosen you, because **our gospel came to you** not only in word, but also **in power** [grace] and in the Holy Spirit **and with full conviction**. You know what kind of men we proved to be among you for your sake. And **you became imitators of us and of the Lord,** for you received the word in much affliction, with the joy of the Holy Spirit, so that **you became an example to all the believers** Macedonia and in Achaia. For not only has the word of the Lord sounded forth from you in Macedonia and Achaia, but **your faith in God has gone forth everywhere**, so that we need not say anything. For they themselves report concerning us the kind of reception we had among you, and *how **you turned to God from idols to serve the living and true God**.*

A redeemed view ponders how these three elements fit together. Going back to John 11 regeneration and resurrection, Martha and Mary's brother and Jesus' close friend Lazarus died. By design, Jesus delayed long enough for Lazarus to die – and be dead for four days. Hebrews knew 4-days-dead was dead! John 11:6 says, "So, when he heard that Lazarus was ill, He stayed two days longer in the place where He was." Jesus comforts the family by saying "I AM the Resurrection and the Life. Whoever believes in Me, though he die, yet shall he live." Jesus was about to accomplish John's Sign #7.

When He arrived at the tomb, after weeping, Christ called Lazarus out of the grave. Jesus called a dead man back to life! This is a clear miracle but it's more. In this real-life parable, Jesus clearly teaches the reality of new birth in the Three Step Process. After Jesus calls "Lazarus, come out!" the once-dead Lazarus comes out! This always happens when He calls people out of spiritual death. We may not hear His command per se, but when He speaks, we come out! Better than E.F. Hutton commercials, when Jesus speaks, we listen!

In the Valley of Dry Bones of Ezekiel 37, the prophet obeys God and commands life to come to a valley of bones; this is another powerful picture of new birth. It's not an exciting proposition to preach to dead bones but God calls prophets, pastors and disciples to do this. We often preach to dead bones and God must bring them to life – a critical qualifier. Those who hear may think they did the work but God's call is critical to our walk from death. Has He called you?

We can easily miss that Lazarus comes out 'dressed' with grave clothes. When we are called from the dead, grave clothes must be taken off. Taking-off-grave-clothes represents repentance – things we take off after we possess new life. **This is why an outside-in approach does not work; we must have inside-out reality**. We can only take grave clothes off after we have new life. Attempts to take off grave clothes before new birth is tantamount to wearing fig-leaf-clothes but this might parallel what a God-fearer does with right motive. Jesus could have taken them off but says, "Unbind him, and let him go!"[1]

I can picture Lazarus walking out like an Egyptian mummy. At first, others start taking his wraps off. As soon as he could, Lazarus happily got involved. Who wants grave cloths on longer than needed? When new life beats in our veins, we want nothing to do with death; we want grave clothes off! Rebirthed ones want their sins and dysfunctional garments off! This unveiling may take time but this unwrapping must occur quickly; if not, something is seriously wrong!

Like Lazarus, we need the help of others to take these stinky wraps off – until we can join in the needful but oft-messy procedure. An objection on Lazarus' part would be pretty stupid but some squeal bloody murder. Why? When we point out sin and hear objections, it's like – "Do you want to stay in those grave clothes or do you want help with them?" Without saying it, some imply they do not want help. I wonder, "Did they come back from the dead or not?" Maybe not!

When one is raised from the grave, we want our death clothes off! When 'resurrected ones' squeal about removing their death clothes, something is wrong – as resurrected life rejoices in repentance. Remember Isaiah 55? Those who come back from the dead rejoice in repentance. Think about it: squealing about others helping us take off grave cloths is totally foreign to one who is given re-created life.

In a tongue-in-cheek way, maybe stillbirths are those called out of the grave who refuse help in getting their grave-clothes off and die because they cannot untangle themselves. Get over the thought; accept the help. Get out of those clothes and start walking in **grace**!

Like egg on our face or a log in our eye,[2] repentance might mean we have sin on our face and need someone to take off what we can't see. If we are upset with those who want to help, we short-circuit necessary repentance. Spiritually speaking, we don't repent of being dead but we repent of baggage we bring from the grave; there is a difference and, further down the road, we do repent of ongoing sin.

King David needed the prophet Nathan to help him see his sin in 2 Samuel 11-12. At times, we need outside help to work through repentance – to check our pride, spiritual temperature, or whether we are alive in Christ. If 'repentance' does not turn us from sin to obedience, we are likely not saved. Do not deceive yourself. Ponder the definition you embrace because it has eternal consequences.

As a doctrine, some see repentance as a one-time act that occurs when we come out of the grave but biblical repentance is seen in a humble ongoing life-attitude. Even redeemed sinners fall short of God's glorious **grace** and need to repent. As taking off grave cloths is necessary for a functional life after resurrection, so repentance is vitally necessary to our functional life in Christ after regeneration. This is why we must approach the Lord's Supper in a repentant manner.

If we are resurrected, a mental-living-correction occurs – look at Jonah. We'll look at the life and experiences of Jonah on page 237-239. This mental correction – or redeemed lifeview – parallels faith. Some wrongly think faith is creative thinking to give us what we want. Spiritual resurrection pursues ongoing-mental-living-correction. I never experienced physical resurrection but I've experienced spiritual resurrection and know it **grace**fully corrects thinking and faith.

As Scrooge in the Christmas Carol, spiritual resurrection causes us to know we are given a second chance at life and we can know that others are brought to Life by a Life-Giving Savior by what we see in their life. Instead of living for ourselves, God lives strong in us through the power of His Word, Gospel, **grace** and Spirit. What an opportunity to refocus, transform, or redeem our thinking to His Will and Ways! This is the reality and transfigurative power of redeemed faith.

Faith is not mysterious. Responding to God's Holiness with obedience is faith-natural for regenerated ones. At its root, faith is God-following action. An October 2012 *Disciple Magazine* article by Justin Lonus: *Obedience is Elementary* quotes Dietrich Bonheoffer from *The Cost of Discipleship* who taught that **trusting God and obedience are inseparable actions**. He stated "Only he who believes can obey! Only he who obeys can believe!" I love that two-sided **grace**ful quote.

Hebrews 11 shows <u>faith – the action of belief</u> – as obedience to God's call. Rather than faith being merely sincere or gracelessly human as some practice, **redeemed faith necessarily obeys God's Will**. His call demands response and redeemed faith gives it! Once we see Faith as changing our thinking to conform to Christ's obedient mind, we realize why the pursuit of a Christian lifeview is critical to our new life.

Against professors who pursue a redeemed lifeview as drudgery, making professed faith suspect, Faith is as natural in the redeemed soul as breathing air is to a healthy human. Faith parallels breathing but requires cognitive and volitional working whereas breathing comes so natural that we seldom think of it as a working reality. In this comparison, a redeemed soul naturally breathes faith.

In regards to salvation, our faith believes in the "Believe in the Lord, and you will be saved!" conditional command – tied to true faith. Like Lazarus, when we hear, we believe! Understanding the link between profession of faith and reality of faith is where many flounder. The Gospel Call is 'Repent and Believe in the Lord Jesus Christ.' **Regeneration, being called from the dead, causes redeemed faith!**

Faith, or resurrected believing, follows Justification. In an ongoing way, <u>faith breathes **grace**</u>. Faith always believes God's Word and Truth. Faith learns His Will. Faith walks in His Ways. Faith learns His Holy Character by **Grace**. Faith knows and obeys His Law through the power of **grace.** Faith lives and proclaims His gospel. The question we must ask is: Where are you in Step Two correction?

After pulling off our grave cloths (#1) and changing our stinking thinking (#2), we put on clothes that demonstrate new life reality (#3). We don't stand naked in repentance, faith puts on **grace**-clothes; in this way, Step #3 parallels and pursues conversion. <u>Conversion</u> puts on Christ, good works and ever-growing **grace**ful sanctification. It can be designated a complete act but should be acknowledged as an ongoing necessary work only complete in glory. With redeemed faith, conversion means we are always in-process. Paul would say, "If the cake resides in you, put icing on it!" Conversion seeks this reality.

Conversion confirms God's work in us by building Christ reflection into our **graced** selves. Conversion confirms God's work in us but it cannot be divorced from repentance and faith. Regeneration requires these three results; visible transformation comes when individuals and churches live and teach these truths. We might not have as many 'decisions' but possession is the law of heaven. Learning to live in right-side behavior manifests conversion with a living faith.

Living in right-side behavior requires holy unction as **Grace** provides. I once heard John Gerstner say, "I would rather die than lie!" I knew what he said was correct but it just about knocked me out of my seat. **Grace** in conversion builds this type of holiness-tenacity. Walking in right-side behavior requires tenacity to not be bamboozled by Satan but to walk in holiness. Genuine repentance spills into conversion.

To demonstrate comprehensive redeemed understanding, it's important to unpack the classic verse that many use for repentance. Many use 1 John 1:9 as a salt shaker of God's mercy. Some define this salt-shaking mercy as grace and I almost go into theological apoplexy. When some sin – if they acknowledge sin at all – they sprinkle a little 1 John 1:9 over their sin and feel they are 'good to go;' some are taught this approach. For them, 1 John 1:9 is a spiritual genie – you rub it and all your problems go away – especially a Holiness-requiring-God.

This generalization depicts perverted understanding because repentance comes full-circle in the Three Step Process. 1 John 1:9 says, "If we confess our sins, He is faithful and just to forgive us our sins and to cleanse us from all unrighteousness." Think of confession after Nathan confronts David's adultery and murder. David squirmed a little under Holy Spirit conviction; we all do until we acknowledge our sin. Acknowledgement might be the hardest part because we must agree with God about how He views our sin – this is true confession.

Some would tell David to sprinkle a little 1 John 1:9 on his *shortcoming*. After all he only failed his kingly duty, committed adultery with a woman who was married to another man, had him killed and covered it up. If we sprinkle 1 John 1:9 on our sin, it does not matter what we did; we think "Everything is okay." Run from this thinking fast.

David could have denied his sin and skated over repentance – he did for a while - but he *knew* genuine repentance. He was tired of betraying His Lord, per his Psalm 51 words. He had a contrite heart, broken with the gravity and depth of his sin. He cried in verse 2, "Wash me thoroughly from my iniquity, and cleanse me from my sin." In verse 7, "Purge me with hyssop, and I shall be clean; wash me, and I shall be whiter than snow." In verse 10, "Create in me a clean heart, O God, and renew a right spirit within me." He wanted forgiveness but he wanted a clean heart more! In effect he was saying, "Lord, plant me in right-side behavior since I fell short of your glory without your **grace**!" In effect, he prayed the **grace**ful redeemed understanding of 1 John 1:9.

In this vein, confessing our sin brings **grace** to show justness, pardon and mercy. The practical explanation of 1 John 1:9 is this: God forgives sin through mercy in repentance as **grace** cleanses us in conversion and faithful sanctification. While repentance can sweep over us, cleansing is brought by God and manifested as we walk in godly behavior. The redeemed promise of 1 John 1:9 is cleansing.

Grace has a default-mode in holiness but faulty eyes make 1 John 1:9 a panacea of wishful thinking and credulity. Redeemed eyes see a divine promise that God will convert us by His Willing and Doing per Philippians 2:13. Submission is required but grace gives it! 1 John 1:9 is the **grace**ful New Covenant fulfillment of Psalm 51. God saves us from sin so **grace** reflects His image. This is not a promise of sinless perfection but God's promise to lead us in **grace** – leading to righteous behavior to glorify His gospel. Psalm 119:11 says, "I have stored up your (Law-Keeping) Word in my heart that I might not sin against you."

Different terms speak the same truth as they come in varied contexts. Puritans referred to repentance as Mortification of the Flesh. Repentance confirms God's work in us but it cannot be divorced from faith and conversion. Faith confirms God's work but it cannot be divorced from repentance and conversion. Puritans referred to new life as Vivification – the coming again of Life. If we do not see mortification of sin and vivification, there is great cause for alarm!

Distorted gospels can make it difficult for some to embrace accurate teaching but true repentance gives **grace**ful victory. One passage caught me years ago and has not let go. Paul gives valuable qualifiers in 2 Corinthians 7: 8-11 as he distinguishes between redeemed and false repentance. Consider what he teaches:

> For even if I made you grieve with my letter [probably a reference to 1 Corinthians 5], I do not regret it – though I did regret it [I was sorry I wrote about that matter in that way], for I see that *that* same letter grieved you, though only for a while. As it is, I rejoice, not because you were grieved, but because you were grieved into repenting. For you felt a godly grief, so that you suffered no loss through us. For **godly grief** [contrition rather than attrition or false sorrow] **produces a repentance that leads to salvation without regret**, [true repentance demonstrated *because of* salvation] whereas worldly grief [sorrow for being caught] produces death. For see what earnestness this godly grief has produced in you, but also what eagerness to clear yourselves, what indignation, what fear, what longing, what zeal, what punishment! At every point you have proved yourselves innocent in this matter.

Faith, repentance and conversion occur **after** regeneration; they are results of new birth. Repentance rejects the old man or sin. Conversion seeks transformation into a new man through faith. Each can be a single act yet more accurately they are ongoing activities and attitudes. They work together like hands in perfect gloves. Together they help us in an upward Christ-reflecting direction through proactive Spirit-empowered change by putting on the new man.

We need **Grace** to perform every aspect of the Christian life. This is partly why Paul wrote in Philippians 2:13; "For it is God which works in you both to WILL and to DO of His good pleasure." This speaks of the majesty of **grace**. If we are regenerated, **grace** will reverberate in our being. When God works in us to Will and Do His good pleasure, God's **grace** magnifies His Will. Galatians 2:20 says, "I have been crucified with Christ. It is no longer I who live but Christ who lives in me. And the life I now live in the flesh, I live by faith in the Son of God, who loved me and gave Himself for me." Paul knew strength came from **grace**; it lived strong in him. It can live strong in us too!

Once we see **grace** this way, we see its majesty throughout Scripture. Consider how Paul teaches **grace** in Ephesians 4:17-24:

> This I say therefore, and testify in the Lord, that you henceforth walk not as other Gentiles walk, in the vanity of their mind, having their understanding darkened, being alienated from the life of God through the ignorance that is in them, because of the blindness of their heart: who being past feeling have given themselves over unto lasciviousness, to work all uncleanness with greediness. But **you have not so learned Christ;** if so be that you heard Him, and have been taught by Him, as the truth is in Jesus: **That you** [1] put off concerning the former [life-style] the old man, which is corrupt according to the deceitful lusts; and [2] be renewed in the spirit of your mind; and that [3] you **put on the new man, which after God is created in righteousness and true holiness**.

If you do not follow God in righteousness and holiness, you should be alarmed. It could be ignorance but, in light of **Grace,** this is difficult to justify. If **Grace** does not reverberate in your being, seek God to see what is missing. If you were Re-Created in Righteousness and Holiness, do not settle for inconsistency. 2 Peter 1:10-11 says:

> Therefore, brothers, be all the more diligent to make your calling and election sure, for if you practice these qualities you will never fall. For in this way there will be richly provided for you an entrance into the eternal kingdom of our Lord and Savior Jesus Christ.

Following God's Ways in practical holiness is the redeemed paradigm to prove that the divinely-empowering reality lives in us! As this occurs, we are assured 'the cake' lives in us and we truly say with

Scripture that we 'Believed in the Lord Jesus Christ, and we are saved!" The typical understanding that suggests "Believe the recipe, and you possess the cake" or "If you are part of a church, you have God's best" cannot compare. The first believes a recipe but redeemed **grace** rejoices that our 'cake' proves the recipe. The second stresses putting our trust in a church and tradition rather than in Christ who makes a living cake in us. An eternal difference exists here!

Possessing the cake is God's Will for your life and the compelling desire or goal of Scripture. With repentance, faith and conversion, we can imitate the Living Written Word – Jesus the Son of God – as God intends. **Holy living is the path of Christ reflectors**. I present this book so we can say with Paul in Titus 2:11-14,

> For the grace of God has appeared, bringing salvation for all people [all who follow], training us to renounce ungodliness and worldly passions, and to live self-controlled, upright, and godly lives in the present age, waiting for our blessed hope, appearing of the glory of our great God and Savior Jesus Christ, who gave himself for us to redeem us from all lawlessness and to purify for himself a people for his own possession who are zealous for good works.

1 Corinthians 15:10 says, "But by the **grace** of God I am what I am, and His **grace** toward me was not in vain. On the contrary, I worked harder than any of them, though it was not I, but the **grace** of God that is with me." I trust salvation has come full-circle in the Three Step Process where repentance, faith and conversion is clearly seen. I trust **grace** lives strongly in you as you mightily endeavor to serve God by His power. **Grace** brings it – and proves it!

Next, Law and **Grace** flow together in redeemed truth. They are not competing thoughts but complementary ingredients of God's Will. We must see them without sin and haze to embrace them.

---

1 John 11:34.
2 Matthew 7:4

Chapter 12 – Possessing the Cake through Grace

I want to give the old college try to present a redeemed picture of the Gospel. The attempt is made to show a 'middle-road-salvation' through the 'eyes' of a cake. Scripture says **grace** calls some to faith in the Cross-Work of the Only Worthy One who <u>effects</u> salvation; this is what I present. THE $64 million dollar question is, "How does this occur?" The Gospel's power unto salvation for those who believe is lived out in reality but how this reality is manifested is seen differently. Gospel discipleship to reproduce saints was the last teaching Jesus gave His disciples before He went to heaven; therefore, how the reality of salvation 'comes into existence' is a crucial consideration.

To get a picture of **grace,** read a story about a man who hired wood cutters. They got paid for cut and stacked wood. He gave each man instructions, a chain saw, plenty of fuel and sent them in different directions. One man struggled more than others. He came back all sweaty and dirty but couldn't keep up. After several days, the foreman was going to perform a mercy killing and called him into his office to fire him. When told of the decision, the man pleaded for his job and begged for one more chance. The foreman asked about his difficulties and decided to check the chain saw. The fuel was full, he set the choke, primed the fuel bulb and when he pulled the cord, the motor roared. The sweaty man jumped back and asked in amazement, "What's that?" Apparently the man knew nothing about the saw's rotary power and used it like an old rip saw without much success.

This funny story deficiently parallels the power of **grace**. First, some never tap into the <u>regenerating power of **grace**</u>. They work hard at religion and never make headway; therefore frustration and futility sets in. Actually **grace** must tap into us but there is a sense that **grace** taps God-fearers on the shoulder to call them out of the grave at some point. As the foreman, God teaches us that His power is necessary for success. Without Christ's power, <u>religious</u> attempts never work. Without **grace**, we will never find God's Will in the Redeemed View of Life.

Second, some regenerated ones do not know how God gives His power to perform His Will. Many think God's grace is given to enable us to be what we want to be – but this is not **grace** talking. **Grace** does God's Will – especially Gospel proclamation and kingdom advancing work. Maturing in **grace** takes time but we can know God's design and purpose by His power that He invests in saints.

Third, some are 'certain' of God's work in their life but need the majestic power of **grace**. They may not know Christ's organic power that exalts His glory through Christ-reflection because they only know Gospel benefits. As people step into the yoke with Christ, He offers His power in the greatest endeavor known to man – this power ultimately leads to true worship for His Work. If Paul needed to learn this power, we do too! Consider Romans 11:33-36, my emphasis:

> Oh, the depths of the riches and wisdom and knowledge of God! How unsearchable are his judgments and how inscrutable his ways! 'For who has known the mind of the Lord, or who has been his counselor? Or who has given a gift to him that he might be repaid?' **For from him and through him and to him are all things. To him be glory forever**. Amen.

God's Spirit brings correction as He changes our future. God's work is required to change someone's soul but we must know and love Him through Christ. Some embrace His benefits without a true biblical relationship with Him or His Gospel. When we love Him, the benefits are ours as a result; however, some 'have' the benefits without any love of God. A redeemed mind can sort through these qualifiers.

The fundamental change of the soul is known as spiritual rebirth or being born again. Jesus confronted Nicodemus with this new-creation-experience in John 3, saying it was necessary prior to entering God's kingdom. Paul says this necessary born-again-experience is new life in Christ and, without regeneration, we are lost in the haze. New birth is presented in John 3, 4, 11 and 2 Corinthians 3-5 and plugs repentant sinners into Christ and eternal life – the power of the saw. Tragically, new creation is often missing in 'conversions' today as many are 'saved' without significant change in their fundamental attitude.

When we say that salvation occurs primarily as a result of what we do – by good works, believing a formula or joining a church (all without new birth) – Jesus' Gospel is distorted. What Jesus did on the Cross is the <u>accomplished</u> foundation of adoption. In new birth, the Spirit <u>applies</u> Justification and empowers Sanctification. As we die in faith, the Spirit causes us to enter Glorification. In all, God finishes salvation in the Cross and – once regenerated – asks us to join Him in declaring His Gospel to 'make' obedient disciples that magnify **grace**.

2 Corinthians 5:17 presents a crucial key, "Therefore, if anyone is in Christ, he is a new creation. The old has passed away; behold the new has come." If New Covenant new-creation has not occurred, salvation has not come! Hard as that sounds, Christ and Paul taught this necessary reality. Sadly this truth is denied today to the church's hurt and eternal destruction of souls. Conversely, once New Covenant occurs in a soul, salvation comes and we walk in newness of life.

Paul actually speaks more about New Covenant truth than the newness of new birth – although that reality is in view. When our focus shifts to the New Covenant that Paul unpacks, we realize redeemed truth. **Grace creates new creations through faith as they enter practical eternal life**. Paul shows New Covenant **grace** against Old Covenant impotence – this is one redeemed contrast he makes.

Many are confused over how Paul presents Justification in the scope of salvation. With that in mind, let's take a peek at salvation-scopes related to Justification, Faith and Salvation to help us chew on and evaluate crucial elements of what we believe and practice in regards to these crucial doctrines seen through **grace**-eyes.

Martin Luther called Justification the doctrine by which "the church either stands or falls." Calvin called it the "hinge of the Reformation." The Council of Trent considered it central. All who profess Christ embrace the doctrine of Justification but we do so from different perspectives. Think of mathematical equations like 1+1 = 2 or 5-3 = 2 as we consider the following. All of the equations use the same words but, as we will see, each use does not mean the same thing.

Justification Scenarios[1]

Liberalism:	Works = Justification − Faith
Neo-Orthodoxy:	*Faith = Justification − Works*
Antinomianism:	Faith = Justification − Works
Roman Catholicism:	Faith + Works = Justification
Evangelicalism:	Faith = Justification + Works
Galatian Heresy:	Faith + Works* = Justification

Be willing to look at <u>Justification</u> from different perspectives. Not only do we see it in different ways and levels, Scripture does too. It's our job to keep these qualifiers straight for right understanding.

1) On the <u>technical level</u> – Justification is God's declaration that sinners are just (in Paul's verbiage) when He regenerates our soul and places us into Christ's Work on the Cross.

2) On the <u>salvation level</u> – (which is how people can typically speak of this reality even though it skews the biblical picture), Justification is how many approach and/or talk about salvation.

3) At the <u>practical level</u> – justification occurs (in James' verbiage) when our actions support our professed faith. The arrow indicates an equal sign or the Cause that leads to the result.

<u>Liberalism</u> starts with man's sinful 'good' works that, at least in their mind, produces justification before God. This is the epitome of

Satan's lie because it's void of redeemed faith and never brings Justification. Most assumed ideas of salvation hang on some variation of the following belief that says "We are justified by our good works and do not need any living Christ-reflecting faith – thank you very much!"

Neo-Orthodox faith is suspect and confusing, especially as necessary good works are denied. According to Scripture, this too is deficient. They may profess "Faith Alone" but when no faith is present, James says it's dead faith – therefore no Justification or Salvation.

Antinomianism starts with supposed faith. By using the 'right' equation they come up with the wrong answer: minus works. This too is biblically deficient. Sadly this represents many, at least at the practical level. This thinking flows from rejecting our duty to God's Moral Law. We cannot reflect God's Justification without necessary obedience!

Roman Catholicism may be a mixture of salvation (#2) and practical levels (#3) rather than the technical level (#1) Evangelicals historically use; this causes unnecessary confusion. They make necessary sanctification (right emphasis) carry justification (wrong context or relationship). In Scripture, Justification carries Sanctification.

Evangelicals posit Faith Alone with necessary works to follow. Faith Alone speaks to the foundation or ground of our faith – essentially Christ's Faith from Habakkuk 2:4 but they are quick to add that it's not by a faith that is alone. Necessary graceful works must follow!

The Galatian issue gives insight into Paul's distinctions; their works were of the faulty rabbinic variety. Their faith was of the Abrahamic-blood-variety rather than the Abrahamic-faith-variety. They sought to merge sinful effort with faulty rabbinic law as the means of Justification – added to (or actually in the place of) faith in Christ. In too many ways, this was a man-made righteousness that was not!

Paul makes it emphatically clear that in New Covenant Faith (#1) – representing Abraham's faith – we are Justified, period! Paul tells us to hang our hats, spurs and eternal life on this point! But if we leave it there – as many seem to do – we end up in a confused state as described in points above. Because of this, qualifiers are necessary.

First, **New Covenant faith manifests graceful obedience**. Abraham believed God and demonstrates belief with necessary works as the Spirit led him to obey specific commands. Even for Abraham, as in the Exodus, Law followed the fulfilled promise of Faith. We struggle to correlate Abraham's perfect **grace**-provoked obedience (sacrificing Isaac) to what God requires of saints in the New Covenant.

Second, when Evangelicals say we are Justified "by Faith Alone," the Reformers always added, "but not by a faith that is alone." We must distinguish but not separate Justification and justification.

Third, technically speaking it's not our faith that saves; it's the objective Righteousness and Faith of Jesus Christ – applied by the Spirit – that saves us. This is the majestic faith of Habakkuk 2:4.

Fourth, our subjective imperfect faith follows directly on the heels of Applied Faith. I've heard this described deficiently and want to make it clear for other strugglers. Against well-intended but distorted teachings that flow in the church today, we can learn much from Paul.

To be clear, Paul left the Galatians in New Covenant Faith that hangs its hat on the Redeemer's Work. He travailed to get them there! With New Covenant Faith – **that God had recently once-for-all-time exposed in its fullness on the Cross** – we should never confuse this clarity with the pollution of a salvation picture that has its roots in hell. The Moral Law has perfect roots in heaven and Paul makes it clear that, on a redeemed level, obedience to the Moral Law is not the issue in the Galatian heresy! Sadly, many stand on a Galatian-distortion.

The Judaizer issue in Galatians is seen in four major points. First, reliance on rabbinic laws and traditions replaced and therefore rejected God's Law. Paul declared "Anathema" or cursing on this position. Second, they didn't accurately understand the Moral Law was their guardian until Christ came to take over. Third, once Jesus was declared the New Covenant Mediator on the Cross – and not before – He took His personal elements to heaven to make eternal intercession for His saints. In one sense, His Work blew up the curtain (His flesh) and the job of guardian was finished and therefore obsolete for them. Fourth, when Christ took over through His Mediator-Faith-Work, all the rules changed. Pretty much everything they trusted in prior to His "It-is-Finished- Work" changed. The motif and Moral Law were the same but everything changed to an eternal redeemed **grace**ful level!

In a majestic curtain-shattering way, the ALREADY was here in New Covenant fullness. With eternal freedom in view, the Galatians went back into bondage by co-opting their victory. Like in the Garden, Satan convinced them to snatch death from the jaws of ultimate victory. This sounds stupid but now we have an idea of what occurred in the Garden and Galatia. Paul encouraged them to make a correction to avoid a car wreck. He challenged New Covenant believers to see the error of their ways. Even professors could avoid the greater car wreck and come to Christ rather than submit to the Pharisaical traditionalism that took them away from Christ and His **Grace**. After all, there is Only One Way – His Way or car wrecks? Your choice!

The concept of regeneration can make people think deeply about salvation reality. Jesus told Nicodemus the Spirit performed this born-from-above reality by Himself, not as a result of what Nicodemus did or could do. Rather than be caused by something we do (common misunderstanding), God works His new-creation-work in us. Confusion abounds about regeneration and how it's gained but the overall picture is clear. **Once regenerated, we gracefully join in sanctification**.

Conversations with people from different backgrounds reveal that many are 'saved' without becoming new creatures. This distorted phenomenon can flow from believing a faulty gospel or 'believing' the true Gospel in a faulty way – making myriad stillbirths. Tragic realities suggest something is amiss in our gospel presentation rather than the

Gospel. Some wrongly teach and think faith causes regeneration; this misunderstanding flows into the tragic reality of still-births. Scripture teaches that regeneration causes faith. Another distortion is belief in a church or tradition with no explicit organic saving power. Since **only live spiritual births enter heaven**, serious consideration is needed here.

To more-deeply consider nominal Christianity, in my years of talking to professing believers, I hear many reasons offered to not pursue the highest relationship with Christ. Try to reflect on where we've been as I paint a vision of what we should passionately pursue. In the call to examine ourselves to see if we are in the faith, do we:

Profess spiritual resurrection while living and eating in the pigpen?

Cling to formulas or redeemed benefits without walking in obedience?

Profess salvation yet cling to a sinful-unredeemed mentality?

Claim Heavenly Life Insurance without a Fire Proof structure of life?

Profess Eternal Life without working through the haze of truth?

Claim Love of Christ without a passionate pursuit of intimacy?

Profess Christ without His Power, Faith and Will?

Profess salvation without a Redeemed View of Life or Christ's mind?

Profess Christ-Likeness without the pursuit of necessary holiness?

Profess salvation without embracing God's Holy Character?

Profess to having Christ's mind while clinging to free-will?

Profess God's Will without leaving the realm of man's wisdom?

Claim salvation without a transformed Son-mind that gladly obeys?

Claim Christ-Likeness without always seeking holiness?

Hear His Word without obediently doing His Word?

Profess Cross-Victory while clinging to the bondage of a sin-view?

Jesus didn't just perfectly keep the Law out of a naked duty to gain salvation for His Sheep – although that was the distinct result – but He necessarily kept the Law because He demonstrates the pursuit of pleasing His Father with perfect obedience. **When we claim to be birthed into Christ, we should not be bashful to live from His Redeemed View of Life that always seeks to please Our Father.**

Faith and obedience are the result of new birth rather than the cause of regeneration. Rather than implicit or assumed faith that many hang eternal destiny on, we need explicit organic faith. The first time I heard that regeneration precedes faith it almost knocked me out of my chair. I had to replay the tape several times because I previously believed that my decision caused new birth. After picking myself off the theological floor,[2] it became clear this is the truth of Scripture!

Knowing that regeneration precedes faith put me on the path to finding God's Will in a redeemed lifeview. Through this, the Spirit led me into my current understanding of **grace**. Now I see that regeneration wasn't from me but totally from God. Post-salvation understanding allows me to praise God for His regenerating work.

Scripture speaks of regeneration as a once-in-time act, distinct from, but an essential part of salvation. It speaks in terms of ongoing salvation; referring to past tense – "we were saved;" present tense – "we are being saved;" and future tense – "we will be saved." The living-in-us mystery of regeneration brings comfort per Romans 8:3-4, 7-17,

> For God has done what the law, weakened by the flesh, could not do. **By sending his own Son in the likeness of sinful flesh and for sin, he condemned sin in the flesh, in order that the righteous requirement of the law might be fulfilled in us**, who walk not according to the flesh but according to the Spirit. . . . For **the mind that is set on the flesh is hostile to God, for it does not submit to God's law; indeed, it cannot.** Those who are in the flesh cannot please God. You, however, are not in the flesh but in the Spirit, if in fact the Spirit of God dwells in you. **Anyone who does not have the Spirit of Christ does not belong to him.** But **if Christ is in you**, although the body is dead because of sin, **the Spirit is life because of righteousness. If the Spirit of him who raised Jesus from the dead dwells in you**, he who raised Christ Jesus from the dead will also give life to your mortal bodies through his Spirit who dwells in you. So then brothers, we are debtors, not to the flesh, to live according to the flesh. For if

you live according to the flesh, you will die, but **if by the Spirit you put to death the deeds of the body, you will live**. For **all who are led by the Spirit of God are sons of God**. For you did not receive the spirit of slavery to fall back into fear, but you have received the Spirit of adoption as sons, by whom we cry, "Abba! Father!" **The Spirit himself bears witness with our spirit that we are children of God**, and if children, then heirs – heirs of God and fellow heirs with Christ, provided we suffer with him . . . .

The notion that accepting-Christ-as-Savior or joining-a-church *equals* salvation sounds great but an eternal difference exists when regeneration does not occur. A mental knowing or church-bloodline-confidence can leave souls in eternal lostness when we embrace Gospel benefits rather than God-in-Christ-life-reality. Presenting Gospel benefits without Gospel reality truncates God's Truth – even as zeal can carry us away at times. As people enjoy marriage benefits without the real thing, **the gospel can be presented as benefit without reality**. Romans 8:16 says The Spirit brings witness to our spirit that we are God's sons. I want *that* assurance as The Spirit does confirm life!

Some testify of prior salvation that 'did not take' or did not result in the new creation, only to give later testimony of a definite work of God in their soul. Amazingly this 'second experience' of God's work alone manifests regeneration. This seems amazing for those who don't know God works this way. I wish I had power to recreate this epiphany but I don't. Only God's Spirit can do this but I want every <u>professor</u> to become a <u>possessor</u> – because possession counts for eternity.

Regeneration results in salvation-confidence unseen in those who put their faith in faulty salvation experiences. This does not mean that trusting in church affiliation or the decision-causing-regeneration scenario does not produce assurance – because it does! Assurance is not the central issue – right assurance on the regenerating redeemed living reality is! This is why I emphasize regeneration, then assurance.

Regeneration leads to redeemed assurance. Those with faulty assurance may not possess behavior to demonstrate regeneration and they may not demonstrate true worship of God. I trust God challenges us to re-examine Scripture's truth in regards to the gospel. Maybe some will question the validity of their salvation experience. Maybe you are regenerated but live in disobedience to God because you have not adopted a Christian lifeview. Either way, please know that God brings joyful obedience through regeneration and wholesome conversion.

I offer my understanding in hope that Scripture brings people *to* Christ in search of a living-recreating-working-faith. God's Work in us produces a living working faith-effort that creates a huge contrast to those caused by mere human decision or church affiliation. Regarding salvation, big struggles surround questions like, "What is it? How do we gain salvation? Can we do something to earn salvation? Is it a God-alone activity or a mutual effort?" We can sort through variables.

The following is crude and exhibits poor English but can help unpack the typical conundrum of salvation. Two questions are: "Do we Do-to-Be?" Or, "Do we Be-to-Do?" In other words, do our actions save? Can we put ourselves in position for salvation? Or, does the work of God cause us to do, after He regenerates us? I believe all three, but with qualifiers. God-fearers "Do" so that God might make them a "Be." But at the same time, God must make us a "Be" before we can "Do!" When God regenerates, we Do – not to gain acceptance with God but **to gain salvation in sanctification**. This is the way James speaks. Good works justify our salvation before God and mankind.

As Christ's Word burned in two disciples as they listened to His teaching on the Emmaus road, told in Luke 24:13–35, reformed teaching burns in my soul. It took years for Reformed doctrines of Gospel, righteousness, regeneration, **grace**, new creation and others to take substantial meaning in my study and life. With understanding comes responsibility to teach and practice what we know.

James says we can be hearers of the Word and not proactive doers; this leaves us deceived and in a fraudulent position. James 1:22

says "But be doers of the word, and not hearers only, deceiving yourselves." James 1:25 says, "But the one who looks into the perfect law, the law of liberty, and perseveres, being no hearer who forgets but a doer who acts, he will be blessed in his doings." Jesus commands us to make disciples – teaching them to observe what He commands in *The Great Commission* from Matthew 28:16-20. It's a privilege and challenge to practice disciple-making as we **grace**fully plod through life.

A redeemed Gospel can help people see God's picture. I disparage common methods – to provoke corrective discussions. Primarily, we have too many professing believers that don't manifest regeneration, and **I don't see still-births in Scripture!** On the other hand, **the only believing, bloodline or church-affiliation assurance-model in Scripture is faulty to the core unless it's built on Cross-reality**. To see a correction in faulty gospels, we must admit a fault in what we present – but this is extremely difficult for many to do.

Let me take a brief detour for a biblical example of what I'm talking about to show why it's difficult to look past our paradigms. Consider the story of the prophet Jonah. Almost everyone believes that when Jonah was thrown overboard, he was immediately 'sucked up' by the great fish and spent three days in the 'God-prepared floating Hilton of his day.' I always heard this – and therefore I believed it. I probably heard this version of the story 100 times until a pastor from England preached on Jonah – giving a completely different version.[3] Let me tell you what I discovered as I looked beyond my paradigm.

From the Jonah text, rather than from the version most hear, there is no doubt Jonah died when he was thrown overboard – if we believe what the text presents. To see this, we must lay down the typical story to see another picture. Let me plainly tell you what the text teaches and then support or prove it by Scripture. Jonah went down into the deep and died – period! He was D.O.A. – Dead On Arrival at the bottom of the Mediterranean Sea. Some may squeal, "That's not what I was taught!" Some might ask, "How then was he thrown onto shore alive?" That's a great question and one that Scripture explains.

First, let's establish that Jonah drowned. The traditional version denies this fact. I'm certain people don't teach this faulty version intentionally; they teach the story intentionally but not intentionally in a faulty way. They probably teach it as they were taught; that's how we live much of life – we parrot the actions, words and teachings of those we love and respect until we learn otherwise.

Jonah's 'first' prayer (2:7-9) creates order-confusion. He prayed, "God if you spare my life, I promise to preach" **before** he died. We assume his prayer was before-the-fact of being swallowed by the fish but his 'second' prayer (2:1-4) is after-the-fact of his resurrection. Jonah's prayer rehearses what happened after he was thrown overboard (including his water-grave-dying-promise) but his prayer is after-the-fact of being brought back from death (v. 2:5). Let's see where he is before the whale-Hilton (coffin) picked him up. He was in the valleys of underwater mountains – wrapped in seaweed and dead (v. 2:6). In review, he talks of his resurrection (v. 2:6) as he remembers moments before his death (v. 2:7).[4] Then his coffin spit him up on dry land alive to keep his dying promise to preach in Nineveh.

If you struggle with my teaching, listen to Jesus' explanation. In Matthew 12:38-41, Jesus presents the 'Sign of Jonah' to Jewish unbelievers. He uses this Sign to chastise Jews who refuse to believe in Him. What Sign? Jesus' Death and Resurrection! Jesus' death parallels what the Jonah text presents – Jonah died, stayed in his coffin three days, was resurrected and cast out of his fish-tomb after the God-appointed time. Check it out. Do you believe Jesus? Jonah's experience directly parallels what Jesus endured as Firstborn.

This sounds strikingly familiar to Jesus's Main Signs and story – that is His point! As THE Prophet, Jesus' repentance message must be heeded! Sadly, the Jewish nation did not repent and believe – and suffered judgment for their refusal. In 70 A.D. they lost their temple and city of Jerusalem; the age of the Jews was over![5] Unbelieving ones were stripped of their evangelistic ministry; this privilege was given to believing Gentiles and Jews per Romans 11. As Jonah was sent to preach to pagans, Christ-followers are sent to disciple the nations.

This Jonah teaching compels three considerations. First, we need encouraged to hold some paradigms loosely. Second, we need to check out Scripture for ourselves like the Bereans in Acts 17:11, as many errors come from well-intentioned teaching. Third, realize that assumptions might lead to eternal error whereas explicit objective reality leads us home to glory. With that, let's get back to salvation.

Salvation-stumbling blocks come out of misunderstanding Scriptural principles in Acts. It's not that Acts tells it wrongly, it's that *we* extrapolate it wrongly – like in Jonah! We pull out wrong meaning without intending to do so but, when this occurs, this can be corrected.

First, we wrongly imagine the mass-salvation of Acts 2:41 – where 3,000 came to Christ – is the norm. It's not! With this wrong idea, in our attempt to duplicate this scenario, we 'fit' our gospel into this misguided framework. We want to see immediate mass conversions. While this is a noble goal, wrong understanding provokes distorted paradigms. Scripture's pictorial teaching provokes a new paradigm.

We often fail to look closely at the text or earlier prophecy to see what transpired to bring about the Jerusalem Pentecost.[6] This misguided frame explains the altar-call-mentality as we desire to see people come to faith in droves. This desire is noble but if our gospel is framed on a distorted picture, I don't think anyone wins. Deluded people certainly don't win! We might send them to hell with the belief that they are saved – a high cost for manipulation and self-delusion.

Wrong extrapolation doesn't mean God can't work quickly and magnificently; Scripture shows He does but the norm becomes clear when we look at the whole. The Scriptural Gospel makes disciples who move from repentance to faith to continual conversion to good works by glorifying Gospel **grace**, starting all over again by making disciples who ... And on it goes. I think we need some redeemed changes.

Second, Acts uses summarizing snippets of evangelization and salvation; we can therefore extract a truncated gospel built around a 'regenerating-causing-decision' without realizing this. When we say that a decision, baptism or church-affiliation **causes** salvation, we flirt with decisional-regeneration[7] or baptismal-regeneration despite contrary cries. Salvation that divorces ongoing sanctification betrays redeemed salvation. Faulty gospels can mean believing **recipes** rather than **reality. Scripture always seeks the reality of the recipe!** Do you?

Let me explain the corrective-thinking that has churned in my soul for almost 40 years. I grant the necessity of a decision but when the salvation-decision is prompted by manipulation, this may be man's ability to enflame an emotional response rather than regeneration. Decision-without-regeneration may manifest the man who didn't know the power of a chain saw (presented later). Christ's Work possesses power unto salvation and the God-alone-act in a soul causes the reality of regeneration and sanctification. We should know that regeneration **causes** a following-decision in the biblical salvation-flow.

For many, "Believe in the Lord Jesus, and you will be saved" (with decisional or baptismal regeneration) is the Gospel! The statement is reality-consequence with God's promise; the difference requires qualifier-understanding. Mickey Nardin (see book dedications) pushed me many times about this very detail. At the time, I'm not sure either of us had an idea of the long-term effect of his provocative questioning. The Holy Spirit used Mickey's provocation to push my salvation-doctrine-explaining-ability further to advance God's Gospel.

An honest assessment of the too-common lack of regeneration and distorted overviews helps us see a different picture. Many want godly results but how this occurs is another matter. Don't put the cart before the horse in the matter of Gospel presentation. I've never seen a mere cart lead a horse, and <u>regenerating-holiness-effecting-</u>**grace** is the horse that leads the way in the redeemed Gospel!

When ones' understanding of salvation is questioned, the angst can run fast and deep. <u>For some, to question their salvation or salvation-paradigm is paramount to challenging Scripture</u>. I've seen it often! A huge difference exists between what Scripture teaches and what we understand that Scripture teaches (remember Jonah). I don't refute the Gospel but faulty logic in gospel presentations. In our zeal to see souls saved, we can offer typical definitions of grace without evaluating stillbirths – with eternal ramifications at stake!

To put this in context, I combined Cornelius the God-fearer in Acts 10 with the Philippian jailer in Acts 16 into a *Salvation through the Eyes of the Baker* sermon to make my point. In both passages, men ask for insight into becoming what God wants them to be. Under different circumstances, both men make decisions for Christ that manifests regeneration. The jailor gives a response that disciple-makers want to hear, "Sirs, what must I do to be saved?" The classic retort is, "Believe in the Lord Jesus, and you will be saved, you and your household." Christians want to see and hear this response.

The Baker analogy allows for an excellent backdrop to distinguish <u>belief in a recipe</u> from the <u>reality of the recipe</u>. Please think deeply about this distinction as we can make a valuable transition in the gospel we proclaim and live. Luke used life-analogies to share the Gospel, and everyday-life can teach us as we approach the Gospel.

Let's consider <u>the decision to bake a cake</u> versus the reality that comes as a <u>result of working the recipe</u>. This simple difference is huge. My mother pushed me as a young boy to perform many chores. Part of her training was to bake things so I made many cakes. We often used a Betty Crocker cookbook as I made cakes from scratch. To make a cake from scratch – for those who only know of box cakes – means to follow a recipe and mix specifically measured ingredients in a proper order. The mixed batter is put into cake pans for baking. With a prepared oven, the batter is cooked according to a given timeframe. After evaluating the complete cooking process by verifying with a toothpick, you pull the cake from the oven for cooling and icing. No matter the recipe origin, I knew if I followed the recipe correctly and baked the batter properly the result was a good tasting cake.

Never once did I think, "If I <u>decide</u> to bake a cake, I now have the cake!" That would be foolish! Yet in a crass way, this is how I hear the common gospel presented today. In like manner, people are told, "If you <u>decide</u> to bake a cake, you now <u>possess the reality</u> of the cake!" To me, this is wrong! In gospel terminology, the presentation is: "If you <u>decide</u> for Christ, then you have the <u>reality</u> of Regeneration!" An associated message is: "If you <u>decide</u> to be baptized into the church, you are eternally secure." The logic of these recipes is: "If you make the decision for Christ or stay in the church, you now possess the cake!" Experience says **this is how <u>stillbirths</u> hear the gospel** – they make professions that don't and maybe can't exhibit the reality.

The Holy Gospel is not wrong or impotent. Admittedly a believe-the-recipe-and-now-I-possess-the-reality-gospel or believe-in-the-church-and-now-I-possess-the-reality sounds great. Some think these recipes represent the true gospel but these distort the Gospel, the Way or process of salvation and God-made-alone-reality. Contrary to noble desire, Scripture doesn't present salvation this way. May God redeem understanding from well-intended misunderstanding to move us out of campgrounds planted on baptismal church affiliations or beliefs that allow for assurance without the regeneration reality. Scripture proclaims that we should bank on cake reality!

When I ask provocative questions about faulty logic, a believe-the-recipe-creates-the-cake idea of salvation, manipulative practices of coercing a person to faith, baptismal regeneration, unregenerate people having false assurance and jumping over sound principles – the first accusation I get is that I don't believe the biblical gospel. I may not believe in these 'gospels' but I certainly believe in the Gospel that redeems. There's a huge difference as God's Gospel regenerates!

If we look a bit closer, I'm convinced **Scripture presents The Gospel in the cake-reality-way**. Please hear me out. In the eclectic vein of Richard Baxter, a redeemed sense of salvation presents the Gospel as a Recipe-toward-the-reality-of-the-cake-scenario with the end result being the cake rather than a decision to believe the recipe. I'm convinced this is the best way to approach the biblical Gospel that allows the Spirit to confirm rebirth in the soul per Romans 8:12-17 rather than offer false assurances. **Spiritual resurrection manifests the cake reality**. A redeemed Gospel tends to prevent stillbirths who stand before God with false assurance of life in Christ. A redeemed Gospel can change a sinner's world through the **Grace**-Full church.

The Spirit, Word and **grace** are valid salvation-qualifiers. Romans 8:16 says, "The Spirit Himself bears witness with our spirit that we are children of God." If salvation-assurance is left to the Spirit, we would be further ahead as Scripture's applied Gospel is manifested and exalted by the cake. In his desire to see people saved I'm convinced Paul asked, "Do you have the Cake reality – Christ in you?" This makes baking, Scriptural and Gospel sense! Does it to you?

The true Gospel is the power of God unto salvation! I believe this to the bottom of my soul and would die to proclaim *that* Gospel. The baking analogy confirms that **when people work the recipe and God bakes the batter, a cake is produced**. Yes, this supposes that we can 'work the recipe' and that's the point of Scripture – seen in the reality of God-fearers – that is often missing today.

The Gospel is God's Work for us in us. If we present The Gospel as the process of a cake-in-waiting, reflecting the reality of the God-fearer rather than as a quickie decision to believe the recipe or as one who abides in a church, this better reflects the redeemed reality of the redeeming Gospel. This perspective helps correct the truncated gospel that flows from a distorted synopsis of gospel responses in Acts. The actualized Gospel manifests **grace** in a regenerated cake.

Granted, some accepting-responses are genuine and reflect regeneration but our extrapolation must not jump over the text to frame a gospel outside of what is portrayed through Scripture. I fear that we create a gospel by our desire more than proper exegesis and hermeneutics. Millions of still-births seem to substantiate my point. A **grace**ful redeemed view can change much. I'm convinced a corrected Gospel can affect needed adjustments in the universal church like:

Redeemed **grace** effects every Gospel glorifying truth and practice!
The cake-teaching parallels *The Way* Teaching in the early church.
This redeemed view can help resolve age-old semantic struggles.
We too can be known as *Disciples of the Way*.
We can truly know whether we are regenerated by God.
A redeemed gospel can affect doctrine in every theological camp.
A redeemed gospel can provoke sincere unifying discussions.
This cake-reality-gospel can repair broken theological fences.
We could see a world-wide provoking unto good works.
People could truly come together for the glory of God's **grace**.
Cake-teaching can help believers seriously pursue sanctification.
This can purify the Church as we disciple regenerate believers.
Regenerated believers will make more Christ-reflecting disciples.
Gospel correction can drive discussions on other crucial doctrines.
The unity Christ died for might finally become clearer and attainable.
Redeemed believers thirst for God's **Grace,** Word and Holiness.
We might 'close ranks' toward true church growth.

I pray these points prime the pump of **grace**-thinking as I am convinced the *Recipe-produces-the-cake-Reality-Gospel* gets us back to Scripture's thrust. I do not charge people with willful distortion of the Gospel but too often we either give lip service to it or cannot properly distinguish between our convictions of the gospel with the biblical Gospel itself. If we mull over the above points and allow the Spirit to make the shoe fit for each of us, good discussion can be the result – even if you don't completely agree with my thoughts.

Surely God *can* make the cake without the recipe-following-process – and seems to at times – but that's the exception rather than the rule. We can think this is the norm from Scriptural snippets, like the woman caught in adultery in John 8 and the jailer of Acts 16 but the norm is "Follow the Recipe to get the cake!" This reflects the disciple-model that Christ taught in Matthew 28. **Follow His rule!**

From a Baker-paradigm – whether a disciple, an evangelist, disciple maker or God-fearing one desiring salvation (speaking in purely human terms) – our duty is to put the recipe together if we want a Gospel-cake. Without working the recipe to 'make the cake,' the tragic void means Christ's Gospel is eclipsed or forsaken. We can't cause the cake-reality by ourselves as an outside factor is needed but it makes sense to proclaim the Gospel proclaimed throughout Scripture. Move past faulty paradigms as **God will take care of the exceptions**.

If the cake-outcome is to become reality, the oven-work is needed. The God-alone-act of making a cake from the batter is a great illustration of the regenerating-oven. Only God can transform the batter into a cake. Only God can take a *battered* sinner and *cook* a spiritually-dead-person into a cake; the puns magnify my point. Only God can perform this God-alone-act that brings regeneration. Yet, at the same time, the baker who wants a cake is responsible to bring the proper ingredients together. When we see salvation through the redeemed eyes of the Baker, **salvation through His recipe is 'workable.'**

Without sliding beyond the parameters of analogy and making salvation all about our effort to make the cake, we should not too easily overlook or dismiss the mixing work involved in putting the necessary ingredients into the batter. That's like dismissing the farmer's spade work that occurs in planting and harvest; Scripture does not show a different model for evangelism and Gospel acceptance. If we place the focus on the mixing ability of those who seek a cake and God who makes the cake, cake-seekers might consistently perform the biblical duties of salvation that reflect God's Ways. If we say God's Ways don't work unto salvation – as some do – what are we saying? Rather than distortion, **the Gospel is exalted with a cake-making scenario**.

Technically speaking, the baker only makes the batter and puts it in the oven. The completed cake *requires* the 'outside factor' of an <u>oven</u> and <u>cooking</u> to transform the batter into a cake even though we often say "I made the cake!" Our ovens today are very controlled but the transformation of batter into cake is beyond the control of the Baker because something occurs in the chemical/organic make-up of cooking whereby you can never go backward in the process. Once our batter is cooked, we can never go backward to individual ingredients. Indeed, the cake (rebirthed soul) is a new organic entity!

A common question is, "What about the once-saved, always-saved teachings?" Or, "If the church is our Mother, aren't we always in the family?" Many answers can be given but consider this – The cake can never go back to being batter. The bigger point is that without the right ingredients and God's baking process, you will never get a cake.

Many are on the wrong side of the baking process. Many cling to a 'decision that makes the cake' without realizing we can't bake the cake or may not possess the cake. Many cling to a church foundation without realizing they may not possess the cake. Many 'Gospel-givers' are happy with a believe-the-recipe-decision without realizing the cake may not exist. Many 'church-foundation-givers' are happy with a believe-in-the-church-decision without realizing the cake may not exist. **Redeemed eyes see salvation from a realized-cake paradigm**.

Scripture shows an ontological organic change when God's **grace** converts sinners to saints. Scripture makes it plain that those rebirthed by God's Spirit follow Him in obedience – without exception.

God-warnings about our walk, in light of applied regeneration, can change many things. In the baking analogy, the cake can never return to batter or individual ingredients, so Paul challenges, "If you are a cake, live like it!" This may be poor English but "As the cake does, so does the regenerated believer" who lives in the power of **grace** to image and likeness Christ by walking in **grace**ful obedience!

When the cake comes out of the oven, the cake-reality occurs because we followed instructions and put the recipe together. Putting an empty pan in the oven – expecting a cake – is not faith but credulity. Sure, we make a decision to make a cake but unless we are an exception, we can't imagine we get the salvation-cake without working the recipe. At times, we allow people to speak as if they make the cake but redeemed thinking knows better. God helps us draw essential connections between the decision and the cake. The cake flows from decision but decision doesn't create the cake. Following the recipe is ' humanly-causal' but the divine baking process makes the cake.

In the best way I know, I presented the picture of applied Gospel. I trust seeing the Gospel described this way provokes us to look again at His Gospel. My prayer is that many will rethink what they believe, portray and preach; the following salvation view may help:

#1 – Election is the Eternal phase	2 Timothy 1:9	
#2 – Justification is the Legal phase	1 Timothy 1:15	
#3 – Regeneration is the Vital phase	Titus 3:5	
#4 – Conversion is the Practical phase	1 Timothy 4:16	
#5 – Glorification is the Final phase	Romans 13:11[8]	

Through redeemed eyes, invite people to put God's ingredients together as God makes the cake a reality. Rather than people waiting for God to strike them down from their horse like Paul, they can decide to possess the cake and get busy putting the recipe together so God might bake the cake in them. This is what happened to Saul – God baked him into Paul. Like Paul, don't let people get away with false assurance; ask them if they possess the salvation cake.

Please don't settle for merely believing the recipe or being baptismally connected to a church; make sure you possess the cake of Christ. **Possessing His cake is God's Will**. Systematically pursue the reality of Christ and get after holiness in the power of **grace**. Preach and live Christ crucified as the only message worth telling and the Spirit will take you higher in sanctification as you go from glory to glory. Walk in **grace** till you find yourself in eternity with Jesus your Lord.

I haven't 'arrived' yet but I look forward to my arrival in His presence to hear, "Enter the joy of my salvation. Well done faithful servant." Cancer was found in my body more than a year ago. Surgery removed a cancerous prostate and biopsies showed cancer in three residual areas. I don't know how much time God will give but His **grace** lives passionately in me to His glory. What's His Story in you?

In some ways cancer ups the expediency-ante of living. Cancer reminds me of my mortality swallowed up in His Cross victory (already) that will someday be realized in totality (not yet). At that point, humanly speaking, my questing mind may be silenced because I will be in the presence of My God and Savior Jesus Christ. What a day that will be! From a redeemed view, I think God will teach us throughout eternity so maybe my questing mind will never be quenched but then I can sit at the feet of One who knows all things – and eternal reality will reign!

I breathe David's words of Psalm 38:9-10, "Oh Lord, all my longing is before you; my sighing is not hidden from you. My heart throbs; my strength fails me, and the light of my eyes – it also has gone from me." As Jesus is life-giving water, David says in Psalm 42:1-2, "As a deer pants for flowing streams, so pants my soul for you, O God. My soul thirsts for God, for the living God. When shall I come and appear before God?" I truly pant after God's Will. I hope you do too.

When we actually possess the cake reality and our salvation is questioned, we can say with David in 119:41-48, emphasis added:

> Let your steadfast love come to me, O LORD, your salvation according to your promise; then shall I have an answer for him who taunts me, for I trust in your word. And take not the word of truth utterly out of my mouth, for **my hope is in your rules. I will keep your law continually**, forever and ever, and I shall walk in a wide place, for **I have sought your precepts. I will also speak of your testimonies** before kings and shall not be put to shame, for **I find my delight in your commandments, which I love. I will lift up my hands toward your commandments, which I love, and I will meditate on your statutes**.

Death is the great equalizer – laying us naked before God. We either stand before Him in our fig-leaf attire or in the Righteousness of Christ. I don't want to stand in any man-centered or man-driven form of self-salvation or fig-leaf attire. I want to be found with the cake of His Righteousness that was completely finished by His Son on the Cross and applied by the Lord of the Universe.

---

1 John H. Gerstner, *Primitive Theology: The Collected Primers of John H. Gerstner* (Morgan, PA.: Soli Deo Gloria Publications, 1996) 264. In the back of my Bible I have the Galatian 'equation' that I think Gerstner added to at some point in his teaching.

2 I heard this from a tape highlighting the teachings of John H. Gerstner. I believe he credited one of his former teachers who said this to him; I believe it was John Orr. R.C. Sproul lovingly referred to Gerstner as his mentor in the faith.

3 The pastor's name was Antony Finny. He pastored a church in Swindon, England. Our church sent a church-planting team and he was the English contact.

4 The confusion in changing our paradigm with Jonah is similar to when we seek to understand Romans 7 but I think the Jonah passage is deeper with bigger implications.

5 Many miss the magnitude and significance of this event because of prevalent Dispensational teaching. An excellent start is *The Last Days According to Jesus* by R.C. Sproul. A further heightened resource is *The Parousia* by J. Stewart Russell.

6 Many think Pentecost was multiplied many times over without realizing that five 'Pentecosts' occur to represent Acts 1:8 fulfillment. Jerusalem and Judean Pentecosts are represented in Acts 2&4; Samaria in Acts 8&10; and the uttermost parts in Acts 19.

7 Decisional Regeneration is the term applied to the idea that regeneration occurs as a result of a decision. An off-shoot is Baptismal Regeneration where baptism, either in water or in a church, creates the result of regeneration. Right understanding of Scripture, where regeneration precedes faith with necessary following, corrects these ideas.

8 Cited from LetGodbetrue.com in *The Five Phases of Salvation* under the salvation tab. I highly recommend this site for some excellent teaching on the differences between a man-centered and man-driven salvation (man's wrong 'Monergism' prompted by Satan's lie) versus the redeemed picture of salvation by the God-alone-act of regeneration. One suggested teaching is *Seven Proofs of Unconditional Salvation*.

Chapter 13 – God's Gospel Seeks Sons

Gospel is Good News! Speaking theologically, Jesus Christ is God's Gospel in Living form. This Christmas message was proclaimed at Bethlehem. The Living and Written Gospels are God's **Good News** unto salvation – to convert sinners into Christ-reflectors. God's Gospel requires radical discipleship in Christ's Ways yet Gospel is about what God has done for His sheep. Paul presents a great synopsis of the power and workability of Gospel in Romans 1:16-17:

> For I am not ashamed of the gospel, for **it is the power of God for salvation to everyone who believes**, the Jew first and also to the Greek. For in it the righteousness of God is revealed from faith for faith, as it is written, "**The righteous shall live by faith**."

At its most basic level, the Gospel is never about what we do but what another has done for us – in fact, what God has done for us through Christ's Cross Work. But if we leave the gospel at *what someone has done for us* however, we can easily make His Gospel into an assumed, implied or universal gospel. Some add the crucial qualifier "in us and for us" without eliminating an assumed, implied or universal gospel. I empathize with those who stumble over this point; this is why I stress the reality of regeneration and the "we, us, and you" of Gospel application. It's pivotal to properly understand who the applied-ones are – to know how the Gospel **for** us is the Gospel **in** us!

When I wrote this book skeleton 20 years ago, the gospel-point of salvation was not the confusing point it is today. Today I see a keen need to expand this point as many professing believers show few signs of being regenerated by God's Spirit. I've taught many times on Holiness and realize this is crucial. Holiness needs to be proclaimed from rooftops and in our hearts because **the end purpose of the gospel is Redemption through Holiness**. Gospel application is God's Gospel bringing the results for what it was designed to bring.

The Gospel is **applied** to redeemed ones. Many know gospel as merely God's Redemption message through Jesus Christ and His Work; to them, it's a done deal! Unconverted ears hear the message speak correction to mankind's car wrecks – promising the benefits behind the message. From the Mount of Transfiguration, with Moses and Elijah in Jesus' presence before the on-looking eyes of Peter, James and John, a voice declared from the overshadowing cloud, "This is my beloved Son; listen to him!" In every way, Jesus is the essence of God's Gospel through Word, action and substance.

Let me take a brief stab at correcting common confusion regarding 'The Gospel.' The four Gospels – Matthew, Mark, Luke and John – declare Good News about Jesus Christ, who He is, what He does and what He declares. **They declare Jesus Christ in distinction from, but in vital connection with the Gospel proper**; therefore we must understand The Gospel in contrast to the Gospels.

In this regard, Paul mostly unpacks The Gospel proper but many fail to understand his calling to unpack mystery after God's unveiling at the Cross. We must work through this haze factor between the four Gospels and The Gospel proper – found in the Finished Work of The Gospel (Jesus Christ) – that is effectively applied to believers. When we don't correctly understand Gospel qualifiers, we confuse The Gospel presented in Acts and beyond – especially the New Covenant perspective that Paul correctly explodes.

After John speaks to the reality of Abraham's blood-sons who reject Jesus, John says "But to all who did receive him [Abraham's spiritual sons], who believed in his name, he gave the right to become children of God, who were born, not of blood nor of the will of the flesh nor of the will of man, but of God."[1] We see qualifiers on Gospel-receptivity so that we cannot claim any essence from three popular and supposed vaults of human merit. First is the claim of physical bloodline. Second is the will of sinful flesh. Third is the will of man; this rules out the notion that freewill can work God's plan of redemption. But, The Gospel finds root in the spiritual sons of Abraham.

It's correct to say The Gospel 'seeks to be planted' in the lives of Abraham's spiritual sons; this is the redeemed way to speak of elect ones – the recipients of His Gospel. As God and His Gospel, Jesus calls the God-fearer Zacchaeus,[2] "Today salvation has come to this house, since he also is a son of Abraham. For the Son of Man came to seek and to save the lost." The Gospel seeks planting spots.

In the mid 1980's, I went to England with the possibility to return for church planting. We learned a tragic statistic about people 'on the other side of the pond.' In the land where historic battles for the faith were fought, people were pagan in thought and life. I was shocked and could not imagine that America would sink deeply into unbelief. But I was proven wrong! As a nation, we too have become pagan.

Some broadly use the term pagan to mean those outside the Christian, Muslim or Jewish religion. Pagan accurately reflects those who claim Christianity or life in God but deny His power – practical atheists or nominal Christians. Several years ago I went to Israel and learned that, shockingly, many Israelites are pagans too. In the land where Christ was born, people deny the redeemed reality of Christ.

> But understand this; that in the last days there will come times of difficulty. For people will be lovers of self, lovers of money, proud, arrogant, abusive, disobedient to their parents, ungrateful, unholy, heartless, unappeasable, slanderous, without self-control, brutal, not loving good, treacherous, reckless, swollen with conceit, lovers of pleasure rather than lovers of God, **having the appearance of godliness, but denying its power**.[3]

When we honestly realize the condition of sinful man without Christ, we see the stark eternal need for the gospel. John Piper said,

> What is God looking for in the world? Assistants? No; the gospel is not a help-wanted ad. It's a help-available ad. **God is not looking for people to work for Him but people who let Him work mightily in and through them.**

It's not just Americans, Englishmen or Israelis that need Christ; every person in the world needs Christ and His Gospel because this is the only 'thing' or Gospel that brings eternal life through spiritual rebirth.

When <u>discipleship</u> and <u>New Covenant rebirth</u> are missing from the gospel we proclaim, faulty reality results. When sin, spiritual death, man's inability, discipleship and necessary regeneration are removed from the gospel, we distort the redeemed **Gospel! Manipulation produces nominal Christians who might be stillbirths**. Even Billy Graham changed to a discipleship approach to be inaugurated in November 2013.[4] This *My Hope America – Matthew and Friends Project* has run for ten years around the globe; look for this project.

Redemptive-history-progression culminates in Christ's death. Due to misunderstanding, some think Old Testament salvation was different but we shouldn't suggest a technical difference if one may not exist.[5] Scripture shows no essential difference yet we struggle to see how Covenant-knowledge impacts our salvation and sanctification.

God's Gospel takes root in those who seek God in Christ. When a person comes alive spiritually through God's gift of Christ's applied righteousness, **grace** magnifies Gospel-works. Redeemed eyes see these results as the <u>Applied Gospel</u>. 1 Corinthians 1:30 says, "He is the source of your life in Christ Jesus, whom God made our Wisdom and our Righteousness and Sanctification and Redemption."

Scripture teaches that repentance, faith, and conversion are <u>resulting fruits</u> of new birth, seen primarily in Ephesians 2:8-10, yet some see these as <u>causal entities</u> that create new birth. Words bring different thoughts in different contexts. Meanings sometimes change and can vacillate in the wind of whimsical cultural change. We must guard crucial words as we meaningfully communicate His truth.

When Holiness or Righteousness is mentioned in the public square, two typical responses occur. Either the subject is addressed from inherent self-righteousness or a blank look appears. The blank look can reflect ignorance, confusion or deep thinking. To engage someone in conversation, the restraint "There are two things you don't talk about: religion and politics" must be overcome. As many violate the latter, they often violate the former; therefore, stick a foot in the door.

Evangelism doors open if we can show how salvation impacts eternity. We use this approach when witnessing to Muslims to provoke interest by making the biblical case that forgiveness is much different in Islamic understanding than biblical understanding. Sin, forgiveness, Justification and salvation can be door openers that encourage us to evangelize in a winsome **grace**ful fashion.

A door-opening presents opportunity to give witness to God's Righteousness in Christ's Gospel. Pursue every opportunity to gain a hearing for the Gospel as people typically speak of righteousness in ways foreign to those that God uses in Scripture. Many use their own faulty version rather than the definition provided by a Holy God. God gives clear understanding for a holy life and empowering **grace** to live in a pleasing way as we follow God's Law and Gospel. In persistent obedient effort, God opens our souls to Himself.

Misunderstanding can range from weak doctrinal instruction to personal beliefs guided by erroneous foundations. We typically accept beliefs of parents or church leaders without mature ability to correctly evaluate the knowledge-process or essence of reality. Socrates once said, "The unexamined life is not worth living." Misunderstanding can be corrected through diligent study and openness to true doctrine as the Holy Spirit works integration through His Word and gifted teachers.

Almost from the beginning of time, error has existed alongside truth. Although God and His truth are eternal, faulty thinking led to Lucifer's downfall. Satan then provoked Adam and Eve's sin in the Garden. History shows schisms and heresies throughout the life of the church. Like Eve, I once imagined that I possessed the power to make error okay. Faulty thinking did not work for her and will not work for us.

Objections flow from two basic areas. Some fall into 1) <u>fatalism</u> when they feel perverted thinking is being overridden by a Holy God. Paul praised God for being 'overridden' by Christ as sinners-turned-saints give up polluted notions of freewill and autonomy. 2) <u>Refusing to believe</u> is not seeing truth from God's perspective. Not believing is our fault. We cannot blame God for this yet many cannot comprehend how *this* God can elect people by His own Purpose. Like Paul, praise God when He overcomes deadness, especially when it occurs in your soul! Indeed, this God-induced reality provokes worship.

To those with ears to hear, eyes to see and hearts to believe, the message and personal reality of Christ's Gospel is truly good news because Christ's Gospel provides our car-wreck remedy. False gospels present 'good news' but ultimately lead to condemning conclusions. On this basis, false gospels must be rejected. Listen carefully: the right Gospel believed wrongly leads to distortion; and I'd like to help.

God's Spirit convicts us to change through the Word but we cannot hear because we are broken or dead after our car wrecks. C.S. Lewis once said of the world's two kinds of people, "Ones who say to God, "Thy Will be done" and those to whom God says, "Alright, then, have it your way." The second ones experience both car wrecks. All the king's horses and men could not put Humpty Dumpty[6] together again but God and His Gospel are sufficient to put us together again. As God put me together again, I'm glad He planted me in various theological camps to provoke my questing mind toward salvation, as you will read.

My questioning mind tends to irritate those who do not think deeply, cogently or consistently – or maybe those who do not want to really think. I do not want everyone to think like me (maybe I do) but everyone is commanded to think with Christ's mind. I want people to pursue thinking and living <u>like</u> God in the Redeemed View of Life.

Gospel variations are often defined by different <u>paradigm-stops</u> in redemption history. People can camp at different places in

Redemptive history – believing they camp where God wants them. Have you ever considered where you camp and why you are in *that* spiritual campground? Are you camped on a doctrinally premature or shrouded campsite? I know my coming qualifiers will step on toes and hearts so, before my gospel review, please read with charity.

God can show us if we are in the wrong campground, with the wrong camping equipment or with no idea where to go – if we open our minds and hearts to hear. Some sit in the wrong campground with no idea that eternal destruction waits – and *that* will be an awful reality! Scripture provides salvation snippets to overcome honest mistakes if we camp in the wrong place. The Redeemed View can tell us that we need to change our camping spot or go to a different campground.

Camping spots can be ignorantly intentional but we must ask serious questions about the salvation paradigm we maintain and believe. We can draw lines in the sand over how we obtain salvation (people do this all the time) but a transformed mind is required to judge correctly. As Abraham did, be willing to pull up stakes to move where God leads – this is the epitome of believing God. If your camping spot is found wanting, God can lead you to the right campground or site.

Consider a few campsite questions. Are we to blame if we choose the wrong site? Yes. Do we have the *right* to believe in whatever salvation we concoct for ourselves? No. Can man pick-and-choose the details he wants – as if God offers smorgasbord Christianity? No. Is it wrong to make God in our image? Yes. Is a waxed-nose approach always wrong? Yes. Can we claim fatalism and Christ's Gospel at the same time? Never!

Texts in Genesis show why we need God's salvation flyover. In *The Gospel of Genesis*, Warren Gage[7] posits Genesis 1-7 as the microcosm of world and salvation-history. With different glasses, we see varied approaches to God, humanity, the Fall and Redemption; without much thinking, these variations often become our paradigms.

Many paradigms compete against God's Gospel and do not reflect New Covenant design or intentions. We can be dogmatic about different salvation-scenarios so grant charity to those who disagree – but only God's Way is sufficiently true. Remember, our opinion falls at the feet of God's Will in His Gospel and Word – subject to the Cross. Primarily, our eternal destiny hangs on God's Will living in us!

Many democratic foundations were built on Scripture but God does not decide Law, Truth or Gospel democratically. Carefully judge your conclusions by the whole Scripture in New Covenant light – especially the Gospel. We might find we are in the wrong campground or campsite so be willing to allow the Spirit to correct your thinking. With these caveats, a redemptive history flyover helps us see different gospels as we seek the big salvation-picture through God's eyes.

The following gospel or campsite review highlights God's plan of redemption. My desire is not to unnecessarily disparage other gospels but I do not know how to provoke evaluation otherwise. I'm not trying to kick church tires but I'm trying to get us to review how we live and drive our faith – to make sure it's God's Faith. If the shoe fits, wear it or change it. Be willing to critique aspects of different gospels even as I lay my convictions before New Covenant light; I trust it helps.

Consider how the following variations stack up against New Covenant regeneration. **Try to frame gospel references in the overarching reality of regeneration**. I drive toward the necessary reality of regeneration as I speak against points of doctrine and denominational teaching. As I seek to provoke needed corrections, I'm not as severe practically as I am theologically. I start generally, move to more specifics, and then back to general specifics near my own camp.

If my words sound rough, hear my heart more than my words. My understanding is not the norm, but Christ's regenerating redeeming Gospel is! Our truth can be contrary to God's Truth that never changes, so admit it if 'your truth' is in a state of flux, even in small degrees. Only in glory (possibly hell too) will we have no erroneous thinking; that's why living from the right foundation is crucial here! As we struggle with doctrine and belief, we should do everything possible to make sure we possess life (The Cake) – the driving result-reality of the Gospel.

I have mercy for those willing to learn or who know they are in a dead-end dilemma – and want out. I talk with many who despair at a failed decision or know little about how to honor God in Christ. As my regenerative-generalities may accurately touch error, ponder how correction can be made. Do not let my minor foibles keep you from considering two Infallible things in this universe – God and His Word.

To get us started, consider the **Whatever gospel** presented in a tongue-in-cheek fashion. This prevailing popular gospel approaches God through a personally-accepted form and then does whatever! Years ago, "Whatever!" became a household phrase to prevent real discussion on essential topics and the Whatever gospel prevents real discussion about God, His exclusive truth and what he wants. Because God does not accept strange fire, He will not accept "Whatever!"

In the Evangelical vein, the '**Christless Christianity gospel**' is a faulty gospel in America.[8] Michael Horton warns against Christianity without an explicit gospel or powerful Christ. His diatribe is a wake-up call to oversights that lead away from biblical Christianity. Many claim to be Christian without regard to Christ, His Will or His Law; he says:

> **Where everything is measured by our happiness rather than by God's holiness, the sense of our being sinners becomes secondary**, if not offensive. If we are good people who lost our way, but with proper instructions and motivation can become a better person, we need only a life coach, not a redeemer. **We can still give our assent to a high view of Christ and the centrality of his person and work but in actual practice we are distracted from "looking to Jesus, the founder and perfector of our faith."** In order to push us off-point, all Satan has to do is throw several spiritual fads, moral and political crusades, and other relevance operations into our field of vision. **Focusing the conversation on us – our desires, needs, feelings, experience, activity, and aspirations – energizes us.**[9]

It's easy to settle for religion that sounds Christian with little Redeemed reality in its mechanics. **Pragmatism** is big; Horton says:

> My concern is that we are getting dangerously close to the place in American Church-life where **the Bible is mined for 'relevant' quotes but is largely irrelevant to its own terms**; God is used as a personal resource rather than known, worshipped and trusted; Jesus Christ is a coach with a good game plan for our victory rather than a Savior who has already achieved it for us; **salvation is more a matter of having our best life now than being saved from God's judgment by God himself**; and the Holy Spirit is an electrical outlet we can plug into for the power we need to be all that we can be.[10]

Sociologist Christian Smith says **Therapeutic Moralistic Deism** is America's faulty gospel today. Smith found <u>professing believers</u> "stunningly inarticulate concerning the actual content of their faith." In contrast to previous generations, "there is little serious ability to state, reflect upon, or examine their beliefs, much less relate them to daily life." I find his commentary true.[11] Smith presents ingredients of this distorted gospel's lifeview; deeply consider its faulty foundations:

1. God created the world.

2. God wants people to be good, nice and fair to each other as taught in the Bible and most world religions.

3. The central goal of life is to be happy and to feel good about oneself.

4. God does not need to be particularly involved in one's life except when needed to resolve a problem.

5. Good people go to heaven when they die.[12]

My experience confirms that Smith's generalizations are tragically true as the above lifeview ensures eternal wrath. Listen to Jesus' words in Matthew 7:21, "And then will I declare to them, 'I never knew you; depart from me <u>you workers of lawlessness</u>.'" Jesus' Gospel rejects sin – with proper regard to God's Law, Character and Truth.

Christianity has a perfectly Holy moral foundation even if it's often misunderstood and rejected. Against common perception,

Christianity does not posit a moralistic deistic approach to God. Because God wrote His-Story, with Jesus playing the lead role and the Spirit carrying out the final gathering, God is more intricately involved in our lives than we admit. Therapeutic Moralistic Deism – a tragic yet valid commentary – is not the biblical gospel despite popular opinion!

The **assumed or implicit gospel** leads many down the wrong road. Tragically this gospel resides in valid camps; the campground is not my point here but the campsite is! Just as Hebrews lived in the campground of Abrahamic faith, many set up campsites that rejected the faith of Abraham. In Scripture, deluded ones believe an assumed or implicit gospel, and assume an implicit faith. Know this – True Hebrews camp on Abraham's Faith in organic reality and explicit faith!

Implicit-gospel-believers camp on the belief that they live next to true possessors; therefore by association, they believe they are ones too! Never mind that they cannot demonstrate that Abraham's faith lives in them – they wrongly cling to implicit salvation. Never mind that God commands a working-**grace**ful-faith. The broad gospel of implicit faith shackles many; I pray some can see beyond their bondage.

The **dispensational gospel** leaves people believing that their decision-in-the-formula or acceptance-prayer creates rebirth and subsequent salvation. This is in stark contrast to the monergistic, single-working-act of the Holy Spirit that **results** in a proper soul-change decision. Regenerated ones make proper belief-decisions on the basis of true faith, but it's another gospel when we make the **decision** the crux of the matter. Many subjective decisions lack the focal point of Christ's Holiness in the Cake. Our faith must stand on Christ's objective work on our behalf, followed by necessary obedience.

The **'decisional-regeneration-gospel'** can become a work to merit God's acceptance. Instant-salvation-provoked-by-a-decision[13] assumes that regeneration occurs as a result of this decision. This equation or formula is built on faulty logic and misunderstanding. Often the foundational premise is faith in faith, or fideism. Redeemed faith knows we are saved by Christ's Faith – and proactive faith follows.

To challenge this 'required decision' is tantamount to starting a riot in some tents.[14] To shake people from untested life-long convictions founded on faulty exegesis, faulty extension and misapplication can require a spiritual 'two-by-four to the head.' At one time in my life, I held this belief so I know doctrinal error may occur from right motive but – hear this – right motive can't excuse wrong theology in salvation doctrine; and I remember the 2x4 I received.

At philosophical and ontological levels we need the true Gospel where a <u>decision</u> to follow Christ with true faith always follows regeneration. Against decisional-regeneration logic, Ephesians 2:1-10 demonstrates that <u>decision, faith, and works</u> don't cause new birth but <u>God and applied-**grace**-alone causes new birth</u>! Our subsequent decision and working faith is an outflow of His causal (oven) work!

The '**Baptism gospel'** is historically a Roman Catholic teaching with Protestant variations; it presents salvation in or through baptism or church membership, where baptism is usually performed on an infant. This gospel may not <u>explicitly</u> speak of regeneration at the baptism but I've heard heavily-weighted <u>implications</u> suggest this occurred. When the implicit becomes the foundation of 'redeemed life,' especially when little biblical warrant exists, this is a dangerous campsite. But the reality of regeneration changes this site!

The **baptismal-regeneration gospel** suggests regeneration occurs as a result of baptism or membership – with a confirmation process to follow. Without suggesting ill intent, this becomes a formula for salvation. For some, this becomes guaranteed salvation. Churches teach this 'means' of salvation where biblical 'warrant' comes from conspicuous extrapolation. This encampment leaves gaping voids with covenant relationship-emphasis for members, an excellent thing by itself, but even confirmation often lacks regeneration reality.

The **Synergism gospel** says we are saved (Regenerated and Justified) by a synergistic joint effort between God and man. The following offers technical flesh against the concept that opposes Monergism – the God-alone-act of regeneration. Ken Silva says,

> **A man-centered gospel is the belief that the determining factor in whether or not a man is eternally saved, in the end, relies** (at some level) **upon an act of his own will i.e. human decision**. This is often called synergism because it is thought to be a cooperative effort between God and man. A God-centered Gospel means that man has absolutely nothing whatsoever to do with causing his salvation by "choosing God," "deciding to follow Christ," "asking Jesus into your heart," and/or any other like phrases so common today. Sola fide and sola gratia [by faith alone and by grace alone] as used in the Protestant Reformation mean that while the sinner is dead in his trespasses and sins God Himself sovereignly regenerates those whom He wills. As His gift, God gives them the faith to believe in Christ, and they repent of their sins. This is actually diametrically opposed to any of the seeker-friendly post-evangelistic movements e.g. the Purpose Driven Life as taught by Rick Warren. The sad fact is that **the contemporary American Christian Church largely believes in synergism** (man cooperates with God), while in stark opposition to the synergism of apostate Roman Catholicism, the Reformers (even before John Calvin) taught Monergism. Yet to a great extent today the Emerging Church movement overall, and voices in this Emergent rebellion against Sola Scriptura [Scripture Alone] like Rob Bell in particular also strongly believe in synergism [at best].[15]

Essential formulations from the Protestant Reformation include five Sola's or Alone-statements that form the skeleton of Reformed tenets. The reformers always declared that salvation was by: 1) Sola Christos – By the Work of Christ Alone; 2) Sola Gratia – By **Grace** Alone; 3) Sola Fide – Through Faith Alone; 4) Sola Scriptura – Through the Scripture Alone; and 5) Soli Deo Gloria – To the glory of God Alone. These five Alone-statements need qualifiers lest they are taken out of context but my purpose is to provide them so readers know the source. Grab a good book to understand necessary qualifiers.

The **Catholic gospel** teaches sacerdotalism – that salvation comes chiefly through the Eucharist and Baptism sacraments; and that righteousness must *inhere* or abide in the person through sanctification **before** Justification occurs. This gospel confuses the order of salvation presented in Romans 8 to besmirch the practical Righteousness of Christ, His atoning work of imputation and the doctrines of Justification and sanctification. Scripture, rather than the church, must be our guide – and **Scripture teaches that Justification produces sanctification**.

Catholic doctrine anathematizes or curses salvation <u>by-grace-alone</u> (#2) through <u>faith alone</u> (#3) yet Paul hangs his theological spurs on these teachings. To my knowledge, regeneration is never mentioned in Catholic circles; near as I can tell their faith is the implicit and assumed variety. Thankfully, despite a skewed salvation-starting-point, many Catholics demonstrate the reality of new birth. Praise God that regeneration trumps wrong and inconsistent theology.

The '**works-righteousness gospel**' exchanges Christ's perfect righteousness with personal goodness – teaching that <u>inclusion</u> in God's kingdom is earned through <u>inherent righteousness</u> – a figment of imagination. This false gospel denies Christ's divinity and sinless life. Without Christ as our applied substitution, Scripture teaches that no salvation is possible. A bumper sticker once said: Know Christ, Know Peace – No Christ, No Peace. That concise statement is so true!

Works-righteousness is often built into first impressions of the moral Law – **for** salvation. Without New Covenant teaching, this could sound valid but when the Gospel, Law and **Grace** are unpacked, we see a different picture. Thinking that embraces the moral Law should never be squashed. Law-keeping from sinners **for** Justification is skewed; it's valid but not savingly. When obedience is seen as the <u>cause</u> of Justification unto regeneration, we need an adjustment in thinking. After regeneration however, God works **grace**ful Covenant-keeping in us to the glory of His Gospel of **grace** through Law-keeping.

Any gospel that presents works as meritorious by any other means than the substitutionary-perfect-work-of-Christ alone is faulty and must be rejected. Any gospel that substitutes man's sinful fig leaves for Christ's-Righteousness-applied-by-the-Holy-Spirit is a false gospel. Any gospel that says anything *but* **grace** causes regeneration must be rejected. We must be clear; James taught that works show our faith. **God designed salvation so that our living demonstrates grace-driven faith** and, in this way, gives assurance of salvation.

The **'Oprah/Chopra gospel'**[16] assumes many names but looks similar. Ravi Zacharias shatters Eastern and Western versions of less-than-biblical spiritualties that are fast becoming accepted religions. At core they are absurd, post-modern, enticingly 'christian' in facade and tempting for any with an antipathy for formal religion. This gospel can be shared with all heresies. We can't have Gospel without Christ or Christ without regeneration; also we can't have Gospel without resulting personal godliness that flows from Christ's Righteousness.

The **'Spirituality-without-Religion-gospel'** presents popular generic salvation in a knowing that allows the god-within to come out. This gospel suggests that inherent sinful human ability is sufficient to make us acceptable to God, despite common sense and His Word. Any gospel that depends on the sinful ability of man is flawed to the core. Any gospel that essentially stands by itself – without God, His Word, Christ's Atonement, regeneration, necessary personal belief and holiness – violates the redeemed Gospel and is false!

The **New Age gospel** denies God's standard of Holiness within necessary regeneration, as it posits a personalized model that comes 'alive to God' because they imagine they are god! This gospel rejects the necessary-second-Adam-approach, does not require conversion, organic rebirth by God, and stands on Satan's exalted sinful autonomous foundation. New Age thinking is as old as Lucifer's fall and his attempt to get us to forsake **Grace** and imagine we can sit on God's throne. We may be our soul's captain but when we are not directed to Life in God's Gospel by The Captain, correction is needed.

The **Rob Bell gospel**[17] posits God's 'saving' Love without Holiness, **grace**, atonement and sanctification; this justification stands on no biblical redemption, pulling in rebels of Evangelical Christianity in various forms. Sadly, what they posit speaks to the carnal nature and buys distortion as God's design – the same lie of Satan.

The **Prosperity gospel** teaches a fundamental prosperity goal where the good news equals benefits of Christ's Work without the Savior. In other words, with prosperity – who needs Christ? Sure, they speak of Christ and His work but their gospel quickly becomes a fundamental prosperity. Scriptural prosperity is far different than they posit but they seem unable to see beyond their man-made paradigm.

This gospel message says, "Send your seed money and God will bless you abundantly. Get on this track and you can have anything your heart desires." Regeneration is never mentioned and, if re-birth is spoken about, it's to a prosperity mindset rather than Holiness. Without knowing the details, my soul was warmed when a popular prosperity teacher said, "Relationship with Jesus changes everything – that's prosperity!" I agree with the words even if I reject his theology.

The **Love gospel** teaches that God's love rather than the holy righteousness of Jesus Christ is foundational. The primary message is that Love trumps everything – faith, holy living, New Covenant Gospel, and empowering **grace**. Love is biblical but it must be subsumed under or through God's Holy Plan, Will, Ways, Word and **Grace.** This gospel makes love the panacea for any God-violating thought or action. When love reigns supreme, who needs regeneration or **grace**?

My gospel-site-review shows that, depending on our paradigm of salvation-encampment, we can build myriad salvation scenarios. This concludes my faulty-gospel overview but many more could be added. I hope the brevity does not diminish my point because there is much to learn in light of the redeemed Gospel that effects salvation through regeneration. Alistair Begg quotes Martin Luther, who said,

As long as a person is not a murderer, adulterer, thief, he would swear that he is righteous. How is God going to humble such a person except by Law? **The Law is a hammer of death, the thunder of hell and the thunder of God's wrath to bring down the proud and shameless hypocrites**. When the Law was instituted on Mount Sinai it was accompanied by lightning, by storms, by the sound of trumpets, to tear to pieces that monster called self-righteousness. As long as a person thinks he is right, he is going to be incomprehensibly proud and presumptuous. He is going to hate God, despise His grace and mercy, and ignore the promises in Christ. **The Gospel of free forgiveness of sins through Christ will never appeal to the self-righteous**. **This monster of self-righteousness**, this stiff-necked beast, **needs a big axe. And that is what the Law is, a big axe**.[18]

We need the Law-axe against anything that keeps us from coming to Christ for salvation. The Law Axe helps us see that sin is anything that violates, denies or marginalizes Holiness, God's Ways, Christ or Christ's Cross. Once the Spirit applies Christ's Gospel and the axe brings us to our knees before the Cross, we can stand up in new life to live in the power of **grace** in Christ-likeness. The reality of Christ's Gospel is that no stillbirths come from His Gospel because He brings all His elect ones to Life through a Faith that saves completely.

Satan – the Father of Lies – is the source behind every false gospel. Each false gospel above can be corrected with regeneration and right living-understanding of redeemed truth. While I cannot correct doctrinal error in others, if we are willing the Holy Spirit can provoke proper thinking and biblical conformity in us. God wants us to examine our campsite as we sit on an Atonement theory, salvation-scope, and gospel. Make sure you are planted on the right site. Study and application of right doctrine is necessary to find God's Will, and the study of theology might be the greatest endeavor of our redeemed lives – as study can lead us to the throne room of heaven itself.

Scripture confirms that we must approach God in Christ in a New Covenant way – through the Word, The Gospel of His Cross and subsequent regenerated living. Many religions do not accept Christ as presented in Scripture, but enough claim to accept Him and are therefore classified or labeled Christian. We must beware of 'accepting' Christ in skewed forms and think we are acceptable to God because we listen to 'qualified' voices. We are called to rightly divide Truth and there is no place more important than the applied Gospel.

I could not put the **Gratitude gospel** in my list above because it *does* teach regeneration-truths. But when the most exalted goal of saints is to offer works to God through 'worshipful gratitude,' this seems skewed; its legitimacy falls short of what **grace** does. Paul's greased doctrinal chute often caused him to slip into doxology where his gratitude flowed freely. But gratitude, as good a foundation as it sounds, falls short of the holy prize. Gratitude flows from **grace** – the redeemed foundation that rebounds every thought and action back to the One who is Worthy of our **graceful** grateful activity. Enough said?

Biblical qualifiers help us consider Christ's Righteousness and how it affects salvation. 1) Righteousness abides in and proceeds from God's Character. 2) Righteousness is the critical element of salvation procured from Christ's perfect life and work. 3) Righteousness is the essence of **grace** – the power of God to Justify, regenerate, produce holiness in, and glorify saints. 4) Christ's Righteousness covers saints through Imputation. 5) Righteousness is the necessary element for entrance into God's kingdom. God works these five points in those with faith, as we share in each point through His application.

God's application of Genesis 3:21 is expanded in the New Testament. Ephesians 1:3-4 says God chose us in Christ before the world's foundation, indicating that – in God's plan – Christ was crucified before He created mankind. As God's eternal crux, we see why God unveils Christ Crucified from the beginning in the Garden, on the Cross and eternally afterward. Difficult questions can almost disappear with redeemed eyes. It amazes me how God reveals the crux through the haze as Ephesians 1:3-10 helps unpack the Gospel:

Blessed be the God and father of our Lord Jesus Christ, who has blessed us in Christ with every spiritual blessing in the heavenly places, even as **he chose us in him before the foundation of the world, that we should be holy and blameless before him**. **In love, he predestined us for adoption through Jesus Christ, according to the purpose of his will**, to **the praise of his glorious grace**, with which he has blessed us in the Beloved. In him we have redemption through his blood, the forgiveness of our trespasses, **according to the riches of his grace**, which he lavished upon us, in all wisdom and insight **making known to us the mystery of his will**, according to his purpose which he set forth **in Christ as a plan for the fullness of time**, to unite all things in him, things in heaven and things on earth.

Paul, like Psalm 1, teaches the beauty of the person who is blessed with regeneration. Paul particularly got my attention because he unpacks Gospel mystery; let's list the points that speak loudly:

1) God blesses saints with regenerative application (v.3);
2) God chooses saints IN Christ before the world's foundation (v.4);
3) He chooses His saints to be holy and blameless (v.4);
4) He predestines our adoption through Jesus Christ (v.5);
5) It's His will to sovereignly choose saints IN Christ (vv. 5-7);
6) His choosing is designed to exalt His glorious **grace** (v.6 & 2:7);
7) His **grace** is fully seen in and through Christ (v.6);
8) In Christ's blood-letting, saints obtain forgiveness (v.7);
9) Mercy, forgiveness and redemption flow from **Grace**'s riches (v.7);
10) By Christ's righteousness the Spirit lavishes **grace** unto us (vv.7-8);
11) By wisdom and illumination, God makes the mystery of His will known to saints in an effective manner (v.8);
12) This perfect unveiling was through Christ from the beginning even though shrouded truth was fulfilled at the perfect time (v.9);
13) God united all things IN Christ as the crux of the matter – the Cross of Christ (v.9) and
14) The reality of the Cross was the perfect bridge between heaven and earth – the fullness of the coming kingdom His saints were taught to pray for in the Sermon on the Mount (v.10).

This passage is chock-full of powerful truth. Paul shares the magnitude of the Gospel as God intended from before the creation of the world. His Gospel sufficiently <u>effectively</u> redeems His people.

The Gospel Paul preached went especially to Gentiles. He took abuse everywhere he went – mostly from his own blood brothers. In 2 Corinthians 11, Paul defends his practice; listen to his defense. He boasts of suffering for preaching The Gospel where it's never been heard. His suffering-message comes full circle – from Christ's Cross-suffering back to His servant full-force – this is redeemed prosperity! In Ephesians, Paul exceptionally highlights the **grace**-message lived by the church through Gospel dissemination; don't miss this!

Without redeemed eyes, we can't fathom someone boasting in suffering. We like to boast in what we see as our accomplishments; Paul is quick to speak of suffering as accomplishment. Imagine that! Paul speaks like this because he knew something many of us do not know. Paul learned what we need to learn and it will work for us too!

Amazingly Paul boasts in the magnitude of his suffering. In light of his 2 Corinthians 11:23-29 litany, my stories pale in comparison. Verse 30 sums up his rantings, "If I must boast, I will boast of the things that show my weakness." Let this sink deep within our ears and souls.

Paul speaks of experiences that most never know. Whether in a vision or several near-death experiences where God sent him back to 'finish his time,' Paul was ushered into heaven to see things he was not allowed to speak about. Maybe this was left to John the Revelator? Paul might be the only man given a revelation and then suppressed by God for that knowledge. To make matters worse, he suffered for this with a thorn in the flesh from Satan – and only a cake can take that!

Paul boasts about 'this man' but minimally about the man who lives in his skin. That takes humility! In the midst of his suffering, Paul asks God to remove this thorn – similar to how Jesus asked The Father to remove the cup of sin while knowing God would not take it away. Paul declares that he asks God three times (2 Corinthians 12:8) – the Hebrew expression of perpetual asking – yet receives a negative answer. We'd think "Enough is enough!" but **grace** keeps Paul ticking.

Paul already knew much about **grace**. He endured much for The Gospel's sake yet God's power pushed him on. God would teach him **grace** in a superlative way. When Paul got the negative answer, he mercifully received commentary from God, "My **grace** is sufficient for you, for my power (**grace**) is made perfect in weakness." Now, rather than being confused by suffering, Paul saw the majestic reason behind the suffering he endured. Like Job, God purposed to show His majestic power of **grace** through Paul's sufferings for the sake of The Gospel as the power of **grace** makes holy-seeking disciples! Is this you?

Against a mercy backdrop in Romans 12:1-2, Paul commands us to put ourselves on the altar of sacrifice. Paul knew the fullness of **grace** as he laid on the altar horns – that's personal example! Paul learned that **grace** is fully revealed in the actuality of suffering for Christ. Now Paul 'got the message.' He needed to perform the mission God gave him! Learning **grace** in this way made Paul the Apostle he came to be. May we learn the message Paul learned! If 2 Corinthians precedes the writing of Romans, maybe now (as Paul Harvey would say) we know the rest of the story of Paul's **grace**-progression.

From Scripture and Colquhoun, God's Law requires 1) perfect obedience of life, 2) perpetual righteousness or holiness of nature, and 3) complete satisfaction for sin. These requirements never go away; they eternally apply before and after regeneration. When I realized these truths, it was like a surgeon's knife opened my redeemed sight.

Gospel majesty is revealed as Jesus provides all three requirements for His saints on the Cross. What a deal! The Spirit takes an eternally damning entity within us (sin and death) and applies something to our account we cannot accomplish. Confusion permeated my thinking before reading Colquhoun's work but his teaching gave clarity. God applies Fulfilled, totally-obeyed Law; listen to Horton:

God is holy. **He has not simply revealed personal preferences, but the law that expresses his own moral character. He has**

not commanded anything of us that is not required by the core of his very being. His commands never spring from a whim, but come from a will that is rooted in his unchanging nature. If the preceding arguments are true – namely, that God has given his law; **his law is the very impress of his unchanging character, and the New Testament commands expand and deepen rather than withdraw or curtail the moral law** – then it follows that we are no less obligated than the Israelites to obey everything that God has commanded in his moral law. This moral law can be easily distinguished from the ceremonial and civil laws that are inextricably connected to the Mosaic theocracy, and is still in force for both believers and even for all human beings, since it is preserved in their conscience since creation.[19]

Let's consider the Gospel in light of God's primary conditions or requirements. #1 – God requires Perfect obedience. #2 – God requires Perpetual (and eternal) Law-keeping. #3 – God requires Perfect Satisfaction for Holiness-replacement and Redeeming Atonement. In these points, the typical gospel explicitly addresses half of point #3; it's a well-intended but partial gospel – less than a half-Cross gospel. Actually, The Gospel is not partial but it's typically communicated in a partial manner, and redeemed eyes can bring a needed correction!

With **Grace** as the applied Holiness-additive in The Gospel and our lives, Christ's Flesh – the veil torn in Hebrews 10:20 – 'remedies' all three requirements and leads to forgiveness. Rather than preach the second half of point #3 (what I contend is the typical gospel) Paul preached the full three-part Gospel in what I call Two Sides of the Cross. My effort in this book seeks to demonstrate a better way.

From the beginning I focused on regeneration, **grace** and salvation – this is my whole-book focus. In light of what I call a half-Cross gospel, I'd like to turn the magnification up a little on what many believe about salvation. This might be meddling but I think it's needed.

Earlier we talked about varied gospel camps and soon we talk about salvation campgrounds. Many embrace Synergism rather than Monergism (p. 262); I want to burrow into this thinking to help some 'explore' my spiritual journey to understand **Grace** from a slightly different perspective. I do not have the power to change someone's mind but the Spirit does – maybe through my experience and words. I promise to keep this magnified meddling to two pages, so hang on.

I want to briefly examine two new points – <u>sovereignty</u> and <u>prevenient grace</u> – as we turn up the magnification. Previously we saw that free will, as most believe, is unattached from God's Will and therefore cannot work God's Will – so let go of this 'right.' We saw that common grace should better be seen as common mercy. In the same way, let's explore these two 'new' points that cause many to stumble.

Almost every believer acknowledges <u>God is Sovereign</u> but not everyone agrees with its 'extent.' Common people think Satan and God are on the same level and sit back waiting to see who wins. Believers in the Christian God believe God Alone is Sovereign, but when it comes to election in regeneration, many posit a power in man similar to the power they deny in Satan. How can this be? Scripture confirms that God is Sovereign over Satan and man – without suggesting man is a robot. In believing that God is Sovereign over Satan, we never suggest Satan is a robot yet some posit this faulty argument for man. How can this be? I do not deny that man can *think* he has sovereignty like pejorative free will, but if we cling to *this sovereignty*, we fundamentally deny the Sovereignty that Scripture proclaims.

When we think of Sovereignty in a redeemed way, **grace** is God-effective and Monergistic. As I present redeemed **grace**, it must be Effective but most Synergists reject the notion of Effectiveness in **Grace**. Sure, they profess to believe in grace but not effective **grace**. In regeneration and Justification, effective **grace** is exalted. If we take any credit for this, we steal God's glory. This is part of the 'job' of **Grace** – to teach us redeemed qualifiers – and I trust we learn.

Let's turn to a common understanding of <u>prevenient grace</u>, even as many don't know the term. Wikipedia says prevenient grace is:

An Arminian doctrine distinctive to Methodism and the broader Wesleyan Movement; it holds that man is so fallen that he is utterly incapable of perceiving the need for salvation, **but God**, in His infinite wisdom **has preveniently** [given before new birth] **extended to humankind sufficient** [but not effective] **grace that we can, through <u>free will</u>, willingly accept salvation.**[20]

The idea of prevenient grace may come from <u>initial innocent grace</u> that I contend man rejected in the Garden – in order to sin – but most reject *this* Garden-thinking. **If man rejected *this* grace and fell from grace, then prevenient grace per se is no longer valid.** If we posit prevenient grace as the God-electing-protection of sinners until God's Spirit applies redemption, then we agree with Scripture but use faulty terms. If we posit prevenient grace as not Effective, Sovereign or Redemptive, then, at best, we refer to mercy that God gives to draw us to Christ through repentance. In this way, prevenient grace could be seen as prevenient mercy to represent God's Ways in the Effective Justification and Regeneration of His Sheep as Scripture proclaims.

Let me summarize my meddling and move on. When we see what our Effecting God sees we begin to see Sovereignty, Justification, **Grace**, Regeneration, Sanctification and salvation in New Covenant light. When we realize **God is indeed the Monergistic Author and Finisher of salvation**, we can take ourselves out of the free-will-seat-of-author that we delusionally hold. Trust me; I know it's difficult to jump off our seat of mini-sovereignty. We somehow think we engineer our own salvation to steal God's glory. This is the same lie Satan told Eve; and we know the outcome of that belief. I trust you see how 'our sovereignty' (free will) is inconsistent with a redeemed lifeview. Once we see that our **Effecting God** sits on the throne, we can rest in His Work for and in us – as we diligently pursue His **grace**. Overall, belief in prevenient grace is a rejection of redeeming effective **grace**.

I deeply respect the work of J.C. Ryle and many pastors who give a <u>mercy-focused gospel</u> because I do not think they preach it out of wrong motives but this shows why a redeemed assessment is necessary. Evaluation can provoke gospel-modifications. Ryle explains the Gospel in typical mercy-focused terms; therefore I add thoughts in brackets to make it a New Covenant Whole-Cross message:

[Where must a man go to recover Holiness?] Where must a man go for pardon? [Where is holiness-correction to be found?] Where is forgiveness to be found? **There is a way both sure and plain, and into that way I desire to guide every inquirers feet**. That way is simply to trust in the Lord Jesus Christ as your [Holiness Model through **Grace** and] Savior. It is to cast your soul with all its sins, unreservedly on Christ—to cease completely from any dependence on your own works or doings, either in whole or in part—and **to rest on no other work but Christ's work**—no other righteousness but Christ's righteousness, no other merit but Christ's merit as your ground of hope. Take this course—and you are a [declared, becoming holy, and] pardoned soul.

Says Peter "All the prophets testify about Him, that through His name everyone who believes in Him will receive forgiveness of sins" (Acts 10:43). [Says Paul in Romans 5:19-21: "...So by one man's obedience the many will be made righteous. Now the law came in to increase the trespass, but where sin increased, grace abounded all the more, so that, as sin reigned in death, grace also might reign in righteousness leading to eternal life through Jesus Christ our Lord."] Says Paul at Antioch, **"Through this Man forgiveness of sins is being proclaimed to you, and everyone who believes in Him is justified from everything."** (Acts 13:38). "In Him," writes Paul to the Colossians, "we have redemption through His blood, even the forgiveness of sins" (Col. 1:14).

[The Lord Jesus Christ, in grace and truth has made a full satisfaction for God's Holiness requirement by giving His Holy flesh for our Righteousness.] The Lord Jesus Christ, in great love and compassion has made a full and complete satisfaction for sin, by suffering death in our place upon the cross. There He offered Himself as a sacrifice for us, and allowed the wrath of God which we deserved—to fall on His own head! [For our holiness, He offered His flesh as eternal merit and sustenance for **grace**-applied-ones.] For our sins, as our Substitute, He gave Himself, suffered, and died—the just for the unjust, the innocent for the guilty—that He might deliver us from the curse of a broken law, and provide a complete pardon for all who are willing to receive it. And by so doing, as Isaiah says—He has borne our sins. **As John the Baptist says—He has taken away sin**. As Paul says—He has purged our sins, and put away sin. As Daniel says—He has made an end of sin and finished transgression.

And now the Lord Jesus Christ is sealed and appointed by God the Father to be a Prince and a Savior, to give [Righteousness and its outflow with] forgiveness of sins, to all who will have it. The keys of [Life and Righteousness, and] death and hell are put in His hand. **The government of the *gate of heaven* is laid on His shoulder. He Himself is the door, and by Him all who enter in shall be saved**. Christ, in one word, has purchased [a full Righteousness and] a full forgiveness, if we are only willing to receive it. He has done all, paid all, suffered all that was needful, to reconcile us to God. **He has provided a *garment of righteousness* to clothe us**. He has opened a *fountain of living waters* to cleanse us. [Through the veil of His flesh, per Hebrews 10:19-25, we have access to the Throne of **Grace**.] He has removed every barrier between us and God the Father, taken every obstacle out of the way—and made a road by which the vilest may return to God. . . . Let a man only do this, and he shall be saved. [By Christ's Righteousness and mercy] His iniquities shall be found completely pardoned and his transgressions completely taken away!

Who, among all the readers of this paper, desires to be saved by Christ, and yet is not saved at present? Come, I beseech you! Come to Christ without delay. Though you have been a great [Holiness rejecter and] sinner, COME! Though you have long resisted warnings, counsels, sermons, COME! Though you have [no Holiness and have therefore] sinned against light and knowledge, against a father's advice and a mother's tears, COME! Though you have plunged into every excess of wickedness, and lived without prayer, yet COME! The door is not shut; the fountain is not yet closed. Jesus Christ invites you. It is enough that you feel laboring and heavy-laden, and desire to be saved. COME! COME TO CHRIST WITHOUT DELAY! Come to Him by faith, and pour out your heart before Him in prayer. Tell Him the whole story of your life, and ask Him to receive you. Cry to Him as the penitent thief did, when He saw Him on the cross. Say to Him, "Lord save me also! Lord remember me!" COME! COME TO CHRIST![21]

Everyone fails to meet the requirements of perfect obedience, perpetual righteousness, and perfect atonement. When we miss the first one, we can't hope to perform the second or third one. In the face of this impossibility, some wrongly imagine they *can* perform them and thereby exclude themselves from inclusion in Gospel reality. God's Gospel supplies Holiness-correction first, then sin-correction.

The only way our car-wreck failures can be reversed is through a substitute who <u>actively</u> performs the first two requirements and <u>passively</u> accomplishes the third. Sin, faith and believing are typically mentioned in evangelical gospel presentations; however, the depth of sin, payment for that sin, conversion, and necessary or ongoing obedience are seldom discussed. Without these necessary elements, the glaring void leaves many with the idea that inherent ability or generic goodness qualifies them for salvation. Some are told that a simple accepting-decision **effects** salvation but Scripture indicates this formula is flawed. At best our accepting-affecting decision confirms the effecting Work of the Spirit and thereby embraces sanctifying **grace**.

The word **Gospel** means **Good News**. The accomplished and applied finished work of Jesus Christ on the Cross is Good News! In this point, I appreciatively remember John Murray's excellent work, *Redemption: Accomplished and Applied.*[22] Truth be told, his work permeates my teaching and preaching. Many gospels minimize or distort the necessity and centrality of Righteousness in salvation, and I reject faulty gospels without essential holiness.

Distinctly, Jesus is the Gospel! Jesus said He – His person and Gospel – is the only way to the Father and eternal life per John 3:16-21. All sinners are without God's requirements but The Spirit applies Christ's work to elect ones at a point in time – not at the time of His crucifixion, as many think. The Finishing is one thing; the application of finished Salvation is completely another as taught in Romans 5:19-21.

Many are entrenched in contrary teaching. I realize the difficulty of this teaching – I used to be there! I struggled against the doctrine of elect ones but the Spirit caused me to reject erroneous beliefs by bringing a paradigm shift.[23] In <u>Christ's two-sided Gospel</u>, #1) **Christ's body is the Holiness-corrective-reality through the overcoming power of grace** and #2) Christ's mercy comes over our sin in clemency and forgiveness; together they are a whole Gospel.

Paul was in a similar position when confronted with the Gospel. From his skewed perspective, he honestly thought he 'glorified' God with murderous activity. He was not about to easily reject the religion he held from birth. After all, he had tenure. It's said he was in line to be the next High Priest; talk about opportunity! That's like being the next Pope. God knocked him off his horse to get his attention – a spiritual 2-by-4 – yet Paul was eternally blessed for being knocked off his 'mountain' as he resisted God's glorious Gospel. He would not have believed without this God-alone activity. Paul was grateful to be **graced**!

I only believe in One Way of salvation – through the applied and believed substitutionary atonement of Jesus Christ – found normatively by walking the Way. Knowing we can camp on varied texts, we must consider how we come to our salvation views or campsites. I offer the following list to help us think thru redeemed principles related to common salvation views or campsites.

Salvation Campgrounds or Campsites

Man is responsible for his thoughts, emotions and actions.
It's not God's fault that man lost Holiness and fell into sin.
Being kicked out of the Garden is God's judgment for sin and death
        because His Tree of Life was ultimately Christ's Cross.
The Fall *is* man's fault but spiritual death can be corrected.
God never allows man's attempts at self-salvation or self-justification.
Man can't earn or merit salvation but lost **grace** can be recovered.
Man's effort at justification is not acceptable to God but being a God-
        fearer might lead to regeneration then sincere effort.
God is not required to offer salvation, but He mercifully does.
Salvation is practically dependent upon how we *image* God.
Salvation is not about man making the rules he will abide by.
Salvation is not found in fig-leaf attire but in God's animal skin attire –
        God's application of Christ's Righteousness.
We cannot balance the scales of God's Holiness with our goodness.
Justification is God's Holy declaration rather than our sinful one.
Justification is dependent on perfect obedience and perfect atonement,
        and hinges on the sacrifice of another – Jesus Christ.

Justification is not a joint effort between man and God but salvation and
    sanctification are proactive efforts of **effective grace**.
Man can *affect* his salvation by being a God-fearer and God-seeker.
Regeneration compares to being called out of the tomb like Lazarus.
Salvation is not about just adding a little Jesus to life's mix.
A Godly make-over through Christ enables us to follow and obey Him.
Salvation is realized in being *re-made* to image or likeness Christ.
Salvation is like Moses being rescued by Someone else – Jesus Christ.
Salvation is like **believing** a serpent on a pole.
Salvation is like Joshua bowing to Jesus as the Commander.
Salvation at the practical level boils down to *how* we approach God.
We cannot be 'saved' and then approach God any way we desire.
Our worship cannot 'bring' salvation but flows *from* salvation.
It's crucial whose bloodline we possess; make sure it's the spiritual
    bloodline of Abraham through the blood of Christ.
We cannot create required justification but we can subjectively affect
    salvation by walking in His Ways through His means.
We cannot presume upon God's **grace** or mercy; it must be explicit
    rather than implicit; and applied rather than assumed.
Salvation is about regeneration and a re-created state through Christ.
Salvation is not about life in the first Adam but in the Second Adam.

Fundamentally, what we believe and think determines our
convictions and actions. Only a small step exists between wrong beliefs
and actions. Until corrected, we all have wrong beliefs. Before we are
regenerated, how we think and live is crucial to our overall life
because mistakes cause consequences that may never be reversed –
and the only person responsible for this is the one in your shoes. If you
think "Someday I will come to Christ, and then everything will be okay"
as if your wild oats won't come home to sprout, consider your basic
foundations as apathy, unbelief and unacceptable. Once we are
regenerated, however, how we think and live is crucial to our joy.

The belief of false doctrine, by itself, will not disqualify you from
salvation but ultimately clinging to unbelief and disobedience will
disqualify you. In regeneration, God corrects faulty doctrine – as He did
in Paul. We all come up short before God's glory (Romans 3:23) and a

difference exists between wrong belief and redeemed belief. Unbelieving ones can't see The Gospel as good news. The Gospel is the two-fold application of mercy and **grace** whereby we are created anew and now marvelously realize repentance, faith and conversion. The Gospel of Jesus Christ is good news for believing ones because it addresses the voids in fallen man. Without the accomplished and applied Gospel, we have no Eternal Hope of Life or abundant living.

Sin-correction – as necessary as it is – does not make us Holy. Remember the check-book analogy and zero balance? This is why **sin-avoidance doesn't work God's Will, but Holiness does**! This is why the blood of bulls and goats couldn't 'take away sin.' **A Holiness-correction adds the necessary positive Holiness that gives right standing with God**. A mercy-focused gospel keeps people trapped in a <u>potential sin-avoidance attitude</u> rather than allow the freedom of being holy – attained through **Grace** and **Grace**ful Law obedience. A New Covenant Whole-Cross Gospel brings the focus to a fully-actualized-and-practical-holiness-gaining-life-practice that glorifies our Holy Redeemer. As we grow in the Holy-actualizing part, I trust this makes holy-sense as you seek God's mind to live in His Will.

Chew on this; Adam and Eve lost Holiness[24] – visibly, morally, ontologically, relationally, spiritually, volitionally, practically, **grace**fully and organically – and it's no wonder they sinned! Redeemed eyes help us see why man sinned when they lost Holiness as Adam was in need of sin-correction because of the Holiness void alone! Listen to my feeble attempt to explain a very difficult reality. <u>The redeemed Gospel of Scripture makes the Holiness-correction ontologically primary with the sin-correction necessary but somewhat secondary</u>. **We need the Redeemer before we can be Redeemed!** We primarily need the Redeemer because He secondarily brings Redemption. Both are necessary but the Redeemer necessarily precedes Redemption. I trust you are beginning to see why re-installed Holiness is necessary.

Early in my life, I thought Scripture taught a synergistic gospel. When the Spirit brought me to understand the Redeemed View of Life, I saw that Scripture taught a monergistic Gospel.[25] Paul preached and taught this Gospel, and is often misunderstood. Paul taught God-alone-Redemption through graceful Law obedience – Christ's obedience rather than ours; however, our graceful obedience follows the application of His accomplished obedience. This is the New Covenant view of Graceful salvation in the Redeeming Gospel.

The Gospel can be given in clear terms but it's often given as a mercy-focused one-sided half-cross gospel. We learn this and may not question it even as it might torment our soul. Paul taught a New-Covenant-Whole-Cross-Gospel that presents Holiness as primary and Forgiveness as complementary, if not secondary. Without recognizing a holiness-void, we can't acknowledge a necessary holiness correction. But a thinking and living correction can come in a Whole-Cross Gospel.

In the attempt to provoke a **grace**/holiness paradigm that should be second nature to redeemed saints, many ask "How does this occur?" The reality of cancer provides a great analogy. When the disease of cancer is in our body, a healthy paradigm **knows** that Life overcomes sickness. One camp believes in 'killing' cancer out of us thru surgery, chemo and radiation. Another camp believes in 'healthing' it out of us thru diet and health. If our body-environment is healthy, cancer can't survive. In the past 18 months, I've done many healthy things – non-GMO foods, no carbonated drinks, Alkaline water, supplements, good home cooking and others. We can 'beat on sin' all we want thru forgiveness - spiritual surgery, chemo and radiation – and it won't do much good. On the other hand if we live holy, sin 'just' leaves. Recently, with PSA numbers escalating, I was told I had to go through radiation. Just before going to print, after a bone and CAT scan I heard, "No visible cancer!" PTL! My point is this – **grabbing hold of holiness through grace leaves little room for sin and unholy living**.

As I write, I often listen to gospel music. On Utube I recently saw and heard Signature Sound. They sang a song that speaks to holiness and how we should embrace it as our watchword and life:

There's A Road Called The Holy Highway
There's a road called the Holy Highway
    that once was a desert land
Very soon, you'll hear the sound of a holy marching band
    Everlasting joy upon them
There's a remnant strong and true

Chorus:
    We bring the song back to Zion,
    We bring the praise back to You!

Did God make a Holy Highway in you? I hope so. Praise God if you are part of His remnant. *The Son*, a story going around the Internet, helps us realize how to approach God and appreciate how God offers His Son as the remedy of a Holiness-rejecting and sinful people.[26]

The Son

A wealthy man and his son loved to collect rare works of art. They had everything in their collection from Picasso to Raphael. They would often sit together and admire the great works of art. When the Vietnam conflict broke out, the son went off to war. He was courageous and died in battle while rescuing another soldier. The father was notified and grieved deeply for his only son.

About a month later, just before Christmas, there was a knock at the door. A young man stood at the door with a large package in his hands. He said, "Sir, you don't know me but I'm the soldier your son gave his life for that day. He saved many lives that day, and he was carrying me to safety when a bullet struck him in the heart and he died instantly. He often talked about you and your love for art." The young man held out his hand, "I know it isn't much. I'm not really a great artist but I think your son would have wanted you to have this."

The father opened the package. It was a portrait of his son, painted by the young man. He stared in awe at the way the soldier had captured the personality of his son in the painting. The father was so drawn to the eyes that his own eyes welled up with tears. He thanked the young man and offered to pay him for the picture. "Oh no sir I could never repay what your son did for me. It's a gift." The father hung the portrait over his mantle. Every time visitors came to his home, he took them to see the portrait of his son before he took them to see any of the other great collected works.

The wealthy man died a few months later. It was published; there was to be a great auction of his paintings. Many influential people gathered, excited to see the great paintings and have an opportunity to purchase one for their own collection.

As people arrived and sat down, the painting of his son was on the platform. The auction began; the auctioneer pounded his gavel to start the bidding, "We'll start the bidding with this picture of the son. Who will bid for this picture?" There was silence. Then someone hollered, "We want to see the famous paintings. Skip this one!" But the auctioneer persisted, "Who will bid on *this* painting? Who will start the bidding? Will someone give $100? $200?" Another voice angrily said, "We did not come to see this painting. We came to see the Van Gogh's, the Rembrandt's. Get on with the real bids."

But the auctioneer continued, "The son, the son, who'll take the son?" Finally, a voice came from the very back of the room. It was the longtime gardener of the man and his son. "I'll give $10 for the painting." Being a poor man, it was all he could afford.

In auctioneer fashion, the auctioneer continued, "We have $10, who'll give me $20?" Someone yelled, "Give it to him for $10. Let's see the masters." The crowd was becoming angry as they did not want the picture of the son. They wanted the more worthy investments.

The auctioneer pounded his gavel, "Going once, going twice. Sold for $10!" A man sitting in the second row shouted, "Now let's get on with the rest of the collection."

The auctioneer laid down his gavel and said, "I'm sorry, the auction is over!" "What about the paintings?" was the cry from the audience. "I'm sorry; when I was called for this auction I was told of a secret stipulation in the will. I was not allowed to reveal that stipulation until now. Only the painting of the son would be auctioned. Whoever bought that painting would inherit the entire estate including the other paintings. **The one who took the son gets everything!**"

What a great story that reflects the Gospel Message and Reality! God gave His Son 2,000 years ago to die on the Cross to save His Sheep. Much like the auctioneer, His message is "The Son, The Son, who'll take the Son?" Because, you see, whoever takes the Son gets everything! Take and possess Jesus Christ in the whole Cross, and you get everything as a joint-heir with Christ. Because of new life that God plants in those who believe, we have everything in the Son!

It's great if you have the Son – but don't make a premature assumption of this reality. A false assumption or wrong conclusion at this point can be an eternally fatal mistake. As God gives me energy and voice, I attempt to shake people in their assumptions but rejoice with those who possess the reality or those who seek the reality. Those with the reality live in the power of the New Covenant – this is our inheritance and Freedom In Christ that **grace** brings.

Let's see how **grace** lives out in those who have been redeemed. When <u>The Redeemer</u> and His <u>applied Holiness-correction</u> are essential to the applied, proclaimed and lived Gospel that flows into <u>merciful forgiveness</u> – we can better understand our needs. His Gospel redeems these two glaring voids by substituting elements we could never supply. **Proclaim His complete Gospel and live the practical reality that flows from the verbal variety**. A direct relationship exists between the lived and proclaimed message but our living flows <u>because of</u> the <u>applied</u> Gospel and <u>from</u> the <u>proclaimed</u> Gospel.

<u>Holiness-correction</u> is an oft-missing key today. If Christianity is mere Moralism, as some charge, much is offered but this falls short of the Gospel. Mere sin-correction (often offered) falls far short. When, however, a Holiness-Correction through Christ's **grace** leads to a sin-correction through mercy – because of the torn flesh and spilled blood on the Cross – the focus is rightly on the **Grace**-providing-Savior.

As I close this chapter about the Gospel seeking sons – and daughters too – we need people to show us the way. Brian Free, of Assurance, sings "*I want to be that Man*" telling of a father-figure role model in the faith. How I hope His Gospel is planted in you. If so, I hope you are a **grace**ful role model for someone else. If not, seek to be one.

I Want To Be That Man

He was awake before the sun with his Bible opened up
Seeking truth with every single page he turned
Anyone could see my daddy lived what he believed
With a gentle heart and passion for Jesus' blood
I know we had our times we disagreed
But the longer I live it's clear to me

Chorus:
I want to be that man
Who loves the Lord with all his heart just like the Word commands
Who takes a stand and leads his family as he holds the Father's hand;
I want to be that man

Society would say there's a new ideal today
Not what you give, it's more about what you can get
But I want to live a life that's marked by sacrifice
Like the Savior who died to show us all the way
So I'll take up my cross and trace His steps
Surrendering is how I serve Him best

Chorus:
Just like Peter, Paul, and all the saints of days gone by
Let me show that kind of faith to those who come behind

Chorus:
I'll lead my family as I hold the Father's hand
I want to be that man.[27]

The words of this song remind me of my father. No matter your age or gender, I hope you can sing and declare "I want to be that man or woman!" God calls us to Image Him. Jesus calls us to Follow Him. Paul says, "Follow me as I follow Christ." Grace calls each of us to lead others in the same way. We too can say, "Follow me as I follow Christ." When God's Gospel is planted and thriving in us, we can help others be a planting pot for God's Gospel as it **seeks** sons and daughters. Follow Christ by seeking other sons who will **grace**fully obey Him.

---

1 John 1:12-13

2 Luke 19:9-10

3 2 Timothy 3:1-5

4 A new program will be launched for Billy Graham's 95th birthday in November 2013. The project, used around the world for the last ten years is called *The Matthew Project*. Check it out. It's a good correction but I wish it went further toward the redeemed Gospel.

5 I say this facetiously because I fundamentally believe there is no difference between salvation in the Old and New Covenants even as I know most people are taught there is a difference. I'd like to correct this shortsighted thinking.

6 The Children's Story *Humpty Dumpty* is a parallel to the Atonement and necessary healing that we gain through Christ's Works that were laid on or manifested in the Cross.

7 Warren Austin Gage, *The Gospel Of Genesis: Studies in Protology and Eschatology* (Eugene, OR.: Wipf and Stock Publishers, 2001), 4-6.

8 Michael Horton, *Christless Christianity: The Alternative Gospel of the American Church* *(Grand Rapids, MI.: Baker Books, 2008)*.

9 Horton, *Christless Christianity*, 15-16.

10 Horton, *Christless Christianity*, 19.

11 Cited in *Christless Christianity*, Christian Smith posits Moralistic, Therapeutic Moralism as the major illness of the American church. The second chapter, *Naming Our Captivity* discusses much of Christian Smith's and Marsha Witten's excellent work.

12 Horton, *Christless Christianity*, 41.

13 The decision-provoked-by-a-decision is a handle to describe what I see across the ranks of Evangelical churches. It's my way to speak a feast-in-a-mouthful with a spoonful.

14 The division mentioned here is between Exclusivism and Inclusivism. Exclusivism contends explicit acceptance of Gospel truth is necessary for salvation. Inclusivism contends this is not necessary. Without getting caught in the crosshairs, neither side focuses on regeneration but on the <u>decision to make a cake </u>rather than the <u>cake reality</u>.

15 Cited from Monergism.com – Classic essays on the gospel.

16 Ravi Zacharias, *Why Jesus? Rediscovering His Truth In An Age Of Mass Marketed Spirituality* (New York, NY.: FaithWords, 2012). This label is 'borrowed' from Ravi's assessment of Oprah Winfrey in Chapter 4 and Deepak Chopra in Chapter 5. For years I've enjoyed reading Ravi. I consider him one of the world's great Christian minds.

17 Rob Bell's gospel is taught in his popular book *Love Wins: A Book About Heaven, Hell, and the Fate of Every Person Who Ever Lived*. Bell teaches things that go against clear biblical teaching. In my judgment, he speaks of a gospel that allows unregenerate people to feel good about their sinfulness – in violation of the Redeemed Gospel.

18 Alistair Begg, *Pathway to Freedom: How God's Laws Guide Our Lives* (Chicago, IL.: Moody Publishers, 2003) 37.

19 Michael Horton, *Introducing Covenant Theology* (Grand Rapids, MI.: Baker Books, 2006) 187-188

20 From Wiktionary.org

21 Cited from Monergism.com – *The Way of Salvation* by J.C. Ryle

22 John Murray, *Redemption: Accomplished and Applied* (Grand Rapids, MI.: Eerdmans Publishing, 1955). I consider this a classic.

23 Besides teaching I heard, *The Death of Death in the Death of Jesus Christ* by John Owen clinched this truth for me. If you are willing to read what I consider the best work of doctrinal exactness on the subjects of election and particular salvation (Jesus only dying for His Sheep), I highly recommend this tough but powerful book from 1684.

24 Some theologians reject the idea that Adam and Eve rejected Holiness and therefore sinned. They give explanations but do not address **grace** as described in the Redeemed View of Life. While I appreciate their effort, I cannot accept their conclusions.

25 Most people think about Justification in terms of synergism – the joint effort of man and God to work technical justification in the soul through the application of Christ's Righteousness. This is the majority report today. Scripture speaks of Justification in terms of Monergism – the God-Alone act of applying Christ's Righteousness to the soul – with the subsequent active faith of salvation being a joint effort. See again pp. 262; 272-3.

26 We should listen well as Jesus unpacks truths about His Kingdom and what we need to hear and do to enter in – not least about the cost of 'buying into' Him and His Work. Matthew 13:44-46 give two pictures of how a God-fearer sells what he has to 'invest his life' in the Pearl of Great Price. Later, Jesus would not cast this Pearl before swine – but most wrongly focus on the unbelief and His refusal to perform miracles. Matthew 13 is also one of the best places where Jesus clearly teaches the truths of the two types of people in the world – the good and bad seeds and their origins. Hear Him!

27 This can be found on many YouTube sites but I got the words from lyrics.com/l-want-to-be-that-man-brian-free-lyrics.html and you can hear the song too.

Chapter 14 – God's Law Applied by Grace

This chapter dissects biblical Law-views to plant Moral Law firmly in the cultivating greenhouse of **grace**; thus the chapter title. **The Law** can be a very complex doctrine. The Law is complex yet simple, mentioned in different contexts and relationships. Being rebels at heart we struggle to submit to God's Law. We must work through our "Blueberries are red when they are green" riddle to embrace redeemed qualifiers of Law in an ever-changing upward-movement.

Let's start with the word/concept of Covenant as understood in America in marriage, church membership and our Constitution. One stumbling block in America surrounds misunderstanding the simple phrase *Separation **of** Church and State* that came from a Thomas Jefferson letter about freedom of religion. Most confusion-problems stem from misinterpreting "of" into "from." Many distort the intended meaning when we twist the statement into "Freedom from religion" rather than "freedom of religion." A huge difference exists between freedom **of** religion and freedom **from** religion!

In like manner a huge difference exists between freedom from Law and freedom of Law in a redeemed sense. Salvation-**Grace** gives saints freedom **from** Law but not freedom **of** Law. In fact, **freedom comes in living the Law through the power of grace.** I want to demonstrate that New Covenant Life is lived through Law by the power of **Grace.** Some think 'we're not under Law' – and we need crucial qualifiers – but **New Life lives from graceful Law-keeping.** Our salvation was gained by **Grace**-Full Law-Keeping and we can discover that **New Covenant life is freedom OF Law!**

At first look, some verses *seem* to suggest the Law is no longer binding on saints. Can this be true? If **grace** is the Spirit's effective empowerment in saints to 'Be and Do holy,' we must rethink these passages. Only a few possibilities can be correct. In Matthew 5:17,

Jesus said, "Do not think that I have come to abolish the Law or the Prophets; **I have not come to abolish them** but to fulfill them." If He did not come to abolish the Law, why do we try hard to do this? His words are only difficult when we twist them. What is the Redeemed Position of Law? Three generalities exist: 1) Law-obedience is the means of Justification in legalism. 2) The Law is thrown out in blatant or inconsistent antinomianism. 3) **The Law is God's Way for salvation through Christ and the Spirit's empowerment to be holy** – to reflect Christ's Righteousness. Let's unpack each point to gain insight.

1) Law-obedience is seen as the means of justification – as in legalism. Without throwing out the baby with the bathwater, eternal sentiment is contained in this point. To maintain orthodox belief through Justification-by-Faith-Alone,[1] we must be careful in legalistic qualifiers. Perfect obedience to the Law is God's eternal requirement and is the technical ground of our Justification. Because Christ's perfect Law-keeping is the ground of our Justification, we should strive for perfect Law-keeping in sanctification ("Be Holy as I am Holy"). Our obedient effort through His Faith, Power and **Grace** reflects or images Christ.

When a sinner pursues technical Justification before God by keeping the Law, this flawed approach is tantamount to fig-leaf clothes. It's not that perfect obedience is not required, but an unholy approach to Law is eternally unacceptable! The perfect obedience of Christ is the only acceptable Righteousness that answers the eternal demand of the Law. Here's the key point that many misunderstand – when Jesus, Paul and Scripture speak of law in the legalistic sense, the reference speaks of 1) seeking technical Justification or 2) yielding obedience to rabbinic law that was held in higher esteem than God's declared Moral Law; this is often seen in traditionalism or extreme fundamentalism. Obedience to the Moral Law, however, is **never** rebuked unless in one of the above two forms. Please know that a holy approach to practical justification through **grace** – after Justification – is always good!

When a saint pursues <u>practical justification</u> by keeping the Law through the power of **grace**, God is always pleased because His Moral Character is esteemed by Christ reflectors. Is there really any other way to honor and Image our Perfectly Righteous Redeemer? **Never see the pursuit of perfect Law-keeping through the power of grace as wrong or as legalism**; this libelous charge doesn't stand up under Scriptural scrutiny. If this statement strikes your ears as strange, check out what Jesus and Scripture explicitly teach about the Law. The diligent pursuit of Law-Keeping through **Grace** allows Christianity to become what God designed it to be. If we please our Father through necessary obedience, our joy and fulfillment escalate exponentially to provide oft-missing but desired and valid assurance.

2) The Law is thrown out or has 'no teeth' in antinomianism. Remember, Antinomianism is an anti or against-Law position. In the blatant version, the Law is totally discarded. Most readily discard this position as erroneous – a redeemed definition of **grace** would correct much of this oversight. To reject blatant antinomianism is good for eternal and redeemed reasons; however, a subtle version occurs when we are a law unto ourselves – as we 'embrace' God's truth.

The more-subtle version replaces God's Law with our law – making the inconsistent antinomianism position a legalistic approach with 'our' tradition. Rather than freedom <u>of</u> Law through the power of **grace**, the antinomian cries, "Free <u>from</u> the Law, oh blessed condition, I can sin as I please and still have remission."[2] This blatant cry of antinomianism inconsistently decries redeemed repentance, faith and conversion, and ignorantly fosters an unholy foundation for salvation and sanctification. From a redeemed Law-Embracing position, this is an awful position for a <u>professing Christ-Reflector</u> to hold! The installation of one word into Law-keeping – **necessary** – could correct this flaw in inconsistent antinomians and drive us back to the **grace** that keeps the Law to the glory of God's Character and Gospel.

For some, the Moral Law is embraced inconsistently as noble, recommended and advisable but not necessary. Many embrace an inconsistent antinomian position – believing this pleases God. I'm not sure why it's so easy to not see inconsistency in ourselves but necessary obedience corrects an inconsistent antinomianism position. Some don't honestly think about this point; for years, I didn't! Jesus told the woman caught in adultery, "Go, and from now on sin no more" in John 8:11 but sadly many don't understand the 'sinning no more' in an honest way. Most inconsistent antinomians profess to be Bible-believing conservative people but 'sinful conformance' or 'sinful Christ-reflection' is an absurdity that we must reject – especially as it rejects the redeemed reality of **grace** in God's **effectual** Gospel.

In *Primitive Theology*, John Gerstner says on Justification:

> What most clearly shows that the absence of works is utterly impossible for a justified person is the relationship of works to faith. **That faith which justifies is a working faith. If justification is by faith, it must be a real, genuine faith**. Everybody who reads this knows we are talking about real, not about counterfeit, faith. The fact that the hat in the window can be bought for $20 does not mean it can be bought with a *counterfeit* $20 bill. The fact that justification may be by faith does not mean it can be bought by a *counterfeit* faith. **A non-working faith is no faith at all, a counterfeit faith indeed. It is conclusive evidence that the person is not a believer that he does not pursue holiness**, without which no one shall see the Lord. Those who are Christians take up their crosses daily and follow Him. **Only those who *abide* in His Word are His disciples** (John 8:31). If a person does not take up his cross, does not abide in God's Word, and does not deny himself, then he simply is not following Jesus Christ. He is not a true believer; he is not an heir to eternal life, he is not going to inherit the kingdom of God.
> The classic passage is James 2:21: "Faith without works is dead." **James** does not say that faith without works is sick. He does not say that faith without works is not very healthy. He does not say that faith without works is dying. He **says bluntly that faith without works is *dead***. It simply does not exist. **Christ said the same thing in the parable of the vine and the branches**. That which does not bear fruit does not abide in Him. It is not in Christ, the vine, if it is not bearing the fruits of good works.[3]

I often relate inconsistent antinomianism to Dispensationalism; this broad-stroke assessment may be unfair even as it might be the majority report in the church. If we honestly approach God's Will and Ways, we must evaluate our approach to the Law. Gerstner says,

> Dispensationalism, past and present, teaches antinomianism, and therein denies justification by faith alone. Until Dispensationalism repudiates its antinomianism, it is going to have to labor under that awful indictment of <u>cutting the heart out of Christianity</u> by a fatally defective view of justification, which is the article by which the church or theology or the individual must stand or fall. No amount of excellencies can compensate for it. Just as a human being may be healthy in some ways except for one fatal ailment, so **it takes a lack of only one ingredient to destroy a theology.**[4]

For years, I was caught in the bondage of Dispensational theology without knowing the term at all. Today my soul bleeds when people profess to believe in Christ's Holiness yet fail to be disciples who live and teach necessary obedience to God's commands. This theological-practical-foil spawned my passion for a redeemed definition for **grace** that excludes every antinomian position.

2) The Law is God's Way for salvation – with Justification through Christ as the ground of our obedience – with **grace** as the Spirit's effecting empowerment to be obediently holy in reflecting Christ's Righteousness. Against the foil of legalism and antinomianism, redeemed **grace** answers the voids in each. Once Justified in the technical sense, the Spirit's sanctifying power causes us to walk in Law-obedience – the epitome of **grace** per Ephesians 2:10. <u>Grace requires necessary Law obedience</u> – even though our less-than-perfect obedience is acceptable in the hand of Christ because His perfect Holiness is the ground of sincere obedience. In this way, **grace** answers the dilemma of mankind for Justification, Sanctification and Glorification – to the praise of the most-Wise Redeeming God.

A small lesson sets the stage for most New Covenant truths. We can speak of the '**already** but **not-yet** reality' of Scripture to demonstrate that some things are given in their objective <u>already</u> entirety but received in an ultimate-realized-state only in glory – thus the <u>not-yet</u>. In the <u>already</u> state of Justification, we receive the perfect gift of Christ but – although the gift is complete – it's <u>not-yet</u> realized perfectly until we get to our glorified heavenly state.

The Moral Law was always an <u>already</u> reality even though at times it was shrouded in a <u>not-yet</u> cloak. This idea gives insight into Old Covenant/Moral Law difficulties we struggle with today. The Moral-Law-<u>already</u>- reality was shrouded in the Mosaic economy and we struggle to extricate a whole picture and see salvation correctly as it comes out of this haze into New Covenant truth. With this in mind, let's see how they work together in salvation.

When the objective <u>technical</u> reality of Christ's Atonement is carried into our practical lives, we can allow misunderstood forgiveness to be a cosmic Band-Aid. Yet Holiness is the correction God designed for our standing before Him. Ephesians 2:4-6 says, "But God . . . 1) <u>made us alive together with Christ</u> – by **grace** you have been saved – and 2) <u>raised us up with Him</u> and 3) <u>seated us with Him</u> in the heavenly places in Christ Jesus." Paul creates three new Greek words to describe these majestic realities in our <u>already</u> state of Justification.

After Justification, we are in the subjective <u>practical</u> reality of Christ's applied Righteousness in our <u>not-yet-finished</u> Sanctification. Because of His perfect applied Righteousness, saints live in the reality of imperfect **grace**ful holiness as our Holiness void 'remedy.' The application of <u>Christ's Righteousness is necessary for Justification</u>; by truth-extension, **grace**<u>ful Law-keeping is necessary for Sanctification</u>. To accomplish this, we must discover and live our freedom in the Law. The practical absence of this necessity exposes our lack of theological understanding. It might also describe the reality of stillbirths.[5]

God wired me to pursue consistency in biblical and practical regeneration and salvation – driving me to highlight inconsistency in those who nakedly claim life in Christ. 2 Corinthians 13:5 says, "Examine yourselves, to see whether you are in the faith. Test yourselves. Or do you not realize this about yourselves, that Jesus Christ is in you? – unless indeed you fail to meet the test." If we fail the test, we might not examine ourselves in this way. Do you see why a negative-reality can be a self-defeating conundrum? A similar dilemma exists in the church; it's easier to call every professor a believer but I refuse to do this. Free-flowing labels rarely work well – be cautious.

Because of God's provocation in me, I differentiate between Christ-professors and Christ-possessors, drawing a distinction between those who are regenerated (possessors) and are therefore saved against those who might only think they are (professors). Jesus makes this same differentiation in Matthew 7:21-23 with different language. Some think they belong to God because they profess a relationship but the Father, Jesus and the Holy Spirit confirm possession is required.

God's litmus test checks for our approach to Law and a love relationship that manifests obedient Christ reflection. Scripture teaches that possession of faith is heaven's Law and manifests obedient Christ reflection. I wish professors and possessors were one-and-the-same but experience and God's Word suggest an eternal difference. We must examine ourselves in this matter. When practical failing boils down to a mere teaching or practical issue, a correction is needed. Corrective teaching is needed to advance the Gospel, lead people to genuine salvation in Christ and lead saints in the process of sanctification – where **the Spirit works in us to proactively make us holy obedient Christ reflectors that manifest possession**.

Christ-professors, whether possessors or not, often disregard the Law or Ten Commandments and live as if God doesn't **regulate** their life by His commands. This leads to exposed contradiction or a charade with false assurance. Some think we can sin with impunity or without consequence but accountability certainly comes. Don't buy the idea that God doesn't require accountability. Consequences and judgment certainly comes! Don't mock God's command to "Be holy as I am Holy!"[6] because Law-violation certainly mocks Him! Pagans and atheists know this – even as they reject God's Gospel. When Holiness doesn't **shine** its Gospel light into the world per Matthew 5:14-17, sinners are further emboldened to mock God and His Law.

God teaches eternal principles in the Old Testament through the <u>Regulative and Retribution Principles</u> – even if this is done in implicit fashion. These principles address vital aspects of salvation and sanctification as God promised "your sins will find you out!" We can learn the foundation, misunderstandings and application of these Principles that bear greatly on practical Christianity. Are you ready?

Hebrew people knew these principles from their youth. Modern Christians don't think or talk in these terms anymore except maybe in a "That was then" mode. We can learn to empathize and appreciate what drove their conduct. At another level, don't easily dismiss principles and leave them in the Old Covenant without New Covenant adjustment.

Here's a synopsis of the Regulative Principle as it applies to Law, obedience, accountability and reap-what-you-sow concepts. The <u>Regulative Principle</u> basically means that **what God gives** in Source, resources, moral Law, commands, warnings and promises **should regulate our life**. This is the way it should be! The Regulative Principles flows from God's Law that regulates life – positively and negatively. Scripture teaches there is no other way. When we forget this, the results are tragic and eternally damning. **We either bow to His regulations, or reject and rebel against them**. Your choice!

God's <u>regulations</u> are lived out in the opposite poles of <u>Covenant keepers</u> versus <u>Covenant breakers</u>. This might be the thrust of the Psalmist in Psalm 14:1, "The fool says in his heart, 'There is no God.'" This speaks to rejection of the Regulative Principle in the soul of those who reject God's authority. Essentially this gives voice to a soul position that says, "I won't have God regulate me!" In another vein, it's rejection of "*that* God with *those* laws." This is not an atheist voice without belief in God but – listen up – <u>a Covenant rejecter who denies God's authority</u>. Covenant rejecters make bold 'atheists' as God's Law indeed regulates all of life! Here's a synopsis of God's Law:

> All laws are fundamentally religious since God is the lawgiver and ruler over everything. There are eight distinct categories of civil law in the Old Testament: 1) laws regulating leaders – exclusion laws; laws about kings, judges, the judicial system, witnesses, law enforcement, refuge cities, and prophets; 2) laws regulating the Army; 3) laws respecting criminals – crimes against God, society, sexual morality, including fornication, adultery, homosexuality, prostitution, incest, bestiality and transvestiture, and an individual's person; 4) laws dealing with crimes – against property, stealing, blackmail and loan fraud, weights and measures, lost animals, and boundaries; 5) laws relating to humane treatment – protection of animals and human beings; 6) laws about personal and family rights – parents and children, marriage, hired servants, slaves, and aliens; 7) laws regulating property rights – lost property, damaged property, unsafe property, land ownership, and inheritance laws; and 8) laws regarding other social behavior.[7]

Tragically many don't know, believe or embrace the fact that **God's Law was given to help us understand the Way or Path to reflect His Character in Salvation**. Many do what the Psalm 14 man does – refuse to bow before God's authority in His Law and Gospel; they 'believe in God' yet reject His rule and the Way of His Salvation. 'Psalm 14 thinking' abides in Law-rejection. Adam and Eve discovered God's radical consequences for sin.

It's easy to miss this Garden-tragedy-reality. Saul discovered this negative reality when he was knocked off his horse on his way to imprison Christians. Covetousness and national snobbery regulated his life. "Kicking against the goads" was eternally destructive per Acts 9:1-6 and 26:14. Once he saw his sin for what it was, his soul was struck to the quick. Paul discovered that regeneration flows into repentant conversion – into eternal life thru Christ-reflecting holiness.

After he was literally, figuratively and spiritually knocked off his 'high-horse,' Paul knew the <u>Regulative Principle</u> flows from God's blessing or wrath related to God's Law. This Principle basically says God's Law regulates our whole life. Some ask, "How so?" Generally speaking, the results relate to what we choose – **either** God, His Life, His Law and **grace**ful obedience **or** the rejection of God, His Life, Law and **grace**. Here's the point: **Paul didn't reject God per se but he rejected Christ** – believing he honored God. He learned that rejecting Christ and His Gospel was really rejecting God and God's Law.

Once he bowed to Christ, he rightly saw the Law and began to learn Grace. More than we know, Paul's conversion was the greatest Law-rejecter parable. As a Pharisee, Paul embraced contrary rabbinic laws – now he could see God's Moral Law for what it was. As <u>the only Pharisee-writer of Scripture</u>, Paul knew the difference; this is why he unpacks the Law as he does and never rejects the Moral Law. He taught that the Holy Spirit helps us learn Christ-reflection-through-**grace**-because-of-the-Atonement by seeing with redeemed eyes. If we get past faulty teaching today, we can hear and perform the qualifiers that Paul makes very clear in regards to our approach to the Law.

The crass rejection of God's Holiness and His Law is a scary manifestation – Paul almost went into spiritual apoplexy when Law-rejection was attached to a polluted understanding of **grace**.[8] Many today believe that grace overrides the need for Law-obedience. Those who know better must live victoriously in God's **grace** and proclaim the vision of walking in God's Thread of Continuity. We can't *bring* people to faith or bring the world into **grace**ful conformity but we can proclaim Law-Holiness and redeemed embracement of the Gospel of **Grace**.

In our typical confusion, many fail to realize the Old Testament often speaks from a redeemed or **grace**ful perspective. But if we are anti-Law or think grace doesn't come until the New Covenant – we don't hear it as such. Here's what we miss: the Old Testament speaks from the voice of the <u>sanctification perspective</u>. It often says, "Because you are redeemed, do this!" The same misunderstanding can carry into how we hear New Covenant salvation. Mere <u>professors</u> often live on assumptions that leave them in a 'donkey position' (making an ass-u-me) – the wrong position to hold when we meet the Master.

The Regulative Principle flows into the <u>Retribution Principle</u> that basically imagines we deserve what we get or get what we deserve. In other words, life-choices receive 'payment.' We know sin leads to negative consequences but it's quite another thing to directly relate suffering or persecution to sin. In this way, the true sentiment of the Retribution Principle is often distorted. On the flipside, **success and prosperity doesn't mean God's Gospel is being magnified**.

Job's three friends erroneously chastise, accuse and condemn him – particularly because of sincere confusion. Jesus' disciples have the same problem in John 9:1-2 when they see the man born blind and ask, "Rabbi, who sinned, this man or his parents that he was born blind?" This is John's Sign #6 and we should learn to guard against wrong judgment. We should be open to what God might do in the circumstance to reveal His glory. Who knows if God will display His Works in someone through the healing of spiritual resurrection?

Given the eternal reign of God's Law, the Regulative Principle is a valuable pointer. For many, this principle strikes our minds as legalism and condemnation rather than as **God's promise to bless the blessed life**.[9] This blessedness is not what many are taught to believe. In Psalm 1, God draws a sharp distinction between <u>Covenant keepers</u> against those who are <u>Covenant breakers</u>. God demonstrates **the necessary prerequisite for following Him – the gift of regeneration** that flows into **grace**ful obedience as the blessed-highway can lead to suffering for righteousness' sake.

Regeneration is the only redeemed salvation-beginning of Scripture; I hope we see this as the only whole-Scripture picture. As in the Redeemed View of Life, God's redeemed people allow principles to positively influence thoughts, attitudes and actions. Israelites knew that blessing flowed from **grace**ful obedience – even if what others saw was not always correct. Paul says that Christ possessors are true Hebrews (Galatians 3:7, 9, 14, 29 and 4:19) who learn **grace**ful Law-keeping.

When God says "Blessed is the man whose delight is in the Law of the Lord,"[10] He highlights the necessity and beauty of regeneration and Keeping Law. **Regeneration is the foundation of redeemed blessing**. Bible translations that use the weak rendering happy for blessed enable a confused concept. **Blessing – the state of being blessed through regeneration – is the foundation upon which Jesus builds His Mount Sermon in Matthew 5**.

Blessing, **grace** and obedience all go together! Sadly, many twist Law-obedience into a works-righteousness that betrays His Gospel and what God taught from the beginning. To **gracefully** embrace practical Law-keeping is not works-righteousness; rather, it's God's means to joyful coherent existence before His Commands. **God's blessing flows into freedom OF graceful Law-obedience**.

Jesus knew Holiness by the pure nature of God-Being but was also practically holy in His humanity. Scripture highlights these facts. Conversely Adam knew holiness in his innocent state at a peripheral level until sin 'was found' in his given-by-God-being. Then, being spiritually dead, Adam knew holiness in a given-by-God-recreated-being through the second birth. Adam didn't experience human birth but **Adam experienced spiritual birth as all saints do**. He received regeneration through application of Christ's Righteousness per Genesis 3:21. From both natures, Jesus knew the joy of keeping the Law.

More than anyone, Jesus knew that salvation hinges on perfect obedience. If we could interview a 1st century redeemed Hebrew, we would discover this person knew that God's Law should regulate everyone's life – this is how it was from the beginning. Many could use a Law correction today to understand negative and positive dimensions of godly principles. To reject or violate Law shifts the Regulative Principle into a negative-consequence-mode (maybe eternally) while redeemed living shifts the principle into a positive-blessing-mode.

When we judge in a legalistic Old Covenant sense as Job's friends did, we can wrongly judge **grace**ful Law-keeping in salvation. Redeemed vision practices Law-keeping so that we can say with David and Jesus, "Oh how I love Thy Law!" Maybe even before there was a Written Word, Job knew what David did.

One difficulty in the church is how Scripture is taught. At first, we understand the <u>Moral Law's eternal viability</u>. Then sadly, many are *taught out of proper belief*. They're taught to un-believe The Law. A simple hermeneutical rule is to read and practice Scripture in a simple sense – but we make it confusing. Some teaching <u>throws out</u> necessary obedience to moral Law on misunderstood passages.

Wrong teaching says Paul 'does away with Law on the basis of faith' despite what Peter warns at the end of his second Epistle. Peter already warned against false teachers and prophets. Then he tells us "be diligent to be found by Him without spot or blemish" and then plugs Paul's difficult teaching. With editing, 2 Peter 3:15 -17 says:

> Just as our beloved brother Paul also wrote . . . in all his letters . . . **There are some things in them that are hard to understand**, which **the ignorant and unstable twist to their own destruction**, as they do the other Scriptures. You therefore beloved, knowing this beforehand, **take care that you are not carried away with the error of lawless people** and lose your own stability.

When we understand the New Covenant through redeemed eyes, Paul speaks more to huge Old and New Covenant contrasts but never speaks of doing away with Moral Law, despite what some teach.

Paul teaches the viability of Law with New Covenant qualifiers in Romans, 2 Corinthians, Galatians and Ephesians. He always upholds the Moral Law through Christ's eyes and rule. Romans 3:31 is about as clear as it can be; it says, "Do we then overthrow the (moral) law by this faith? By no means! On the contrary, **we uphold the law**." I stand upon this to declare that we must work through qualifiers and implications to live Law in a God pleasing **grace**ful way.

The Holy Spirit works through the Word to bring conviction toward Righteousness per John 16:4-11. **Redeemed eyes help us see salvation as essentially the same in both Testaments**. I declared this; now I will make the New Covenant case in light of God's Law. Pulling right understanding of God's Moral Law through the haze into the majesty of the New Covenant is difficult but we must do this to honor the eternal majesty of His **Grace**, Law, Word and Gospel.

So what constitutes a proper view of the Law? Once we see that Whole-Bible salvation is the same throughout Scripture, we can embrace **grace**ful obedience because this glorifies Holiness, God's Holy Gospel, Law and Christ's Work on behalf of His sheep. Both Testaments present salvation through true faith manifested in following Law through the power of **grace** – this is Scripture's **grace** premise. We don't gain technical Justification by keeping any Law! This is why Adam and Eve could never re-gain eternal life by keeping Law after they lost Holiness and sinned. To say we can't gain Justification by keeping the Law doesn't mean we can't significantly impact salvation and Sanctification after Justification – by keeping the Law.

At its basic level, the Law says, "Do this!" In broader form, the Law says, "Do this and live!" **Scripture teaches that we find life in following the Law – but only through Gospel grace because it's built on Christ's Righteousness**. When God gives a moral command, He tells humans what He wants and never changes His requirements. We may misunderstand God's meaning and implications of Christ's fulfillment but we must not teach contrary to God's Law.

God requires perfect obedience to the Moral Law – He always has and always will! This is the foundation of The Gospel and what He commands. As some struggle to process this detail, we must sort through what God expects without dismissing His Law. Since Gospel **grace** gives the power to do what God commands, fleshed-out implications help us see how we can **grace**fully live out His Law.

Law is the foundation of life, even as New Covenant believers know that life comes through Christ and **grace**. Law is the foundation of New Covenant life so, in this sense, Law is the foundation of our life in Christ. When Christ commands "Go therefore and make disciples . . . teaching them to observe (obey) all that I have commanded you," He gives this command as risen Savior and God – the author and King of the Law. Think about this: if we produce disciples who keep the Law, disciple-makers must do the same; and Law-necessity is transferable!

The fulfilled-Law-foundation of Life is seen through and from the Cross, confirming the technical start of the New Covenant at the Cross. God never approaches Law democratically nor does He seek consensus from those it rules over. Sadly however, many don't know this or live from God's perspective; many don't live with the Regulative Principle and Christ's **grace** as their modus operandi. Rather than being naked law (if there is such a thing) – the Law that flows from the Cross-view is the fulfilled foundation of Life. It's not just normative, although many don't believe this anymore, it's fulfilled normative – this is why Jesus is the Ultimate Example to emulate and why the Moral Law becomes a higher law for saints *after* the Cross.

From our Continuity Thread, God's Word can be replaced with God's Law and Gospel without significant loss of meaning. Jesus is God's Living Word and the Bible is God's Written Word – so listen well to His Word. The Canon was being formed at the time of New Testament writings so when 21st century believers hear a reference to God's Word, we can think of the whole Bible but that wasn't 1st century reality. The Word mentioned in the Old Testament and Gospels most often refers to God-Written words in an Old Covenant setting of Law.

A practical theological question asks "How does the Law fit into the Gospel?" Some answer, "Not at all!" but Scripture presents a different answer. The Law encompasses and points to Gospel as the Gospel fully embraces the moral Law. Two John Murray books made my Top Ten All-Time list. I consider *Principles of Conduct* a classic. In the Foreword, J.I. Packer called this his masterpiece; listen well:

> It is best read as an exploring and fleshing out, and thereby a testing and verifying, of three hermeneutical hypotheses: (1) that **a single, perfectly coherent divine-command ethic** is taught from Genesis to Revelation, and thus **remains in force from history's beginning to its anticipated end**; (2) that the **grace** of God is intended not to lead away from, or beyond, a life of law-keeping, but **precisely to enable sinners for it**; (3) that **law-keeping belongs to the purest expression of pure religion**.[11]

Praise God for men who proclaim the eternal majesty of God's Law. The obscuring, marginalization, and rejection of God's Law may be the biggest tragedy in the church and world today. Murray writes:

> The Ten Commandments, it will surely be admitted, furnish the core of the biblical ethic. When we apply the biblico-theological method to the study of Scripture it will be seen that **the Ten Commandments** as promulgated [made official and published] at Sinai were but the concrete and practical form of enunciating [announcing and stating definitely] principles which did not then for the first time come to have relevance but **were relevant from the beginning**. And it will also be seen that, as they did not begin to have relevance at Sinai, so **they did not cease to have relevance when the Sinaitic economy passed away**. It is biblico-theological study that demonstrates that these commandments embody principles which belong to the order which God established for man at the beginning, as also to the order of redemption. In other words, we discover they belong to the organism of divine revelation respecting God's Will for man.[12]

Gospel and Law are two planks of biblical salvation. Colquhoun teaches the interrelationship between Law and Gospel. You may have to wade slowly; if you must, grab the floaty and listen slowly:

> The subject of this treatise is, in the highest degree, important and interesting to both saint and sinner [regenerate and

unregenerate ones]. **To know it experimentally is to be wise unto salvation; to live habitually under the influence of it is to be at once holy and happy**. The law and gospel are principal parts of divine revelation, or rather the center, sum, and substance of all the other parts. Every passage of Scripture is either law or gospel, or is capable of being referred either to one or the other. Histories of the Old and New Testaments are narratives of facts done in conformity or opposition to the moral law, and done in belief or disbelief of the gospel. The ordinances of the ceremonial law were grafted on the commandments of the moral law and were an obscure revelation of the gospel. Precepts of the judicial law are reducible to commandments of the moral law. All threatenings are threatenings either of the law or gospel; and every promise of one or the other. Prophecy is a declaration of things obscure or future, connected either with the law or gospel, or both; and there is not one admonition, reproof, or exhortation that does not refer either to the law or gospel. **If a man cannot distinguish rightly between the law and gospel, he cannot rightly understand a single article of divine truth.** If he does not have spiritual and just apprehensions of the holy law, he cannot have spiritual and transforming discoveries of the glorious gospel; and, on the other hand, if his view of the gospel is erroneous, his notions of the law cannot be right.

If the speculative knowledge which true believers have of the law and the gospel is superficial and indistinct, they will often be in danger of mingling the one with the other. If they blend the law with the gospel or works with faith, especially in the affair of justification, they will obscure the glory of redeeming grace and prevent themselves from attaining joy and peace in believing. They will, in a greater way than can be conceived, retard their progress in holiness as well as in peace and comfort; but **if they distinguish well between law and gospel, they will, under the illuminating influences of the Holy Spirit, discern the glory of the whole scheme of redemption, reconcile all passages of scripture which appear contrary to one another, try whether doctrines are of God, calm their own consciences in seasons of mental trouble, and advance resolutely in evangelical holiness and spiritual consolation.**[13]

My hope is that Colquhoun whets your spiritual appetite to pull up a chair and sit down to a feast. Accept my challenge to buy his book, #2 on my all-time list to digest its eternal truth. His wise teaching expounds distinctions and similarities between the Law and Gospel. If we open our spiritual mouth wide as a baby bird, God is pleased to 'feed' saints qualifiers about His Will contained in Law and Gospel. I could offer many quotes but I share another from Colquhoun's *The Establishment of the Law by the Gospel* chapter, emphasis mine:

> According to the doctrines of grace in general, and to the doctrine of a sinner's justification by faith without works of the law in particular, the law in that form is, . . . of standing use to convince sinners of their sin and misery, to discover to them their need of a better righteousness than their own, and **so to render Christ and His perfect righteousness precious to such as believe.** A sinner must first be convinced by the law **that justification on the footing of his own obedience is absolutely impossible** before he will listen to what the gospel says of Christ and His righteousness (Rom. 7:9). Accordingly, the Spirit of God does not lead a man to Christ by the gospel **without first convincing him of sin and of his want [lack] of righteousness by the law.**[14]

My book is not a Treatise on the Law and Gospel but great space is given to Law and Gospel through **grace** eyes. Feast on nourishing redeemed food by getting on the same page with Murray and Colquhoun; it's worth every bite – then embrace God's Law.

God's patience is designed to promote repentance rather than disrespect for Him or His Word. Through Christ, God can forgive but may not take away the consequences of death that we see nationally, psychologically, emotionally, spiritually, relationally and physically. Death is the inherent consequence of every sin, dysfunctional method, thought, behavior or violation of the Law, even in violations covered by His blood. Even though Christ took the eternal curse and consequence of His Sheep's sin, confusion in the church fosters contradictory approaches to the Law in saints and sinners alike.

As in the days of Ezra and Nehemiah, we need a recovery of God's Law in the church today. For too long the Law has been buried theologically and practically. Look around at our crumbling culture, marriages, homes, government, schools and churches. If the church and saints recover the Law, we could anticipate Gospel acceptance in the world. In *The Law and The Gospel* Foreword, Tom Ascol says,

The spirit of our present age insists that relativism is the only truth, and tolerance is the only virtue. **Absolutes are seen as archaic**; and right and wrong are forgotten categories. The church, rather than effectively standing against this spirit, has been infected by it. **We have lost our moorings**. We have forsaken our foundations. Until they are recovered, God's people will lack the spiritual ability to resist the onslaught of cultural decadence.[15]

Truer words to describe our culture, church and confused believers are hard to find. Many things would change if the church recovered the Law and lived it correctly. The recovery effort needs all hands on deck. In his Introduction, Reisinger cites J. Gresham Machen,

A new and more powerful proclamation of that law is perhaps the most pressing need of the hour; men would have little difficulty with the gospel if they had only learned the lesson of the law. . . . So it always is: a low view of the law always brings legalism in religion; **a high view of law makes a man a seeker after grace. Pray God that the high view may again prevail**.[16] [Amen!]

Machen's points are spot on in their assessment of our need, view of the Law and **grace**-pointing ability. He points the way for an envisioned recovery. Typically we don't think about sin and its correction deeply enough. At times, people think God is pleased to forgive sins. Many seek forgiveness per 1 John 1:9 as a spiritual Band-Aid rather than as a **grace**ful remedy to provoke holiness.

Forgiveness is essential but, contrary to popular opinion, God is not excited about forgiving sin. Instead, God is pleased with righteousness and holiness as they glorify Him and **grace**. Jesus' blood was eternally necessary and sufficient for salvation but we are hard pressed to say God is pleased with blood. God's Holiness is supreme in heaven, with no sin allowed, so let's talk about a new paradigm.

Popular opinion avoids the sin problem by positing a cosmic universal salvation – "No problem; we're all saved!" In light of faulty views, almost no one deals with lost Holiness. Common paths don't deal with spiritual death yet everyone has an opinion about how to bridge the chasm between God and sinful man. Deficient solutions ironically imply that correction comes by substituting 'righteous' acts; therefore, sinners crudely support the idea of exchange for right standing with God as they imply that sin can be overcome by man's goodness. Amazing! In word, they support the Gospel they reject.

If they could see clearly, they might believe God and seek Him through Christ. After Adam and Eve sinned, God <u>corrected</u> their holiness void and death by perfect Holiness to the Law – ultimately it took Jesus' death to correct the Holiness-void and sin. **Jesus is the Only Eternal Answer!** Blood is required for Atonement and God gave correction through the applied blood of Jesus. Holiness is required for right relationship and the Holiness-void was corrected by the Imputation of Holiness - as Jesus' Cross-death truly saves His Sheep!

A redeemed view of the Law realizes God is not pleased even with the blood of bulls and goats. First, the blood of His Son is the only sufficient 'thing' to adequately cover sin. Second, He is pleased with Holiness – this is why the perfect Law-keeping body of Christ is the only sufficient thing to provide **grace**. Because Jesus laid His perfect practical Holiness on the Cross for our sin and holiness-void, **graceful Law-keeping is the remedy God designed for His saints**. There is a huge difference between <u>transgressed Law</u> and **grace**<u>fully-obeyed</u> <u>Law</u>. God can apply mercy to the former; the latter magnifies **grace**.

Redeemed eyes allow us to see the eternal majesty of this difference. **Adam and Eve's Law-breaking was *corrected* by Perfect Law-keeping**. Perfect blood was applied to their sin. The forthcoming Messiah Jesus Christ's perfect perpetual obedience was the remedy for lost Holiness, ultimately corrected by Jesus' perfect **Grace**-Full Law-keeping. Hear this point clearly: In the practical realm, saints' sins are 'corrected' by imperfect **grace**ful Law-keeping – the essence of God-pleasing obedience in sanctification. Paul denounces distorted Law-thinking throughout his writings. Despite this, the church continues to seek consensus beyond clear meaning.

Let's consider conflicted teachings that add to the haze. Some teach that Law only applies to Jews. Some see a distinct separation between Old and New Testament believers regarding Law. Others see a dichotomy between Law and Gospel, or Law and Grace. Galatians and 2 Corinthians 3 seem to indicate the Law itself – in God-Written tablets – is no longer binding. Questions abound as to what it means when Jesus fulfilled the Law. Some teach the Law was abrogated, done away with and is no longer applicable or binding. Some misunderstand the 'disagreement' between Paul and James. Jesus Fulfilled all Law – ceremonial, civic, casuistic, sacrificial and Moral – but we must not add confusion and misunderstanding to the mix. It's easy for our theology and paradigms to lead to false conclusions. We must diligently study so that His Law-Word guides our paradigms. **Once we realize obedience to Law is God's Will, we can live accordingly**.

Law questions surely need answers. Confusion causes some to throw up their hands and give up on understanding Scripture about the Law. Redeemed understanding requires diligent study to wade through the plethora of questions and qualifiers to come to consistent, Christ-reflecting, New Covenant answers. Be patient but don't throw out the baby of Law-keeping with the bath water of Old Covenant confusion. Consider how James 1:22–25 relates directly to the Law,

> But be doers of the Word [Law] and not hearers only, deceiving yourselves. For if anyone is a hearer of the Word and not a doer, he is like a man who observes his natural face in a mirror; for he observes himself and goes away and at once forgets what he was like. But **he who looks into the perfect law, the law of liberty, and perseveres**, being no hearer that forgets but a doer that acts (by **grace**ful obedience), **he shall be blessed in his doing**.

Without the Law, we are like ships at the mercy of a raging sea – without charts, compass and navigational tools, without a navigator, rudder, lighthouse, landmarks, stars, destination, momentum, power or a safe harbor. This futility is similar to those who claim guidance from God's Word but throw out The Law in practice.

Without proper understanding of Law, we can't perform God's Will or know His Ways. **We will never find God's Will if we throw out the Law in mind or practice**. Chaos results when we forsake the necessary foundation of God's Law. During Israel's history, unbelief and idolatry revealed neglect or denial of God's Law. **Only as the Israelites recovered, respected, and obeyed the Law did they obtain God's blessing**. This truth is denied today. Our Supreme Court recently declared the Defense of Marriage Act (DOMA) unconstitutional (imagine that!) as storms and fires raged, killing 19 special fire-fighters in one tragedy. When we forsake God's Law as a country, church or as individuals, God's judgment and wrath will fall – and we wonder why.

A Law-recovery-message needs to be shouted from rooftops. To reflect God's Image requires the recovery of and obedience to the Law in New Covenant understanding and power. Yes it's through **grace** that obedience follows the Law but lack of proper esteem for the Law is one key reason why many church folks – nominal Christians who claim to reflect Christ and Image – don't reflect God's Holiness.

David realized **grace** to live God's Law. Because of this, David saw God's Word and Law as practically synonymous. We should too! We read this in Psalm 19, 40 & 119; consider Psalm 19:7-11,

> **The law of the LORD is perfect, reviving the soul**; the testimony of the LORD is sure, making wise the simple; the precepts of the LORD are right, rejoicing the heart; the commandment of the LORD is pure, enlightening the eyes; the fear of the LORD is clean, enduring forever; **the rules of the LORD are true, and righteous altogether**. More to be desired are they than gold, even much fine gold; sweeter also than honey and drippings of the honeycomb. Moreover, by them is your servant warned; **in keeping them there is great reward**.

The Law consists of God's testimonies, commandments, precepts and ordinances or rules. David highlights descriptive terms that apply to God's Law. He said God's Law is perfect, sure, right, pure, clean, true, precious, sweet, and profitable – that's quite a list!

David further said that obedience to The Law results in revival of the soul, wisdom, joy of the heart, an enlightened mind, eternal life, righteousness, warning, discernment, dependence upon God, and acceptable living. David's list sounds like New Covenant salvation – and he rejoices in the Law! Listen to a few excerpts from Psalm 40:

> He also brought me up out of a horrible pit (v.2) and set my feet upon a rock and established my steps. He has put a new song in my mouth (v.3). Blessed is that man who makes the LORD his trust (v.4). Sacrifice and offering you did not desire; my ears You have opened (v.6). Then I said, "Behold, I come; in the scroll of the book it is written of me. **I delight to do Your will, O my God, and Your law is within my heart** (vv.7-8).

David fully knew that God brought him out of a pit of sin and death, set his feet on a salvation rock and 'opened his ears.' David knew **gracefully living the Law is the way to please His Lord**.

Despite the clear teaching of Romans 1, many don't honor God; Law-violation demonstrates this tragedy. When people seek pre-eminence and discovery in their disobedience, they are self-deluded. We mock God's Word when we hide our sin. Adam and Eve discovered this principle was alive in Eden as their sin and hiding exposed their nakedness. Hiding and nakedness speak to the exposed person who imagines their sin is invisible. Listen to Warren Gage discuss Law:

> The relationship of the Ten Commandments to the creation of the cosmos is more than merely analogical. It instructs us that when we disobey the moral Law of God we introduce chaos into our culture. **To the extent that we defy the Law of God** expressed in His Ten Commandments, **we destroy the very foundations of the social order that makes life itself possible**. Moses set before us the law of life and death. He instructs us to choose life that we might live (Deut. 30:19). The commandment, as the apostle Paul assures us, is "holy, just, and good" (Rom. 7:12).[17]

John Colquhoun sees the Moral Law of Mount Sinai as a two-sided giving between Hebrews entrenched in bondage who 'find' their righteousness in themselves versus True Israel who finds Justification in God – with proof manifested in **grace**ful obedience. Both Gage and

Colquhoun provide **grace**ful clarification. Godly men can provoke us to consider, fully embrace and then live truth through The Law as they help us correctly sort through this difficult subject. Please listen.

As clearly as I know, I present regeneration as the primary key to redeemed understanding throughout the Bible. The remaining pages flesh-out this conclusion. **To live the regeneration-reality is essential if we are to manifests the reality of graceful Law-obedience**.

The practical difference in Moses' two-sided-giving is quite easy to see once we see from a New Covenant perspective. Moses contrasts two salvation perspectives. On one hand, he presents a tongue-in-cheek salvation obtainable with human 'perfection' through a Covenant of Works. When we misunderstand his tongue-in-cheek offer, we misunderstand why people wrongly throw out The Law. Across the board, he presented the coming salvation brought by Jesus Christ.

Many <u>professors</u> said with determination, "We can do that!" It sounds good but their response is no different from those who say they can live acceptably before God's face without His input, Word or **grace**. From a New Covenant perspective, we know better! They sufficiently failed yet continued to think this failure was acceptable to God because of their bloodline. This approach would never work! Christ's personal, perfect and perpetual obedience is the only ground of Gods' acceptance and our **grace**ful obedience. Against common teaching, this is why His Law-obedience heightens our obligation.

To add insult to injury, if you will, we must understand how their thinking applied to sacrifice. After God taught them to perform animal sacrifices for sin, they 'fulfilled' what God required as they continually performed sacrifices for sin. We must give them some credit; they felt they did as God required – even though God told them they 'missed the boat' by thinking God freely accepts the 'sacrifice' of asking for mercy in the face of merry-go-round-sin. They were wrong on several counts. We too fail to understand what God made clear in His teaching.

Many discard Old Testament ideas of salvation but Exodus has parallels for our experience today. Were you offered works-salvation? Were you baptized into <u>the faith</u> from birth? For those who embrace the altar call, did you do as the man-of-God said and follow his directions for salvation? Did you walk the aisle and 'accept Jesus as your Savior?' Were you promised eternal life if you walked and accepted? Many who 'submit' to this formula are told "You're saved; you possess salvation!" When *this* salvation is questioned, they hang onto whatever they believe; this is why some fail to sufficiently examine themselves in light of Matthew 7:21-23. Don't rest on a faulty notion of salvation no matter who said what – because **believing a false reality is insufficient**.

It matters little if you misunderstood what God's man offers, even if it was Moses. We're responsible for what God means and clearly proclaims in His Word. If one fails to perfectly communicate God's Gospel terms, this doesn't free us from responsibility. Wrong teaching on the Law doesn't free us from culpability. Some 'good-sounding teachings allow' us to throw out the Law with the 'blessing' of the church, parent or man of God. We must rethink this approach because it sounds like we've bought Satan's promise – The Big Lie.

The Law basically says, "Do this perfectly and live!" As Adam's sons, we change God's requirements only a bit. We think, "A minor word adjustment to God's Word can't be crucial." Some say, "You're not going to tell me we have to obey perfectly are you?" What they often mean is, "We're not really going to obey – but if there's a question, we basically try to be good." Some say, "We were born and baptized in a church; our parents are saved; and we occasionally take communion." Others say, "We're Americans you know!" Either way, that's a far cry from what the Law and Gospel requires. The implication of Law points to the Perfect Fulfiller and Atoner of Law – Jesus Christ and believing Him and His Work; there is no other way to eternal life. The Law is not to blame for anyone's failure. Neither is God!

A key issue is misunderstood gospel **grace** – the regenerating power to be saved and then **grace**fully keep the Law as God's family rules. Most Hebrews missed Moses' ultimate point. This may explain why Jewish leaders argued vehemently with Jesus – believing He was wrong. After all, they had bloodline, law and history to show they were right. But they were dead wrong because they would not believe the One to whom the Law directly pointed.

The majority heard the "Do-to-Be" gospel of self-salvation. They heard "Obey the Law *for* salvation," never realizing God offered the substitutionary Atonement of Christ to make them adopted sons. They were determined to make rebellion work into righteousness with the 1 John 1:9 saltshaker method used today. They never heard God's offer through Abraham's faith; they were convinced their bloodline in Abraham was sufficient. They never heard God's offer of **grace** through the free-woman Sarah and her Seed; they were determined to make error work by the bond-woman Hagar even as they wanted Isaac's redemptive blessing. They did not hear that **grace**ful Law-keeping was an outflow of regeneration; rebellion made them hear a distorted giving – thinking their 'obedience' merited salvation or that 'their works' gained salvation. **They didn't hear the True Gospel that they rejected.**

Sadly it was little different when Jesus came onto the scene. Maybe it was worse, probably similar to today. John Owen suggests the Jews of Jesus' day were the most decadent of all time. They deserved every "Woe" Jesus declared against them for their unbelief in the Prophet/Savior who taught and ministered in their midst. He called for repentance and belief like Jonah per Matthew 12, and they did not listen. The Old Covenant trap led many to think their bloodline and 'commitment' – rather than personal-justification-through-Christ – was their ticket to the Promised Land. Their bloodline, per se, got them to the Promised Land but not to a necessary regenerating experience with Christ. Their commitment got them as far as demons, per James 2:19.

For salvation, they needed the blood of a different line – that of the God/Man Jesus Christ. Hebrews from Moses' time, Jesus' time or today all need the Atonement of a perfect substitute. We all need these two things – the blood and body of the Second Adam who died on the Cross. This is why **the Cross is our eternal answer – through the Law in the Gospel**. With it, we can have salvation. Without it, we have God's wrath and separation; it's your choice. Rather than blame God for our rebellion and what it deserves – His eternal wrath – seek the gift by **believing** the Giver of Life. We all need different blood.

On the other hand Moses offers the same Gospel, but elect ones hear the *other side* of his two-sided approach to the Law. Using the same words to speak to God's sheep – later known as the Old Testament remnant – Moses offers a different approach to the Law. It's the same Gospel but heard from the right foundation. Redeemed people hear the True Gospel of **Grace** in the Mosaic administration. In this light, Moses presents salvation that was obtainable with 'human perfection' through a Law-keeping Covenant. He offers the same words to everyone but how they hear sheds light on which person they are – covenant-breakers or covenant-keepers. This is the same with Gospel preachers today – they give the message; how hearers hear is the essential difference. The choice is yours but the right choice only flows through Jesus Christ and His Faith. Will you choose that path?

The difference is that **God's Sheep hear Moses' words as a grace offer in Christ's hands for regeneration unto graceful obedience because of Christ's substitutionary Atonement**. This point is so important. They hear Moses' words as the regenerating power for effective salvation and **grace**ful Law-keeping thru believing. We can't reject this, even if it confuses our sentiments. When they said, "We will do this!" they committed to believe and follow their Messiah. As they knew the "Be-then-Do" cries of Law through the power of **grace**, they saw with redeemed eyes and did with redeemed faith!

Matthew 7:13-14 describes a picture of redeemed **grace** in the few elect ones in the broader many of professing believers; Jesus said,

> Enter by the narrow gate [Jesus Christ]. For the gate is wide and the way is easy that leads to destruction [our car wrecks], and those who enter by it are many. For the gate is narrow and the way is hard that leads to life, and those who find it are few.

We are often confused with this elect ones reference and what they do in the face of the Gospel but this depicts the same reception-quotient that Moses faced. All Israel [bloodline] was not Israel [Abraham's Faith in Christ] as Paul later made clear. Despite what Paul taught, we still hear teaching that 'all Israel was spiritual Israel' – a skewed picture.

We get a clear picture of this stark reality with the prophet Elijah as he confronts the 450 prophets of Baal and 400 prophets of Asherah under the evil king Ahab. The people of Israel had forsaken God and gone whoring after false gods who could not deliver. Speaking of odds Elijah faced, twice he said, "I, even I only, am left a prophet of the Lord, but Baal's prophets are 450 men." After God consumed the sacrifice of meat, stones and water, they had a Come-to-Jesus-meeting after which Elijah killed the false prophets. It's certain some Hebrews truly repented but bobble heads were also in attendance.

Against Elijah's complaint that 'he alone was left,' God later told him, "Yet I will leave [I had] seven thousand in Israel, all the knees that have not bowed to Baal, and every mouth that has not kissed him."[18] The remnant is not God's Special Forces but those with redeemed Faith – God's Army! God always has an elect remnant but it's not as big as many imagine. **Grace** enables us to be part of the elect remnant because we believe God in Christ and **grace**fully keep His Law.

We too can miss Moses' ultimate point but I hope that unveiled New Covenant reality is now easier to hear and see. I ask, "What do you see? How do you hear the Law as it relates to the Gospel? Do you hear it as a means of self-salvation? Do you hear the Law as a grace-based offer to accept, only to earn the rest of salvation in your power? If so, this is faulty thinking. It matters how we hear the call of the Law in respect to the Gospel – as obedience is the outflow of applied Gospel.

I hope you hear Moses' offer as the remnant did. If so, you hear the Law correctly and look for God's mercy and **grace** through Jesus Christ and His substitutionary Atonement – to then live in a God-pleasing **grace**ful manner in regards to God's Moral Law. This is what David knew as he said, "O, how I love thy Law!" Because he lived in the power of Christ and **grace**, he knew New Covenant truth.

Consider two quotes that speak to this two-sided offer of Moses on Mount Sinai. In *Grace To Stand Firm, Grace To Grow,*[19] Carol J. Ruvolo teaches 1 & 2 Peter. Her books can help those who want to grow in grace. Ruvolo quotes Edmund Clowney and Martyn Lloyd-Jones who now know these truths through heavenly glorification. Clowney said, "The indicative [redemptive declaration] of what God has done **for us and in us** precedes the imperative [command] of what we are called to do for Him."[20] Essentially Clowney endorses the "Be-then-Do" scenario. In other words, God does for and in us and then we do because He gifts us with His power of **grace** to reflect Christ.

Ruvolo says, "Dr. Martyn Lloyd-Jones, also in a sermon on 2 Peter said that 'the gospel isn't interested in our behavior – until after we're saved."[21] We often get the order of salvation confused as we wrestle with the Law and Gospel. We can struggle with what we are to believe, how we are to act according to doctrine, etc. What we do matters, but it matters greatly after we are regenerated! Ruvolo says,

> The gospel is not a call for us to be saved by doing something; it is a proclamation that we have been saved because something has been done for us. However, **once we are saved, the gospel demands that we do a lot.**[22]

Jesus taught that God's Law is binding. In paraphrase fashion, **we are obligated to obey** – not <u>for</u> salvation but <u>from</u> salvation **grace**.

As the Living Word, Jesus hearkens back to when the Word literally and physically came into <u>Living-Written-Being</u> on Mount Sinai. John 1 speaks of how the Word became flesh in a different way.[23] Scripture often refers to Itself as God's Written Words as Jesus – God's Living Word – makes this point. <u>Moses</u> obeyed God's command and <u>was the only human treated to a book signing when God's finger wrote two tablets</u>. Yet we now have a much better record than Moses.[24]

Albert Mohler Jr., president of Southern Baptist Theological Seminary writes in *Words From the Fire;* he says,

> **If God has not spoken, then there is no one who is right, and there is no one who is wrong**. If God has not spoken, then all you have is the end game of postmodernism – nihilism without knowledge. But if God has spoken, everything is changed. **If God has spoken, then the highest human aspiration must be to hear what the Creator has said**.[25]

Mohler doesn't use the term lifeview but correctly frames our thinking around Law. I highly recommend his book, not just because he is my seminary president. Here are some of his abbreviated points:

> First, **if God has spoken, we do know**; and if God has spoken, we must know... And **having heard, we cannot feign ignorance** . . . Second, if God has spoken, we know only by mercy . . . Third, if God has spoken, we too must speak. . .Fourth, if God has spoken, then it is all about God, and it is all for our good. . . Fifth, if God has spoken, it is for our redemption . . . Sixth, **if God has spoken, we must obey**. . . Seventh, if God has spoken, we must trust . . . Eighth, if God has spoken, we must witness.[26]

Mohler quotes the late Francis Schaeffer who was a great theologian and philosopher who often taught the Christian Worldview. I have *The Complete Works of Francis Schaeffer* and recommend them. He was the impetus behind the film series *How Shall We Then Live;* my book could be viewed as a partial microcosm of Schaeffer's work.

Mohler cites *The Francis A. Schaeffer Trilogy* that rebukes common thinking that denies culpability by claiming the right to dismiss truth with an epistemological excuse. Epistemology is the science of how we know with a practical question: "How can we really know?"[27] "For the Christian who understands the doctrine of revelation, there is no real epistemological crisis; there is only a moral and spiritual crisis. **All that remains is whether we will obey**."[28] For those who reject the knowing-duty as conjecture, there's no hope without repentance. **We never find God's Will without walking in His Will** in ever-growing Christ-likeness through **grace**ful covenant Law-obedience.

It's said, "The Old Testament is the New Testament concealed; the New Testament is the Old Testament revealed."[29] The question we must ask is, "Do we define the New Covenant by Old Covenant law or Old Covenant Law by a New Covenant redeemed-view perspective?" Many hide behind a false dilemma where we do the first and claim the second. Correction is needed, and this is what I passionately seek. We must embrace Law through New Covenant eyes and living.

Let me throw out two scenarios to see how you hear and/or believe them. First scenario: <u>Adam and Eve would experience eternal life and complete New Covenant salvation if they hadn't sinned</u>. Have you heard this or believe it? We must distinguish between <u>potential possibilities</u> from the view of innocence versus the reality that **Christ's Cross was God's eternal redemption plan despite their innocence**. **Grace** through Christ's Cross was not God's "Plan B;" it is His eternal plan! In that light, God's applied redemption in Genesis 3:21 was the <u>already</u> as they waited for the <u>not-yet</u> of later redemption history and glory. The reality of the Tree of Life in the center of the Garden was symbolic of the Cross – part of their not-yet reality and our haze.

The second scenario: <u>Israel as a nation could experience complete Covenant promise with Christ's inaugurated Kingdom if they manifested complete Covenant obedience</u>. Have you heard this or believed it? We must make a distinction between <u>plausible reality</u> against the reality that was revealed with Christ's Cross and complete salvation. Redeemed Israelites had the <u>already</u> but not the <u>not-yet</u>-New

-Covenant-time-reality. They had to wait for the Incarnated One who would bring complete salvation through His substitutionary atonement to inaugurate or 'bring in' the New Covenant. When we propose possibilities that deny the necessary reality of Redemptive History in Cross fulfillment, we provoke answers that don't fit Redeemed salvation. I enjoy discussing these matters but a better discussion is redemptive-history-actuality. We must guard against inconsistent answers by always protecting and applauding **grace**ful obedience.

Let me offer another teaching to highlight redemptive history in a redeemed light – with the help of our already/not-yet perspective. In other words, without the objective not-yet aspect of salvation, we don't have complete salvation in an already-valid sense. If you can't absorb this, pass over it. While the tree of life in the center of the Garden of Eden represents the Cross – **without the not-yet Cross-reality, the Tree of Life couldn't be used**. This is why Adam and Eve were dispelled from the Garden, not because God didn't want to apply the remedy (He already had!) but because the Reality of the Tree was yet future. They lived in the yet-future-already-reality but it was not in their midst as we speak of salvation in not-yet-completed terms. The Tree's presence had more to do with future redemption than current reality.

A similar scenario applies to Hebrews who leave Egypt to make their way to the Promised Land. God manifests Himself in several already-realities to point redeemed Hebrews to the not-yet-reality of completed Cross-salvation. The Serpent-on-a-Pole scenario of Numbers 21:4-9 is one. The pole's already-salvation compares to the not-yet reality of the future-promised Cross but we can't deny the Cross with hypothetical conjectures – remember the Son!

Since the Cross is the crux of God's revelation-matter, **we must consistently see Old Covenant redemption by a redeemed New Covenant perspective**. Many claim this but fail to be consistent. Why is all this important? It's crucial because redeemed perspective significantly impacts and frames our Gospel understanding, presentation and living as His Cross and **Grace** span man's history.

Four common approaches are unpacked in Chapter 15; consider them as I reject the first three. 1) We can throw out the Law, believing the New Covenant supersedes the Law's necessity for possessors. 2) We can *allude only* to Law in gospel presentations and Justification. 3) We can present the Law in Evangelism – similar to Jesus – from noble desire but without necessity. 4) We can teach the Reformers' three uses of Law with an emphasis on Law as a mirror for empowered conduct before God.

A New Covenant perspective helps us sort through important qualifiers to see **Grace** in the Redeemed lifeview. The Law is corrective encouragement because it provokes us to see how redeemed **grace** significantly transforms the Christian life. As Americans used to cry, "Remember the Alamo!" **Grace** affects our view of the Law because we DO find life in **grace**ful Law-keeping and must "Remember the Law!" To see **grace** through Law helps us discover or recover New Covenant truth. Remember, redeemed ones have freedom OF Law – live like it!

A redeemed view of the Law can live strong in us and we need many voices to declare this redeemed truth. The Army says "Be all you can be!" God says "My power can make you all I want you to be – as you seek to likeness my Son!" **Grace**ful Law-keeping can be realized in already-reality – what are you waiting for? Saint Augustine said, "The human will does not attain **grace** through freedom, but freedom through **grace**." We have freedom from law through Christ's Work and freedom of Law to obediently keep the Law through the power of **Grace** that flows from His Work – and living this dual-distinction **finds** His Will!

---

1 Justification By Faith Alone is the typical orthodox saying of salvation that speaks particularly to how we are technically Justified before God – by Faith Alone as the reformers stated this point. Their doctrinal handle is often misconstrued and slandered but it speaks the truth of Ephesians 2, "For by **grace** are we saved through faith."

2 John H. Gerstner, *Primitive Theology: The Collected Primers of John H. Gerstner* (Morgan, PA.: Soli Deo Gloria Publications, 1996) 279. For those who like to surf the Internet, look up The Antinomian Way of Justification by John Gerstner from Ligonier as his chapter on Justification is given; www.ligonier.org/blog/antinomian-way-justification. Gerstner probably did not have a dispensational sentiment in his body and his teaching is greatly needed in our day as he calls dispensational antinomianism on the carpet.

3 Gerstner, Primitive Theology, 284

4 Gerstner, Primitive Theology, 281

5 I use the term stillbirth to describe a regeneration-violating 'reality' that is visible in the visible church. In humanity, we speak of stillbirths to describe a baby that is born dead. In reality, this technically means that life existed in the fetus. In the spiritual variety, life never existed but people speak as if this was true; therefore, the term stillbirth. Correctly, in light of regeneration, the term stillbirth is invalid because it's likely that no spiritual life existed. Nonetheless, this is a tragic reality in the church.

6 Galatians 6:3-8 is a great passage with verse 7 saying, "Do not be deceived: God is not mocked, for whatever one sows that will he also reap." Mocking God is something many do not consider today.

7 Ronal F. Youngblood, *Nelson's New Illustrated Bible Dictionary* (Nashville, TN.: Thomas Nelson Publishers, 1995) 748-755.

8 Romans 6:1-4

9 *The Blessed Life* of Scripture speaks fundamentally of the majesty of the new birth being created in our soul. So often we speak of Shalom or blessing in a way that overlooks the reality of regeneration – Scripture would help us do this if we listen clearly. We must rethink how we view these verses. Redeemed vision sees blessing as planted ontologically and organically in regeneration. Psalm 1 paints a great picture to show this reality; we are firmly planted in regeneration and, because of this, we are blessed.

10 This is a contraction of Psalm 1:1-2.

11 John Murray, *Principles Of Conduct: Aspects of Biblical Ethics* (Grand Rapids, MI.: Eerdmans Publishing, 1957) 5-6. The other John Murray book in my top ten is *Redemption: Accomplished and Applied.*

12 Murray, *Principles of Conduct,* 7-8.

13 John Colquhoun, *A Treatise On The Law And The Gospel* (Morgan, PA.: Soli Deo Gloria Publications, 1999) vi-vii. To share my passion; this book holds the #2 spot on my all-time list. Every serious student of the Word should digest a copy of this work.

14 Colquhoun, *A Treatise on the Law and The Gospel,* 179

15 Ernest C. Reisinger, *The Law and the Gospel (Phillipsburg, NJ.: P&R Publishing, 1997),* xi.

16 Reisinger , xv.

17 Warren Austin Gage. (2005, February) *The Lord of the Law. TableTalk* 29,16-19

18 1 Kings 19:18

19 Carol. J. Ruvolo, *Grace To Stand Firm, Grace To Grow* (Phillipsburg, NJ.: P&R Publishing, 2003).

20 Edmund Clowney, cited by Ruvulo in *Grace To Stand Firm,* 41.

21 Martin Lloyd-Jones, cited in Ruvulo, 171.

22 Ruvolo, 171

23 John 1:1-18.

24 Luke 16:27-31.

25 R. Albert Mohler Jr., *Words From The Fire: Hearing the Voice of God in the 10 Commandments* (Chicago, IL.: Moody Publishers, 2009) 16.

26 Mohler, *Words From The Fire,* 17-22. These points form the foundational chapter themes in this book.

27 Epistemology is the philosophical study that basically asks, "How do we know!"

28 Francis Schaeffer, cited in Mohler, *Words From The Fire,* 17.

29 I have no idea the origin of this statement; I only remember hearing this many times at the church in which I cut my spiritual teeth.

Chapter 15 – God's Gospel Grace Lived With Law

People often teach the Moral Law as a stand-alone entity in the Old Covenant **without** the power of **grace**. In this vein, the picture makes about as much sense as the first time we hear "Blueberries are red when they are green." Some true statements require relationship-differentiation to accurately qualify – as they may initially sound contradictory. When we see Law practically fulfilled in believers through the power of **grace**, many paradigms change. God wants this truth lived out in saints – this is His Will for His Sheep! I boldly present the New Covenant perspective that sees obedience to God's Moral Law – lived out in the power of **grace** – as the Christian faith.

Some may ask, "Why do you present Law and **Grace** in this way?" Jesus perfectly kept the Law and was the full essence of Truth and **Grace**.[1] Jesus' Example is not mere coincidence but the Essence of God's standard. Jesus' perfect Law-keeping is the essence of His body that He laid on the altar of the Cross. Consider that His body represents the burning flesh of Old Testament sacrifice, making the aroma of His sacrificed flesh a sweet-smelling savor to the Father. These points give the synopsis of my **Grace**/Law foundations.

In many ways, <u>we struggle to pull the burning flesh of the Old Testament sacrifice intact through the haze into New Covenant **grace**</u>. I contend this is the missing doctrinal key. Without redeemed **grace** in doctrine and practice, God's Gospel and our testimonies are shortchanged. The fallout is that **many don't understand how Christ's Righteousness pertains to our graceful Law-keeping**.

Many 'posit' Holiness in salvation but not through sacrificed burning flesh from the Old Testament sacrificial Law. It's like we have a mental lapse between the Two Testaments – we bring the blood and forget the body or flesh. The Holiness picture many understand in the

Gospel is <u>God's generic Holiness</u> rather than <u>Christ's necessary perfect Holiness</u>. Could this flaw allow some to posit 'unnecessary' holiness in sanctification? This incomplete understanding leaves many voids – a big one tied directly to the Cross and 'sacrificed Holiness.' **God's redemption in Christ's sacrificed flesh helps us actually live right knowledge of Law – through and because of grace!**

Many affirm God's eternality yet struggle to affirm the eternality of God's Moral Law that flows from His Character. This indefensible contradiction is tragic! God's Moral Laws are eternal despite contrary teaching and inconsistent living. Few things please the Father more than **graceful** Christ-reflecting obedience – so let's open the haze curtain a bit to see how the Law lives in the greenhouse of **grace**.

David shows Law through a needed (new) paradigm. David challenges us to think and live differently. Rather than a "Don't confuse me with the facts; I already have my mind made up" attitude, I trust we live an old perspective. Only God wrote the last chapter of Scripture.[2]

A misunderstood qualifier leads some to tragically reject the Law and embrace an anti-law position. Ernest C. Reisinger calls us to reflect upon common antinomian or legalistic approaches to the Law:

> **The law, like Christ, has always been crucified between two thieves – antinomianism on the one side and legalism on the other.** The antinomian sees no relationship between the law and the gospel except that of being set free. The legalist fails to understand that vital distinction between the two. Some preach the law instead of the gospel. Some modify them and preach neither the law nor gospel. Some think the law is the gospel, and some think the gospel is the law; those who hold these views are not clear on either.[3]

I remember playing the game *Kick the Can*. Usually a fast person guarded the can and everyone went off to hide or make themselves unrecognized by the guard. The guard's goal was to capture people by finding them while 'guarding' the can from someone kicking the can – to release all captives. The guard had to capture everyone to win. If someone legally kicked the can they hollered out a freedom-saying to release all captives. Then, everyone ran and hid again. If someone won, we'd pick a new guard and keep playing.

Antinomians treat our approach to the Law as a spiritual game of Kick the Can. According to their game, God does His best to capture people with the Law and Satan or someone else sneaks in to kick the can – and holler freedom to all captives. This Kick-the-Can freedom-call is the epitome of the antinomian approach to Law. Former captives are free to do as they want – go hide in the bushes again with the belief that Law can no longer capture them. But Scripture paints a different picture and I trust we see how God 'wins the game' through Law.

Legalists, on the other hand, play the game of *Life*. By their decisions, they 'control' life. When it comes to the Law in their control, they make more of the law than God does – if that's possible. As they go around their board, they put others under their domination of traditionalism. Scripture obliterates the rules of this game too!

When we discard or ignore the Law, a crucial salvation-ingredient is lost. With that cost in mind, it's no wonder those who discard the Law struggle in their salvation and contrived sanctification. It could be that they don't possess the blessing of regeneration; therefore they can't **grace**fully obey. If they do possess regeneration, the Spirit leads in **grace**ful obedience – but we must follow. Are you?

I can't accept the oft-heard phrase, "Jesus kept the Law so we don't have to!" This is not the redeemed cry; rather it's the cry of a practical or actual antinomian. Jesus perfectly fulfilled Old Covenant sanctions and curses (one meaning of His Law-keeping) so that **New Covenant saints <u>can</u> keep the Moral Law in His Power to please the Father**. God adopts sons and gives His power – Christ's **grace**-ability to effectively provoke **grace**ful Law-keeping.

Solomon refers to Wisdom as a woman – as she calls in the streets – so we see a definite cause/effect relationship regarding our behavior when God's moral Law regulates our behavior. We don't earn or merit right relationship with God *through* obedience, but **grace**ful rebirth provokes obedience to God's Law to please the Father, Son and Spirit. I believe this cause/effect relationship shouts **grace**.

Proverbs 2:1-4 speaks eight **If's** that believers **will** follow in obedience. Consider these Wisdom <u>IF-Statements</u> that show us how to approach God's Law and its **grace**-ought-compelling nature.

1) **IF** you receive my words (v.1) – **meaning do them;**

2) **IF** you treasure my commandments (v.1) – **wholeheartedly incline your heart to understand;**

3) **IF** you make your ear attentive to wisdom (v.2) – **listen attentively to study and diligently obey;**

4) **IF** you incline your heart to understanding (v.2) – **discipline your heart and mind to *know;***

5) **If** you call out for insight (v.3) – **beg God for insight into your sin and pray for the power to overcome;**

6) **IF** you raise your voice for understanding (v.3) – **wrestle with until you know or possess the needle;**

7) **IF** you seek it like silver (v.4) – **commit time and work to find the silver shaft;** and

8) **IF** you search for it as hidden treasures (v.4) – **use every means to *mine* nuggets of truth; this is wealth.**

Wisdom basically says, "**IF** you do these points, **THEN** you will have God's promises! By the <u>blessing of **grace,**</u> you can perform His Will! There are no better promises for redeemed people that reflect the Gospel. Do you want what God has for us? **IF** so, **THEN** follow His plan. **IF** not, **THEN** you have your desire! These **IF**'s can be positively pursued through **grace** or negatively rejected from pride or rebellion; either way **THEN**'s come into play. In verses 5-22, four main **THEN**'s with qualifiers support the compelling nature of **IF** statements:

1) **THEN** you will understand the fear of the LORD and find God's revelation; vv. 5-8.

2) **THEN** you will understand righteousness, justice, equity and every good path; vv. 9-15.

3) **THEN** you will be delivered from spiritual and physical exploitation; vv. 16-19.

4) **THEN** you will walk in the good way and stay on the righteous path; vv. 20-22.

Essentially **Jesus kept the above If/Then statements so that His sheep can keep God's family rules by grace**. In practical and salvific ways, **our life is framed by how we live God's Law**; this applies to regenerate and unsaved ones alike. Approaching the Law in a cold **grace**less way never works. We must approach His Law as God-fearers pursue His Ways – the essence of fearing the Lord.

Moses gave God's written stones to the Israelites to reaffirm the blessing/curse options for obedience. Proverbs' Wisdom says that God guards and directs our steps when we follow the eight If's. If we want God's promises, Wisdom says, "**Then** follow the Law!" with the four Then's listed above to honor God's Law through **grace**.

When asked, "Teacher, what good deed must I do to have eternal life?" Jesus asked the rich young ruler "What does the Law say?" In Matthew 19:16-22, Jesus responds "**If you would enter life, keep the commandments**." Jesus' words sound strange to our modern sentiment and theology. At first glance, many wrongly think Jesus speaks a legalistic gospel. No matter our perspective, we think, "Why would Jesus say this?" Many don't know what to do with Jesus' response – but this is God speaking. Without dismissing His words too quickly, consider the interchange.

After rehearsing the commandments, the man asked, "What do I still lack?" Many struggle with Jesus' reply as He essentially tells him to practically submit to or obey the Law in order to be perfect – or to obtain salvation. We can take this in two valid ways. First is that 'obedience to the Law is the Path to salvation' – this speaks directly to the God-fearing approach that represents Scripture. Second is that 'graceful obedience is the path to prove who follows.' Persistent non-following indicates an opposite proof. Jesus speaks as an accepted Rabbi but this man refuses to follow and be Jesus' disciple. We too are called to be a disciple of this God-ONLY-approved God-Rabbi. What's your answer? The other two approved rabbis – Hillel and Shammai – couldn't pass muster with God's requirements. **Only Jesus qualified, and took His position to the Cross-altar to prove it!**

In view of the If-Then presentation, Jesus basically said, "**If** you are one of Abraham's sons as you claim, **then** obey in the power of **grace**." By his refusal, this man demonstrates blatant rebellion or, more likely, that he isn't one of Abraham's Faith-sons. Maybe he believed rabbinic laws were higher than what Jesus taught. This Law-distinction is significant as many worldly 'rabbis' today call people to follow a faulty path. Make no mistake – Only One Unique Son/Rabbi fits the bill – and **Jesus doesn't hesitate to connect Law and Salvation. Neither should we – in our Gospel and living!**

When Paul argued the finer points of Justification by faith alone in Romans 3:31, he asks "Do we then overthrow the (moral) law by this faith?" "By no means! On the contrary, we uphold the law!" Throughout Scripture, God's moral Law is always upheld! If you think otherwise, look again. If Moral Laws are the family rules of God's Kingdom obeyed through the power of **grace** received at the Throne of **Grace**[4] per Hebrews 4:16, we must approach the Law from a Redeemed View.

Tragically, obedience to the Law is often seen as legalism. This perceived legalistic flavor causes many to disrespect and reject the Law. <u>When I embraced the Law as something good and necessary for my spiritual welfare – doctrinal and practical things fell in place</u>, leading me to learn the Redeemed Lifeview. Colquhoun gives insight here:

> The obligation of the natural [moral] law upon mankind, then, as resulting from the nature of God and from the relations between

God and man, is such that **even God Himself can't dispense with it.** It can't cease to bind so long as God continues to be God and man to be man – God to be the sovereign Creator and man to be His dependent creature. **Since the authority of that law is divine, the obligation flowing from it is eternal and immutable.**[5]

The Law in God's Thread of Continuity is a mirror that reflects the Image, Glory, Character and Holiness of God. Colquhoun helps:

> It [The Law] is given to believers as a rule to direct them to holy obedience. It has the sovereign and infinite authority of Jehovah as a Creator as well as a Redeemer to afford its binding force. His nature is infinitely, eternally, and unchangeably holy; and therefore **His law, which is a transcript of His holiness, must retain invariably and eternally all its original authority** (Leviticus 11:44; 1 Peter 1:15-16). The law as a rule, then, is not a new perceptive law, but the old law, which was from the beginning, issued to believers under a new form. This law issues to true Christians from Christ . . . It proceeds immediately from Jesus Christ, . . . **it is given** to all who believe in Him, and who are justified by faith, **as the only rule of their obedience.** The Apostle Paul accordingly calls it "the law of Christ" (Galatians 6:2). It is a law which Christ has clearly explained, and which He has vindicated from the false glosses of the scribes and Pharisees; His new commandment which He has given and enforced by His own example, and whose obligation on the subjects of His spiritual kingdom He has increased by His redemption of them from their bondage to sin and Satan. It is a law which He, according to the promise of His gracious covenant inscribes by His Holy Spirit on their hearts; a law too which He calls His yoke, and which, in comparison to the law of works, is a light and easy yoke.[6]

When we live the moral Law that manifests our re-creating and redeeming God, it becomes the centerpiece of covenantal relationship, the Gospel and life-practice. Warren Gage says 'God spoke Ten Words into chaos to create cosmic order' in Genesis 1: 3; 6; 9; 11; 14; 20; 24; 26; 28 and 29. Then 'God spoke Ten Words to create social order' in Deuteronomy 5:7; 8; 11; 12; 16; 17; 18; 19; 20 and 21.[7] Gage says,

> When we disobey the moral law of God, we introduce chaos into our culture. **To the extent that we defy God's Law expressed in His Ten Commandments, we destroy the very foundations of the social order that makes life itself possible.**[8]

Consider how the Ten Commandments apply to American life and our Constitution; Warren Gage says,

> **We best understand the <u>necessity</u> of the commandments when we recognize that the essence of the Law is the protection of human life and happiness. Each commandment protects some vital aspect of the life of man.** The first commandment announces that there is only one God, thus protecting the truth of man's theological understanding about God. The second prohibits graven images, thus protecting the true expression of acceptable worship. The third prohibits taking God's name in vain, thus protecting the sanctity of the Lord among men. The fourth requires remembrance of the Sabbath Day, thus protecting the theology of grace. Jesus said the Sabbath was made for man, and not man for the Sabbath. The fifth requires the honoring of one's father and mother, protecting respect for the authority of the home. The sixth proscribes murder, thus protecting a man's life. The seventh forbids adultery [and fornication], so protecting the integrity of a man's family. The eighth is against stealing, thus protecting a man's livelihood. The ninth forbids false witness, thus protecting a man's reputation. The tenth prohibits coveting of any kind, so protecting the purity of the heart.[9]

God's commandments relate to everyday life for every person. **To reject or deny the Commandments is perilous – especially for those who claim to reflect God's character**. If we don't see the moral Law as our Path for **grace**ful faith in Christ, re-examine your paradigm.

The elliptical[10] aspect of Law illustrates how the elastic aspect of Law stretches beyond a hard-and-fast characterization. The elliptical effect is seen in Jesus' teaching as He – the Author and Expounder of Law – expands the meaning of Law in the Sermon on the Mount. The elliptical nature of Law shows contrasts, extensions, qualifiers and expansions to help us live the Law's beauty and majesty.

John Colquhoun's *A Treatise On The Law And The Gospel* helped me in three key areas: 1) the contrast between the Old and New Covenants; 2) God's three requirements that form the basis of Christ's Atonement; and 3) the practical magnitude of **Grace**. Speaking of the moral Law as somewhat of a litmus test for believers, Colquhoun says,

All true believers, through faith, not only do not make void the moral law, but on the contrary establish it or make it stand in all its force. <u>To establish the law . . . is to make all the infinite authority and obligation of it stand firm</u>, or to place them on their original and immovable basis, and instead of invalidating to confirm or strengthen them. **Believers, then, by faith, that is, by the doctrine and the grace of faith, establish the law.**[11]

Each point significantly impacts how we approach the Law. In his classic book, *Holiness,* J.C. Ryle says,

Genuine sanctification will show itself in habitual respect to God's law, and habitual effort to live in obedience to it as the rule of life. There is no greater mistake than to suppose that a Christian has nothing to do with the law and Ten Commandments *because* he cannot be justified by keeping them. The same Holy Ghost who convinces the believer of sin by the law and leads him to Christ for justification, will always lead him to a spiritual use of the law, as a friendly guide, in the pursuit of sanctification.[12]

A <u>spiritual use of the Law</u> is driven by **grace**, The Word and Spirit. Colquhoun says Law is the New Covenant family rules in the hand of Christ. Ryle suggests that many disregard the Law either because they know they can't keep it or were taught they shouldn't try because their Justification already occurred – but justification is a continuous practical pursuit. Rather than obedience as a cold duty, it's the lifeblood for ones called to His purpose per Romans 8:28-29.

How we see Law and **Grace** definitely impacts how we live with both. Great confusion exists about God's Law as many confuse Law references and essential differences between the moral, civic, purification, casuistic, dietary, rabbinic, and temple laws. Historically the church unflinchingly embraced the moral Law but today it's slighted, disregarded and abandoned by professing believers – to the possible damnation of their soul. **The essential performing-power of grace is seen in the practical Doing of Law – to Christ's glory and Gospel.**

I was raised and bred in a holiness environment that laid the foundation for my later full-circle understanding and appreciation of holiness. For years, I was caught in wrong teaching that I now decry. I was in a church culture that skewed a redeemed understanding of how we should approach the Law. Sadly, when people initially hear my words, the first response is one of running from legalism. I deny any legalistic teaching but this caveat can't keep people from accusing me of legalistic notions of holiness, but a closer look refutes that charge.

Putting ourselves in the Way of salvation[13] properly shifts the focus to where it belongs. **The charge of legalism can't stand in the face of the regenerative sanctifying power of grace that Christ's body and righteousness brings to the salvation-table.** Many miss these qualifiers, even in the salvation they proclaim. Often, those who reject 'my' notion of **grace** – either through ignorance or disregard – are actually perpetrators of Legalism. Our righteousness can't merit right standing with God; however, after we are rebirthed, essential obedience must camp on the Law in our re-created nature.

Throughout Scripture, salvation and Gospel are based on GraceFull promise provided through Law. The **GraceFULL** promise for Law-keeping is through adoption and sonship. Moses presents and touts the Law. Prophets proclaim the Law. Many kings proclaim the Law. Jesus – the Law Giver Himself – proclaims and expounds the Law. The Apostles proclaim the Law. The New Covenant proclaims the Law; therefore we miss something when we reject the Law or don't embrace it as God designed – so that we Image or Likeness Christ.

Sadly, many are taught against Legalism and therefore reject every notion of God-pleasing **grace**-driven Law-keeping activity. This is why many throw out the baby of <u>God-natural holiness</u> with the bathwater of residual sin nature. If you find yourself standing here, I plead with you to re-examine what you think and do.

On another level, those who charge Legalism don't often examine the root or impetus of the obedience in question. Let me turn the tables a bit. Why would we think that obedience is bad? When disobedience caused the Fall, why do we think obedience is wrong? When God commands perfect obedience, why think obedience is not His design? When disobedience displeases the Father, why flinch about offering pleasing actions? When the Son perfectly kept the Law, why not strive for this with His power? When the Spirit is grieved with disobedience, why walk down that road? When God gives Resurrection power, we should never disparage the Law yet Satan's Lie permeates thinking in the church and gets many to practically reject the Law.

Most discussions of Legalism start with confused points. They typically don't start with 1) regeneration, 2) a New Covenant picture of biblical salvation and 3) **grace** as God's empowerment to be holy. Unless they start at the right place, the whole discussion is skewed. Most start with a wrong view of salvation; this is why I shift the focus to Monergism and regeneration. Confusion over the organic reality of regeneration might explain why many are confused with Jesus' words to the rich young ruler about inheriting eternal life. Jesus quickly took him back to the Law – a great starting point for one schooled in the Law and supposedly seeking salvation. What a novel thought for evangelism![14] Our evangelism should start with the Law as Christ examples – and not just to expose sin and reveal the blood-corrective.

As the Law basically says, "Do this perfectly, and live!" this can be a depressing thought to those dead in sin and without God's empowerment of **grace**. By itself, the Law offers no Law-keeping power. In deadness, we have no divine power to keep the Law. **We can never _effect_ new birth through obedience but we can _affect_ our approach to God's Will and Ways**! Maybe the rich young ruler misunderstood what Jesus meant but he likely completely understood and wasn't about to follow this Only-Accepted **Grace**-giving Rabbi. Look what he missed by refusing to follow the Law – salvation itself!

The Gospel presents a shifted paradigm but the same message. The Gospel of **grace** says, "Because you Live; Do this!" We can embrace God-glorifying, Christ-reflecting, **Grace**-magnifying, and Gospel-overcoming effort every time! I often put the Gospel in a "Be-to-Do!" scenario as it promises, "<u>IF</u> (when) God re-makes you to be (regenerated), <u>THEN</u> do!" This "Be-then-Do" Gospel-scenario is a different paradigm than most consider. **When God rebirths us, we have the grace-ability to do as He commands**; live and proclaim this!

Let me present a salvation-paradigm from the Exodus. Many confuse God's salvation *before* the Law and imagine Law precedes salvation; this thinking can lead to a legalistic approach to salvation. This faulty view is the energy behind rejections of Law-keeping but God demonstrates salvation for 19 chapters *before* giving the Law. But even Law-giving in *this* context seems to be a stumbling block for many.

Throughout Scripture God demonstrates that regeneration always occurs before grace-driven activity occurs. <u>Most realize this but struggle to plant this reality in man before The Fall.</u> This might be the missing point that breeds confusion in the church with a twisted understanding of Free Will and Image-ability without regeneration. Adam and Eve were the only created humans – with innocence and **grace**. Everyone else was birthed in spiritual death and without **grace**. But, if we think about it, salvation is and **must** be the same, even if we are confused with the reality of Adam and Eve's innocent state.

To me, **the missing puzzle piece is that grace was required *before* the Fall**. But we don't often hear or read of this necessity. We must use '*redeemed investigation*' to discover and understand the redeemed view of the Cross to see that **salvation comes only to those who are re-created or re-birthed in Christ's Grace and Faith**.

Some reject 'my' approach to Law and **Grace** but I say God doesn't write the New Testament to expose the Old Covenant; there's a sense that <u>He writes the Old Testament to explode the New Covenant</u>. A great explosion from the Cross unveils **grace** to drive regeneration, salvation and sanctification – everything we need to overcome!

God applies New Covenant salvation to Adam and Eve in Genesis 3:21. From this, regeneration and **grace**-empowerment are required throughout Scripture! **With the person and work of Christ as the True Model, Adam and Eve needed grace and regeneration from the beginning!** Normatively, regeneration is **particularly** applied by **grace** – **effectively** soon after their innocence was shattered.

Before and after the Fall, God requires perfect obedience. This requirement helps us realize why Christ's perfect Law-keeping is the ground of God's salvation. **When Christ's Work is applied to us by the Spirit, grace-empowered obedience pleases Him because of His Finished Work.**[15] Without regeneration and empowerment, the actuality of godliness is impossible and moralistic. With necessary **grace** before the Fall we can avoid confusing Garden-questions that are the fool's errand; this is why **grace** was voided or denied before Adam and Eve could sin. Adding 'voided-**grace**' back to the 'equation of mankind' helps put **grace** in the middle of salvation where it belongs.

To understand necessary regeneration – even as Adam and Eve's innocence *hazes* us – we can realize that lost 'innocent-Holiness' was the impetus for sin. This understanding, disputed by some, makes it simpler to unpack Genesis. Understanding this qualifier allows us to see life differently as the unveiling is more-complete. From the split veil, with Scripture-writing occurring for several years after Jesus' death, we see the redeemed view of life – in light of Law and Gospel. At the same time, we can draw eternal and necessary connections from Law to obedience because of God's effective empowerment of **grace**.

After applying salvation, God institutes the Law as the family rules of Christ's Kingdom. If we see this as legalism, we posit a contradictory message. If we embrace antinomianism, we posit a God-denying message because **God never terminates the obligation of perfect graceful Law-keeping**. The Spirit leads in **grace**ful joyful obedience, a far cry from Legalism or Antinomianism of any stripe.

When we allow faulty paradigms to control our convictions, it's almost impossible to accept valid qualifiers. In a *TableTalk* article, Mark E. Ross gives a summary that represents my desire.

> How easy it is for theologians, whether amateur or professional, to denounce uncharitably those with whom they disagree. To be sure, doctrinal error must be exposed. Scripture requires it. The 'essentials' of the faith must not be reduced to the barest minimum while the remainder is left to personal preference. The whole counsel of God must be taught, and deviations from it must be opposed. **Teachers must guard the good deposit entrusted to them** [1 Tim. 6:20], **and we must contend for the faith delivered once for all** [Jude3]. At the same time . . . we must be sure our speech does not contain unwholesome words but only that which builds up, as fits the occasion, that it may give grace to those who hear [Eph. 4:29]. **We must always hold fast to the truth but how we hold fast to it is just as important.**[16]

In our doctrinal understanding, it's easy to fall into theological camps based on taught or learned perspectives. We learn through varied means – television or radio programs, denominations (types of church), devotionals, hermeneutics (how we interpret Scripture), exegesis (how we pull out meaning), personal study or through friends (where opinion often rules) and we can easily make wrong conclusions.

With this in mind, let me open the window a little wider into salvation-camps. Some see salvation through mere Law. Some see salvation through mere gospel. Some see salvation through a mix of Law and Gospel. Some see salvation through mere man's effort. Some see salvation through man's effort based on what God does for us, in us, with us, or all three. Some see salvation through God-working-alone because of Christ's work. Exposure to various camps sparked in me a love for deep theology that bears on crucial questions of doctrine.

Christianity falls into two major religious categories. Some think what they do *earns or merits* right relationship with God so salvation boils down to a Do-to-Be formula, often with man as the focus and causal agent. Others understand that God must regenerate dead men before they can walk in resultant new birth reality so salvation is a <u>Be-then-Do</u> scenario with God as the focus and causal agent. I believe the second because it teaches Monergism and regeneration. Still others maintain man has the ability to 'come to God' on His terms, in the middle of the first two categories. Regarding the God-fearer, this seems like a biblical Way. As we observe, it could be that some God-fearers are already regenerated and are proactively being sanctified; this adds haziness to our perspective so we must carefully evaluate.

Redeemed understanding glorifies God's **Grace** by proclaiming a **grace** Gospel that exalts God's necessary God-Alone-Work. In Romans 11:33-36, Paul highlights and exalts this necessary point. I wish we could always keep Paul's understanding straight in our lives:

> Oh, the depth of the riches and wisdom and knowledge of God! How unsearchable are his judgments and how inscrutable [mysterious and unfathomable] his ways! "For who has known the mind of the Lord, or who has been his counselor? Or who has given a gift to him that he might be repaid?" For from him and through him and to him are all things. To him be glory forever.

In clear terms, Paul indicates that regeneration and Justification come through God's Monergistic work. I don't read synergism in verse 36 but – to **confirm** necessary regeneration – Paul immediately calls us to put ourselves on God's altar for worshipful service in Romans 12:1-2.

A Hobby Lobby advertisement from many years ago gives a middle-road summary. It showed the inside view of an empty tomb and speaks to a lifeview – speaking to the difference between <u>religion</u> and <u>Christianity</u>. Isaiah 55:6-7 is quoted, speaking of repentance; it said:

> You choose your beliefs, your neatly tied package of what can and cannot be. With these beliefs we weave the fabric of our religion. But what if God refuses to be defined by what we consider believable? What if truth is not something we create, but something we discover, and embrace? What if God is actively and aggressively looking for you? What if He really desires to spend eternity with you? What if He rose from the dead to prove it?[17]

Steve Green cites Josh McDowell speaking of truth's exclusivity,

The same is true about Christianity. If the claims of the Christian faith are true – and many people accept them as true – these people are no more intolerant for their belief than those people who accept Washington D.C. as the United States capital. They are either correct or mistaken about how God revealed Himself in the world. If they are right, then there really is no other way to God but through Christ. If they are wrong, then Christianity is false. The question of tolerance isn't the issue. The question of truth is.[18]

When I discuss Christianity, I often distinguish between religion and Christianity. I find this distinction necessary because many speak of religion in a pejorative sense rather than from the sense God requires and designs. As **grace** and regeneration are necessary for right relationship with God, the New Covenant paradigm shines. In a simple religious/religion mindset where man is the captain of his soul with freewill, there is little hope of making a proper Gospel connection.

I seek clarity on the essential difference between religion and Christianity. Most see Christianity as just another religion because they don't see it through God's eyes. **True Religion is Christianity** but this is not how most think or communicate. As I speak, consider religion with a lower case 'r' and true Religion with an upper case 'R.'

In religion-distinctions, I define 1) religion as man's sinful attempt to find or reach God, describing the world's population that 'seeks' God. Never mind that God clearly presents His Ways, Word and Gospel in Christ. Yet many have the audacity to think it's okay to make their own way – and call it religion. As they define it, it's mere religion but they rarely see it this way. Whether through embracement or rejection, most people speak of religion in this sense without realizing **man's form can never please God** with its sinful human-focused starting point. In this sense, religion always competes against Christianity because it never bows to the Redeemed View of salvation.

I define 2) Christianity (True Religion) as God seeking out a people called to His plan by His power and redeeming them through

His means or Ways. This book essentially presents what I consider True Religion. In this sense, Religion is a good thing – with God and Christ's Atoning Righteous Work as the starting point. When people pursue true Religion, God leads them to become God-fearers who pursue right relationship to God's Law that unrepentant sinners can never do in a holy sense. In this sense, **Religion is the pursuit of God's Way through Christ's Atonement – realized in the Cross**.

According to Scripture, **Christianity is God finding and saving people by His grace for His glory**. Christianity – taught well – accurately reflects God's work for His people's salvation. This is why I earlier stated that the Bible is God's Plan for the Redemption of His people. **The directional flow between religion and Christianity is huge and gives insight into struggles of <u>professed</u> believers to adopt a Christian lifeview**. Scripture presents these truths so that individuals will change their theology, pursuit and practice.

The third category is what I call 3) the 'christian religion.' This <u>nominal</u>-hybrid allows sinful man the opportunity to cause salvation on terms other than what Scripture posits, leaving the door open for great confusion. When we imagine that we cause our salvation by righteous acts – <u>even the act of faith</u>, no matter that we deny the ability to earn salvation – we distort The Gospel. The 'christian religion' syncretizes religion with Christianity, leaving a co-opted reality that uses similar terms and concepts but falls short of a biblical Gospel with practical **grace**ful duty. This may be due to faulty interpretation or a desire to 'catch more fish' but the fallout is severe. **Without the possessed cake, nominal Christianity is the 'default mode' today**.

In my opinion, much of the Evangelical church falls into this third category to the detriment of a pure church and Gospel. This prevalent salvation-culture produces a hybrid picture – with many _professors_ rather than _possessors_ in the church. Jesus said tares look like the wheat until just before the harvest comes, but Scripture teaches that only true saints can perform God's will. Tares don't produce wheat any more than they can obey God's Law without **grace**. Tares may look like wheat but can't **grace**fully act like wheat. We often teach and attempt to do what Jesus calls impossible;[19] but we can't make tares into wheat any more than we can raise the dead. Only God can do this!

Jonathan Leeman wrote a small book on church membership. Some of what he says is valid here, especially the holiness-focus as he speaks to a membership-standards-guide 'from' the Beatitudes:

> **Look for ones** who are poor in spirit, who mourn their sin; who aren't entitled, always insisting on their own way, but are meek; **who are sick to death of sin and all its nonsense and so therefore hunger and thirst for righteousness like it is water. When you find people like that, make sure they know who Jesus is. Make sure Jesus is the one who fills their impoverished spirit**, who has forgiven their sins, who receives their life and worship, and whose righteousness they depend upon and pursue. When you find such people, tell them to join! Notice that it's not a person's moral perfection that qualifies him or her for church membership. It's just the opposite; **it's his or her recognition of a lack of moral perfection coupled with a hunger for it**. It's not the people who never sin; **it's the people who fight against sin. A church's judicial work is to affirm**, not the righteous but **the unrighteous who thirst for righteousness** – the righteousness only God in Christ can give. Here's one more way to say it: **What makes people acceptable to a church is** not their own moral purity, but Christ's – not what they have done to save themselves, but **what God has done to save them**.[20]

By himself, man can 'cause' his own salvation by walking in God's Way *unto* salvation! Jesus let people walk away to show **an obedient-all-in-following-attitude is required**. This was the epitome of Jesus' invitation to the rich young ruler. Against many pleas for different gospel-approaches today, God never suggests an emotional 'I'd like to try a different approach.' I don't know why the church freely accepts faulty messages as noble and sufficient.[21]

As we consider distinctions Jesus made between Law and Gospel, we must leave God's work in His realm yet work diligently to perform what He desires on our end. For this reason I dismiss most 'christian religion' options although godly desire can flow from this category. I'm convinced that camping in #1 or #3 short-circuits the Gospel. **Scripture teaches that presentation of Law with Holy Spirit conviction can bring the required application of the Gospel**. We should do pre-evangelism by discipling with The Law – with hope that God brings true knowledge of the Gospel. **Grace-driven Law highlights God's Way and brings people to right understanding of Gospel grace**. Without manipulation, The Law shows people their need for Christ so they may follow Him and His Way for salvation and **grace**:

> **The law in the hand of the Spirit renders the grace of the gospel precious and desirable in the eyes of convinced sinners; and this grace, when it is received, makes the law salutary and pleasing to them** (Romans 7:22). The law is an awful commentary on the doctrines of the gospel, . . .And **the gospel is a delightful commentary on the high demands and sanctions of the law**. . . The gospel exhibits in the wonderful person and work of Christ the highest proofs of the infinite authority and perpetual stability of the law. . . **To such an infinite degree is the consummate righteousness of Jesus Christ the fulfillment of the law and the glory of the gospel; that sinners of mankind are peremptorily commanded in the law, and earnestly invited in the gospel, to accept the gift of it, and to present it in the hand of faith to the law** in answer to its high demand of infinite satisfaction for sin, and of perfect obedience as the condition of eternal life. **Thus the law, as it is the covenant of works, is in harmony with the gospel. The law, likewise, as a rule of life to believers agrees with the gospel. When the law as a covenant presses a man forward, or shuts him up to the faith of the gospel; the gospel urges and draws him back to the law as a rule** (Leviticus 11:44). The law is his schoolmaster to teach him his need of the grace of the gospel; and **this grace will have his heart and his life regulated by no rule but the law** (2 Peter 1:15-16). **Nothing is gospel-obedience but obedience to the law in the hand of Christ as a rule of duty**. The gospel is no sooner believed than obedience is yielded, both to the law as a covenant and to the law as a rule. The righteousness of Christ in the hand of faith is obedience to it in the former view, and personal holiness of heart and life to it in the latter. **If the law commands believers, the grace of the gospel teaches them to love, and to practice universal holiness** (Titus 2:11-12). **What the law as a rule of life**

binds them to perform, the grace of the gospel constrains and enables them to do (Leviticus 20:8; 2 Corinthians 5:14-15). **That which the precept of the law requires as a duty, the promise of the gospel affords and effects as a privilege** (Ezekiel 18:31; 36:26-27). **Whatever holds the place of duty in the law holds the place of privilege in the gospel.**[22]

A foundational tenet of Christianity is that <u>God seeks those He wills to save</u> per Romans 11:33-36. **Those God wills to save are unsaved until God draws them to gracefully and joyfully become part of His Redeemed People**; however, this doesn't mean we wait for God to save, as <u>fatalism</u> suggests. Some are told in <u>Quietism</u>, "Sit back, let go and let God;" this doesn't work either. Some may see my view as a middle-of-the-road salvation, and Scripture shows **grace** in this view.[23] **As we approach salvation in the Redeemed way, we see God *work* His Will through our working – to glorify His grace.**

I don't present the above points as an either/or generalization of Religion. Rather I try to answer disturbing dilemmas I see in the church, evangelism and Gospel. My convictions lead me to a position where we disciple in the "Be-to-Do" vein and trust God to bring the redeemed "Be-then-Do" regeneration reality. Common objections to Monergism imply that we would become robots controlled by God but this is never seen in Scripture or **grace**ful experience. If ever there was a straw-man argument, this is it! If however, we claim that God's power of **grace** doesn't control us, what does this mean? <u>Monergism gives praise to God for what He does, requiring **grace** for what He commands – and God blesses those who approach Him by His Way.</u>

The presence of God-fearers in Scripture indicates that people can put themselves in the position of salvation and God rewards this pose with salvation in His timing. Cornelius in Acts 10 was one; and salvation came to his house. Rahab in Joshua 6:17 and Zacchaeus in Luke 19 were others; salvation came to them. God-fearers don't perform self-salvation but do something significant that few do today.

The Law commands "Repent, Believe and be Converted!" We hear, "Freely submit" – and God is pleased to regenerate God-fearers.

Many discard moral Law for various reasons but **everyone must give an account to the Law in light of the Gospel**. We can't accept the Gospel without a reckoning to the Law. **Once God regenerates us, He <u>empowers</u> us to proactively and diligently please Him by the Word, Spirit, Truth and Graceful obedience.** Scripture shows this pleasing to be through the power of His <u>**grace**</u>.

Salvation is given to elect ones in the Great Exchange of <u>Double Imputation</u>. The application of Christ's perfect righteousness is exchanged for our sin – the New Covenant double exchange-essence from Genesis 3 onward. God imputes the sin of elect ones onto Jesus Christ on the Cross. On the flip side, God imputes Christ's Righteousness to our account, completing this double imputation – a most blessed doctrine for blessed ones. 2 Corinthians 5:20-21 says,

> Therefore, we are ambassadors for Christ, God making His appeal through us. We implore [beg] you on behalf of Christ, be reconciled to God. For our sake He made Him to be sin who knew no sin, so that in Him we might become the righteousness of God.

Without this double exchange, we have no hope for salvation. When we understand **effective redemption**, we know <u>we must have God's work</u>. If we become <u>the Righteousness of God</u> per 2 Corinthians 5:20-21 and Romans 5:17-21, **we must perform graceful Law-obedience after His Righteousness is applied**.

From the application of this <u>double-exchange</u>, the Spirit makes sinners into new-creation-saints in Christ per 2 Corinthians 5:17, causing us to come alive to His Holiness per Ephesians 2:10. 2 Corinthians 5:17 speaks of making a new creation but the higher focus is that the 'phasing out' of the Old Covenant results in the 'coming in' of New Covenant reality through the Cross ministry and Unpacked **Grace** of Christ. Even the coming in of New Covenant reality speaks to this double exchange – from a Covenant perspective.

Because we get so excited about the New Covenant reality coming within us, we often don't give enough attention to the greater truth that the New Covenant has come! Our epiphany can overlook the majesty of the New Covenant Cross but <u>the application of this 'New-Covenant-has-come' greater truth results in sinners becoming new creations</u>. **A new organic creation is made by the regenerating work of The Spirit**. Against misunderstandings of legalism and antinomianism, living in New Covenant reality changes everything.

If we put 2 Corinthians 5 into its context, Paul poignantly highlights New Covenant distinctions and realities to contrast the fading glory of the Old Covenant. The Old Covenant was glorious but its shine fades in light of the New Covenant. Paul's contrast helps us see that the Mosaic Covenant is not the devilish thing it's often painted to be today. As the shine disappeared from Moses' face, the shine was fading from the Mosaic Covenant. As the moon compares to the sun, the New Covenant has greater glory. We should glory in unveiled truth.

Imagine sanctification as a practice-run toward heaven. Scripture hints that our heavenly experience will be perfect **Grace-Full** obedience and God-likeness. Our practice-run on earth, while it displays less than perfect obedience and Christ-likeness, should mirror the heavenly reality. **Grace**ful obedience to the Law pictures Christ's Lord's Prayer words, "Thy Will be done on earth as it is in heaven." **Nowhere does Scripture say the moral Law is rescinded, not even in heaven**. In fact, eternity itself will not change the moral Law; we should therefore not imagine the Law is rescinded for Christ reflectors.

Do we ever think about why sin will not be in heaven? I think God will cause **grace** to reside eternally in our glorified bodies – that's why and how no sin will be in heaven. Our response to the moral Law here should be the same as it will be in heaven – **grace**ful willing obedience. This is the essence of the Lord's Prayer in Matthew 5:10. In a different setting, consider 2 Corinthians 3:7-18:

Now if the ministry of death, carved in letters on stone, came with such glory that the Israelites could not gaze at Moses' face because of its glory, which was being brought to an end, will not the ministry of the Spirit have even more glory? For if there was glory in the ministry of condemnation [Old Covenant], the ministry of righteousness [New Covenant] must far exceed it in glory. Indeed, in this case, what once had glory [OC] has come to have no glory at all, because of the glory that surpasses it. For if what was being brought to an end came with glory [OC], much more will what is permanent have glory [NC]. Since we have such a hope, we are very bold, not like Moses, who would put a veil over his face so that the Israelites might not gaze at the outcome of what was being brought to an end. But their minds were hardened. For to this day, when they read the old covenant, that same veil remains un-lifted, because only through Christ is it taken away. Yet, to this day, whenever Moses is read a veil lies over their hearts. But when one turns to the Lord, the veil is removed [NC]. Now the Lord is the Spirit and where the Spirit of the Lord is, there is freedom. And we all, with unveiled face [those living in the reality of the NC], beholding the glory of the Lord, **are being transformed into the same image from one degree of glory to another**. For this comes from the Lord who is the Spirit.

Consider also 2 Corinthians 4:3-7; 4:11-12 and 5:1-5 as they build to 5:17: "Therefore, if anyone is in Christ, he is a new creation. The old [OC] has passed away; behold, the new [NC] has come." With redeemed eyes, God's message comes through loud and clear.

We often say good works never merit salvation but Scripture shows this is precisely how salvation is accomplished! **Christ's Law-Keeping rather than our imperfect Law-keeping, merits salvation**. Without this, there's no hope of salvation. Salvation gained through Christ's merit sacrificed on the Cross is the essential requirement of Law and applied Gospel. **A difference exists between Christ's Essential Righteousness and our personal righteousness built on His Righteousness – but personal righteousness is necessary**.

Our good works don't merit salvation but the perfect Works of Christ sufficiently merits salvation for His sheep – the ground of effective salvation. Technically, salvation comes through Law fulfillment as Paul confirms in Romans 3:20-31. Practical salvation comes through our imperfect but sincere obedience to the Law even as we are Justified by the obedience Jesus laid on the Cross-altar.

Being <u>IN CHRIST</u> is Paul's favorite saying that refers to born-again-ones. Paul refers to being <u>In Christ</u> 35 times in Ephesians. Those who are <u>In Christ</u> are not under the curse, condemnation, ceremony, judgment or sacrificial system of the Law but **all these qualifiers say nothing directly against the moral Law**. We must work through qualifiers so that we don't discard responsibility to God's moral Law.

The Finished Work of Christ took away (expiated) God's wrath for His Sheep by perfectly fulfilling or completing God's Levitical Law. Some imagine Christ's fulfillment means we don't have to keep the moral Law. This faulty thinking wrongly interprets <u>fulfilled</u> because He <u>kept</u> the Law for more than technical Justification. We shortchange what He fulfilled when we abolish the Moral Law; Scripture never teaches this! We are <u>technically Justified</u> by Law-keeping (Christ's) and <u>practically justified</u> by **grace**ful Law-keeping (ours) – to reflect Christ's personal Holiness. We magnify God's **Grace** in Law-obedience.

Some erroneously think, "If God's chosen people failed to obtain <u>fulfillment</u> of the Law as they pursued it, wrongly though it was, why should we bother?" As said earlier, some throw out the baby of **grace**-works with the bath water of self-salvation or wrong fulfillment. This is a distortion on two levels. First, as we uphold the Law we see different bath water. Second, some Hebrews tried to fulfill what only Christ could fulfill – Law-obedience on the wrong side of merit.

Wrong teaching provokes some to begrudgingly discard the Law. Some erroneously think Jesus condemned the requirement of necessary obedience when He condemned the Pharisees because they kept <u>the letter of the law</u>. Listen carefully – Jesus was never against Law-keeping but was against the law-keeping of God-violating traditionalism! **Jesus rebuked their law-keeping because it denied God's Moral Law**, but <u>many misunderstand His necessary qualifier</u>.

Jesus said statements like, "You have heard it said (Rabbinical teaching), but I say to you (as Lord of the Law)." Misunderstanding imagines Jesus spoke over, rewrote, or re-interpreted God's Law but this is not so! When Jesus made these statements He refers to man-made laws or **grace**less interpretation rather than God-given Moral Law. Jesus' valid teaching in Matthew 15:1-20 discards the faultiness of man-made laws that put people in bondage with no hope of escape. As **Full-of-Truth GraceFull** Authority, **Jesus discards faulty rabbinic traditions rather than God's Law-Path that brings Life**.

Jesus fully supports God's Law-intentions with the preface "But I say to you!" Jesus always embraces God's Moral Law! In fact, as God in humanity, Jesus embraces and expounds God's Law. Let's not add to the Pharisees' error by denying God's moral Commandments. **The Law is a "But I Jesus – Your God and LORD – say unto you" reality;** therefore Christ reflectors must keep God's Law!

Jesus said graceless-works-salvation-law kills but He never said graceful-regenerated-Law-obedience kills. Confusion causes many to tragically throw out the Law – believing they somehow obey Christ by rejecting God's Law. Imagine that! When Law-keeping refers to efforts of guilty sinners for Justification, the Law kills but can drive us to Christ! King David said that **grace**ful regenerating Law brings Life – and Scripture confirms this truth throughout its pages.

As Author of the Law, Jesus expounds Eternal Moral Law. He never truncates or abolishes Commands. A prevalent teaching draws a distinction between God's Moral Law and Christ's Two-Law summary of the Law – what some call The Great Commandments. This position is really a 'glorified antinomianism.' Those who hold this view pat themselves on their back for rejecting God's Moral Law as they bask in the reality that they keep 'Christ's Commands' without seeing a glaring contradiction. Summarizing the two Tables of the Law – to God and Man – in no way 'does away' with eternal Law and we should not slander Christ for perpetrating a God-violating suggestion. If you wrestle with my thoughts, take a Berean approach back to Scripture.

When saints attempt to keep the Law without God's power, graceless effort kills sanctification but we can correctly find sanctified life through Christ and the Applied Gospel.[24] Any attempt to imitate Christ without the Spirit or **grace** is futile! Once you discover **Grace** in its fullness, the Law becomes a cherished entity within salvation.

When professors reject **grace**ful holiness or Law-obedience, they fall; Jesus confirms this in Matthew 6:22-24. Jesus contrasted graceless Law or letter-of-tradition-law against Spirit-driven Law-obedience that is Life-empowering; Christ reflectors embrace this! Christ always pleased His Father by perfectly keeping the Law; we can please our Father as we Keep His Law too! As Christ did through prayer, seek **grace** to keep the Moral Law to please the Father. *This* obedience magnifies His Gospel **grace** and brings joy.

Although Jesus rejects the Pharisee's misinterpretations and additional laws that put people in bondage, Jesus never rejects right Moral Law obedience! Indeed, He said the world would pass away before any Moral Law would become null or void per Matthew 5:17-20. What don't we understand about this? In speaking to the Pharisees, Jesus applauded **grace**less Law-keeping as better than no Law-keeping – but **Graceful Law-keeping is the goal and requirement**.

As Adam and Eve rejected God's Holiness and **grace** – and didn't keep the Law – they initiated The Fall so redeemed **grace** points **Grace** back before The Fall per Ephesians 1:3-9. **When we teach that grace is necessary for obedience and is available at the Throne of Grace per Hebrews 4:16, obedience to the moral Law is much different in New Covenant reality**. We can only approach the Throne of **Grace** through Christ because of **grace** in regeneration.

In New Covenant understanding, our sense of duty to the moral Law is heightened because of the complete Word, indwelling Spirit and

grace. Jesus fulfilled every moral Law so that – through Him – His Sheep can gracefully obey the Law. David Wells says,

> This moral reality [judgment] is at the center of our universe and God's dealing with it. **In the end, it is upon Christ's death and wrath that our hope rests,** for he is the last line of resistance to the triumph of what is evil and fallen. It is because of his judgment, because of the day **when he will put truth forever on the throne and evil forever on the scaffold,** that hope can be sustained in the midst of a world in which there is not only much corruption but in which **what is corrupt is so often rewarded and triumphant.** God, who is at the moral center of the world and who sustains the moral order, is also the one who has provided in Christ the answer to the profound moral dilemma that his presence evokes.[25]

In our bobble-head culture where people profess to know, yet lack God's moral fortitude or character to pull it off, we are in a dilemma of our own making. Alistair Begg cites The Westminster Confession:

> **The Moral Law does forever bind all,** justified persons as well as others, **to the obedience thereof**; and that not only in regard of the matter contained in it, but also in respect to the authority of God, the Creator, who gave it. Neither does **Christ in the Gospel** any way dissolve, but rather **strengthens this obligation.**[26]

Hear John Murray speak about law and **grace**; he said:

> But when we arise from our prostration before the Cross, it is not to find the moral law abrogated [done away with], but to **find it by the grace of God wrought into the very fiber of the new life in Christ. If the Cross of Christ does not fulfill in us the passion of righteousness, we have misinterpreted the whole scheme of divine redemption.**[27]

The Westminster Confession puts it like this: "**The Spirit of Christ subdues and enables the will of man to do that freely and cheerfully which the Will of God, revealed in the Law, requires to be done.**"[28] Samuel Bolton says, "**It is no infringement to our liberty in Christ to be tied to the performance of duty.**"[29] John Owen said "**A universal respect to all God's commandments is the only preservative from shame.**"[30] Amen! We can learn so much when we embrace the Law as God desires. Begg further says:

The believer has been changed inwardly, given a new heart, the same shape as the Law of God. It is a perfect fit. There is nothing irksome or uncomfortable about it. **There is no conflict between that heart and the requirements of holy living.** We make progress into a life of obedience to God's Law (Romans 6:13). How striking that the work of regeneration is here defined in terms of the Law being written on the heart and mind of the believer. As we heed the warnings and rest upon the promises of Scripture, **the Holy Spirit works in our lives a supernatural principle which cannot be acquired by fulfilling our duties but it is preserved by them** [our duty to the Law].[31]

Grace compels believers to keep the Law as a rule of life in the hands of Christ; Colquhoun shows how Law and grace work together:

The law, as a covenant of works and a rule of life, demands nothing of sinners but what is offered and promised in the gospel; and in the gospel everything is freely promised and offered to them which the law, in any of its forms, requires of them. The gospel presents to them for their acceptance the consummate righteousness of Jesus Christ, the Surety of such sinners as believe, which fully answers every demand of the law in its covenant form, and so magnifies it in that form and makes it honorable. It also exhibits to them, in its offers and promises, the infinite fullness of Christ from which they may be regenerated and sanctified, and **so be enabled to yield such obedience to the law as a rule of life as will in due time become perfect.** While it reveals and offers righteousness to satisfy the law as a covenant, **it promises and offers strength to obey the law as a rule. It promises all the supplies of grace and strength which are necessary for the acceptable performance of every duty** that the law as a rule of life requires of believers. The righteousness, too, which the law as a covenant demands, and which the gospel affords, being imputed to believers, merits for them that holiness of heart and life which the law as a rule requires, which the gospel promises, and which is perfect in parts here and will be perfect in degrees hereafter. **Thus, in general, the law and the gospel agree together or mutually subserve each other.**[32]

We started out with an honest search for God's Will. I trust you find His Will in **Grace**ful Law-obedience – even if blindsided by a spiritual tsunami. I trust you <u>believe God</u> and pursue His Will with **grace**ful effort with His <u>overcoming effective power</u>. In summary, with deep admiration, I respectfully allow Colquhoun the final word,

In the doctrine of faith, the eternal obligation of the law on them [saints] is declared; obedience to it is enforced by the strongest motives, and represented as performed under the best influences, from the best principles, and for the best ends. **According to that doctrine** [of faith], **all believers are bound by infinite authority to obey; they are enabled to sincerely obey; they are constrained by redeeming love to obey; they resolve and delight in dependence on grace, to obey; and they cannot but obey the law as a rule of duty.** The love of Christ, as revealed in the gospel, urges them; the blood of Christ redeems them; **the Spirit of Christ enables them;** and **the exceeding great and precious promises of Christ encourage them to obey and yield spiritual and acceptable obedience.** The holy law as a rule is written on their hearts, and therefore **they consent unto it that it is good, and delight in it after the inward man. While they do not obey it for life, but from life, they account obedience to it not only their duty, but their privilege and their pleasure. Thus, according to the doctrine of faith, they present, in the hand of faith, perfect Righteousness to the law as a covenant of works; and they perform, as a fruit of faith, sincere obedience to it as a rule of duty.** And **so effectually do they, by the doctrine of faith establish the law as a rule of duty** that they never account their obedience to any of the precepts of it sincere and acceptable but in proportion as their performance of it flows from the unfeigned faith of that doctrine. **In their view, nothing is obedience to but what proceeds from evangelical principles, and is excited by evangelical motives.**[33]

The Moral Law is a beautiful goldmine when we understand regeneration and **grace**. With His empowerment in our effort, we can say with David, "Oh how I love thy Law." **Spirit-passioned graceful effort** forever changed my life – I hope it does yours too!

---

1 John 1:14.

2 O. Palmer Robertson, *The Final Word: A Biblical Response to the Case for Tongues and Prophecy Today*, (Edinburgh, Eng.:The Banner of Truth Trust, 1993). Robertson presents the Bible as God's Final Word. Despite claims that God speaks in other ways today, Jesus was His Final Word! 1 Cor. 13:10 & Heb. 1:2.

3 Ernest C. Reisinger, *The Law and the Gospel* (Phillipsburg, NJ.: P&R Publishing, 1997) xvi.

4 From especially Hebrews 4:16 I am convinced the *Throne of Grace* replaces the Mercy Seat. This ground breaking New Covenant news is thrown in quietly but this does not diminish what the writer of Hebrews teaches. This teaching is expanded later.

5 John Colquhoun, *A Treatise On The Law And The Gospel* (Morgan, PA.: Soli Deo Gloria Publications, 1999), 7-8

6 Colquhoun, 26-27

7 Warren Austin Gage. (2005, February) *The Lord of the Law. TableTalk*, 29, 16-19

8 Gage, *TableTalk*, 18.

9 Gage, *TableTalk*, 17-18.

10 The term elliptical properly means to have the form of an ellipse. In theological language, this refers to the full-orbed teaching contained in a certain doctrine. We often think doctrine or teaching is constricted to a given slant but the elliptical reality of Jesus Christ opens up qualifiers for our understanding and growth.

11 Colquhoun, *A Treatise on the Law and the Gospel*, 178.

12 John Charles Ryle, *Holiness* (Webster, NY.: Evangelical Press, 1979), 26.

13 *The Way of Salvation* is a difficult concept because for too long we have distorted the biblical understanding of salvation even if this was not intentional. You should begin to see a Way of Salvation similar to what the Puritans used to present.

14 This starting point is confusing because many set the Law aside out of rebellion or ignorance. Ray Comfort and Kirk Cameron present the gospel this way through *The Way of the Master* teachings. My friend Tom Bear presents the gospel this way in his *Stones-Cry-Out Ministry. The* majority of people in Dearborn, MI are primarily Muslims.

15 At the practical salvation level, grace-empowered-obedience ultimately comes only because of and through the Cross Work of Christ in its historical setting even though its effect was applied as early as Genesis 3:21 – way before its actuality.

16 Mark E. Ross, *TableTalk: Guarding Our Speech* (Lake Mary, FL.: Ligonier Ministry, October 2012) 62.

17 Steve Green, *Faith in America: The Powerful Impact of One Company Speaking Out Boldly* (Decatur, GA.: Looking Glass Books, 2011) 48

18 Green, *Faith in America*, 45 – citing Josh McDowell, *The New Evidence That Demands a Verdict: Evidence I and II* (Nashville, TN.: Thomas Nelson, 1999), x-xi.

19 Matthew 19:16-30; Jesus contrasts rich against the poor in spirit who seek Him.

20 Jonathan Leeman, Church Membership: How The World Knows Who Represents Jesus (Wheaton, IL.: Crossway, 2012), 88-89

21 It's not my intent to go in-depth against false gospels. The negative influence of the Health, Wealth, and Prosperity gospel is huge in the church. Many good books clearly qualify errors as I make broad-brush rebukes across the board to glorify **grace**.

22 Colquhoun, 166-167

23 We were on this very topic when Dave Mercer graduated to heaven.

24 Applied Gospel is what John Murray presents in *Redemption: Accomplished and Applied*. In the gospel chapter, I examine different gospel campsites of salvation. Many views are taught. I want people to think of the deep reality of salvation. Is the gospel implicit and therefore given to all? Is the gospel merely believed at the intellectual level? Is it believed at the heart level? Is the gospel necessarily applied? Is it an assumed or an explicit gospel? Is the gospel a fiduciary decision? Is the gospel an organic change? Excellently, Murray posits the accomplished and applied version I embrace.

25 David F. Wells, *Losing Our Virtue: Why the church must recover its moral vision* (Grand Rapids, MI.: Eerdmans Publishing, 1998) 36.

26 Alistair Begg, *Pathway to Freedom: How God's Laws Guide Our Lives* (Chicago, Il.: Moody Publishers, 2003), 26.

27 Cited in Begg, *Pathway to Freedom*, 40.

28 Cited in Begg, 41.

29 Cited in Begg, 42

30 Cited in Begg, 42

31 Begg,43

32 Colquhoun, 161-162

33 Colquhoun, 181-182

The Conclusion of the Matter

God wants Trophies Of **Grace**. Are you one? Ingredients of life cause emotions, desires and effort to ebb and flow. Despite changes, Scripture teaches God's people to use **grace**ful effort to imitate Christ. When we possess the eternal required-reality of the salvation-cake we are a Trophy of **Grace – put on display for His Glorious Gospel**.

God's Will is closer than we imagine – it's found in His Word through the Way of Salvation that leads to the cake-reality. As God gives spiritual breathe through re-creation, a Cross-picture helps us understand and reflect Christ. I offered paradigms that revolutionized my life to help you embrace redeemed seeing, life and action. A new vision of Law changed my life and I work to provoke this in others per the mandate of Hebrews 10:25. I seek to live my granted time for God's Will to glorify the **grace** of God's Gospel. I trust you do too.

Years ago, The Spirit applied the Cross reality and I now possess His salvation cake. This application and my Christ-reflecting-following helped me overcome the damnation of nominal Christianity that sets on many Christ-professors today. With realities of the Spirit, **grace** and cake you too can overcome the scourge of nominal faith.

By itself, <u>mere believing in a recipe</u> does no good but believing and pursuing the recipe that brings salvation allows God to bless us with Regeneration so that we possess the cake reality. Possessing the cake saved me from both car wrecks as God brought organic new birth to my soul. Ongoing repentance, faith and conversion transform my mind and actions into the redeemed reality of Christ-reflecting activity that honors God and His Law. I seek to live at a recipe-reality-level every day to know God and to see Him one day at a glorified level.

Until then, I endeavor to leave a legacy for my children, those I pastor and those I influence in varied ways. By getting here, I hope the fog has lifted in your mind and obedience. God continues to clear the haze to help me pursue and practice Christ-like holiness through **grace**ful Law-keeping. A redeemed lifeview provokes me to walk boldly in God's Will, Word and Ways as I live with Abraham's faith.

Drawing this labor of love to a close, Revelation 22:17 calls: "The Spirit and the Bride say "Come." And let the one who hears say, "Come." And **let the one who is thirsty come**; let the one who desires take the water of life without price." Jesus knocks at the soul's door of His Sheep saying, 'Come and find soul-peace through My Word and Ways. Walk **grace**fully in My Holy Will.' **There are no greater words than "Come out of the tomb and follow me**." I heard His voice and I'm still following – seeking a home beyond this world.

I continue to seek His Will in the Cross because salvation was finished there. I praise God that Christ's Cross-Work lives in me and I can obediently pursue His eternal **Image in Christ**. As I give **grace**ful effort to that Holy Goal, I encourage others to believe and work the recipe so they too can possess the cake to find joy. Seek until you come out of the hay holding the Christ-Likenessing needle with joy unspeakable! I hold it high so others will play, look and find.

Joy fills my soul as Christ and **grace** lives strong in me. I realize this mostly when I tell others of His sufficient saving Gospel. As I walk boldly in **grace**, the vision gets clearer every day. Even in the midst of suffering for righteousness's sake, God gives abundant **grace** to magnify His saving Gospel as I incarnationally proclaim His Gospel. I proclaim His Gospel to reproduce disciples who glorify His **grace**.

Join me in finding the joy of living God's Will through **Grace**. Exalt in practical Cross-holiness and you will be living God's Will. As you find God's Will in the Redeemed View of Life, you too will proclaim the Gospel of **Grace** to see others brought to cake-life in Jesus through God's Word. If not before, now you know why I typically sign off,

In His Grace (the heartthrob of my soul), Tim Parker

Appendixes

Appendix 1 – Life Experience

Some details of my life are not necessary to repeat (some betray Christ) but I offer the following so some may be encouraged to know that others struggle in similar ways. **My life is not normative but God's regeneration at some point in our history is normative** to those who are in Christ. **Salvation is** not something to be assumed, implicit or taken for granted but **something to be known, explicit and proven in our life through biblical manifestation**. In the midst of playing in the hay of God's Word and truth, God is pleased to bring us from the haze with the needle in our hands so that – through His power – we can build a pleasing life to the glory of His Holiness.

I was raised from birth in a Free Methodist Bible-practicing home with many opportunities to learn the faith. As a young boy, I remember hearing about Catechism but the program must have been shelved before I took it. Growing up under godly parents, I had a warm heart for what I heard about the faith and at the age of seven – after 'accepting' Jesus as my Savior – I asked to be baptized, a great foundation. For us, church consisted of Sunday School, Worship service, with Sunday and Wednesday evenings. I remember many extra-curricular activities designed for fellowship and maturity-building. I often attended summer camp or family camp in Jackson, Michigan.

At the age of ten, right after John F. Kennedy's assassination, I suffered another bout of rheumatic fever that left me with a heart murmur, an enlarged heart and six months of bed rest with little hope of activity beyond that window. For a boy, that was devastating news. It was during this time that I fell in love with quartet music as I often listened to *Quartet Time* on Christian radio. The elders of the church prayed for me but I had little hope that God would intervene in a way that a healthy boy could imagine. But God did intervene and I lived a pretty normal life after this major incident.

We had Christian Youth Crusade (CYC) that paralleled Awana, Royal Rangers or Boy Scouts today. More than badges and receiving the highest award possible, the best thing was Scripture memorization. I was active in this program and summer Bible programs. For older teens, we had Holiness Youth Crusade (HYC) at the Detroit Institute of Arts; this was quite a monthly event. Between church services and Holiness Youth Crusade – with many altar calls – I probably 'went forward' a hundred times in my life, either believing I was getting saved, getting saved again, to seek forgiveness or sanctification, rededicating my life or something of this nature. I was never sure 'it' stuck and was not about to be left behind – before we had a *Left Behind* book series.

In my late teen years, as much as I thought my faith was valid, either it was overshadowed by selfish living or was nominal at best. My parents would argue for the first but something was missing. I knew the Bible stories and most of the answers (so I thought) but was not satisfied in my soul. One day the Holy Spirit asked me a question, "What is salvation?" Because I knew the common answers, I gave a response that He did not accept; His question and my found-wanting-answer provoked me to really dig into the Word for the first time in my life in search of not just the answer but a living answer for my life.

After this year-long process, I came out knowing God had regenerated my soul. I was not sure when, but knew it occurred. I'd like to say everything was upward moving at that point but that would not reflect reality. One great thing happened afterward, though I no longer believe in happenstance. I attended the *Institutes of Basic Youth Conflicts* by Bill Gothard. For me, this was my Catechism and God used this to significantly build a viable foundation in my life. The Institute-teachings dealt with just about every imaginable reality of life and taught a biblical perspective to issues we all struggle to understand and overcome. Today it's called *Institutes of Basic Life Principles* and is a valid recommended foundation. While regeneration was part of the Spirit's answer and a foundation for this book, the more complete answer of life-long **grace**-learning is given throughout this book.

As with most, my life took many turns. My Chrysler career spanned 37 years but layoffs and a desire 'to get ahead' pushed me into other jobs that expanded my horizons. For God's reasons and my stupidity thrown in for good measure, an undiagnosed broken neck led to an emergency neck fusion five years later. God used this as my 'thorn in the flesh' event – similar to Paul – to teach me **grace** as I think Paul learned. God teaches us much through life's trials and much more through ministry. If our life-ship is not moving in God's direction – with His power to advance the gospel – we need an adjustment. God used neck surgery as my adjustment, and it's never been the same since He leads where I would not choose, without His **grace**.

Whenever we get hot after God's Will, Satan gets hot after our trail to put up roadblocks in our path if he cannot stop us. He seeks to stop us one way or another. For me, Satan destroyed a marriage of over 27 years. I felt like Joseph when he was thrown in prison after adequately serving his master and being falsely accused by Potiphar's wife. God continued to teach me through this difficult time, as the shambles of divorce can be like a prison that we can't escape. Only in God's timing are we let out. On the backside of my prison-sentence, my friend Al Titus (one to whom I dedicate this book) invited me to teach my **Grace** *Series* at his church. In that series, I met my wife Elizabeth and stayed over ten years before God pushed me into other paths.

Elizabeth provoked me to return to school to get my degree – little knowing it would put me on a difficult but joyous path that has not stopped. Even though she struggles in her role as a pastor's wife – not asking for this role – she inspires me greatly. I still have no idea where my schooling will end but I'm enrolled in God's life-long school that will see graduation in glory. Still 'enrolled' in Southern Baptist Theological Seminary, I have an unfinished Master of Divinity degree in process. I retired from Chrysler with the belief that God would push me into other things; some of His vision for me was to pastor Smiths Creek Bible Church and lead my flock and others to reflect Christ.

As a bi-vocational pastor and substitute teacher, I seek to walk in God's Will for my life. God's Will might not be so much a discovery or destiny as an attitude and lifeview. This partly explains why I wrote – so others can share in a God's-Will-lifeview. I trust some of my life experiences encourage readers to seek God's face in regeneration and then rest in God's sovereignty as we learn from His Ways, Word, Will, **Grace** and Cross to walk boldly in Law-obedient Christ reflection.

The struggle to embrace the Law in a redeemed manner seems to be difficult for many who profess Christ. I'm not sure if this is due to wrong teaching, wrong believing or a combination of the two. Wrong teaching is sure prevalent and entrenched in the church! Wrestling with the Law can be seen as a before-Christ reality but is better seen as an after-Christ reality that is often linked with the early stages of our redeemed life. Make the Law personal before His face!

Like Jacob, my challenge caused me to wrestle with God over who was going to be Sovereign. For too long, I had been the boss of my own life. Like Jacob, I messed things up because I failed to submit to God's authority. When we maintain sovereignty to do what we want to do – under the false notion of free will or whatever excuse we hang onto – God is not Sovereign in our life. Our approach to Law ultimately boils down to who is sovereign in our life. As Jacob discovered, when God wins the wrestling match, we might walk with a limp because we are humbled before His Will. I walk with a limp because of spinal cord damage and surgery but also because God humbled me in our wrestling match. I will be eternally grateful that He won! More than anything, my limp reminds me that I wrestled with God and He won!

We are taught to be 'captain of our soul' and we struggle to give the wheel to the Eternal Captain. When the Captain shows up, as He did in Joshua 5:13-15 – as the Commander of the Army of the LORD – we must bow before Him and His Word. Some of us struggle to do this. Why? What are we thinking? These are questions I asked myself. **When I bowed, all of a sudden – almost magic-like – what to do was not the real issue but how I did it was adequately framed by His Moral Law that reflects His Character**. The answer for how He wanted me to live was all too plain once I bowed before The Commander. He's still Commander and I love to bow before Him.

I struggled with the message "to be holy as He is Holy" but once I really looked, didn't excuse my merry-go-round disobedience and saw necessary obedience I was on the way across the bridge to **grace**ful joy. I went through a time of internal argument – waffling between old teaching and redeemed truth – but **once I laid down this internal dialogue to follow His Law through Grace, God has been teaching me redeemed truth ever since**. I needed an Isaiah 6 moment where the LORD – High and Lifted up – confronted me with the Holiness of One who sits on the Throne, and it was not the same me after I saw things correctly! I did as Isaiah did; God brought healing and gave me the tongue-scorching soul-burning reality of **grace**.

Once I saw the absurdity of 'non-conforming-Christ-likeness' and 'Law-keeping-without-the-Moral-Law,' it was a no brainer to submit to His rule. Submission brings joyful worship and I want this for you! God walked me across this bridge to discover joy in graceful Law-obedience. By His **Grace,** I have never looked back. I call others across this bridge because Scripture says this is the redeemed key to finding God's Will, and I missed it for years.

I pray you do not miss it for years. Go to the Throne of **Grace** and The Cross of Calvary to bow before the Commander of the LORD's Army. By doing so, you will discover the Redeemed View of Life for yourself. You too can find peace and joy as you say with Isaiah, "Send me!" or with Paul, "What do You want me to do?" As you follow in **grace**ful Law-obedience, He is glorified to lead by His **grace**.

I know because I'm <u>By and In His Grace</u>, Tim Parker

Appendix 2 – John's Son-of-God References

John uses seven great Signs as a backdrop for his Gospel. This is one reason that John's Gospel is different from the Synoptic Gospels (Matthew, Mark and Luke) that follow a story approach to Jesus' life and ministry. John's Signs point to who Jesus claims to be and He proves His point. John demonstrates that Jesus is God's Son (The Sent-God) through these Signs. John highlights these seven to make his Case for Christ as God's Only Unique Son. As an eye-witness, John also saw Jesus in His revealed Glory – **without any haze!**

Another difference is that John does not record Parables as people understand from the Synoptic Gospels. I'm convinced **John presents Parables of the Living/Miracle/Sign variety**. I grant this perspective is initially foreign to many but consider this possibility. Once we see John's Signs as Living/Miracle/Parables, there is much to learn from what Jesus does and demonstrates through His Signs.

John demonstrates what Jesus claims – directly or indirectly through verbiage, demonstration, or highlighting these points in his gospel presentation. Everything John says is geared to show Jesus as God for redemption and salvation. John and Jesus unturn many conceivable arguments if we would listen. Those who believe-not-to-believe can't see through John's presentation, but we can believe.

Jesus' Seven Great Signs

#1 – Making water into wine at the wedding in
      Cana of Galilee – John 2:1-11
#2 – Jesus cleans the Temple – John 2:13-22
#3 – Healing the nobleman's son by speaking the word in
      'abstentia;' also in Cana of Galilee – John 4:46-54
#4 – Healing the 38-year infirm man in Jerusalem at the
      Pool of Bethesda – John 5
#5 – Feeding of the 5,000 that flows into the
      Bread of Heaven Discourse – John 6:14
#6 – A man born blind receives his sight and flows into His
      Good Shepherd Discourse – John 9-10
#7 – Jesus raises Lazarus from the tomb – John 11

As the seven Signs point to the Cross that flows into the Resurrection – as the icing on the Gospel cake – the Cross is the biggest point John makes for Jesus' purpose and destiny.

I believe *The Gospel of John* is the concerted declaration that Jesus is God's Son. I trust my provocation helps us see John's Gospel from a different paradigm – a compilation of significant events that support John's major premise or purpose statement in John 20:30-31.

With broad-brush consideration, John presents crucial events leading to the completion of salvation on the Cross to demonstrate that Jesus is exactly who He claimed to be – God in **graceful** humanity.

Jesus was and is God – as God's Son – meaning He is fully a member of the Triune God. We often get stuck on seeing the miracles, Parables and Signs for what they are in themselves rather than as Jesus intended – the means to look further to see Him as the prophesied Messiah that would be crucified on the Cross. May we see the majesty of who He is – to our benefit and for God's Glory. I did not use sources for this list; and it's offered in simple form as a beginning.

I take liberty here but think it's close to what John and the Spirit desires for us to see. If we see what John saw, we see the majesty of the Son of God. Granted, it takes believing eyes – eyes that have been given new sight - but that's exactly John's and Jesus' point. I think you will be amazed at how many things John highlights. 16 points were given in a fuller way on pages 132-135 (underlined here); here they are given as one-line entities. Most statements begin with **"I AM:"**

1) **"I AM the Eternal Word of God"** – John 1:1

2) **"I AM the Word who is God"** – 1:1

3) **"I AM God from the Beginning"** – 1:2

4) **"I AM the One who Created all things"** – 1:3

5) **"I AM the One who has Life in His Being"** – 1:4

6) **"I AM the Source of recreated life in man"** – 1:4

7) **"Because I AM the Re-Creator, I AM the light of men"** – 1:4

8) **"I AM Light because I shine into dark dead souls"** – 1:5

9) **"I AM the Illuminator of darkness"** – 1:5

10) **"I AM the One who John, the witness, speaks about"** – 1:6-7

11) **"I AM the One on whom you are to believe!"** – 1:7

12) **"I AM the One who the witnesses unveil FOR salvation"** – 1:8

13) **"I AM the One who every man should Know in salvation"** – 1:9

14) **"I AM the Sent One who came into the world"** – 1:10

15) **"I AM the One whom God-rejecters do not know"** – 1:10

16) **"I AM the One whom My own people reject"** – John 1:11

17) **"I AM the Life-Giver to God-fearers"** – 1:12

18) **"I AM the One on whom God-fearers believe"** – 1:12

19) **"I AM the One who makes Children of God-fearers"** – 1:12

20) "I Alone AM the One through whom God-fearers are Re-birthed and adopted into God's family" – 1:13

21) "I AM the Eternal Word that descended from heaven to permanently take on flesh" – 1:14

22) "I AM the Descended One who tabernacles with man" – 1:14

23) "I AM the Revealer of God's Glory" – 1:14

24) "I AM God's Only Begotten Son" – 1:14, 3:16

25) "I AM full of Grace and Truth" – 1:14

26) "I AM the One who gives My sheep fullness and grace" – 1:16

27) "I AM the One who brings a New Paradigm of salvation" – 1:17

28) "I AM the Exposer and Declarer of God's heart" – 1:18

29) "I AM the LORD of whom the Wilderness Crier – John the Baptist – preached and declared" – 1:19-26

30) "I AM God's Baptizer into Life and the Spirit" – 1:26-34

31) "I AM the Lamb of God" – John 1:29 & 36

32) "I AM the One who can take away sin because I will make Perfect Atonement and make holy" – 1:29

33) "I AM the One on whom the Spirit descended upon in its fullness and eternality" – 1:32

34) "I AM the One whom the Wilderness Crier called the Son of God" – 1:34

35) "I AM the Great Rabbi; men who are called by God willingly follow Me wherever I go" – 1:35-51

36) "I AM the Promised Messiah" – 1:41, 4:25-26

37) "I AM the One who regenerates; they come to Me and I give new ones new names" – 1:42-43

38) "I AM the One who can see True Israelites" – 1:47

39) "I AM the Son of God and King of Israel acknowledged by Nathanael's testimony" – 1:43-50

40) "I AM the Great Revealer to my sheep" – 1:50

41) "I AM Jacob's Ladder" – John 1:51, 3:31, 6:45-46, 61-62

42) "I AM, with certainty and without a doubt, God's Son" – 1:51

43) "I AM the New Covenant wine" – John 2:1-13

44) "I AM the Purifier and Completer of Ceremonial Law" – 2:6

45) "My works are signs that point to the Cross" – 2:1-11

46) "I AM the Temple; God is present in me!" – 2:13-22

47) "I AM the One who will not allow any mockery of
My Ways as you come into My presence" – 2:13-22

48) "I AM the One whose greatest sign is the Cross" – 2:18-19

49) "I AM the One who talks in Riddles until after My Cross Event
and then all things will be plain for My sheep" – 2:18-22

50) "I AM the Discerner of Hearts" – 1:43-50, 2:23-5, 6:64-70, 8:6-47

51) "I AM acknowledged as Rabbi by Nicodemus (God-fearer) who
will be regenerated by Me; he sees my signs" John 3:1-2

52) "I AM the Door to God's Kingdom!" – 3:3

53) "I AM declares that rebirth is required before you
can even SEE the Kingdom of God" – 3:3

54) "I AM declares that Re-Birth by the Water and Spirit is required
before you can enter into God's Kingdom" – 3:5

55) "I AM declares that Re-Birth is a strange thing for unredeemed
flesh to understand; the Spirit reveals this mystery" – 3:6

56) "I AM the One Who Re-Births in Water and Spirit" – 3:5-8

57) "I AM Israel's Teacher" – 3:10-12

58) "I AM declares Only God's Truths" – 3:11-12

59) "<u>I AM the Serpent On The Pole</u>" – 3:14-15, 12:30-33, 18:28-40

60) "I AM the Giver of Eternal Life to My sheep" – 3:15-16

61) "I AM God's Salvation to everyone who believes!" – 3:15-17

62) "I AM declares that those who believe IN Me will not
see the second death but have Eternal Life" – 3:15-16

63) "I AM declares that God sent me into the world to
obtain and declare salvation through Me" – 3:17

64) "I AM the Law-Condemnation Remover" – 3:18

65) "I AM declares that all who do not believe in the LORD – the
Only Begotten Son of God – are condemned!" – 3:18

66) "I AM declares, in eternally certain terms, that you must
trust in Me to avoid condemnation and obtain Life" – 3:18

67) "I AM declares that evil men (common sinners who love
their darkness) will not come to Me for Life" – John 3:19-20

68) "I AM declares that Light-rejecters who do not want their sin exposed will not come to Me" – 3:20

69) "I AM declares that Light-Reflectors (redeemed ones) come to the Truth for Life and salvation" – 3:20-21

70) "I AM declares that Light-Reflectors appreciate that God exposes their sin and gracefully causes obedience" – 3:21

71) "I AM the Light of the World" – 3:19, 8:12, 9:5

72) "I AM the Sin-Zapper for saints" – 3:20

73) "I AM the Grace-Giver to bring holiness" – 3:21

74) "I AM the Great Baptizer" – 3:22-23, 4:1-2, 15:26-27

75) "I AM the Bridegroom of God's Wedding" – 3:27-31

76) "I AM the One who Reveals ALL Truth" – 3:27

77) "I AM God's True Testimony" – 3:33

78) "I AM the Fullness of God's Spirit" – 3:34-35

79) "I AM tells of God's Wrath for Covenant Breakers" – 3:36

80) "I AM the Great Evangelist – seeking lost ones" – John 3 & 4

81) "I AM better than Jacob's well" John 4:6

82) "I AM comes into town at high noon as the New Sheriff" – 4:6

83) "**I AM the Gift of God**" – 4:10

84) "**I AM the Living Water**" – 4:10-14

85) "I AM the Great Prophet" – 4:16-20

86) "I AM the Great Place of Worship" – 4:21-24

87) "I AM the Source of Spiritual Food (Grace)" – 4:31-34

88) "I AM the Great Apostle" – 4:34, 6:38, 7:18, 7:28-31, 8:42

89) "I AM the Great Harvester" – 4:34-38

90) "I AM God's Sure Testimony" – 4:39-41

91) "I AM God's Gospel that brings Salvation" – 4:39-42

92) "I AM can speak Life into someone at any time" – 4:50

93) "I AM the Great Healer – in absence" – John 4:50, 5:8-9

94) "I AM God's Great Sign-Post" – 4:46-54

95) "I AM better than the Pool of Bethesda" – John 5:1-16

96) "I AM declares only those who want healing find it in Me" – 5:6

97) "I AM declares that I can bring Regeneration through many means of outward appearances" – 5:8-14

98) "I AM declares that when I make someone New through Re-Birth, they can overcome sin through My Grace" – 5:14

99) "I AM working My Father's Plan" – 5:17

100) "I AM, lest there be any doubt, equal with God" – 5:18

101) "I AM the Son with the Father's Authority" – 5:19-21

102) "I AM declares that the Son of God perfectly reflects the Father in Character, vision and action" – 5:19

103) "I AM can raise dead ones to Redeemed Life" – 5:21

104) "I AM the Judge of all mankind" – 5:22-27

105) "I AM declares that ones who are given Eternal Life are ones who hear and obey my Word" – 5:24

106) "I AM declares that My sheep who have Eternal Life pass from the Old Covenant to the New Covenant" – 5:24

107) "I AM declares that My sheep pass from death to Life" – 5:24

108) "I AM declares that the Time for Spiritual Resurrection and Re-Birth is now here in Me!" – 5:25

109) "I AM declares that, lest there be any doubt, the same Eternal Life that exists in the Father exists in Me" – 5:25-27

110) "I AM Eternal Life and can give Life" – John 5:25-29, John 11

111) "I AM declares everyone should make it a priority to make sure that you have Life when you die" – 5:27-29

112) "I AM gives perfect Judgment at the end of the age" – 5:30

113) "I AM is glorified with human testimony" – 5:30-35

114) "I AM's salvation can be testified by human testimony" – 5:33

115) "I AM glorified with God's testimony" – 5:36-37

116) "I AM declares that My Word only abides in those who hear and obey me – in My sheep" – 5:38

117) "I AM authenticated by Scripture" – 5:38-47

118) "I AM the True Judge of thoughts and motives" – John 5:42

119) "I AM the Epitome of God-Honoring obedience; only those who are found in Me honor God" – 5:44

120) "I AM says that whatever you trust in will judge you" – 5:45

121) "I AM declares that whoever properly believes in Moses' Administration and Law will believe in Me" – 5:46

122) "I AM declares that belief in Moses is required for you (Jews and maybe everyone) to believe in Me" – 5:47

123) "I AM the Pied Piper of Signs; sheep follow me" – John 6:1-2

124) "I AM the Exponential Multiplier of God's Food" – 6:8-14

125) "I AM the One who can walk on water" – 6:16-19

126) "I AM the One who can quiet your fears" – 6:20-21

127) "I'M God's sealed Sign delivered; will you believe?" – 6:27-29

128) "I AM the True Bread from Heaven" – 6:32-33

129) "<u>I AM the Bread of Life, the Wilderness Manna</u>" – 6:35

130) "I AM the Father's Fruit Gatherer and final inspector" – 6:37

131) "I AM the Eternal-Life Guard-ian" – John 6:39

132) "I AM the Eternal Will and Covenant Protector" – 6:39-40

133) "I AM God's Heavenly Magnet, drawing My sheep" – 6:44

134) "My flesh is God's Bread!" – 6:51-52

135) "My body and blood are the Lord's Supper Elements" – 6:53-6

136) "I AM Eternal God who has and gives Eternal Life" – 6:57-58

137) "I AM the Spirit that can overcome flesh" – John 6:63

138) "I AM the One who takes all the Father sends" – 6:65-66

139) "I AM the CHRIST – the SON of the Living God" – 6:68-69

140) "I AM the Heavenly Chooser" – 6:70

141) "I AM God's Approved Rabbi" – John 7:14-19

142) "I AM the Sinless ONE!" – 7:18

143) "I AM the Heavenly Ultimate Provoker" – 7:19

144) "I AM the Heavenly Irrefutable Scholar" – 7:20-24

145) "I AM the One with Righteous Judgment" – 7:24

146) "I AM from God because He Sent Me" – 7:29

147) "I AM in charge of His-story's Time Clock" – John 7:32-34

148) "I AM Sovereign over your evil deeds and desires" – 7:34

149) "I AM the Eternal Spiritual Thirst Quencher" – 7:37

150) "I AM the Source of the Spirit that can flow thru you" – 7:38

151) "I AM the Spiritual Mesmerizer" – 7:40-52

152) "My Word (I AM) is truth, even if you are confused" – 7:51-52

153) "I AM the Eternal Temple; in Me, sinners can find forgiveness, wholeness and graceful obedience" – John 8:1-12

154) "I AM a Rabbi without sin; therefore I can forgive sin" – 8:7

155) "I AM can bring conviction with authority and dirt" – 8:8-10

156) "I AM One who does not condemn justified sinners" – 8:10-11

157) "I AM Eternal Sinlessness; therefore I can grant ability to walk in graceful freedom without Law's judgment" – 8:11

158) "I AM The CAUSER of Righteousness in My sheep" – 8:12

159) "My self-witness declares I AM God" – 8:13-16

160) "I AM One with the Father, and our witness is True" – 8:16-18

161) "I AM the Father-Revealer; believe Me!" – 8:16-19

162) "I AM going to die on the Cross and will go heaven; if you do not believe in Me, you will go to Hell!" – 8:21

163) "Hell is your destiny if you do not believe Me (I AM)" – 8:21-24

164) "I AM the Father's Representative" – 8:25-27

165) "The Cross will prove that I AM He!" – 8:28

166) "I AM a Total God-Pleaser, like you should be" – 8:29-30

167) "I AM the True Vine; eternal life resides in Me" – 8:31-2, 15:1, 5

168) "I AM Truth and will make you free if you abide in Me" – 8:32

169) "As the Son of God, I can make you free" – 8:34-35

170) "I AM Abraham's Seed and Son" – 8:37-41

171) "I AM God's VERY Words" – 8:42-47

172) "I AM perfectly honors God" – 8:49

173) "I AM One who seeks God's Perfect Glory" – 8:49-50

174) "I AM will give Life to those who obey My Commands" – 8:51

175) "I AM Greater than Abraham and the Fathers" – 8:52-53

176) "I AM Knows God and obeys His commands" – John 8:54-55

177) "Abraham rejoiced to see Me (the I AM) in his day" – 8:56

178) "I AM the LORD that appeared to Abraham" – 8:56-57

179) "Before Abraham was, I AM!" – 8:58

180) "I AM the Revealer of God's Plans in individuals" – John 9:3-4

181) "I AM works God's Works while it is day" – 9:4

182) "I AM the Light of World – Divine Holiness and Justice" – 9:5

183) "I AM the Authoritative Healing Rabbi!" – 9:6-7

184) "I AM heals blind eyes; the bigger point is that I AM can heal
spiritually blind eyes to bring true seeing" – 9:6-7

185) "True seeing sees I AM for who He is" – 9:5-38

186) "I AM makes former blind ones into God-worshippers
who proclaim My Healing ability and Work" – 9:5-38

187) "I AM better than the water in the Pool of Siloam;
My water can bring soul healing too" – 9:11

188) "I AM LORD of the Sabbath; My recent in-your-face
healing easily proves this" – 9:13-16

189) "When others excommunicate you or make you an
outcast because of what I performed in you, I AM
watches out for your spiritual welfare" – 9:13-35

190) "When you are brought before the courts to testify of My
Work in you, I AM gives words of defense" – 9:13-34

191) "I AM calls broken people – lame, deaf and blind ones whom
I restore into my service" – 9:6-41

192) "I AM the Son of Man!" – 3:13, 9:35-37, 19:5

193) "When I AM comes along side – as a Paraclete – sight
is perfected through redeemed sight" – 9:35-38

194) "I AM doesn't hesitate to call blind ones Blind ones – 9:39-41

195) "I AM does not hesitate to call a kettle black" – 9:39-41

196) "I AM declares that ONLY ONE WAY of salvation exists and,
lest there be any confusion, I AM that Way!" – 10:1

197) "I AM declares that anyone who tries another way other
than through Me – is a thief and robber" – John 10:2

198) "Since I named My sheep, I AM knows their names and
they follow Me when I call to lead them out" – 10:3

199) "I AM leads My sheep because they Know My voice" – 10:4

200) "I AM puts an internal radar in My sheep so that they
do not follow strange teachers" – John 10:4-5

201) "I AM the Door of the Sheepfold" – 10:7, 9

202) "I AM let's my sheep in and out to find rich pasture" – 10:9

203) "I AM gives Abundant Life to My sheep" – 10:10

204) "I AM the Good Shepherd" – 10:11

205) "I AM the Giver of Eternal Life" – 3:15-16, 10:10, 27-28

206) "I AM gives His life on the Cross for His Sheep" – 10:11

207) "I AM defines My leaders as protectors of My sheep" – 10:12

208) "Lest you missed My purpose and claim, I AM will lay down His life for His sheep!" – 10:15

209) "I AM has other sheepfolds but they are sheep who come the same way – through Me" – 10:16

210) "I AM Only has one flock" – 10:16

211) "I AM has the power to lay down His own life when He is called to do so by the Father" – 10:17-18

212) "Because I AM God, I AM is greater than Solomon's Porch in the Temple - I cannot say this any plainer" – 10:22-30

213) "The Works that I do (My seven Signs) bear Witness of Me – the Eternal I AM" – 10:25

214) "I AM knows His sheep because other sheep-looking creatures do not follow Me" – 10:27

215) "I AM gives My sheep Eternal Life so that they will not die the second death" – 10:28

216) "I AM able to keep my sheep from perishing – no one can steal their life unless My Father allows it" – 10:28

217) "My Father gave Me – the I AM – My sheep and no one can snatch them out of His Hand" – 10:29

218) "My Father and I – I AM – are one in essence, purpose, Work, Plan, Truth and Grace" – 10:30

219) "Lest there be any doubt, I AM God!" – 10:30

220) "I AM shows only Good Works from the Father; for which Good Work do you seek to kill me?" – John 10:32

221) "I AM never blasphemes God because I AM God" – 10:33

222) "I AM KNOWS Scripture and it says I speak Truth" 10:34-36

223) "I AM is confirmed and defined by Works" – John 10:37-38

224) "Listen again; "<u>I AM the Son of God</u>" – 10:36-38

225) "Lest there be any doubt, I AM God" – 10:37-38

226) "The more you see and believe, the more your thinking and action will conform to the I AM" – 10:40-43

227) "The time of regeneration and spiritual resurrection is in the hands of the I AM" – John 11:1-4

228) "When I AM delays, look past the obvious to see His Plan and your part in His Will" – 11:1-7

229) "When I AM retraces His steps, follow closely and learn from Him" – 11:7

230) "I AM is not afraid to walk back into the lion's teeth or lead His sheep there – with My presence" – 11:8

231) "I AM has Light to tread between scorpions" – 11:9-10

232) "I AM readily declares His intentions" – 11:11

233) "I AM speaks riddles that confuse the scoffers" – 11:11-15

234) "I AM makes promises that I will keep" – 11:23

235) "<u>I AM the Resurrection and the Life</u>" – 11:25

236) "I AM the Teacher and I call for you" – 11:28

237) "I AM seeks those who are dead and laying in sin" – 11:34

238) "I AM shows real emotions of spiritual sorrow" – 11:35-37

239) "I AM order the steps that lead to resurrection" – 11:39

240) "Dead stinking flesh does not stop I AM from bringing dead ones back from death to Life" – 11:39

241) "I AM speaks hope to those outside the tomb to believe that I can bring spiritual resurrection" – 11:40-42

242) "My Father always hears I AM because I always seek His Will – so that other Sheep will believe" – 11:41-42

243) "I AM calls My Sheep out of spiritual death by name" – 11:43

244) "When I AM calls, My Sheep come out" – 11:44

245) "I AM draws Sheep because of His Signs" – 11:45

246) "Those who refuse to believe I AM are driven away by my Works and Message" – 11:46-48

247) "I AM's Sacrifice is Eternally Expedient – and God's Will can be 'called for' by My rejecters" – John 11:49-52

248) "Until My time, I AM knows when to stay out of the limelight – then I will boldly walk in" – 11:53-57

249) "When My time comes, I will be anointed for investigation and prepared for death and burial" – John 12:1-3

250) "Evil people seek to kill those who the I AM brought back to life because their words testify of Me" – 12:9-11

251) "When My people hear that I AM is coming to town, they come out in droves to worship Me" – 12:12-15

252) "I AM-rejecters cannot understand why people come to worship Me as Eternal King" – 12:16-19

253) "When I AM calls, even those 'outside of the faith' come at the sound of my call" – 12:20-26

254) "I AM declares that unless someone falls Into My Cross, you cannot escape the second death" – 12:23-24

255) "I AM calls to my sheep, "Come and die;" if you do this, you will be exponentially productive" – 12:24-26

256) "Where I Am is, my servants are there too" – 12:26

257) "If anyone serves Me – the I AM – he follows Me" – 12:26

258) "I AM freely submits to the Father's Will – even as what I will go through is difficult" – 12:27

259) "I AM acknowledges that I came for this very hour" – 12:27

260) "I AM's obedience will Glorify My Father's name" – 12:28

261) "God glorifies Me and My Work from Heaven" – 12:28-33

262) "When I AM is put on the Cross, the judgment of the world will come and Satan will be cast out" – 12:31

263) "All of I AM's Sheep will come to Me because of and through My Cross Work" – 12:32

264) "Strange as it sounds, I AM – the Eternal One – will die to bring about God's Plan of Redemption" – 12:34

265) "You can only become sons while the Light – I AM – is in your presence – believe Him while you can" – 12:35-36

266) "I AM provokes either positive or negative belief" – 12:37-43

267) "Spiritual belief, sight, and hearing the I AM equals belief in God" – 12:44-47

268) "I AM-rejecters are God rejecters and they will be

judged for their rejection of the I AM" John 12:48

269) **"Those who obey God's command and Come to I AM, they can have Eternal Life through Me"** – 12:49-50

References below are from the Upper Room Discourse or beyond to magnify fulfillment rather than the particular declaration that looks forward to fulfillment. Fulfillment was performed in the Cross and implicitly, or by later extraction, John intimates Jesus would declare these statements if given the chance. Throughout the whole book, I believe John presents Jesus as he knew Him to be – after he got redeemed vision. I trust we obtain redeemed vision to sit up and take notice if we have any doubts about who Jesus is.

270) **"I AM loves My Sheep to the end"** – John 13:1

271) **"Satan's kids deny God's Son"** – 13:2

272) **"I AM knows how to model God-reflection"** – 13:2-6

273) **"I AM's foot-washing symbolizes washing My Sheep in the water of regeneration"** – 13:2-11

274) **"I AM is not greater than the Father; therefore you are not better than others – live like this"** – 13:12-17

275) **"I AM knows whom I choose; when some deny Me, you will know that I speak the truth about regeneration"** – 13:18-22

276) **"When I deem it necessary, I AM can expose those in our midst who are not part of us"** – 13:23-30

277) **"The Great Commandment I AM leaves with you is the same: love God and your neighbor to fulfill the Law"** – 13:31-35

278) **"I AM declares that you cannot join Me in the Cross that I endure but afterward you will follow"** – 13:36-38

279) **"I AM is going away to build a dwelling place as a tribute to our marriage in the Lamb"** – John 14:1-4

280) **"I AM The Way, The Truth, and The Life"** – 14:6

281) **"I AM gives Grace – empowerment to do My Will"** – 14:12-14

282) **"If you love I AM, keep My Commandments"** – 14:15-18

283) **"I AM only manifests Himself to those who believe His Word – despite the magnitude of Signs"** – 14:22-24

284) **"I AM will send The Holy Spirit who will lead you into the mysteries that are still shrouded by My Cross"** – 14:25-3l

285) "I AM the True Vine; you only Live In Me" – John 15:1-8

286) "Abiding in the Love of the I AM is seen in
      keeping My Commandments" – 15:9-17

287) "I AM The Great-Commandment-essence" – John 15:12-17

288) "I AM the eternal Master" – 15:18-25

289) "I AM the sender of the Holy Spirit" – 15:26-27

290) "I AM All of God's Truth Personified" – John 16:12-15

291) "I AM the Great High Priest" – 16:16-24

292) "I AM the Great Revealer" – 16:25-28

293) "I AM Eternal Peace" – 16:29-33

294) "I AM Salvation to those chosen by the Father" – John 17:1-5

295) "I AM Noah's Ark in regards to salvation" – 17:6-12

296) "I AM the Eternal Joy-giver" – 17:13-16

297) "I AM the Great Sanctifier" – 17:17-19

298) "I AM the Great Reconciler" – 17:20-26

299) "I AM Jesus of Nazareth, prophesied Messiah" – John 18:1-11

300) "I AM the Spotless Passover Lamb" – 18:12-27

301) "I AM King of the Jews" – 18:33-40

302) "I AM King of another world" – 18:36

303) "I AM God's Truth Herald" – 18:37

304) "I AM the Day-of-Atonement-Sacrifice" – John 19:1-11

305) "I AM the Spotless Lamb of Passover" – 19:4, 7

306) "I AM the Silent Lamb waiting for slaughter" – 19:10

307) "I AM the Day-of-Atonement-Scapegoat" – 18:39-40, 19:12-16

308) "I AM the One with All-Power to lay my life down on the
      altar/cross and take it up again" – 19:11

309) "I AM Abraham's Redemption Sacrifice" – 19:17-22

310) "I AM God's Finished Salvation" – 19:28-30

311) "I AM the Eternally-Pleasing Sacrifice taken into the
      Holy of Holies" – 19:31-37

312) "I AM Eternally the Resurrection and Life – 19:38; 20:10

313) "I AM the Sacrifice on the Mercy Seat" – John 20:11-12

314) "I AM the Mercy Seat, the presence of a
   forgiving God – 20:13-16

315) "I AM the Risen, Reigning and soon to be
   Coronated King – 20:17-18

316) "I AM the First-Fruits of the Glorified Bodies" – 20:19

317) "I AM God's Apostle; now I send you" – 20:21

318) "I AM the Returned High Priest because God accepted
   My Sacrifice" – 20:20-23

319 (As God breathed life into Adam) "I AM breathing
   The Holy Spirit into you" – 20:22

320) "I AM giving you the power and authority to forgive
   or retain sins in the church" – 20:23

321) "My Resurrected Body that has the Crucifixion proofs
   is Proof that I AM who I claim to Be" – 20:24-29

322) "I AM LORD of the New Covenant Harvest" – John 21:1-14

323) "I AM LORD of the Church and will direct your efforts toward
   Evangelism, missions and growth" – 21:6

324) As Lord of the Harvest, "I AM the Designer and Source of your
   direction and strength; no independent spirit here" – 21:6-10

325) If you follow my design and lead, "I AM able to complete
   the harvest and sustain you in the work" 21:11-13

326) "I AM Lord of My Table; I feed you with elements that I spread
   before you – therefore receive for your need" – 21:13

327) As My sheep follow Me, "I AM the Loving God who
   focuses on graceful obedience and downplays doubt,
   denials and disobedience" – 21:15-18

328) "I AM the Restorer and Lead Ox" – 21:15-19

329) "I AM The Christ-professor-Examiner and the
   Christ-possessor-Encourager" – 21:15-19

330) In My Sovereignty, "I AM the One who directs the lives,
   mission and death of my sheep" – 21:19-23

331) "I AM the One you should keep your focused devotion
   upon rather than on what others do; whatever you
   (any of us) do, follow Me!" – 21:22

To see this overview as I think John gave it suggests John's Gospel doesn't necessarily present a chronological history of Jesus' life per se – but specific snapshots demonstrate Him to be God's Son with special emphasis on the last days of His physical presence on earth. If we see His Signs as Living/Miracle/Parables and hear these "I AM" statements we begin to see the majesty John boldly describes. This understanding allows us to acknowledge a beautiful encouraging view. Work through your understanding of who Jesus is because it directly affects the **grace**ful model of how we should live.

Without making this overview too long, I was amazed at 331 declarations from John's Gospel. Certainly more exist but this is a noble beginning. As we understand Gospel application, we can learn much from John's declarations – whether directly or implicitly in action or words. The Eternal Question is, "Do you believe in *This* Jesus that John presents?" Many believe in a Jesus they 'make' but we must believe in *This* Jesus! Which one do you believe in and follow?

A favorite quartet song – *John Saw* – gives voice to how John's vision related to the heavenly Jerusalem and the throne contained in Revelation. This *Gold City Quartet* song can be heard on YouTube:

Chorus: John saw jasper walls; oh my, oh my, what a vision
John told of shining streets of gold
Where all God's saints shall forever stroll
I've wondered time and again; how could it have been
To gaze upon that heavenly throne
But I'll wonder no more when I step on that shore
To walk upon the golden ground that John saw.

John saw a land I know I'll share; he saw a river flowing there
John tell me more, John tell me more, John tell it all
John saw a throne so bright and fair; he saw the gate with beauty rare
Someday I want to walk the golden ground that John saw. (Chorus)

John heard a voice from heaven say "I'll brush the tears, all tears away"
John tell me more, John tell me more, John tell it all
He said, "No death shall enter there, no grief or pain for us to bear"
Oh, how I long to walk the golden ground that John saw
Just in the midst of paradise, John saw a tree, a tree of life
John tell me more, John tell me more, John tell it all
The sun and moon no longer shine; the Lamb of God shall be the light
Forever shining on the golden ground that John saw. (Chorus)

I like this song but I'd like to hear a song on God's Son as <u>John Saw</u> when he penned his Gospel. The story he gives is majestic. I think the majesty he saw in Revelation is the same 'vision' he shares with redeemed vision in his Gospel to expose the flesh-God through Signs.

Appendix 3 – Book Suggestions

I attempt to place suggested books under the best chapter but sometimes they don't fit accordingly. I'm sure I missed many great books (that I haven't read) but this is an attempt to offer expansion for the topics. I know God stretches us as we make ourselves available to His Will; if we push ourselves to read, God is pleased to teach us. Become a life-long learner and God will bless as you pursue His Will in Christ and **Grace**. Personally I rate some books higher but not here.

Chapter 1 – From the Haze to The Cross

Biblical Theology: The History of Theology from Adam to Christ by John Owen
No Place for Truth: Whatever Happened to Evangelical Theology
        by David Wells
Above All Earthly Pow'rs: Christ in a Postmodern World
        by David F. Wells (2 books)
The Disappearance of God by R. Albert Mohler Jr.
The Presence of a Hidden God by D. James Kennedy & Jerry Newcombe
The Truth War by John MacArthur
Making Sense of the Old Testament: Three Crucial Questions
            by Tremper Longman III
Knowing Jesus Through The Old Testament by Christopher J. H. Wright
The Bondage of the Will by Martin Luther
The Jesus Who Never Lived: Exposing False Christs and Finding The Real
        Jesus by H. Wayne House
Culture Shift: Engaging Current Issues with Timeless Truth
        by R. Albert Mohler Jr.
Can Man Live Without God? by Ravi Zacharias
The Invisible Hand by R.C. Sproul
A Shattered Visage by Ravi Zacharias
Is God a Moral Monster? Making Sense of the Old Testament God
        by Paul Copan
Misreading Scripture With Western Eyes: Removing cultural blinders to better
        understand The Bible by E. Randolph Richards & Brandon J. O'Brien

Chapter 2 – Approaching God's Will

The Instructed Christian by William Lyford
Lifeviews by R. C. Sproul
Classical Apologetics: A Rational Defense of the Christian Faith and a Critique of Presuppositional Apologetics by R.C. Sproul, John Gerstner & Art Lindsley
I Don't Have Enough Faith to Be an Atheist by Norman Geisler & Frank Turek
The Universe Next Door: A Basic Worldview Catalog by James W. Sire
Christianity in Crisis by Hank Hanegraff
In His Image by Paul Brand and Phillip Yancey

How Do I get to Know God? D. James Kennedy
Will the Real Jesus Please Stand Up? by Paul Copan
"True For You But Not For Me!" by Paul Copan
The Cry of the Soul: How our Emotions Reveal our Deepest Questions about God by Dan B. Allender and Tremper Longman III
When Skeptics Ask by Norman L. Geisler and Ronald M. Brooks

Chapter 3 – In Pursuit of God's Will

Finding Deeper Intimacy With God by John Guest
The Way to True Happiness by Robert Harris
In The Face Of God by Michael Horton
The Ultimate Priority by John MacArthur
Handbook to Happiness by Charles Solomon
Getting Closer to God by Erwin Lutzer
Desiring God by John Piper
Scaling the Secular Wall by J.P. Moreland
Not a Fan: Becoming a Completely Committed Follower of Jesus by Kyle Idleman
Think: The life of the Mind and the Love of God by John Piper
Losing Our Virtue: Why the Church must recover its Moral Vision by David F. Wells

Chapter 4 – God's Thread of Continuity

Institutes of the Christian Religion by John Calvin – 2 volumes
The Christian's Reasonable Service by Wilhelmus a` Brakel – 4 volumes
A Puritan Theology: Doctrine for Life by Joel R. Beeke and Mark Jones
Celebration of Discipline: The Path to Spiritual Growth by Richard J. Foster
Essential Truths of the Christian Faith by R.C. Sproul
A Guide for Young Disciples by J.G. Pike
Knowing God by J.I. Packer

Chapter 5 – God's Will

Knowing Christ by Jonathan Edwards
Religious Affections by Jonathan Edwards
Before the Face of God: Book 2 by R.C. Sproul
Why Jesus: Rediscovering His Truth in an Age of Mass Marketed Spirituality by Ravi Zacharias
The Kind Of Preaching God Blesses by Steven J. Lawson
The Conviction To Lead: 25 Principles for leadership that matters by Albert Mohler

Chapter 6 – God's Ways

Tempted and Tried: Temptation and the Triumph of Christ by Russell D. Moore
The Freedom of the Will by Jonathan Edwards

Pressing Into The Kingdom by Jonathan Edwards
Pleasing God by R.C. Sproul
The Gospel-Driven Life by Michael Horton
Love Your God With All Your Mind by J.P. Moreland
Become Like Jesus by Jim McKeever
The Kingdom of Self by Earl Jabay
Classic Christianity: Life's too short to Miss the Real Thing by Bob George
Seeing With New Eyes: Counseling and the Human Condition Through the Eyes of Scripture by David Powlison

Chapter 7 – God's Word

The Stranger on the Road to Emmaus by John R. Cross
Wrongly Dividing the Word of Truth by John Gerstner
Scripture Alone by R.C. Sproul
What's In The Bible? A Tour of Scripture from the Dust of Creation to the Glory of Revelation by R.C. Sproul and Robert Wolgemuth
Truth and Power: The Place of Scripture in the Christian Life by J.I. Packer
Therefore Stand by Wilbur M. Smith
The Case for the Real Jesus by Lee Strobel
The Case for Christ by Lee Strobel
Words From The Fire: Hearing the Voice of God in the 10 Commandments by R. Albert Mohler, Jr.
Recovering Jesus: The Witness of the New Testament by Thomas R. Neufeld

Chapter 8 – God's Holiness

The Hole In Our Holiness: Filling the Gap between Gospel Passion and the Pursuit of Godliness by Kevin DeYoung
Trust and Obey: Obedience and the Christian by Soli Deo Gloria Publications
The Pursuit of Holiness by Jerry Bridges
Principles of Conduct: Aspects of Biblical Ethics by John Murray
Heaven Opened: The Riches of God's Covenants by Richard Alleine
Desiring God by John Piper
The Holiness of God by R.C. Sproul
A New Call to Holiness by J. Sidlow Baxter
Rediscovering Holiness: Know the Fullness of Life with God by J.I. Packer

Chapter 9 – God's Character

Our Great and Glorious God by Jonathan Edwards
Altogether Lovely by Jonathan Edwards
The Character of God by R.C. Sproul
Seeing and Savoring Jesus Christ by John Piper
Still Sovereign by Thomas R. Schreiner and Bruce Ware
The Glory of Christ by John Owen
Mighty Christ: Touching Glory by R.C. Sproul

Chapter 10 – God's Grace versus Mercy

Grace Gone Wild by Robert Jeffress
Grace: God's Unmerited Favor by Charles Spurgeon
Holiness by Grace: Delighting in the Joy that is our Strength by Bryan Chapell
Grace to Stand Firm, Grace to Grow by Carol J. Ruvolo
Loved by God by R.C. Sproul
Dispensationalism: Rightly Dividing the People of God? by Keith A. Mathison
Saved by Grace by Anthony A. Hoekema
By His Grace and For His Glory by Thomas J. Nettles
Grace Unknown: The Heart of Reformed Theology by R.C. Sproul
Grace and Power by Charles Spurgeon

Chapter 11 – Repentance, Faith and Conversion

Turning To God: Reclaiming Christian Conversion as Unique, Necessary, and Supernatural by David. F. Wells
Overcoming Sin and Temptation by John Owen
Richard Baxter and Conversion by Timothy Beougher
Gospel Conversion by Jeremiah Burroughs
Repent or Perish by John Gerstner
Revival by Martin Lloyd Jones
Revolution in The Church by Michael L. Brown
Faith Alone by R.C. Sproul
Trusting God: Even when Life Hurts by Jerry Bridges
Know Why You Believe by Paul E. Little
The Marks of God's Children by Jean Taffin

Chapter 12 – Possessing the Cake Through Grace

Classic Christianity: Life's Too Short to Miss the Real Thing by Bob George
Lifetime Guarantee: Making Your Christian Life Work and What to Do When It
Putting Amazing Back Into Grace by Michael Horton
Living The Resurrection: The Risen Christ in Everyday Life
         by Eugene H. Peterson
Transforming Grace: Living Confidently in God's Unfailing Love
         by Jerry Bridges
Grace Awakening by Charles Swindoll
Basic Christianity by John R.W. Stott

Chapter 13 – God's Gospel Seeks Sons

The Church of God: As an Essential Element of the Gospel by Stuart Robinson
The Explicit Gospel by Matt Chandler
Gospel Reconciliation by Jeremiah Burroughs
Justification and Regeneration by Charles Leiter
The Spirit of Revival by R.C. Sproul and Archie Parrish
Justification by Faith Alone by Soli Deo Gloria Publications

What Jesus Demands From The World by John Piper
Grounded in the Gospel by J.I. Packer and Gary A. Parrett
The Cross of Christ by John Stott
Preaching The Cross
        by Mark Dever, C.J. Mahaney, Ligon Duncan, R. Albert Mohler Jr.
Him We Proclaim by Dennis E. Johnson
Gospel and Kingdom by Graeme Goldsworthy
Don't Waste Your Life by John Piper
Evangelism and the Sovereignty of God by J.I. Packer
Tell the Truth: The Whole Gospel to the Whole Person by Whole People
        by Will Metzger
The Joy of Preaching by Phillips Brooks
The Way of The Master by Ray Comfort
Hell's Best Kept Secret: Discover the Crucial Key Needed to Unlock the
        Unbeliever's Heart by Ray Comfort
Telling The Truth: Evangelizing Postmoderns by D.A. Carson
The Gospel and Personal Evangelism by Mark Dever
Getting the Gospel Right by R.C. Sproul
The Deliberate Church: Building your Ministry on the Gospel
        by Mark Dever and Paul Alexander
The Hole in Our Gospel by Richard Stearns
Tortured for Christ by Richard Wurmbrand
What Is the Mission of the Church? Making Sense of Social Justice, Shalom,
        and the Great Commission by Kevin DeYoung and Greg Gilbert
Introducing Covenant Theology by Michael Horton
The Christ of the Covenants by O Palmer Robertson

Chapter 14 – God's Law Applied by Grace
Chapter 15 – God's Gospel Grace Lived With Law

The Law and the Gospel by Ernest C. Reisinger
A Treatise On The Law And The Gospel by John Colquhoun
The Law And Its Fulfillment by Thomas R. Schreiner
Before the Face of God: A Daily Guide for Living From the Old Testament –
        Book 3 by R.C. Sproul
Turning Toward Integrity: Face Life's Challenges with God's Strength and New
        Resolve by David Jeremiah
Deliver Us From Evil by Ravi Zacharias
The Ten Offenses by Pat Robertson
The Cross and Christian Ministry by D.A. Carson
The Core of Christianity: Rediscovering Authentic Unity and Personal
        Wholeness in Christ by Neil T. Anderson
Silver Refined: Learning to Embrace Life's Disappointments by Kay Arthur

About The Author

I, Tim Parker, could easily be an Ivory Tower Theologian – spending my remaining days tucked away in seclusion to study God's Word and Truth – but his passion in me is to make God's truth understandable for fellow-travelers in order to glorify God's Gospel **Grace**. **Grace** is my soul's passion that flows into every Christ-reflecting doctrine in Scripture. My prayer is that Christ-followers learn this effective power so that our lives praise His regenerating sanctifying work in our lives. This overarching theme that proceeds from Christ's Cross Work continues to drive my life – now and into eternity.

How to Contact the Author

I may never get the opportunity to sit across the kitchen table or drink a cup of coffee with you to discuss this book or its teaching but I want to give opportunity to contact me with questions or comments. Feel free to contact me in one of five ways:

#1 – Mail: Smiths Creek Bible Church

249 Henry Street

Smiths Creek, MI 48079

#2 Website: www.SmithsCreekBibleChurch.com

#3 – Email: timparker1953@gmail.com

#4 – Phone: 810 305 1954

#5 – If you're in my area, give me a call and we'll see about that coffee. I love to teach at an official level but thrive at the kitchen table.

I'm always learning to Image Christ By Growing In Grace, Tim Parker

Made in the USA
Charleston, SC
04 March 2014